D1273989

Systematic Theology

VOLUME V

CHRISTOLOGY

By

LEWIS SPERRY CHAFER, D.D., Litt.D., Th.D.

President and Professor of Systematic Theology
Dallas Theological Seminary

PUBLISHED BY

DALLAS SEMINARY PRESS

DALLAS, TEXAS

First Printing, March, 1948, 2,500
Second Printing, November, 1948, 2,500
Third Printing, May, 1950, 2,500
Fourth Printing, December, 1953, 2,500
Fifth Printing, October, 1957, 2,500
Sixth Printing, January, 1962, 2,500
Seventh Printing, October, 1964, 2,500

PRINTED IN THE UNITED STATES OF AMERICA
BY THE VAIL-BALLOU PRESS, INC., BINGHAMTON, N. Y

TABLE OF CONTENTS

CHRISTOLOGY

CHRISTOLOGY

CHRISTOLOGY

CHAPTER I

THE PREINCARNATE CHRIST THE SON OF GOD

INTRODUCTION

CHRISTOLOGY (Χριστός, λόγος), to which this entire volume is devoted, is the doctrine respecting the Lord Jesus Christ. In attempting to write on His adorable Person and His incomprehensible achievements—which achievements when completed will have perfected redemption, exercised to infinite satisfaction the divine attribute of grace, manifested the invisible God to His creatures, and subdued a rebellious universe in which sin has been permitted to demonstrate its exceeding sinfulness—the limitations of a finite mind which is weakened by a faulty perception are all too apparent. Samuel Medley expressed this sense of restriction when he sang:

"O could I speak the matchless worth,
O could I sound the glories forth
　　Which in my Saviour shine,
I'd soar, and touch the heavenly strings,
And vie with Gabriel while he sings
　　In notes almost Divine."

Thus, again, the same inability is felt and expressed by Charles Wesley:

"O for a thousand tongues to sing,
　　My great Redeemer's praise;
The glories of my God and king,
　　The triumphs of His grace."

Of this incomparable One it is said that "in the beginning was the Word, and the Word was with God, and the Word was God. The same was in the beginning with God"; yet such an One, who thus occupied the highest place of Deity in company with the Father and the Spirit, "was made flesh, and dwelt among us." He who is from everlasting to everlasting was born of a woman and died on a cross. He who according

3

to the mind of the Spirit is Wonderful, was spit upon by men. He who, by the same mind, is Counsellor is rejected of men. He who is The mighty God is crucified in abject weakness. He who is The everlasting Father, is a Son who learned obedience by the things which He suffered. He who is The Prince of Peace must Himself tread the winepress of the fierceness and wrath of Almighty God, for the "day of vengeance" must yet be in His heart and He must yet break the nations with a rod of iron and dash them in pieces as a potter's vessel. He who said, "I am among you as he that serveth," also said, "Think not that I am come to send peace on earth: I came not to send peace, but a sword." He who is the chaste, wooing Lover of the Canticles is the King of glory who is mighty in battle. He who created all things occupied an infant's cradle. He who is holy, harmless, undefiled, and separate from sinners was made to be sin in behalf of others. He who was the Bread of Life was Himself hungry. He who was the giver of the supernatural Water of Life was Himself thirsty. He who was God's Gift of Life to a lost world was Himself dead. He who was dead is alive forevermore.

The range of the life and influence of the Lord Jesus Christ, as disclosed in the Sacred Text, is such as to comprehend things infinite and finite, of God and of man, of the Creator and the creature, of things in heaven and things on the earth, of eternity and of time, of life and of death, of supernal, celestial glory and of mundane sufferings and sacrifice. No greater spread of realities can be conceived than is done when predicating of one Person that He is both very God and very man. It may be inquired how God could be born in a human fashion and die, how God could grow in wisdom and stature, how God could be tempted, how God could be made subject to law, how God could be in need of prayer, how power could be given unto Him which was not His before, or how He could be exalted beyond what He was before. Thus, too, it may be inquired how a visible, identified man on the earth could heal all manner of diseases by His own authority, how He could still the waves with a word of command, how He could discern the thoughts of all men, how He could finally and authoritatively forgive sin, how He could be in complete dominion over angelic spheres, how He could be associated with the Father and the Spirit in majestic ascriptions of heavenly glory, how He could be linked with the titles, the attributes, and the worship belonging to Deity. The answer is found in the revealed truth that this One, as no other could ever be, is both God and man, yet one adorable Person. None need be surprised that this Being is different and, for want of a parallel in the history of the universe, is incomprehensible to finite minds. Were He only man, even the greatest of men, His fellow men might apprehend Him, but He is, first of all, the God of all eternity; and because of that aspect of His incomparable Person, the finite mind may never plumb the immeasurable depths or scale the limitless heights of His Being.

An uncounted number of devout men and even those who lack a due recognition of divine authority have vied with each other in the effort to define or circumscribe the Person of Christ. Christology purposes to set forth this unrivaled Person; but a true Christology, unlike the straitened treatment imposed in Theology Proper, should extend to the life, to the activities of Christ, and above all else to the redemption He has wrought, and to His eternal power and glory.

No apology is offered for the reconsideration in one connected thesis of truths which have already been contemplated as they, in their appropriate order, have appeared in the course of a full-rounded system of doctrine. There is benefit, sufficient to justify the effort, in gathering into one continuous dissertation the essential features of divine revelation respecting the Person and work of the Second Person of the Godhead—as there is equal advantage in a comprehensive contemplation of the Person and work of the Third Person of the Godhead. Were these vast themes to be broadened to incorporate the history of these doctrines, the subject matter would greatly transcend the plan of this work. Historical features here, as everywhere throughout this work, are eliminated in the main with the expectation that these will be accounted for in another discipline in the student's course of study, namely, the *History of Christian Doctrine*.

The larger and usual division of Christology is twofold—Christ's Person and His work. The work of Christ, being generally restricted to the redemption He has achieved, does not include other essential features—His life on earth, His teachings, His manifestation of divine attributes, His offices as Prophet, Priest, and King, or His relationships to angelic spheres. It is with this larger consideration of Christology in view that a sevenfold division of this extended theme will be pursued: (1) the preincarnate Christ (chap. I), (2) Christ incarnate (chaps. II–VIII), (3) the sufferings and death of Christ incarnate (chap. IX), (4) the resurrection of Christ incarnate (chap. X), (5) the ascension and session of Christ incarnate (chap. XI), (6) the second advent and kingdom of Christ incarnate (chaps. XII–XIII), and (7) the eternal kingdom of Christ incarnate (chap. XIV).

A true and worthy estimation of the Person of Christ is the founda-

tion of a befitting Christology. The cursory computation or valuation
of Christ which extends to no greater lengths than to say He began with
His human birth, lived thirty-three years on earth, died by crucifixion,
was raised, and ascended into heaven, is, in the light of the human story
which the Gospels set forth, a natural deduction. Such an inference is
nonetheless incommensurate and is therefore misleading. The harmful
effect of such a restricted comprehension of Christ is felt not alone in
a field of truth which extends merely to temporal and mundane issues;
it involves man's proper recognition of his God and Creator. In such
realms, no estimation with regard to the effect can be placed on the
enormity of the error. The difference is great indeed whether a highly
endowed and divinely favored man began to exist when Christ was born
of a woman, or whether a Person of the eternal Godhead became incarnate in human form. The natural disposition of the human mind to
think of Christ as a man to whom unusual divine elements were added
enters, perhaps unwittingly, into very much modern religious thought.
That Christ is God in the most absolute sense and that through the incarnation a member of the adorable Godhead has entered the human
family by becoming a part of it, is a far different proposition. The question of who Jesus Christ is becomes the fundamental issue in Christology. If He be very God, as He is, then His birth, His life on earth, His
teachings, His death, His resurrection, His session in heaven, and His
return assume proportions which are as limitless as infinity. On the
other hand, if Christology be occupied merely with a man, be he ever
so exalted and favored of God, these features respecting him are no
more than details of that human exaltation. It is therefore essential,
before any worthy investigation into the great realities which enter into
the divine undertaking in and through the Lord Jesus Christ can be pursued, that the mind and heart of the student be made conscious to a
degree which dominates all his thinking that *Christ is God*. The absolute, dogmatic declaration that Christ is God is the basic premise in
all logic respecting the Person and work of Christ. Without a complete recognition of His Deity, every feature of Christology must be at
fault to a baleful degree. As is the case in a great number and variety
of themes, the only source from which information may be drawn respecting the Person of Christ is the Sacred Text. In that Text God has
spoken regarding the Deity and eternal existence of Christ—this, too,
not in a limited way, but at every point where the subject rightfully
appears in the Word of God; and not so much as one passage, when
properly expounded, implies the contrary. Those who have questioned

the truth that Christ is God have done so either through a limited under-standing of that which is written, or through wanton rejection of what is doubtless the clearest of all revelations. To the theologian whose task is to discover, arrange, and defend the truth which God has spoken, the assignment relative to the absolute Deity of Christ is simple indeed. The joining of the doctrine of Christ's humanity to the doctrine of His Deity does create a problem which demands the most exact and careful consideration; but the doctrine respecting Christ's Deity when standing alone is without complications.

The general divisions of the divine revelation regarding Christ's pre-existence may be comprehended under a sevenfold arrangement of truth: (1) Christ is God, hence His pre-existence; (2) Christ is the Creator, hence His pre-existence; (3) Christ is a party to the before-time cove-nant, hence His pre-existence; (4) the Old Testament anticipation of Messiah which Christ answered is that of Jehovah God, hence He pre-existed; (5) the Old Testament angel of Jehovah is Christ, hence He pre-existed; (6) indirect Biblical assertions declare Christ to have pre-existed; and (7) direct Biblical assertions declare Christ to have pre-existed.

I. THE DEITY OF CHRIST

The line of evidence which demonstrates the pre-existence of Christ on the ground of the truth—as stated above—that He is God, is wholly uncomplicated. Being God, He has existed from all eternity and will be the same yesterday, today, and forever. To the spiritually minded believer the procedure which undertakes to prove the Deity of Christ is redundant; yet to the unbeliever a restatement of this overwhelming evidence will always be advantageous, if perchance there is sufficient candor to receive it. Such a declaration of Christ's Deity is called for in any attempt to develop a worthy Christology. The line of argument to be followed should be clear, namely, that, as the Deity of Christ is verified, both His pre-existence and His eternal existence are assured. In this the Arian assumption, which contends that Christ pre-existed but was a creation of God and therefore not equal with God, is refuted. Of God, the *Westminster Confession of Faith* declares:

There is but one only living and true God, who is infinite in being and perfection, a most pure spirit, invisible, without body, parts, or passions, im-mutable, immense, eternal, incomprehensible, almighty, most wise, most holy, most free, most absolute, working all things according to the counsel of his own immutable and most righteous will, for his own glory; most loving, gracious, merciful, long-suffering, abundant in goodness and truth, forgiving iniquity, transgression, and sin; the rewarder of them that diligently seek him; and withal most just and terrible in his judgments, hating all sin, and who will by no means clear the guilty. God hath all life, glory, goodness, blessedness, in and of himself; and is alone in and unto himself all-sufficient, not standing in need of any creatures which he hath made, nor deriving any glory from them, but only manifesting his own glory in, by, unto, and upon them: he is the alone fountain of all being, of whom, through whom, and to whom, are all things; and hath most sovereign dominion over them, to do by them, for them, and upon them, whatsoever himself pleaseth. In his sight all things are open and manifest; his knowledge is infinite, infallible, and independent upon the creature, so as nothing is to him contingent or uncertain. He is most holy in all his counsels, in all his works, and in all his commands. To him is due from angels and men, and every other creature, whatsoever worship, service, or obedience, he is pleased to require of them. . . .

It is probable that no more comprehensive declaration respecting God has been framed than this; yet it is precisely this infinity of Being which the Scriptures predicate of Christ. There is nothing which is said to be true of God which is not said to be true of Christ and to the same degree of infinite perfection. It is true that He took upon Himself the human form and that in so doing important problems arise regarding the theanthropic Person which He became. These problems have been considered under Theology Proper and will yet be resumed later when contemplating the incarnation and earth-life of the Savior. The fundamental issue is that Christ is God. This has also been proved earlier and is now to be demonstrated again. The student is enjoined not to pass over these proofs without having attained to a profound conviction of the Deity of Christ. If he wavers respecting this foundational truth, he should recanvass every argument and attempt no forward step until this credence is definitely acquired, for apart from this conviction no true progress will be made. If, on the other hand, such a conviction is not gained, the student is fundamentally wrong and can, under such abnormal unbelief and want of amenableness to the Scriptures, serve no worthy purpose as an exponent of the Sacred Text. The Lord has Himself declared that "all men should honour the Son, even as they honour the Father" (John 5:23). The Son is dishonored when assigned a lower place than that of the Father. Such dishonor to the Son is displeasing to the Father, and a ministry is vain indeed which, though sincere, advances under the displeasure of God. The Deity of the Father is all but universally admitted, so also the Deity of the Spirit; but the Deity of the Son is challenged. Such a doubt would not have arisen had the Son not become incarnate. It is His entrance into the human sphere that has provided a field for unbelief. Thus it is required the more that the exact testimony of the Word of God should be given in its full authority. As though the divine Author anticipated the temptation to unbelief which would exist through misunderstanding of the theanthropic Person, the strongest evidence is supplied concerning the Deity of Christ. The Scriptures are as clear and conclusive in their expressions respecting the Deity of Christ as they are respecting His humanity. His humanity is revealed by the natural method of ascribing to Him human titles, human attributes, human actions, and human relationships. Similarly, His Deity is disclosed in the same manner by ascribing to Christ divine titles, divine attributes, divine actions, and divine relationships.

1. THE DIVINE NAMES. The names found in the Bible—especially those applied to divine Persons—are far more than empty titles. They define as well as indicate the Person to whom they belong. The name *Jesus* is His human designation, but it also embodies the whole redemptive purpose of His incarnation (cf. Matt. 1:21). Similar titles such as "The Son of man," The son of Mary, "The son of Abraham," "The son of David," assert His human lineage and relationships. In like manner the designations "Word," or Logos, "God," "Lord," "The mighty God," "The everlasting Father," "Immanuel," "Son of God," connote His Deity. Among these divine names, some are final in their implications.

a. DESIGNATIONS OF ETERNAL RELATIONSHIP: *Logos* (Λόγος). As language expresses thought, so Christ is the Expression, the Revealer, the Manifester of God. The term *Logos*—used only by the Apostle John as a name of the Second Person—indicates the eternal character of Christ. As Logos He was in the beginning, He was with God, and He was God (John 1:1). He likewise became flesh (John 1:14) and thus is —according to divine functions—the manifestation of God to man (cf. John 1:18). In His manifestation, all that may be disclosed relative to the Person of God was not only resident in Christ—"In him dwelleth all the fulness [πλήρωμα] of the Godhead bodily" (Col. 2:9)—but all the competency of God—knowledge-surpassing, indeed—was resident in Him. No stronger declaration of the Deity of Christ can be made than is indicated by the cognomen *Logos*. Without the use of this specific title the Apostle Paul also has written both in Colossians and in Hebrews of the same pre-existence of Christ; and concerning the origin of this title and the fact that the Apostle John employs it without explanation—suggesting a general understanding of its meaning—collateral reading may be pursued (cf. Dean Alford, M. R. Vincent, and in the *International Standard Bible Encyclopaedia, s.v.,* Alexander).

Bishop Lightfoot, in his commentary on Colossians, chapter 1, verse 15 ff., has declared the meaning of *Logos* and its use in the Sacred Text. He writes:

As the idea of the *Logos* underlies the whole of this passage, though the term itself does not appear, a few words explanatory of this term will be necessary by way of preface. The word λόγος then, denoting both "reason" and "speech," was a philosophical term adopted by Alexandrian Judaism before St. Paul wrote, to express the *manifestation* of the Unseen God, the Absolute Being, in the creation and government of the World. It included all modes by which God makes Himself known to man. As His *reason,* it denoted His purpose or design; as His *speech,* it implied His revelation. Whether this λόγος was conceived merely as the divine energy personified, or whether the conception took a more concrete form, I need not stop now to enquire; but I hope to give a fuller account of the matter in a later volume. It is sufficient for the understanding of what follows to say that Christian teachers, when they adopted this term, exalted and fixed its meaning by attaching to it two precise and definite ideas: (1) "The Word is a Divine Person," ὁ λόγος ἦν πρὸς τὸν θεὸν καὶ θεὸς ἦν ὁ λόγος; and (2) "The Word became incarnate in Jesus Christ," ὁ λόγος σὰρξ ἐγένετο. It is obvious that these two propositions must have altered materially the significance of all the subordinate terms connected with the idea of the λόγος; and that therefore their use in Alexandrian writers, such as Philo, cannot be taken to *define,* though it may be brought to *illustrate,* their meaning in St. Paul and St. John. With these cautions the Alexandrian phraseology, as a providential preparation for the teaching of the Gospel, will afford important aid in the understanding of the Apostolic writings.—8th ed., pp. 141–42

Only Begotten (μονογενής)—*John 1:14, 18.* This, one of the highest of titles ever employed, bears an indication of the eternal relationship existing between the Father and the Son. Here R. Govett in his *Exposition of the Gospel of St. John* declares:

This glory was of "the *Only-begotten* from the Father." These words, then, refute the ideas of some of "the men of intelligence," that there were many like emanations proceeding from God. No! *He* is the *Only* begotten. He is related to the Father, as an only son is to an earthly father. He is "begotten, not made," partaker in full of His Father's Godhead. "But if so, do you not introduce another difficulty? If He be the begotten Son of God, proceeding from the Father, do you not imply, that He is not eternal, but had a beginning, after the Father?" At this point two errors may seek to enter, "Jesus Christ is *God;* therefore not a *Son* of God." Then arises Tritheism, or the doctrine of three Gods. Or, "Jesus Christ is *Son*—therefore He is not *God.*" Then Arianism comes in. We testify on the contrary, then, with Scripture, that

Jesus Christ is the Eternal Son of God, and is God. "Eternal decrees" contains as great a difficulty as "Eternal Son." Eternity introduces difficulties
beyond our plumb-line. Jesus is "the Only-begotten" in relation to the many
figurative "sons of God." Angels are sons of God by *creation;* but in the sense
in which Christ is so, they are not sons at all. He stands alone. In another
sense those begotten anew of the Spirit become *adopted* Sons of God. But they
begin to be so, after having become men. Christ was Son from all eternity.
Still further, to set the matter clearly, the Spirit of God adds—"Only-begotten
from the Father," as distinct from Him eternally, and sent forth from the
Father. Jesus uses this phrase in reference to Himself (iii. 16–18). The word
is then to be taken in the loftiest sense of which it is capable; for the giving
of Jesus Christ is alleged to be the very greatest gift which is possible. The
higher the person of Christ, the greater the glory of God in the gift of His
Son.—I, 23–24

Image (εἰκών)—*Colossians 1:15. Image* connotes more than mere
likeness; it implies that there is a prototype and that the image is its
revealed reality. On this term Dean Alford may be quoted:

. . . the image of the invisible God (the adjunct invisible is of the utmost weight to the understanding of the expression. The same fact being the
foundation of the whole as in Phil. ii.6 ff., that the Son *subsisted in the form of
God,* that side of the fact is brought out *here,* which points to His being the
visible manifestation of that in God which is *invisible:* the *word* of the eternal
silence, the *shining forth* of the *glory* which no creature can bear, the *expressed
mark* of that *Person* which is incommunicably God's; in one word, the *declarer*
of the Father, whom none hath seen. So that while the epithet invisible includes in it not only the *invisibility,* but the incommunicability of God, the term
image also must not be restricted to Christ corporeally visible in the Incarnation, but understood of Him as the manifestation of God in His whole Person
and work—pre-existent and incarnate. It is obvious, that in this expression,
the Apostle approaches very near to the Alexandrian doctrine of the *Logos*
or *Word:* how near, may be seen by an extract from Philo: "As they who
cannot look upon the sun, behold the sunshine opposite to him as himself,
and the changing phases of the moon as being himself: so men apprehend *the
image of God, His Angel the Word, as being Himself.*" St. Paul is, in fact,
as St. John afterwards did, adopting the language of that lore as far as it
represented divine truth, and rescuing it from being used in the service of
error.—*New Testament for English Readers,* New ed., II, 446

Exact Image (χαρακτήρ)—*Hebrews 1:3, Gk.* M. R. Vincent states,
"Here the essential being of God is conceived as setting its distinctive
stamp upon Christ, coming into definite and characteristic expression
in his person, so that the Son bears the exact impress of the divine nature
and character" (*Word Studies in the New Testament,* IV, 383).

First-Begotten (πρωτότοκος). This title—sometimes translated
First-Born—indicates that Christ is First-Born, the elder in relation

to all creation; not the first created thing, but the antecedent to all things as well as the cause of them (cf. Col. 1:16). Of this title Dr. John F. Walvoord writes, "This term is used twice in the New Testament without referring to Christ (Heb. 11:28; 12:23), and seven times as His title. An examination of these references will reveal a threefold use: (a) Before all creation (Rom. 8:29; Col. 1:15). As the 'firstborn of every creature' (Col. 1:15), the title is obviously used of Christ as existing before all creation, hence, eternally self-existent. (b) Firstborn of Mary (Matt. 1:25; Luke 2:7; Heb. 1:6). Here the reference is plainly to the fact that Christ was the first child born to Mary, a usage in contrast to that speaking of His eternal sonship. The term is used, then, of His preincarnate Person, and also of His incarnate Person. (c) Firstborn by Resurrection (Col. 1:18; Rev. 1:5). The meaning here is that Christ is the first to be raised from the dead in resurrection life, hence, 'the firstborn from the dead' (Col. 1:18). In relation to the eternity of Christ, this title is another proof that Christ is the self-existent, uncreated God spoken of in Romans 8:29; Colossians 1:15; and that in view of His eternal Person, He also has the honor of being the first to be raised from the dead in resurrection life" (*Outline of Christology,* unpublished ms., pp. 5–6).

A consideration of these designations cannot but impress the devout mind with the truth that the Lord Jesus Christ existed as God from all eternity, and that He will so exist throughout eternity to come.

b. THE PRIMARY DESIGNATIONS OF DEITY: *God.* Though in a few instances the name *God* is used with an inferior application, it is almost universally a reference to Deity. When applied to Christ, as many times it is, it declares Him to be of the Godhead and therefore to have existed from all eternity. The use of this designation for Christ begins in the Old Testament and continues throughout the New. Abundant evidence may be cited which makes Isaiah 40:3 turn out to be an anticipation of Christ's first-advent ministry as heralded by John. The passage reads, "The voice of him that crieth in the wilderness, Prepare ye the way of the LORD, make straight in the desert a highway for our God." In this Scripture the Holy Spirit asserts that the Messiah, or Christ, is both Jehovah and Elohim. In the same manner the same prophet by inspiration writes of Christ: "For unto us a child is born, unto us a son is given: and the government shall be upon his shoulder: and his name shall be called Wonderful, Counsellor, The mighty God, The everlasting Father, The Prince of Peace. Of the increase of his government and peace there shall be no end, upon the throne of David, and upon his kingdom, to order it, and to establish it with judgment and with justice from henceforth even for ever. The zeal of the LORD of hosts will perform this" (9:6–7). Christ alone is the member of the Godhead of whom it could be said that He would be born and that He would sit on David's throne. So, also, Isaiah declares the coming One to be *Immanuel* and identifies Him as One who would be born of a virgin (Isa. 7:14). Matthew interprets the name *Immanuel* as being "God with us" (Matt. 1:23). The significance of this title is more than that God is present with His people; it is that, by the incarnation, God has become one of the human family. Luke reports the angel as saying of Christ that John would turn many to the Lord their God (Luke 1:16); and this is to turn them to Messiah. Thus, also, over against all the revelation relative to Christ's humanity which the New Testament sets forth is the disclosure in the same Testament of the truth of His absolute Deity, made by the repeated application to Him of the name *God*. As seen above, the Apostle John, when introducing Christ as the subject of his Gospel, states that the Logos is God, and at once adds that it is this same Logos (who is God) who created all things. When Thomas beheld the Savior's wounds he said, "My Lord and my God" (John 20:28). Such an utterance, were it untrue, would be idolatry and reprehensible sin; yet Christ did not reprove Thomas, but rather states that, by so much, Thomas has come to believe that which is true of Him. As certainly as it is Christ who is to come again, so certainly He bears the title of Great God and our Savior (Titus 2:13). It was God who shed His blood to purchase the Church (cf. Acts 20:28). When Psalm 45:6 is quoted in Hebrews—clearly referring to Christ—the message states, "Thy throne, O God, is for ever and ever." It is thus in the most express terms that Christ is said to be *God,* and reason asserts that, if He be God, He existed from all eternity. He is the "True God," the "God Blessed for ever," and "God who is over all."

Jehovah. Lastly, it is to be observed that the highest of all appellations of Deity, that of *Jehovah,* is freely and constantly applied to Christ. Of the exalted character of that name it is written, "I am Jehovah, that is my name; and my glory will I not give to another, neither my praise unto graven images" (Isa. 42:8, R.V.). The name *Jehovah* is proper to but One; it can never be rightfully applied to another. Other titles of Deity, such as *Elohim,* imply a correspondence with others. "That men may know that thou, whose name alone is JEHOVAH, art the most high over all the earth" (Ps. 83:18). It is Jehovah who speaks in Zechariah 12:10, yet only Christ could be identified as the One who was pierced. Thus the prophet writes, "And I will pour upon the house of David, and upon the inhabitants of Jerusalem, the spirit of grace and of supplications: and they shall look upon me whom they have pierced, and they shall mourn for him, as one mourneth for his only son, and shall be in bitterness for him, as one that is in bitterness for his firstborn." John seems to be considering this Scripture when he said, "Behold, he cometh with clouds; and every eye shall see him, and they also which pierced him: and all kindreds of the earth shall wail because of him" (Rev. 1:7). To have both Deity and humanity in view as in Jeremiah 23:5–6, is certain evidence that it is of Christ that the prophet writes when he says, "Behold, the days come, saith the LORD, that I will raise unto David a righteous Branch, and a King shall reign and prosper, and shall execute judgment and justice in the earth. In his days Judah shall be saved, and Israel shall dwell safely: and this is his name whereby he shall be called, THE LORD OUR RIGHTEOUSNESS." It is Christ who is made unto the believer *righteousness* (1 Cor. 1:30; 2 Cor. 5:21). In Psalm 68:18, Jehovah again appears. The passage reads, "Thou hast ascended on high, thou hast led captivity captive: thou hast received gifts for men; yea, for the rebellious also, that the LORD God might dwell among them." And it is this very Scripture which when quoted by the Apostle in Ephesians 4:8–10 refers definitely to Christ. Psalm 102, which names Jehovah at least eight times, is quoted in connection with Christ in Hebrews 1:10 ff. thus, "And, Thou, Lord, in the beginning hast laid the foundation of the earth; and the heavens are the works of thine hands . . ." So, also, in Isaiah 8:13–14 He is said to be the Stone of stumbling, "Sanctify the LORD of hosts himself; and let him be your fear, and let him be your dread. And he shall be for a sanctuary; but for a stone of stumbling and for a rock of offence to both the houses of Israel, for a gin and for a snare to the inhabitants of Jerusalem." Of this prophecy of Christ Peter writes, "Unto you therefore which believe he is precious: but unto them which be disobedient, the stone which the builders disallowed, the same is made the head of the corner, and a stone of stumbling, and a rock of offence, even to them which stumble at the word, being disobedient: whereunto also they were appointed" (1 Pet. 2:7–8). Upon the important passage— Isaiah 6:1–13 in its relation to John 12:41, Dr. William Cooke writes:

In John 12:41, the evangelist, speaking of Christ, says, "These things said Esaias, when he saw his glory, and spake of him." The things which Esaias spake are stated in the preceding verse, and we find this prophecy revealed in Isaiah 6. The evangelist states that the prophet saw Christ's glory at the time of the revelation; and there we find the sublime manifestation referred to, and the seraphs veiling their faces before his awful majesty. But he whom the evangelist speaks of as CHRIST, in his humbled and incarnate state, the prophet identifies in his pre-existent glory as "JEHOVAH," and the seraphs adore him as "*Jehovah of hosts.*" The passage is too important and sublime to be omitted. "In the year that king Uzziah died I saw also *the Lord* sitting upon a throne, high and lifted up, and his train filled the temple. Above it stood the seraphs: each one had six wings; with twain he covered his face, and with twain he covered his feet, and with twain he did fly. And one cried unto another and said, Holy, holy, holy, is Jehovah of hosts: the whole earth is full of his glory." The evidence that Christ is here called Jehovah of hosts is too bright to be resisted, and the authority too sacred to be impugned. Now, let the reader remember the declaration we previously adduced from the word of God, which proclaims that "He whose name *alone* is Jehovah is the Most High over all the earth," and then compare this assertion with the fact before us, that the name "Jehovah," and its various combinations, as "Jehovah God," "Jehovah our righteousness," and "Jehovah of hosts," are applied to Christ, and he will have before him a complete demonstration of the proper Deity of Christ. The New Testament being written in Greek, the name Jehovah, which is Hebrew, does not occur in it; the word is not used by evangelists or apostles in reference to either Father, Son, or Spirit. Indeed, that name had ceased to be pronounced, except by the high priest in the temple. In the Septuagint version the word Κύριος, LORD, is used instead of Jehovah, and so it is by the New Testament writers. When they quote from the Old Testament such passages as contain the name Jehovah, they use the word Κύριος, LORD, in its stead, whether that name be applied to the Father, Son, or Spirit; and, indeed, in their own compositions this word is constantly applied to the Deity, whichever person may be intended. This word, in its radical meaning, signifies existence, like the word Jehovah; and though custom has not restricted it to God alone, yet when applied to him it must be understood to represent the meaning intended by the name Jehovah. This will not be disputed in reference to the Father; but as we have abundantly shown that the word Jehovah, with all its sacred combinations, is applied to Christ, it will necessarily follow that the word Κύριος, LORD, is also applicable to him in its highest sense—as the substitute for Jehovah, in the same sense in which it is applied to the Father, and is thus applied to him in a multitude of instances. The numerous passages quoted from the Old Testament, and applied by the apostles to Christ, so fully establish this, as to show that the names "Jehovah" and "Lord" are convertible terms as applied to Christ, and the word "Lord" is applied to the Redeemer about a thousand times in the New Testament. Sometimes, both in the Old and New Testament, a *periphrasis* is used to express the same idea as Jehovah—that is, several words are employed as explanatory of its meaning. A few examples will make this quite clear. "Hearken unto me, O Jacob, and Israel my called: I am he; I am the first, I also am the last." Again, "I Jehovah, the first, and with the last, I am he." Once more, "Thus saith Jehovah, the King of Israel, and his Redeemer, Jehovah of hosts; I am the first, and I am the last; and beside me there is no God" (Isa. 48:12; 41:4; 44:6).

From these passages it is clear that the terms "THE FIRST AND THE LAST" are not only titles of Deity, but are explanatory of the name Jehovah—are expressive of Him who is eternal in his existence and unchangeable in his nature. Now, these Divine titles are ascribed to our Lord and Saviour: "I am Alpha and Omega, the beginning and the end, the First and the Last. I Jesus have sent mine angel to testify unto you these things in the churches." "And when I saw him, I fell at his feet as dead. And he laid his right hand upon me, saying unto me, Fear not; I am the FIRST and the LAST: I am he that liveth, and was dead." "I am Alpha and Omega, the Beginning and the End, saith the Lord, which is, and which was, and which is to come, the Almighty" (Rev. 22:13, 16; 1:17, 18; 1:8). The two former passages most clearly refer to Jesus; and that the third does, is highly probable, both from the context and the identity of the phraseology. Since, then, the title, "The First and the Last," is the periphrasis for Jehovah in the Old Testament, and this is applied to Jesus in the New, it furnishes an additional declaration of his proper Deity. In the texts we have just adduced, several other terms are introduced expressive of the same meaning. He is called Alpha and Omega. Alpha is the first and Omega the last letter in the Greek alphabet, and the import is, that he is the origin and object of all things. He is called the "One WHO IS, WHO WAS, and WHO IS TO COME;" and this is but another periphrasis for Jehovah—another mode of expressing his eternal and unchangeable nature. It appears that he is also here called the ALMIGHTY, which word explains itself as an appellative suited to him alone who in the highest sense is God. The word ($\pi\alpha\nu\tau o\kappa\rho\acute{a}\tau\omega\rho$) *Almighty* is frequently used, and it always means, as Schleusner says, "The Omnipotent Being, who has all things in his own power, and on whose will and pleasure all created beings are dependent;" and (*est nomen soli Deo proprium*) "is a name proper only unto God." The following passage illustrates and confirms this view: "Great and marvellous are thy works, Lord God Almighty; just and true are thy ways, thou King of saints. Who shall not fear thee, O Lord, and glorify thy name? for thou only art holy" (Rev. 15:3, 4).—*Christian Theology*, pp. 97–99

Much may be said of the titles *Jehovah of the Temple* and *Jehovah of the Sabbath* as applied to Christ. To the Jew the temple was greater than all else excepting the One who was pleased to dwell there. Malachi declared that Jehovah would come to His temple (3:1), and Christ fulfilled that prediction. Of the temple Christ said, "Ye have made my house a den of thieves," and "My house shall be called the house of prayer." The temple could not be Christ's house unless it be true that Christ is Jehovah. In like manner, the Sabbath was Jehovah's day. He ordained it and He was to be honored by it; but Christ styled Himself as "Lord also of the Sabbath." The Sabbath was Jehovah's day also in the sense that it came to be His own through the sequence of six creative days. Thus when Christ announced Himself to be Lord also of the Sabbath He, by so much, assumed the place of the Creator of all things.

Yet more may be said of the name which Christ bears. Salvation is through His name (cf. Acts 4:12); and all gatherings of the people of God are unto His name, who therefore is God.

It is thus demonstrated that every divine name is ascribed as freely to Christ as to the Father, and if these titles do not assert the Deity of the Son then, in candor, they do not assert the Deity of the Father. Since it is declared by these names that Christ is God, then it follows that He has existed as God before His incarnation.

2. THE EVIDENTIAL ATTRIBUTES. Equally conclusive that Christ is God is the evidence which is drawn from His attributes. Only a portion of this material need be indicated.

Eternity. A distinction should be maintained between that which is merely extended and indefinite with respect to time and that which is eternal in the absolute sense. Millions of ages may have been marked off, but no multiplication of ages can ever make an eternity. Of Christ it is said that His goings forth are "from of old, from everlasting" (Mic. 5:2). In the English text, the words "In the beginning" serve to open both the book of Genesis and the Gospel by John. The Genesis beginning, however, is comparatively modern history as compared to that mentioned by John. Genesis relates to the origin of material things, while John is straining language to its last degree of expression to declare that which is eternal. In a beginning which antedates all creative acts the Logos *was*. He did not then begin to be, but was Himself as old and as all-sufficient then as now. This Logos that *was* has been identified as the Lord Jesus Christ. He it is whom John is introducing as the Subject of his Gospel. Thus, also, by the application of the Jehovah name "I am" (John 8:58), Christ claimed in respect of Himself that He is Jehovah, and no stronger assertion could be made by Him regarding His eternity than to assume that designation. That He is Jehovah is a truth to which no creature might bear conclusive evidence. He must witness thus of Himself, and this might be, as it was, confirmed by the Father and the Spirit. Christ's own witness to Himself is sustained by His unimpeachable character. In this He was neither self-deceived nor ignorant. Similarly, and by the authority of the Holy Spirit's inspiration, Christ is said by Isaiah to be The everlasting Father, which declaration is better rendered *The Father of Eternity*. The Apostle declares that "he is before all things, and by him all things consist" (Col. 1:17).

He who existed before aught was created is of necessity Himself un-created and eternal. John states that Christ is "The first and the last." This is one of the strongest declarations of Jehovah respecting Him-self (cf. Isa. 41:4; 44:6; 48:12). Ages past and ages future are in-cluded in this proclamation. How, indeed, could the Savior be the source of life eternal to all who believe and He Himself not be eternal? True, with reference to the beginning of His humanity, He is related to time, though His humanity will know no end.

Immutability. The unchangeableness of Deity is ascribed to Christ. When Jehovah announces, "I am the LORD, I change not" (Mal. 3:6), He is stating that which belongs to the Godhead alone. All else is sub-ject to change. It is significant, therefore, that of Christ it is written, "They shall perish; but thou remainest; and they all shall wax old as doth a garment; and as a vesture shalt thou fold them up, and they shall be changed: but thou art the same, and thy years shall not fail. . . . Jesus Christ the same yesterday, and to day, and for ever" (Heb. 1:11–12; 13:8).

Omnipotence. The Almighty is an appellation which can belong only to Deity; yet of Christ it is said that He is "able even to subdue all things unto himself" (Phil. 3:21), and at the end of the thousand-year conquest of all angelic enemies "all things shall be subdued unto him" (1 Cor. 15:28). No particular reference to the power displayed in His mighty works while here on the earth is needed when it is remembered that He is repeatedly said to be the Creator of all things.

Omniscience. Again, another attribute which belongs only to Deity is in view, and in many instances both directly and indirectly this limitless competency is predicated of the Lord Jesus Christ. That omniscience is a characteristic of Deity is disclosed in many Old Testament passages. "For thou, even thou only, knowest the hearts of all the children of men" (1 Kings 8:39); "I the LORD search the heart, I try the reins, even to give every man according to his ways" (Jer. 17:10; cf. 11:20; 20:12). Of Christ it is said that He knew the mind and the thoughts of all men. He needed not that any man should tell Him what was in man. He "knoweth the thoughts of man." It is not a contradiction of this great truth when Christ said of Himself, "But of that day and that hour knoweth no man, no, not the angels which are in heaven, neither the Son, but the Father" (Mark 13:32). It would be wholly within the range of that theanthropic Person to know perfectly on the divine side and yet not to know on the human side. How He could know and not know is beyond human understanding, but not impossible with God;

however, it is probable that the Savior is employing a form of speech which is common to the Word of God. As the Apostle said to the Corinthians, "I determined not to know any thing among you save Jesus Christ and him crucified" (1 Cor. 2:2), so Christ may have been speaking. In this statement to the Corinthians the Apostle is saying that he determined to limit his message to the one theme. Certainly he did not become ignorant for the time being of all else that he had known. It is easily believed that it was not and is not the purpose of God to reveal the day and the hour of Christ's return. Speaking from the glory, Christ said, "And all the churches shall know that I am he which searcheth the reins and hearts: and I will give unto every one of you according to your works" (Rev. 2:23). How conclusive relative to Christ's omniscience is John 10:15; and also Matthew 11:27, "All things are delivered unto me of my Father: and no man knoweth the Son, but the Father; neither knoweth any man the Father, save the Son, and he to whomsoever the Son will reveal him."

Omnipresence. Of Jehovah it is written, "But will God indeed dwell on the earth? behold, the heaven and heaven of heavens cannot contain thee; how much less this house that I have builded?" (1 Kings 8:27); "Am I a God at hand, saith the LORD, and not a God afar off? Can any hide himself in secret places that I shall not see him? saith the LORD. Do not I fill heaven and earth? saith the LORD" (Jer. 23:23–24). In the same manner Christ presents Himself as One to be present wherever two or three are gathered in His name, and to be with every witness even to the consummation of the age. He likewise promised that He with His Father would come and make His abode with all who love Him (John 14:23).

As definitely might it be pointed out that the divine attributes of infinite *love, holiness, justice,* and *truth* are predicated of Christ as they are of the Father. Each divine attribute belonging to Christ is an indisputable evidence that Christ is God and therefore one who existed from all eternity.

3. THE EVIDENTIAL MIGHTY WORKS. This aspect of proof respecting Christ's Deity and pre-existence need not include His miracles while here on earth, which theme will be viewed in later pages. Vast undertakings, such as man cannot even comprehend, are assigned to Christ. Some of these are:

Creation. Though according to the Bible the work of creation is assigned to each of the Persons of the Godhead in turn, it does not lessen the scope of that work in the case of any one of them. Some have con-

tended that John 1:3 asserts that the Father created through the Son as
Agent, and that the Son was not, therefore, the original cause of creation. On this important distinction Dr. William Cooke has written thus:

In order to neutralize the force of this argument for the Saviour's Deity
[that He created the universe], it has been alleged that our translation in
John 1:3, "All things were made *by* him," is too strong for the original, and
that the Greek preposition δι' more properly denotes the instrument *through*
whom a thing is done, than the *agent by* whom it is done; that, therefore,
though Christ may be the *instrumental* cause, he cannot be the *efficient* cause;
and in support of this view we are referred to the passage, "By whom also he
made the worlds" (Heb. 1:2). But this criticism will not stand the test of
examination; for, in the first place, διά, with a genitive, is evidently used for
the efficient cause in numerous passages. Thus it is applied to the Father,
whose efficient agency will not be disputed; hence, we read, "God is faithful,
by whom (δι' οὗ) ye were called unto the fellowship of his Son" (1 Cor. 1:9. See
also Rom. 11:36; Heb. 2:10, where διά expresses the direct agency of the
Father). If, then, the word denotes efficiency when applied to the Father, we
must admit it denotes the same when applied to the Son, unless we are prepared to violate the common principles of language, to sustain a falling system.
But it should be remarked that διά is not the only preposition employed in
reference to the operation of the Saviour's power. The preposition ἐν is used,
and this, too, is expressive of immediate and efficient agency, as in Col. 1:16,
17. As to the passage, "By whom also he made the worlds," while this implies
the agency of the Father, it does not exclude the agency of the Son, but denotes their united agency, for the work of creation is ascribed efficiently to the
three persons in the glorious Trinity; and perhaps the passage implies that
the agency of the Son was as in some ineffable manner especially displayed in
this work.—*Op. cit.*, pp. 107–8

Passing over the truth that creation is everywhere only a divine
undertaking, it is pertinent to note that there are four direct statements
in the New Testament which aver that Christ created all things. These
passages read, (1) "All things were made by him; and without him was
not any thing made that was made" (John 1:3). In a positive sense, all
things were created by Him, and, in a negative sense, apart from Him
not anything was made. (2) "He was in the world, and the world was
made by him, and the world knew him not" (John 1:10). A strange relationship is here asserted: He was in the world which He had made.
(3) "For by him were all things created, that are in heaven, and that
are in earth, visible and invisible, whether they be thrones, or dominions,
or principalities, or powers: all things were created by him, and for him"
(Col. 1:16). Christ is said to be not only the Creator but the Object of
all creation. All was created by Him and for Him. (4) "And, Thou,
Lord, in the beginning hast laid the foundation of the earth; and the

heavens are the works of thine hands" (Heb. 1:10). This Scripture serves to seal all that has gone before, and in the light of these Scriptures none will with candor deny that Christ is the Creator of all things. If He creates, He is God; if He is God, He existed as God eternally.

Preservation. Whoever constructed this vast universe also upholds it and preserves it. All this is assigned to Christ. In Hebrews 1:3 it is said that He, Christ, "upholdeth all things by the word of his power." Similarly, in Colossians 1:17 the Apostle states, "And he is before all things, and by him all things consist." Thus the limitless system of worlds is said to be held together by none other than the Savior of mankind, even He who was nurtured in a human mother's arms.

Forgiveness of Sin. None on earth has either authority or right to forgive sin. None could forgive save the One against whom all have sinned. When Christ forgave sin, as He certainly did, He was not exercising a human prerogative. It is Jehovah that "blotteth out thy transgressions," and Christ, it is said, was the exalted Prince and Savior who gives repentance to Israel and forgiveness of sins (Acts 5:31). The Apostle writes, "Forbearing one another, and forgiving one another, if any man have a quarrel against any: even as Christ forgave you, so also do ye" (Col. 3:13). Since none but God can forgive sins, it is conclusively demonstrated that Christ, since He forgave sins, is God, and, being God, is from everlasting.

The Resurrection of the Dead. Christ assigned to Himself the exalted divine title of *The Resurrection, and the Life.* It is God who raiseth the dead and therefore Christ announced Himself to be God. It is written, "Verily, verily, I say unto you, The hour is coming, and now is, when the dead shall hear the voice of the Son of God: and they that hear shall live. For as the Father hath life in himself; so hath he given to the Son to have life in himself; and hath given him authority to execute judgment also, because he is the Son of man. Marvel not at this; for the hour is coming, in the which all that are in the graves shall hear his voice, and shall come forth; they that have done good, unto the resurrection of life; and they that have done evil, unto the resurrection of damnation" (John 5:25–29); "For since by man came death, by man came also the resurrection of the dead" (1 Cor. 15:21).

All Judgment. In view of the truth that to sit in judgment is the highest function of any government, it is indicative that all judgment is said to be committed to the Son. In such an exercise of authority and power the Judge must know the secrets of all hearts and the history of every creature. He must Himself be the righteous One upholding all standards of His righteous government. In Psalm 9:7–8 it is written of Jehovah, "But the LORD shall endure for ever: he hath prepared his throne for judgment. And he shall judge the world in righteousness, he shall minister judgment to the people in uprightness." Yet it is asserted that the Father judgeth no man, but hath committed all judgment unto the Son (John 5:22), and it is also said, "Because he hath appointed a day, in the which he will judge the world in righteousness by that man whom he hath ordained; whereof he hath given assurance unto all men, in that he hath raised him from the dead" (Acts 17:31). In conformity to this great disclosure, it is seen that the judgment of the nations is performed by the King on David's throne (cf. Ps. 2:7–9; Isa. 63:1–6; Matt. 25:31–46; 2 Thess. 1:7–10; Rev. 19:15), that He judges Israel (cf. Matt. 24:37—25:13), that He judges the believer's works (cf. 2 Cor. 5:10), and that He will yet judge all angelic powers (cf. 1 Cor. 15:25–26). Since He is God and all judgment is committed unto Him, it is He who sits upon the great white throne in judgment of the wicked dead (cf. Rev. 20:12–15). As His consort, His Bride will also sit in judgment with Him.

The mighty works, like His names and His attributes, point to the truth that Christ is God, and, being God, is eternal.

4. THE TRIUNE RELATIONSHIP. As a further and final evidence to be advanced in proof of the Deity of Christ, it may be observed that in every disclosure respecting the triune relationship the Son occupies a place of essential equality with the Father and the Spirit. To the Son are ascribed the same worship, the same honor, and the same glory. There is no ground for any supposition that the Father or the Spirit are more to be revered than the Son. Whatever is true of the Father and the Spirit in this relationship is, in every instance, as true of the Son. The Scriptures maintain this testimony in spite of the unmeasured condescension of the Son in the incarnation, and in spite of the truth that He remains incarnate in human form throughout eternity to come. The humanity of Christ, as has been seen, though perfect, has the limitations of that which is human; but in no instance does His humanity restrict His Deity. He remains what He is, namely, not God *mutilated* by the flesh, but God *manifest* in the flesh. The fact that Christ is to be worshiped and this on the authority of the inspired Sacred Text is indicative of that which He is in the Godhead relationship. He accepted the worship of men, and He, as much as the Father or the Spirit, is to be adored. He asked the rich young ruler who addressed Him as "Good master," "Why callest thou me good?" The entire meaning of this ques-

tion depends on where the emphasis is placed. Evidently Christ did not say, "Why callest thou me *good?*" but He did say, *"Why* callest thou me good?" By so much He drew out, so far as could be done, the esteem in which this ruler held the Lord. There is no basis here for the Unitarian claim that Christ did not believe in His own Deity. Those who think mostly in the terms of Christ's humanity naturally shrink from what to them seems to be the worship of a man. The correction of this impression can come only as the attention is drawn to the truth, which is as perfectly established, that He is God.

To those who believe the testimony of the Bible regarding the triune mode of the divine existence, there can be no doubt that Christ is the Second Person in that Trinity; nor can doubt be entertained reasonably whether the Second Person is in every feature equal to the First or the Third.

In concluding this division bearing on the Deity of Christ, it may be restated that the fourfold proof—His names, His attributes, His mighty works, and His rightful place in the Trinity—has established the truth that *Christ* is *God,* and, since He is God, He has existed from all eternity.

II. CHRIST AND CREATION

So far-reaching in its evidential value respecting the Deity of Christ is the truth that Christ is the Creator that it must reappear in this discussion. Already it has been listed among His mighty works. At this point the theme is introduced as a major proof of Christ's pre-existence. While four major passages bearing upon Christ as Creator have been cited above, only one of these is to be developed further under this division of this thesis.

In itself, the act of creating is an incomparable undertaking. In His creation of material things, God called them into existence out of nothing. Such a declaration is far removed from the notion that nothing has produced something. It is obvious that out of nothing nothing of itself could arise. The Biblical declaration is rather that out of infinite resources of God everything has come into existence. He is the Source of all that is. The self-determining will of God has caused the material universe, as stated in Romans 11:36, "For of him, and through him, and to him, are all things: to whom be glory for ever." In this Scripture the creation of all things is predicated of God; but, in Colossians 1:16–17, it is asserted in the same general terms that all things were created by Christ and for Him, that He is before all things and by Him all things consist. This is a reasonable pronouncement only to the extent that Christ is God. The power to create—whether it be production of a universe, of a new creation, or of a new heaven and a new earth—belongs alone to God, and is predicated alike of each of the three Persons of the Godhead. It is certain that if Christ is God He is able to create all things. However, the statement with which this division of this theme is concerned is that, since Christ is said to have created all things, He is by a right reasoning none other than God.

The one passage now to be considered is Colossians 1:15–19. Having declared the redemption which is provided through the blood of Christ and the remission of sins on the ground of that blood (cf. Col. 1:14), the Apostle enters upon an extended and revealing description of the Son who thus redeems. This whole context should be compared with Hebrews 1:2–12 and is distinctive in that it sets forth the Deity of the Son with no direct reference to His humanity. This exalted proclamation of Christ's Deity, as in Hebrews, chapter 1, is followed by a portion of Scripture which announces His humanity. These verses of Colossians 1:15–19 will be considered separately.

Verse 15. "Who is the image of the invisible God, the firstborn of every creature."

But recently in an earlier discussion the two eternal titles employed in this verse have been considered. To this may be added that to assert, as the Apostle does at this point, that Christ is the εἰκών or image of God is equivalent to John's statement regarding the λόγος—that He is not only the manifestation of God, but that He is God. No greater assertion respecting Christ could be made than the statement here advanced, that He is the exact image of God. Thus, again, in Hebrews 1:3 it is declared that Christ is the effulgence of the Father's glory and that all divine fullness—πλήρωμα—is in Him.

Verse 16. "For by him were all things created, that are in heaven, and that are in earth, visible and invisible, whether they be thrones, or dominions, or principalities, or powers: all things were created by him, and for him."

In this verse the reason is given for assigning to Christ the title found in verse 15, namely, "Firstborn of every creature." As this designation places Christ, in point of time, before all creation, He must have existed before all things. This passage, as Bishop Lightfoot points out, does not teach that Christ was Himself created before all other creations; it rather asserts "the absolute pre-existence of the Son" (*Op. cit.*, p. 144). Concerning a revelation such as this which assigns to Christ the causation of all things—far removed from the idea that He is Himself one of those created things—and includes things celestial and things terrestrial, and things visible and things invisible, it is to be expected that scholars of all generations would have written at length. The precise exegesis of this verse should be followed; however, for the purpose desired in the present treatise, it will suffice to assert, as above, that the text predicates of Christ the origination of all things. The suggestion that Christ was merely an agent through whom God wrought in creation is refused by all who are not prejudiced respecting the absolute pre-existence and creatorship of Christ. Upon the well-established rule that repetition of a truth in the Sacred Text is for emphasis, it is exceedingly significant that the phrase "all things were created by him" occurs twice in this one verse. The enumeration of things that were created by Christ reaches into celestial spheres. There are things visible in heaven as well as invisible and there are things invisible—as the souls of men—as well as visible on the earth. In fact, though mundane things are mentioned by no more than a reference to things that are in the earth, here the contemplation is largely of things which are in heaven. A proper proportion is probably preserved at this point regarding the relative importance of these two spheres. There is no slighting of mundane things. It is only that heavenly things are far more extensive. Thus is accentuated the surpassing creative work of the Son of God. Were this the only reference in the Bible to Christ's work in creation, it would, naturally, stand alone on its own declaration; but, as before stated, this same revelation occurs in other Scriptures, notably, John 1:3, 10; 1 Corinthians 8:6; Ephesians 3:9; Hebrews 1:10. The enumeration of heavenly things is restricted to celestial beings. The passage in Hebrews 1:10 assigns to Christ the laying of the foundation of the earth. Otherwise, that which stands first in the divine estimation is not material things, but living creatures; and the living creatures of heaven appear to exceed far in importance the living creatures of earth. In this connection, it will be observed that in the matter of the judgments of Christ upon all living creatures the time assigned to the two spheres—earth and heaven—is very unequal. The judgment of the people of the earth—Jew and Gentile —is at most a matter of a day or days, while the judgment of angelic empires, according to 1 Corinthians 15:24–26, may require the whole millennial period.

The Apostle has twice recorded the various ranks or divisions of celestial beings. In Ephesians 1:21 he discloses that when Christ ascended into heaven He was exalted to the right hand of the Father "far above all principality, and power, and might, and dominion." This fourfold enumeration is not quite identical with that of Colossians 1:16, all of which suggests that the listing in either case is partial, that the items are named only to answer a general purpose. The same Apostle names the angelic groups when declaring the subduing reign of Christ (cf. 1 Cor. 15:24–26). There he speaks of rule, of authority, of power, and implies that these are "enemies" who must be put under Christ's feet. Among these enemies is death—a factor which in itself is impersonal and in no way to be classed with responsible creatures. Thus, broad indeed is the contemplation of the enemies of the kingdom of God.

The all-important averment of Colossians 1:16 is gathered up in the second declaration, namely, "All things were created by him." The act was His and with a view to glorifying Him. Christ is the *end* of creation. It was *for* Him. In this connection, two passages in Revelation present added truth, "And the angel which I saw stand upon the sea and upon the earth lifted up his hand to heaven, and sware by him that liveth for ever and ever, who created heaven, and the things that therein are, and the earth, and the things that therein are, and the sea, and the things which are therein, that there should be time no longer" (10:5–6); "Thou art worthy, O Lord, to receive glory and honour and power: for thou hast created all things, and for thy pleasure they are and were created" (4:11).

Verse 17. "And he is before all things, and by him all things consist."

This portion of the context adds the important revelation that it is by the direct and unceasing application of Christ's power that all things consist, or more literally, *hold together*. Again there is a parallel to this truth in Hebrews where in 1:3 it is said, "And upholding all things by the word of his power." The disclosure is thus made that He who created all things unceasingly sustains them.

Verse 18. "And he is the head of the body, the church: who is the beginning, the firstborn from the dead; that in all things he might have the preeminence."

Not only is Christ Head over creation, but He is Head over the New Creation—the Church. With respect to the Church, Christ is its beginning and the First-Born from the dead. 1 Corinthians 15:20, 23 proclaims Christ to be the First-Fruits of them that slept. Revelation 3:14 styles Him "the beginning of the creation of God." This is doubtless a reference to the New Creation in which He is a part. Because of all this, to Him be the pre-eminence! To Him who created all things, who sustains His creation, who is Head of all creations the pre-eminence belongs.

Verse 19. "For it pleased the Father that in him should all fulness dwell."

It is according to the design and purpose of the Father that the pre-eminence should be given unto the Son. In the Son all the πλήρωμα dwells (cf. Col. 2:9). Thus the Father's purpose is realized and thus the Father is glorified in the Son.

The declaration that Christ pre-existed is sustained to the last degree by the revelation that He created all things.

III. THE BEFORE-TIME COVENANT

Expositors have not agreed on the exact nature of the covenant which is mentioned in Titus 1:2, which reads, "In hope of eternal life, which God, that cannot lie, promised before the world began" (cf. 2 Tim. 1:1, 9). By some it is believed that reference is here made to an agreement between the Persons of the Godhead which embraced and provided for the whole plan of redemption, that it assigned to each His part in the undertaking. To others the text indicates no more than the foreknowledge of God concerning the promise which the gospel would proclaim. Of the latter view Dean Alford writes, "The solution of the difficulty, that no promise was actually made till the race of man existed, must be found by regarding, as in the place in 2 Tim. [1:9], the construction as a mixed one,—compounded of the actual promise made in time, and the divine purpose from which that promise sprung, fixed in eternity. Thus, as there God is said to have given us grace in Christ from eternal ages, meaning that the gift took place as the result of a divine purpose fixed from eternity, so here He is said to have promised eternal life before eternal times, meaning that the promise took place as the result of a purpose fixed from eternity" (*Op. cit.*, II, 580). On the general theme of a before-time covenant, Dr. A. A. Hodge presents seven points, "1st. As shown at the opening of this chapter [XXII] such a Covenant is virtually implied in the existence of an eternal Plan of salvation mutually formed by and to be executed by three Persons. 2d. That Christ represented his elect in that Covenant is necessarily implied in the doctrine of sovereign personal election to grace and salvation. Christ says of his sheep, 'Thine they were, and thou gavest them me,' and 'Those whom thou gavest me I have kept,' etc. (John 17:6, 12).

3d. The Scriptures declare the existence of the promise and conditions of such a Covenant, and present them in connection (Isa. 53:10, 11). 4th. The Scriptures expressly affirm the existence of such a Covenant (Isa. 52:6; Ps. 89:3). 5th. Christ makes constant reference to a previous commission he had received of his Father (John 10:18; Luke 22:29). 6th. Christ claims a reward which had been conditioned upon the fulfillment of that commission (John 17:4). 7th. Christ constantly asserts that his people and his expected glory are given to him as a reward by his Father (John 17: 6, 9, 24; Phil. 2:6–11)" (*Outlines of Theology,* p. 371).

It is certain that the triune Godhead existed from all eternity, that all things were predetermined, and that an agreement existed between the Persons of the Godhead concerning the part to be executed by each. If the triune Godhead existed from all eternity, the Second Person existed and Christ, being that Person, existed from all eternity.

IV. THE OLD TESTAMENT MESSIAH

What is too often overlooked is the fact that the Messiah anticipated in the Old Testament is repeatedly declared to be Jehovah. It is also to be observed that, within the mystery of the Trinity, Jehovah and the Messiah are two separate Persons. In Psalm 2:2, R.V., it is said of the kings and rulers of the earth that they will yet "set themselves against Jehovah, and against his anointed." (Here *Anointed* is better translated 'Messiah.') Though the finite mind hesitates for want of ability to understand that which is declared, there are many passages of unquestioned interpretation in which the Messiah is said to be Jehovah. In fact, this is true in the great majority of Messianic predictions. Some of these may well be indicated.

Deuteronomy 30:3. "That then the LORD thy God will turn thy captivity, and have compassion upon thee, and will return and gather thee from all the nations, whither the LORD thy God hath scattered thee."

In this passage, which is the first mention within the Sacred Text of the second advent, it is Jehovah Elohim who proclaims that He will return; but He cannot return if He has not been here before. It is alone true of Christ that He has been here and departed, that He will return, that when He returns, as asserted in this passage, He will regather Israel, and that He will reign on the earth. No optional interpretation is available. It is Christ alone who answers this description and He is here identified as Jehovah Elohim.

Jeremiah 33:14–17. "Behold, the days come, saith the LORD, that I will perform that good thing which I have promised unto the house of Israel and to the house of Judah. In those days, and at that time, will I cause the Branch of righteousness to grow up unto David; and he shall execute judgment and righteousness in the land. In those days shall Judah be saved, and Jerusalem shall dwell safely: and this is the name wherewith she [basically, he] shall be called, The LORD our righteousness. For thus saith the LORD; David shall never want a man to sit upon the throne of the house of Israel."

From this prophecy it may be seen that the Branch, or Son, of David will complete the promise that David shall never lack for one to sit upon his throne. The line of rightful kings continued from David to Christ, but no other king need ever arise, nor will one arise. Of Christ it is declared that His is an everlasting kingdom (cf. Dan. 7:14), and He shall reign forever and ever (Rev. 11:15). In his announcement to Mary of the birth of Messiah, the angel said her Son would be the Son of the Highest, that He would sit on David's throne, and that He would reign forever. This Son, having no human Father, is the Son of God (Luke 1:31–35). It is thus conclusively demonstrated that Christ is Jehovah.

Isaiah 9:6–7. "For unto us a child is born, unto us a son is given: and the government shall be upon his shoulder: and his name shall be called Wonderful, Counsellor, The mighty God, The everlasting Father, The Prince of Peace. Of the increase of his government and peace there shall be no end, upon the throne of David, and upon his kingdom, to order it, and to establish it with judgment and with justice from henceforth even for ever. The zeal of the LORD of hosts will perform this."

Incomparable titles are here ascribed to that unique Person who is never duplicated in heaven or on earth, who combines both humanity as a child born and Deity as a Son given. He is here said to be Wonderful, Counselor, The mighty God, The Father of eternity, and The Prince of Peace; yet this is that One—Jehovah—who, as declared above, shall sit on David's throne. All that can be ascribed to Jehovah Elohim is ascribed directly to Christ, and therefore Christ is Jehovah.

Zechariah 9:9. "Rejoice greatly, O daughter of Zion; shout, O daughter of Jerusalem: behold, thy King cometh unto thee: he is just, and having salvation; lowly, and riding upon an ass, and upon a colt the foal of an ass."

In the fulfillment of the prediction, as recorded in Matthew 21:1–14 and John 12:12–15, Christ is proclaimed to be the Son of David who comes in the name of the Lord (Jehovah); and as He entered the temple

He cast out the moneychangers, saying that they had made "my house" a den of thieves when it is properly styled "the house of prayer." Malachi anticipated that Jehovah would thus come to His temple. It was Jehovah's temple and Christ asserts that He is Jehovah when He called the temple "my house." So Zechariah 9:9 is a Messianic prediction which makes Messiah to be Jehovah, and Christ fulfilled this prophecy. The conclusion is that Christ is Jehovah.

Zechariah 1:4, 9, 16. "Be ye not as your fathers, unto whom the former prophets have cried, saying, Thus saith the LORD of hosts; Turn ye now from your evil ways, and from your evil doings: but they did not hear, nor hearken unto me, saith the LORD. . . . Then said I, O my lord, what are these? And the angel that talked with me said unto me, I will shew thee what these be. . . . Therefore thus saith the LORD; I am returned to Jerusalem with mercies: my house shall be built in it, saith the LORD of hosts, and a line shall be stretched forth upon Jerusalem."

The predictions of the Bible know of but one King, of one throne, and one Son of David to reign forever on David's throne. That Christ is that King and therefore the Messiah need not be demonstrated again; but Zechariah distinctly declares the Messiah-King is none other than Jehovah. He shall be worshiped because He is Jehovah.

Isaiah 40:1–3. "Comfort ye, comfort ye my people, saith your God. Speak ye comfortably to Jerusalem, and cry unto her, that her warfare is accomplished, that her iniquity is pardoned: for she hath received of the LORD's hand double for all her sins. The voice of him that crieth in the wilderness, Prepare ye the way of the LORD, make straight in the desert a highway for our God."

John the Baptist fulfills the prediction of one who in preparation for the advent of Messiah is a voice crying in the wilderness. He himself said that he was that voice (John 1:22–23; cf. Matt. 3:3; Mark 1:3; Luke 3:4–6). It matters not that on account of the rejection of the King the complete fulfillment of this expectation is delayed until His second advent. John was the voice preparing the way for Messiah and Isaiah's prophecy asserts that the voice was to prepare the way for Jehovah.

Jeremiah 23:5–6. "Behold, the days come, saith the LORD, that I will raise unto David a righteous Branch, and a King shall reign and prosper, and shall execute judgment and justice in the earth. In his days Judah shall be saved, and Israel shall dwell safely: and this is his name whereby he shall be called, THE LORD OUR RIGHTEOUSNESS."

The King who shall reign and prosper is Messiah, the Son of David. He it is who shall execute judgment and justice in the *earth*. He it is who will save both Judah and Israel (cf. Isa. 63:1; Rom 11:26–27). He it is who shall be designated *Jehovah our Righteousness*—not as a meaningless title, but because He is Jehovah.

Though but a limited selection of passages has been introduced, it will be seen that Messiah is always declared to be Jehovah, and since He is Jehovah He has existed from all eternity.

V. THE ANGEL OF JEHOVAH

One of the most compelling and indisputable proofs that Christ pre-existed is found in the truth that He is the Angel of Jehovah whose various appearances are recorded in the Old Testament. On this doctrine Dr. John F. Walvoord has written an analysis which may well be included in this text:

Definition. A theophany is a manifestation of God in visible and bodily form before the incarnation. Usually the term *theophany* is limited to appearances of God in the form of man or angels, other phenomena such as the Shekinah glory not being considered a theophany. The theophanies are chiefly appearances of the Angel of Jehovah, who is clearly distinct from angelic beings.

The Angel of Jehovah Identified as Jehovah. A study of the references to the Angel of Jehovah in the Old Testament will reveal that He is frequently identified as Jehovah Himself. When the Angel of Jehovah spoke to Hagar (Gen. 16:7–13), He is identified as Jehovah (vs. 13). The account of the sacrifice of Isaac (Gen. 22:11–18) affords the same identification of the Angel of Jehovah and Jehovah Himself. Other passages confirm this interpretation (Gen. 31:11–13; 48:15, 16; cf. 45:5; Ex. 3:1 ff.; cf. Acts 7:30–35; Ex. 13:21; 14:19; Judg. 6:11–23; 13:9–20).

The Angel of Jehovah as a Distinct Person from Jehovah. While many passages identify the Angel of Jehovah as Jehovah, other passages almost equal in number distinguish the Angel of Jehovah as a distinct Person. In Gen. 24:7, for instance, Jehovah is pictured as sending "his angel." The servant of Abraham testifies to the reality of this in Gen. 24:40. Moses speaks of Jehovah sending an angel to lead them (Num. 20:16). A clear instance is found in Zech. 1:12–13 where the Angel of the Lord speaks to Jehovah, "Then the angel of the Lord answered and said, O Lord of hosts, how long wilt thou not have mercy on Jerusalem and on the cities of Judah, against which thou hast had indignation these threescore and ten years? And the Lord answered the angel that talked with me with good words and comfortable words." Other passages make a similar distinction (Ex. 23:20; 32:34; 1 Chron. 21:15–18; Isa. 63:9; Dan. 3:25–28). There are some passages which affirm the deity of the Angel of Jehovah, but do not specifically identify Him as Jehovah or as a person distinct from Jehovah (Judg. 2:1–5; 2 Kings 19:35).

The Angel of Jehovah is the Second Person of the Trinity. While to the natural mind the seeming disparity in terminology and usage of the term *Angel of Jehovah* is irreconcilable, the difficulty is easily dissolved when it is realized that Christ is the Angel of Jehovah. As such, Christ is Jehovah, and at the same time, as a Person He is distinct from the Trinity, being the Second Person. Thus when the Angel of Jehovah is identified as Jehovah, it is a declaration of His deity. When the Angel of Jehovah is distinguished from Jehovah, it is the distinction of the Persons of the Godhead, in all probability the Father in distinction to the Son. This solution is in keeping with the doctrine of the Trinity as unfolded in the entire Scriptures. Granting that the Angel of Jehovah is God, it is a minor problem, relatively, to prove that He is the Second Person, not the Father nor the Holy Spirit.

The proof that Christ is the Angel of Jehovah is supported by four lines of evidence: (a) *The Second Person is the Visible God of the New Testament.* When we turn to the New Testament, the Second Person is found to be the incarnate God, possessing a human body and being visible to all. While the Father's voice is heard from heaven, and the Holy Spirit is seen descending in the form of a dove, Christ, the Second Person, is the full manifestation of God in visible form. It would be logical that the same Person of the Godhead who is visible in the New Testament should also be the chosen One to appear in the form of the Angel of Jehovah in the Old Testament. (b) *The Angel of Jehovah of the Old Testament No Longer Appears after the Incarnation of Christ.* The Angel of Jehovah is exceedingly active throughout the Old Testament period, appearing to many people in widely separated periods. In the New Testament, while there are references to angels as such, not a single instance is found where the Angel of Jehovah appears. It is a natural inference that He now appears as the incarnate Christ. (c) *Both the Angel of Jehovah and Christ Are Sent by the Father.* The Old Testament reveals the Angel of Jehovah as sent by Jehovah to reveal truth, to lead Israel, and to defend and judge them. In the New Testament, Christ is sent by God to reveal God in the flesh, to reveal truth, and to become the Savior. In the nature of the Trinity, it is the Father who sends the Son and the Spirit, the First Person never being sent Himself. The similar character of ministry of the Angel of Jehovah and Christ would serve to identify them. (d) *The Angel of Jehovah Could Not Be Either the Father Or the Holy Spirit.* By process of elimination, it can be demonstrated that the Angel of Jehovah must be the Second Person. According to John 1:18, "No man hath seen God at any time; the only begotten Son, which is in the bosom of the Father, he hath declared him." This verse in effect states that only Christ was visible to man, no one being able to see God the Father or the Holy Spirit in their glory. As the Angel of Jehovah is the Sent One, He could not be the Father, the First Person. As the Angel of Jehovah is God in bodily form, He could not be the Holy Spirit, as the attribute of immateriality is always possessed by the Holy Spirit, and His ministry is never characterized by physical attributes. There is not a single valid reason to deny that the Angel of Jehovah is the Second Person, every known fact pointing to His identification as the Christ of the New Testament.

Appearances of Christ Other Than As the Angel of Jehovah. A number of illustrations are afforded in the Old Testament of appearances of Christ in form other than the Angel of Jehovah. In Gen. 18:1–33, Jehovah appears as a man, accompanied by two other men who are probably angels. Jacob's experience of wrestling with God also involves in all probability the appearance of Christ to him in the form of a man (Gen. 32:24–32). The appearance to the elders of Israel of the God of Israel is probably to be identified as an appearance of Christ (Ex. 24:9–11). The cloud of the Lord, the glory of the Lord (Ex. 40:38), and the "cloudy pillar" (Ex. 33:9–23) are also forms of appearance of Christ in the Old Testament. It is probable that every visible manifestation of God in bodily form is to be identified with the Lord Jesus Christ (Josh. 5:13–15; Ezek. 1:1–28; Dan. 10:1–21).

The Theophanies a Proof of the Pre-existence of Christ. The theophanies of the Old Testament, being the manifestation of Christ, the Second Person, in visible form constitute an argument for pre-existence in history, as contrasted to the direct statement of the New Testament. The abundant witness to the vital ministry of Christ in the Old Testament period and His evident relationship to so many scenes of revelation in the Old Testament are a convincing proof of His pre-existence. An examination of the character of His ministry as the Angel of Jehovah and His manifestation in other forms will not only reveal His pre-existence but will also demand recognition of His deity. As the Angel of Jehovah, He is God, and the revelation of Him in the Old Testament while sometimes devoid of His inherent glory even as He is found during His life on earth after incarnation is nevertheless clearly a display of the attributes of God.—*Op. cit.,* pp. 6–8

VI. INDIRECT BIBLICAL IMPLICATIONS

There are many phrases used in the New Testament which imply Christ's pre-existence. He said of Himself that He was sent into the world (John 17:18); it is written that He became flesh (John 1:14); that He partook of flesh and blood (Heb. 2:14); that He was found in fashion as a man (Phil. 2:8); that He said, "I am from above" (John 8:23); and, "I am not of the world" (John 17:14); He claimed to have descended out of heaven (John 3:13). Other Scriptures worthy of note in this connection are: John 1:15, 18, 30; 3:16–17, 31; 6:33, 42, 50–51, 57–58; 7:29; 8:23, 42; 9:39.

VII. DIRECT BIBLICAL ASSERTIONS

This the final evidence of Christ's pre-existence is that which is direct and positive. The Word of God asserts His pre-existence in terms which cannot be questioned by a devout person. Though before noted in a previous volume, some of these passages are listed here.

John 1:1–4, 14. "In the beginning was the Word, and the Word was with God, and the Word was God. The same was in the beginning with God. All things were made by him; and without him was not any thing made that was made. In him was life; and the life was the light of men. . . . And the Word was made flesh, and dwelt among us, (and we beheld his glory, the glory as of the only begotten of the Father,) full of grace and truth."

Not only is Christ here presented as Creator of all things, but, as far as language can express thought, He is declared to have existed from all eternity. In that beginning which preceded all creation, when the universe—such as it may have been—was inhabited only by the triune God, the *Logos* has existed, that is to say from all eternity. In a depth of meaning which is beyond human understanding, the *Logos* was both with God as a fellow to be distinguished separately and He was God. He is none other than the one God.

John 6:33, 38, 41, 50–51, 58, 62. In these seven texts, which need not be quoted, the sevenfold declaration is made by Christ that He came down from heaven (cf. John 3:13, 31). The more extended revelation of John 6:62 is conclusive: "What and if ye shall see the Son of man ascend up where he was before?" Only the most obdurate unbelief will reject an unveiling of heavenly truth as unanswerable as is set forth in this sevenfold assertion by Christ Himself. The Socinian invention that Christ sometime after His birth was received up into heaven that He might be instructed in heavenly things and that from there He came forth, is perhaps as good an explanation as could be made—if it had a vestige of truth on which it could be based. The devout mind revolts at such impiety and must inquire why any effort is made to save a Christ so humanized that His existence ceases to be of any moment. He came down from heaven where He, as God, had ever had His abode. Every Scripture fully sustains this claim.

John 8:58–59. "Jesus said unto them, Verily, verily, I say unto you, Before Abraham was, I am. Then took they up stones to cast at him: but Jesus hid himself, and went out of the temple, going through the midst of them, and so passed by."

Dean Alford's comment on this passage is included here, "As Lücke remarks, all unbiassed explanation of these words must recognize in them a declaration of the essential pre-existence of Christ. All such interpretations as *'before Abraham became Abraham,'* i.e. father of many nations (Socinus and others), and as *'I was predetermined, promised by God'* (Grotius and the Socinian interpreters), are little better than *dishonest quibbles.* The distinction between was made (*or was born*) and am is important. The present, **I am**, expresses *essential exist-ence,* see Col. 1:17, and was often used by our Lord to assert His divine Being. In this verse *the Godhead of Christ is involved;* and this the Jews *clearly understood, by their conduct to Him.* . . . Probably there were stones (for building) lying about in the outer court of the temple, where these words seem to have been spoken. The reason of the Jews' doing this [v. 59] is given by them on a similar occasion, ch. 10:33, *for that thou, being a man, makest thyself God"* (*Op. cit.,* I, 547).

John 17:5. "And now, O Father, glorify thou me with thine own self with the glory which I had with thee before the world was."

The peculiar circumstances in which the Savior is addressing the Father before He returns to heaven—circumstances wholly apart from any intercourse with men and characterized by that high degree of truth which must obtain when two Persons of the Godhead converse—make this reference on the part of Christ to His pre-existence in heaven of solemn import—such indeed as only those who lack all capacity for respect toward God might question. In his *Exposition of the Gospel of St. John,* R. Govett remarks on this passage:

As the result of such glorification of the Father, He asks for His own glorifica-tion. And for an especial form of it—the restoration to Him of the divine glory which He possessed before He became man. He here testifies His pre-existence, and His abiding with the Father, and in His divine glory, before creation began. Jesus, then, is the Eternal Son of the Eternal Father. He is not one who began to be at creation. As Paul says, He was in "the form of God," and stooped and emptied Himself of glory in His becoming man. Now the bitterest part of that humiliation—the death on the cross—is at the door; but, beyond that, He anticipates so perfect a passage across the darkness, that the Father will be obliged to exalt Him above all creatures as His Son. This appears also in Hebrews 1. Jesus, by His eternal generation, was *the Son;* above all angels, in a sense that cannot justly be assigned to them. But Paul goes on to testify, that by His perfection of service during His incarnation, He has re-won the place of superiority to angels. He has again been saluted as "the Son," on the Father's raising Him from the dead (Heb. 1:5). That place no angel has ever by his obedience earned. The unfallen angels by their obedience just fulfil the work demanded of them, but no more. They are not meritorious servants of the Most High, who can claim a reward, and *such* a reward, as their desert. Neither God nor His Son began to be. The world did begin. There were ages uncounted before it was created. On the other hand, the Father speaking to the Son, after His work on earth, owns His Godhead; and assigns to Him the kingdom as the result of His perfect love and right-eousness, and hatred of iniquity (Heb. 1:8, 9). There are, then, three aspects of the matter presented in this verse. (1) Jesus, as the Son, had glory with the Father before all creation. (2) He stripped Himself of that glory to become the servant. He has so lived on earth, as that the Father has been glorified, and He can claim glory in the day to come, when the Most High shall assign to each the reward of his works. Nay, the glory is to begin at once. "Now." "Glorify Me *with* (that is, 'beside') *Thyself.*" Jesus' glory is to begin at once in the presence of the Father on His ascension; and the same divine glory which He enjoyed before His human birth, is to be restored to Him. Who of mere men could say such things with truth? Who could put forth such pretensions without blasphemy? and the Father's eternal displeasure? "But may not 'the glory which I had with Thee before the world was' mean only, that Christ had that glory in the counsels of the Father, before the Christ had any existence?" So speak some, whose aim is just the opposite to that of the Father; to diminish as much as may be, the honour given in Scripture to the Son. Whenever you find this, be on your guard! No! First, if Jesus be a mere man, how did He know what was the glory destined Him, before creation existed? Secondly, this was nothing peculiar to Himself. God had destined a special glory for Abraham, David, and others as well. Thirdly, the natural sense of the words imports—that Jesus not only existed ere creation, but dwelt in glory in the presence of the Father. Fourthly, this is sustained by many other passages, specially of John's Gospel and Epistles. "The Word was God. *The same was in the beginning with God.*" His was glory before creation; for He created all, and the cause must be before the effect; while the glory of the Creator must be infinitely above that of the creature. Again, "What and if ye shall see the Son of Man *ascend up where He was before?*" "Before Abraham was *born, I am.*" "Who being in the form of God, emptied Himself" (Phil. 2). "He that hath not the Son of God, hath not life." "He that progresseth, and abideth not in the doctrine of the Christ, hath not God" (2 John 1:9). Observe how the "we" in this prayer sets Jesus on a level with the Father (ver. 11, 21, 22). The Object of worship and Giver of life is the Son.—II, 284–86

Philippians 2:6. "Who, being in the form of God, thought it not robbery to be equal with God."

An extended comment on this text and its setting by Dr. John Hutchison (*Lectures on St. Paul's Epistle to the Philippians,* pp. 90–93) will serve to emphasize the testimony of this passage:

The passage is one of no ordinary difficulty. The controversies of the ages have gathered around it. Years would probably not suffice to master its whole literature. Almost every word in these verses has been a battlefield of contention. A sense of confusion therefore may well settle down upon the mind in trying to study this theme; and yet the more we do study it, the sense of its grandeur grows the more overmastering. It is the theme of all Scripture. Its teaching is the meeting-point of all humble, believing hearts. Yet the exposition of it cannot but be feeble, when what is to be expounded "makes breath poor and speech unable,"—transcends, in a word, all mortal thought. We must content ourselves with the simple endeavour to bring out the meaning of the words into clearer light. In the choice of the terms employed, we see how the apostle wrote, as it were, with the point of a diamond. As Farrar (*Messages of the Books*, p. 299) well puts it, "The chief truths of the profoundest Christology could not have been expressed more grandly, and at the same time more tersely, than in this swift outline of Christ's passage downwards, step by step, from the infinite heights into the uttermost abyss of self-humiliation, and then His re-ascent upwards into the super-exaltation of unimaginable dominion." Or we might use the words of Daillé, the worthy French Reformed theologian of the seventeenth century: "The meaning is so noble and so well-established that nothing more powerful could be imagined; the apostle battering down in these few words all that hell has ever invented against this sacred and inviolable foundation of our faith." Or, going back much farther in the literature of the Church, it is worthy of notice how, in the two very striking sermons of Chrysostom, this passage in its several clauses is used as a weapon by which all the varied heresies of his time are broken to shivers. We have, however, to remember throughout our exposition that the apostle is in no sense purposely formulating the doctrine of our Lord's divinity and humanity, and atoning work and mediatorial glory and dominion. All this, indeed, is done; yet the one direct and immediate aim is simply to enforce and illustrate the preceding words, "Not looking each of you to his own things, but each of you also to the things of others." It is simply as the supreme enforcement of this Christian duty that the awfully profound and mysterious truths herein taught about Christ Jesus are to be contemplated. "Who," that is, He whom we now adore alike as the eternal Son of the eternal Father, and as Jesus Christ, the Son of man. But the necessities of the context make the reference to Him as in the bosom of the Father before His incarnation. "Being in the form of God"—the word "being" is emphatic. It means "subsisting," "being to begin with" (Webster and Wilkinson), or, as in the margin of the Revised Version, "being originally." It lays stress upon the reality of His existence, not necessarily, however, upon eternal pre-existence, though this indeed is involved in the clause taken as a whole. He is described then as thus existing "in the *form* of God." The word is striking in such a connection as this. It certainly does not mean "fashion" or "mere semblance," on the one hand, nor does it mean exactly "nature, essence," on the other. It rather shades off into both meanings. It represents actual specific character—that which manifests the essential nature. Of course this word, as applied to our Lord, implies His possession of the divine attributes, for, as Chrysostom says, "It is not possible to be of one essence, and to have the form of another;" and besides, it is placed in apposition to "the form of a servant," and as this latter means assuredly true condition, so must the former. Our passage, then, is in reality identical with the unapproachably grand yet simple opening words of the prologue to the Fourth Gospel: "In the beginning was the Word, and the Word was with God, and the Word was God. The same was in the beginning with God." The choice of the word "form" is yet further significant. It directs our thoughts specially, not to the divine nature itself, but rather to the infinite majesty and glory pertaining to it. This is put by none so well as by Daillé: "To be in the form of God signifies not only to be King, to possess majesty and power, but also to have the insignia of royalty, its courtly train and equipage. . . . Thus formerly among the Romans we might call the form of a consul, the equipage and pomp with which the laws and customs of that people invested those who exercised the office; the purple, the ivory chair, the twelve lictors with their fasces and rods, and such-like. When, then, the apostle here says that the Lord, before taking our nature upon Him, was in the form of God, he does not merely intend that He was God in Himself, and that He had the true nature of the divinity; but, further still, that He possessed the glory, and enjoyed all the dignity, majesty, and grandeur due to so high a name. This is precisely what our Lord means in St. John by the glory which He says He had with the Father before the world was." It was this alone that in His humiliation He renounced. He could not empty Himself of His essential perfections, for, indeed, one of these perfections is unchangeableness itself.

In concluding the discussion of this exalted declaration set forth in this verse, the paraphrase by Bishop Lightfoot of verses 5 to 11 is here quoted: "Reflect in your own minds the mind of Christ Jesus. Be humble, as He also was humble. Though existing before the worlds in the Eternal Godhead, yet He did not cling with avidity to the prerogatives of His divine majesty, did not ambitiously display His equality with God; but divested Himself of the glories of heaven, and took upon Him the nature of a servant, assuming the likeness of men. Nor was this all. Having thus appeared among men in the fashion of a man, He humbled Himself yet more, and carried out His obedience even to dying. Nor did He die by a common death: He was crucified, as the lowest malefactor is crucified. But as was His humility, so also was His exaltation. God raised Him to a preeminent height, and gave Him a title and a dignity far above all dignities and titles else. For to the name and majesty of Jesus all created things in heaven and earth and hell shall pay homage on bended knee; and every tongue with praise and thanksgiving shall declare that Jesus Christ is Lord, and in and for Him shall glorify God the Father" (*Epistle to the Philippians,* p. 110).

CONCLUSION

The arguments which prove the pre-existence of Christ are conclusive and there is every reason to ascribe to the Lord Jesus Christ all that belongs to Deity. To fail to do this is to rob Him of that worship and honor which is rightfully His.

CHAPTER II

INTRODUCTION TO THE DOCTRINE OF
CHRIST INCARNATE

I. THE DOCTRINE AS A WHOLE

IN PURSUING an orderly consideration of Christology, the next theme—
extended indeed—is that of the incarnation, which theme includes the
Old Testament anticipations, the birth of Christ, and the life and ministry of Christ on the earth. Though the incarnation doctrine reaches
on to all that Christ will ever be and do in eternity to come, it is not
traced here beyond the life and ministry, the death and all that follows
being reserved for later divisions of this thesis. The importance in the
divine estimation of this second division of Christology is betokened
by the fact that a little less than half of the New Testament—the four
Gospels—is devoted to His life and ministry, to say nothing of the Old
Testament anticipations of that life and ministry. The Scriptures, as
has been seen, do not underestimate the importance of Christ's pre-
existence or of other features of Christological doctrine—His death,
His resurrection, His session, or His coming again; but the three and
a half years of His ministry on the earth as the incarnate Son of God
is treated in what might seem to be a disproportionate degree. Such a
divine emphasis should be recognized and reflected in a true Christology.
The historical Christ is set forth in the Synoptics, as by John also, but
while Matthew and Luke declare the human birth of the Savior and so
account for His humanity, John in his Gospel brings one of the Godhead
Three into the human sphere and therefore must develop the major body
of truth respecting the incarnation. In reference to John's account of
Christ's advent into the world, Dr. B. B. Warfield writes thus somewhat at length in the *International Standard Bible Encyclopaedia* (IV,
2343–44):

John tells us that it was this Word, eternal in His subsistence, God's eternal
fellow, the eternal God's self, that, as "come in the flesh," was Jesus Christ
(1 Jn. 4:2). "And the Word became flesh" (Jn. 1:14), he says. The terms he
employs here are not terms of substance, but of personality. The meaning is
not that the substance of God was transmuted into that substance which we

39

call "flesh." "The Word" is a personal name of the eternal God; "flesh" is an appropriate designation of humanity in its entirety, with the implications of dependence and weakness. The meaning, then, is simply that He who had just been described as the eternal God became, by a voluntary act in time, a man. The exact nature of the act by which He "became" man lies outside the statement; it was matter of common knowledge between the writer and the reader. The language employed intimates merely that it was a definite act, and that it involved a change in the life-history of the eternal God, here designated "the Word." The whole emphasis falls on the nature of this change in His life-history. He became *flesh*. That is to say, He entered upon a mode of existence in which the experiences that belong to human beings would also be His. The dependence, the weakness, which constitute the very idea of flesh, in contrast with God, would now enter into His personal experience. And it is precisely because these are the connotations of the term "flesh" that John chooses that term here, instead of the more simply denotative term "man." What he means is merely that the eternal God became man. But he elects to say this in the language which throws best up to view what it is to become man. The contrast between the Word as the eternal God and the human nature which He assumed as flesh, is the hinge of the statement. Had the evangelist said (as he does in 1 Jn. 4:2) that the Word "came in flesh," it would have been the continuity through the change which would have been most emphasized. When he says rather that the Word became flesh, while the continuity of the personal subject is, of course, intimated, it is the reality and the completeness of the humanity assumed which is made most prominent. . . . That in becoming flesh the Word did not cease to be what He was before entering upon this new sphere of experiences, the evangelist does not leave, however, to mere suggestion. The glory of the Word was so far from quenched, in his view, by His becoming flesh, that he gives us at once to understand that it was rather as "trailing clouds of glory" that He came. "And the Word became flesh," he says, and immediately adds: "and dwelt among us (and we beheld his glory, glory as of the only begotten from the Father), full of grace and truth" (1:14). The language is colored by reminiscences from the Tabernacle, in which the Glory of God, the Shekinah, dwelt. The flesh of Our Lord became, on its assumption by the Word, the Temple of God on earth (cf. Jn. 2:19), and the glory of the Lord filled the house of the Lord. John tells us expressly that this glory was visible, that it was precisely what was appropriate to the Son of God as such. "And we beheld his glory," he says; not divined it, or inferred it, but perceived it. It was open to sight, and the actual object of observation. Jesus Christ was obviously more than man; He was obviously God. His actually observed glory, John tells us further, was a "glory as of the only begotten from the Father." It was unique; nothing like it was ever seen in another. And its uniqueness consisted precisely in its consonance with what the unique Son of God, sent forth from the Father, would naturally have; men recognized and could not but recognize in Jesus Christ the unique Son of God. When this unique Son of God is further described as "full of grace and truth," the elements of His manifested glory are not to be supposed to be exhausted by this description (cf. 2:11). Certain items of it only are singled out for particular mention. The visible glory of the incarnated Word was such a glory as the unique Son of God, sent forth from the Father, who was full of grace and truth, would naturally manifest. That nothing should be lacking to the declaration of the continuity of all that belongs to the Word as such into this new sphere of existence, and its full manifestation through the veil of His flesh, John adds at the close of his exposition the remarkable sentence: "As for God, no one has even yet seen him; God only begotten, who is in the bosom of the Father—he hath declared him" (1:18, margin). It is the incarnate Word which is here called "only begotten God." The absence of the article with this designation is doubtless due to its parallelism with the word "God" which stands at the head of the corresponding clause. The effect of its absence is to throw up into emphasis the quality rather than the mere individuality of the person so designated. The adjective "only begotten" conveys the idea, not of derivation and subordination, but of uniqueness and consubstantiality: Jesus is all that God is, and He alone is this. Of this "only begotten God" it is now declared that He "is"—not "was," the state is not one which has been left behind at the incarnation, but one which continues uninterrupted and unmodified—"into"—not merely "in"—"the bosom of the Father"—that is to say, He continues in the most intimate and complete communion with the Father. Though now incarnate, He is still "with God" in the full sense of the external relation intimated in 1:1. This being true, He has much more than seen God, and is fully able to "interpret" God to men. Though no one has ever yet seen God, yet he who has seen Jesus Christ, "God only begotten," has seen the Father (cf. 14:9; 12:45). In this remarkable sentence there is asserted in the most direct manner the full Deity of the incarnate Word, and the continuity of His life as such in His incarnate life; thus He is fitted to be the absolute revelation of God to man. This condensed statement of the whole doctrine of the incarnation is only the prologue to a historical treatise. The historical treatise which it introduces, naturally, is written from the point of view of its prologue. Its object is to present Jesus Christ in His historical manifestation, as obviously the Son of God in flesh. "These are written," the Gospel testifies, "that ye may believe that Jesus is the Christ, the Son of God" (20: 31); that Jesus who came as a man (1:30) was thoroughly known in His human origin (7:27), confessed Himself man (8:40), and died as a man dies (19:5), was, nevertheless, not only the Messiah, the Sent of God, the fulfiller of all the Divine promises of redemption, but also the very Son of God, that God only begotten, who, abiding in the bosom of the Father, is His sole adequate interpreter. From the beginning of the Gospel onward, this purpose is pursued: Jesus is pictured as ever, while truly man, yet manifesting Himself as equally truly God, until the veil which covered the eyes of His followers was wholly lifted, and He is greeted as both Lord and God (20:28). But though it is the prime purpose of this Gospel to exhibit the Divinity of the man Jesus, no obscuration of His manhood is involved. It is the Deity of the man Jesus which is insisted on, but the true manhood of Jesus is as prominent in the representation as in any other portion of the New Testament. Nor is any effacement of the humiliation of His earthly life involved. For the Son of man to come from heaven was a descent (3:13), and the mission which He came to fulfil was a mission of contest and conflict, of suffering and death. He brought His glory with Him (1:14), but the glory that was His on earth (17: 22) was not all the glory which He had had with the Father before the world was, and to which, after His work was done, He should return (17:5). Here too the glory of the celestial is one and the glory of the terrestrial is another. In any event, John has no difficulty in presenting the life of Our Lord on earth as the life of God in flesh, and in insisting at once on the glory that belongs to Him as God and on the humiliation which is brought to Him by the flesh. It is distinctly a duplex life which he ascribes to Christ, and he attributes to Him without embarrassment all the powers and modes of activity appropriate on the one hand to Deity and on the other to sinless (John 8:46; cf. 14:30; 1 John 3:5) human nature. In a true sense his portrait of Our Lord is a dramatization of the God-man which he presents to our contemplation in his prologue.

No human mind can ever grasp the significance of the occurrence and consequence of the incarnation. That a Person of the Godhead should become one of the human family—the sphere of His own creation—with a view to remaining in that form, though glorified, and throughout eternity must continue an insoluble mystery to the creatures of this world. What light is shed upon the problem is contained in the divine revelation which unfolds the advantage of redemption both to God and to man. Through the mediation of the theanthropic Person the heart of God is satisfied in the exercise of grace and the sons of men become the sons of God and heirs of God forever.

The analysis of the truth concerning the incarnate Christ which is advanced here will be pursued under these general divisions, namely: (1) the Old Testament expectation respecting the incarnate Christ, (2) the birth and childhood of the incarnate Christ, (3) the baptism of the incarnate Christ, (4) the temptation of the incarnate Christ, (5) the transfiguration of the incarnate Christ, (6) the teaching of the incarnate Christ, and (7) the miracles wrought by the incarnate Christ.

II. THE OLD TESTAMENT ANTICIPATIONS

While, as has been seen, the preincarnate Christ appears in the Old Testament as the Angel of Jehovah, He, with regard to His earth-life, is also anticipated in both type and prophecy. To the student of Scripture in the former dispensation, there was released sufficient foreshadowings of the incarnate Christ whereby a comprehensive understanding might have been gained respecting His parentage, His birth, His life, His death, His resurrection, and His second advent. It was then, as now, largely a matter of believing in their natural interpretation the things that are written. A somewhat complete Christology may be constructed from the Old Testament Scriptures. This fact serves as an effective contradiction to the persistent contention that the Old Testament is lacking in vital truth. With the unlimited material provided in both Testaments which is so interdependent and interwoven, there is little to be gained by the segregation of that found in the Old Testament; yet the student will be enriched by a study of the Christology of the Old Testament. The two foreshadowings it has may well be considered separately.

1. THE TYPES. Dr. John F. Walvoord in his unpublished notes on Christology has drawn off under the head of the major types of Christ a listing (which appears, but without comment, in the index of the Scofield Reference Bible) of forty-one well-defined types of Christ. This list is inserted into this text and should be studied with care.

1. *Aaron:* as Priest (Ex. 28:1; Lev. 8:12). 2. *Abel:* Christ as Shepherd (Gen. 4:2). 3. *Acacia Wood:* the humanity of Christ and His origin as a "root out of dry ground" (Ex. 26:15; Isa. 53:2). 4. *Adam:* Christ, Head of the New Creation as Adam is of the Old Creation (Gen. 5:1; Rom. 5:14; 1 Cor. 15:22). 5. *Altar of Brass:* Type of cross upon which Christ was offered (Ex. 27:1). 6. *Altar of Incense:* Type of Christ our Intercessor, through whom our prayers and praises ascend to God (Ex. 30:1; John 17:1–26; Heb. 7:25; 13:15; Rev. 8:3, 4). 7. *Ark of the Covenant* (Ex. 25:10): Cf. Scofield Bible, p. 101, note 1. 8. *Ark of Noah:* Type of Christ as salvation from judgment (Gen. 6:14; Heb. 11:7). 9. *Beauty and Bands* (Zech. 11:7): Cf. Scofield Bible, p. 975, note 1. 10. *Benjamin* (Gen. 35:18; 43:34): a. *Ben-oni:* Son of Sorrow, to his mother. b. *Benjamin:* Son of my right hand, to his father. See Scofield Bible, p. 51, note 3; p. 62, note 1. 11. *The Two Birds* (Lev. 14:4): a. *The Slain Bird:* death of Christ. b. *The Live Bird Dipped in Blood:* resurrection of Christ. 12. *Sacrificial Blood* (Lev. 17:11): See Scofield Bible, p. 150, note 1, 2. 13. *Burnt-Offering* (Lev. 1:3): See Scofield Bible, p. 126. a. *Ox:* patient and enduring servant. b. *Sheep or lamb:* unresisting surrender to death of cross (John 1:29; Isa. 53:7). c. *Goat:* typifies Christ as sinner's Substitute. d. *Turtle-dove or pigeon:* mourning innocency and poverty of Son of man. 14. *Golden Candlestick* (Lampstand): Type of Christ our Light (Ex. 25:31; cf. John 1:4; Isa. 11:2; Heb. 1:9). 15. *Corn of the Promised Land:* Type of Christ Risen and Glorified (Josh. 5:11). Cf. Scofield Bible, p. 263, note 2. 16. *David as King* (1 Chron. 17:7): David first shepherd, then king. Cf. Scofield Bible, pp. 475–76, note 2. 17. *First Three of Feasts of Jehovah* (Lev. 23:1–14): a. *Passover:* Christ our Redeemer (Ex. 12:11; 1 Cor. 5:7). b. *Unleavened Bread:* Holy Walk of Believer with Christ (1 Cor. 5:6–8; 2 Cor. 7:1; Gal. 5:7–9). c. *First-fruits:* Christ risen (1 Cor. 15:23). 18. *Gate or*

Door: only one door to the tabernacle (Ex. 27:16; John 10:7). 19. *The Two Goats* (Lev. 16:5–10). a. *Goat sacrificed:* typical of Christ's death satisfying all of God's righteous demands (Rom. 3:24–26). b. *Scapegoat:* typical of Christ taking our sins from before God (Heb. 9:26; Rom. 8:33, 34). Cf. Scofield Bible, p. 147, note 1. 20. *Isaac* (Gen. 21:3; 22:9; 24:1): a. *As obedient unto death* (Gen. 22:9). b. *As bridegroom of called-out bride* (Gen. 24). Cf. Scofield Bible, p. 31, note 2; p. 33, note 1; p. 34, note 2. 21. *Joseph* (Gen. 37:2). Cf. Scofield Bible, p. 53, note 2. 22. *Joshua* (Josh. 1:1): Name means, "Jehovah-Savior." Cf. Scofield Bible, p. 259, note 1. 23. *Kinsman-Redeemer* (Lev. 25:49; Isa. 59:20; Ruth 2:1; 3:10–18; 4:1–10). Cf. Scofield Bible, p. 161, note 1; p. 765, note 1. 24. *Laver:* Type of Christ cleansing from defilement (Ex. 30:18; John 13:2–10; Eph. 5:25–27; 1 John 1:9). 25. *Light:* Type of Christ the Light of the World (Gen. 1:16; 1 John 1:5). 26. *Manna:* Type of Christ as the Bread of Life come down from heaven (Ex. 16:35; Josh. 5:11). Cf. Scofield Bible, p. 91, note 1; p. 263, note 2. 27. *Meal-offering:* Christ in His perfect humanity tested by suffering (Lev. 2:1). Cf. Scofield Bible, p. 127, note 3. 28. *Melchizedek:* Type of Christ as Resurrected King-Priest (Gen. 14:18; Psa. 110:4; Heb. 6:20; 7:23, 24). Cf. Scofield Bible, p. 23, note 1. 29. *Moses:* Type of Christ as Deliverer and Prophet (Ex. 2:2). Cf. Scofield Bible, p. 72, note 1. 30. *Nazarite:* Separated wholly to God (Num. 6:2). Cf. Scofield Bible, pp. 173–74, note 2. 31. *Peace-offering:* Christ made peace, proclaimed peace, is our peace (Lev. 3:1; Col. 1:20; Eph. 2:14, 17). Cf. Scofield Bible, p. 128, note 4. 32. *Ram:* Type of Christ our Substitute (Gen. 22:9; Lev. 16:3; Heb. 10:5–10). 33. *Red Heifer:* Sacrifice of Christ as ground of believer's cleansing (Num. 19:2; 1 John 1:7, 9). Cf. Scofield Bible, p. 192, note 1. 34. *Rock:* Christ smitten to make possible the outpouring of the Spirit (Ex. 17:6; Num. 20:8; Matt. 21:44; 1 Pet. 2:8; 1 Cor. 10:4). Cf. Scofield Bible, p. 193, note 1. 35. *Rod of Aaron:* Type of Christ in Resurrection (Num. 17:8). 36. *Serpent of Brass:* Type of Christ made sin for us (Num. 21:9; John 3:14). 37. *Showbread:* Type of Christ as Bread of Life (Ex. 25:30). Cf. Scofield Bible, p. 102, note 1. 38. *Sin-offering:* Christ seen in sinner's place (Lev. 4:3). Cf. Scofield Bible, p. 129, note 1. 39. *Sweet Savor Offerings:* Christ in His perfections offering His merit for us (Lev. 1:9). Cf. Scofield Bible, p. 127, note 2. 40. *Trespass-offering:* Christ atoning for injury of sin (Lev. 5:6; 7:1–7; Psa. 51:4). 41. *Veil of Tabernacle:* Type of Christ's body, through which we have access to God (Ex. 26:31; Matt. 26:26; 27:50; Heb. 10:20). Cf. Scofield Bible, p. 104, note 1.—Pp. 9–11

2. THE PROPHECIES. Again, there is incorporated into this text the admirable listing of Old Testament prophecies respecting Christ which is also used in Dr. Walvoord's unpublished notes on Christology:

Introduction. The word *Messiah* is a modified form of the Greek representation of the Hebrew or Aramaic *māshīah,* the equivalent Greek word being *Christos.* Its root meaning is that of *the anointed one,* used in adjective form for priests in the Old Testament (Lev. 4:3, 5, 16; 6:22), and for kings as a noun (cf. Saul, 1 Sam. 24:6, 10; David, 2 Sam. 19:21; 23:1; Zedekiah, Lam.

4:20). Cf. *International Standard Bible Encyclopaedia, s.v.,* 'Messiah.'
Two types of Messianic prophecies may be observed in the Old Testament particularly:

(1) *General:* language only a Messiah could fulfill. Illus., 1 Sam. 2:35.

(2) *Personal:* connected with the Messiah by some specific term. Illus., Isa. 7:14, *Immanuel.*

Both types of Messianic prophecy are genuine and contribute vitally to the sum of the doctrine. Naturally, when prophecy is connected with the Messiah by some specific term its Messianic character is more easily established.

Four important characteristics of Messianic prophecy may be observed:

(1) *Prophecy purposely in obscure language.* An examination of Messianic prophecy will reveal that it is frequently given in obscure language such as only Spirit-led believers will discern as constituting genuine Messianic prediction. This feature, of course, may be noted in prophecy on most subjects. The entire content of Scripture is designed to require spiritual illumination for its understanding.

(2) *Prediction frequently in figurative language.* While figurative language is not necessarily uncertain in its meaning, the predictions of the Messiah are often clothed in language which requires interpretation. For instance, Christ is spoken of as a "rod out of the stem of Jesse," and as "a branch" which "shall grow out of his roots" (Isa. 11:1).

(3) *The future is often regarded as past or present.* As in all prophecy, Messianic prediction is often viewed as an account of events already past. For instance, the great prophecies of Isa. 53 are largely in past tense. The Hebrew frequently uses the perfect for prophecy. According to A. B. Davidson's Hebrew Grammar, "This usage is very common in the elevated language of the Prophets, whose faith and imagination so vividly project before them the event or scene which they predict that it appears already realized. It is part of the purpose of God, and therefore, to the clear eyes of the prophet, already as good as accomplished (*prophetic perfect*)" (pp. 156–57). The use of the perfect tense, then, in the Old Testament merely conceives of the event as certain of completion without specifying whether it is past, present, or future.

(4) *Prophecy is seen horizontally, not vertically.* While the order of prophetic events is generally revealed in Scripture, prophecy does not necessarily include all the intermediate steps between the great events in view. The great mountain peaks of prophecy are revealed without consideration of the expanse of valleys between the peaks. Hence, Old Testament prophecy often leaps from the sufferings of Christ to His glory without consideration of the time which elapses between these aspects. It is not unusual for great periods of time to separate prophecies closely related (cf. Isa. 61:1–2; Luke 4:18–19).—Pp. 11–12

An Old Testament Theology which aims at completeness will include its Theology Proper, its Angelology, its Anthropology, its hamartiology, its Soteriology, its Pneumatology, and its Christology. No work like this exists and the theological world has long awaited its appearance. The value of such a work beyond the effective truth it develops will be both to demonstrate the scope of truth accorded the Old Testament saints and to enhance the esteem and veneration of the Old Testament which is due it and yet so generally withheld from it.

CHAPTER III

THE BIRTH AND CHILDHOOD OF
CHRIST INCARNATE

ATTENTION IS again called to the distinction between the birth of Christ and the incarnation, the former being but an incident of all that enters into the latter. The incarnation—that stupendous enterprise of God —comprehends the advent of the Second Person of the Godhead into the human family and with a view to an everlasting participation therein. This advent is one of the seven greatest divine undertakings in the history of the universe—the creation of the angels, the creation of material things including life on the earth, the incarnation, the death of the incarnate One, the resurrection of the incarnate One, His return in glory, and the creation of the new heavens and the new earth. The enormity of the meaning of the incarnation could not be comprehended by human understandings. It belongs to the sphere of heaven, though the gracious redemptive purpose affords some light on that work which would otherwise be inexplainable.

I. THE BIRTH

Granting that it was the divine purpose that the Second Person should enter the human realm and become truly man, by what method might He best attain that end? He must have His own identified human spirit, soul, and body; but these would not be secured if He merely took possession of or appropriated some existing human being. That kind of arrangement would result in no more than an indwelling. On the other hand, He would not simply appear among men as one of them without a natural human origin. In such a case His true humanity could never be established nor His rightful relation to the people of the earth. It thus became essential that a member of the Godhead when entering the human family should enter as all others do. By such a procedure no question may be raised about the genuineness of His humanity or the permanency of it. It is true that, because of His unchangeable Deity, He could not be born of a human father. Had He been born of a human father and mother there would have been nothing to identify His humanity as the rightful property of His Deity. On the other hand, had He appeared with no relation to human parentage, there would have been no legitimate basis for the fact of His humanity. The divinely wrought arrangement by which He is generated of the Holy Spirit and born of a woman is the perfect solution of the problem. Cavil about whether the mother may impart a complete human nature and perpetuate a racial stock is silenced by the testimony of the Scriptures to the truth that He, though generated by the Holy Spirit, did possess a complete humanity—spirit, soul, and body. He is of the seed of Abraham, of the tribe of Judah, and the Heir to David's throne. To this body of evidence for His complete humanity may be added the genealogies which trace His human origin back to Abraham and to Adam. This perfect human kinship was demanded if He, as Mediator, undertook the work of redemption. He must be of the Adamic stock with the clearest title and the Fulfiller of the Abrahamic covenant of promise, which covenant stipulates that through Abraham's seed all nations of the earth would be blessed. To the end that this unique Person might sit on David's throne, He must be in the direct line of David and the rightful heir to that throne. Accordingly and in the faithfulness of God, the Second Person in becoming man is born into the Adamic race and became the rightful Fulfiller of the covenants by being born of the stock of Israel, of the seed of Abraham, of the tribe of Judah, and of the kingly line of David.

In presenting this incomparable theanthropic Person, the Scriptures assert by another line of incontrovertible testimony that, in the incarnation, this Person retained His Deity undiminished and untarnished. With respect to the presence of Deity in this unique Person, it may be observed that since a person—divine or human—cannot be divided, increased, or decreased, there could be no lessening of the divine presence. Deity is either present or not present at all—other than as He is omnipresent. To aver that God was in Christ is to aver that all of God was in Christ, and to this sublime truth the Scriptures testify: "For it pleased the Father that in him should all fulness dwell" (Col. 1:19); "For in him dwelleth all the fulness of the Godhead bodily" (2:9). It is therefore certain that from that moment when Christ became a theanthropic Person—whether at birth or before—undiminished Deity was present in Him, not as a Person of the Godhead now indwells the believer, but present in the sense that Deity was the essential feature of that Person. As other men are threefold in their beings—body, soul, and spirit—

this incomparable Person is fourfold, namely, Deity, human body, human soul, and human spirit. In so far as a Person of the Godhead may be localized or maintain an identity of existence, the localized Second Person is where this unique theanthropic Person is. For thirty-three years He was here on the earth; since then He has been seated at the Father's right hand in glory. That incomparable Person will return to the earth and reign. As an accommodation to the human emphasis upon material things it is natural to imply that wherever His humanity is there His Deity is also. On the other hand, the true consideration would be that wherever His Deity determines to be, there His humanity must of necessity be. While thus recognizing the true and perfect humanity which the Second Person acquired through the virgin birth, it is, nevertheless, the undiminished and unalterable Deity which is the primary factor in this unique theanthropic Christ of God.

Similarly, in spite of the fact that the Second Person entered a race every member of which without exception, other than Himself, is utterly ruined by sin, yet is Deity in no way injured by that kinsmanship. Since it is universal, it is natural to suppose that the sinfulness of mankind is an integral feature of a human being. However, it will be remembered that sin entered as an intrusion into the lives of those who by creation were without the taint of sin upon them. Therefore, it should not be deemed incredible that another Adam should arise who is equally unsullied and that He, being very God, could never fall through sin. The humanity of Christ presents certain parallels as well as contrasts when compared to the unfallen humanity of Adam.

First, an important distinction is to be seen in the manner in which these two Adams entered upon their human career. The first Adam was a direct creation of God and therefore was possessed of a sin-free existence through his creation. Sinlessness is guaranteed in the first Adam on the ground of the truth that God would create no sinful being. Over against this, the Last Adam entered into this human existence by a birth; yet is protected from the virus of inherited sin by a special divine intervention. Here two factors must be valued: (1) with regard to the generation of the humanity of the theanthropic Person it should be noted that the Generator is also a member of the Godhead and that His contribution or impartation is thus from a sinless source. It was the Spirit's work to beget the humanity of Christ. (2) This is a different matter than it would be if it were a begetting of Christ's Deity. It has too often been assumed that Christ received His Deity from the divine Parent and His humanity from the human parent; but on the divine side He was never thus generated or in any sense the product of another. He was Himself Deity, and that which He had always been was joined in everlasting identification with His humanity. The generating work of the Holy Spirit remains a mystery; nor is the generating work of a human father free from that which is mysterious. He who creates all things causes a virgin to conceive and thus to bear a Son. This creative act is to the end that the humanity of Christ may be secured. It follows, therefore, that whatever part of this unique child is wrought by the Holy Spirit will be as sinless as the Creator who produced it. A difficulty arises in some minds respecting the mother who herself acknowledged her need of a Savior (cf. Luke 1:47). Though it be declared in Hebrews 4:15 that the Lord Jesus Christ was without a sin nature, the central text on this truth is found in Luke 1:35, which records the words of the angel to Mary. The passage states, "And the angel answered and said unto her, The Holy Ghost shall come upon thee, and the power of the Highest shall overshadow thee: therefore also that holy thing which shall be born of thee shall be called the Son of God." Mary had been told previously (cf. vs. 31) that she would bring forth a son. In this statement no unnatural procedure is implied; but when she is told that the Generator would be the Holy Spirit she is also told that the child would be Himself holy and legitimately and properly the Son of God. The fallen nature of the mother is divinely precluded. This is the meaning of the assurance that the son she would bear would be holy. Care must be exercised in this contemplation lest the impression obtain that God who is not human could not generate the humanity of Christ. He who created the first Adam can generate the humanity of the Last Adam. In this the Holy Spirit is not so much a progenerator as He is a Creator. The unfallen estate, which in the case of the first Adam was guaranteed by the direct creation of the holy God, is in the case of the Last Adam guaranteed by revealed truth that it is generated by the Holy Spirit with a divine control of that which the woman might contribute.

Second, another and equally important difference between the unfallen humanity of Adam and that of Christ is that Adam stood alone with no relation to any other, while the humanity of Christ was and is indissolubly joined to Deity. It is true that unsupported humanity, such as that belonging to Adam, might sin; contrariwise in the case of the theanthropic Person, human traits which involved no moral issues —such as weariness, hunger, thirst—could be experienced, but it is equally true that whatever the humanity of Christ did His Deity also did. Since God cannot be compromised with evil, the normal capacity of unfallen humanity to sin, as that humanity was represented in Christ, could never be exercised to the slightest degree. An unfallen human nature which is welded to God cannot sin since God cannot sin. Some theologians have been satisfied with the weaker contention that Christ, because of His wisdom and divine strength, *would* not sin, and no more assurance of Christ's impeccability is claimed by them. This position ignores the truth that God *cannot* sin. To say that God cannot sin does not deprive Him of any divine attribute or competency. Sin is that accursed thing which has ruined God's creation, but it cannot ruin God. Those who assert that Christ could have sinned must aver that either Christ is not God or that God may Himself be ruined by sin. Since every position held by the Christian is gained only by the fact that he is in the resurrected Christ, it would be a serious jeopardy to those positions if it were true that the Last Adam might fall as the first Adam fell. If Christ could have sinned on earth, He can sin in heaven. He is the same yesterday, today, and forever. If He can sin now, there is no final assurance that He will not sin and thus bring every human hope based on redemption into ruin. Such conclusions are an insult against God and cannot be tolerated by those who bow in adoration before the Christ of God.

Christ might be styled the super-supernatural One, since He was not only supernatural in His original divine existence, but when Deity and sinless humanity are combined in one Person that which is utterly new both to Deity and to humanity emerges. The two natures combine in one Person. He is no longer God alone, nor is He man alone. He is not two Persons; He is one. He is the theanthropic Person—the first, the last, and the only One of His kind in heaven or on earth. Deity has not in this instance taken loosely an indeterminate or equivocal relation to humanity. In Christ, Deity and humanity are joined in one Person as the immaterial and material are joined in one human being. The two natures in Christ may be considered separately, but they cannot be separated.

Writing of the peculiar characteristics of this unique Person and the manner in which He is presented in the Scriptures, Dr. B. B. Warfield says:

The doctrine of the Two Natures of Christ is not merely the synthesis of the teaching of the New Testament, but the conception which underlies every one of the New Testament writings severally; it is not only the teaching of the New Testament as a whole but of the whole of the New Testament, part by part. Historically, this means that not only has the doctrine of the Two Natures been the invariable presupposition of the whole teaching of the church from the apostolic age down, but all the teaching of the apostolic age rests on it as its universal presupposition. When Christian literature begins, this is already the common assumption of the entire church. If we wish to translate this into the terms of positive chronology, what must be said is that before the opening of the sixth decade of the first century (for we suppose that I Thessalonians must be dated somewhere about 52 A.D.), the doctrine of the Two Natures already is firmly established in the church as the universal foundation of all Christian thinking concerning Christ. Such a mere chronological statement, however, hardly does justice to the case. What needs to be emphasized is that there is no Christian literature in existence which does not base itself, as upon an already firmly laid foundation, on the doctrine of the Two Natures. So far as Christian literature can bear testimony, there never has been any other doctrine recognized in the church. This literature itself goes back to within twenty years or so of the death of Christ; and of course—since it did not create but reflects this faith—has a restrospective value as testimony to the faith of Christians. . . . Thus we are brought to the final issue. The two-natured Christ is the synthesis of the whole mass of biblical data concerning Christ. The doctrine of the Two Natures underlies all the New Testament writings severally, and it is commended to us by the combined authority of all those primitive followers of Christ who have left written records of their faith. It is the only doctrine of Christ which can be discerned lying back of our formal records in pre-written tradition; it is the aboriginal faith of the Christian community. It is the only alternative to a non-existent Christ; we must choose between a two-natured Christ and a simply mythical Christ. By as much as "Jesus lived," by so much is it certain that the Jesus who lived is the person who alone is witnessed to us as having lived—the Jesus who, being Himself of heavenly origin and superior to the very angels, had come to earth on a mission of mercy, to seek and save those who are lost, and who, after He had given His life a ransom for many, was to come again on the clouds of heaven to judge the world. No other Jesus than this ever lived. No doubt He lived as man, His life adorned with all the gracious characteristics of a man of God. But He cannot be stripped of His divine claims. We have already had occasion to advert to the gross contradiction which is involved in supposing that such a man as He was could have preserved that fine flavor of humility toward God which characterized His whole life-manifestation and yet have falsely imagined Himself that exalted being in whose fancied personality He lived out His life on earth. The trait which made it possible for Him to put Himself forward as the Fellow of God would have made the humility of heart and demeanor which informed all His relations with God impossible. Our modern humanitarians, of course, gloze the psychological contradiction; but they cannot withhold recognition of the contrast of traits which must be accredited to any Jesus who can really be believed—even on their postulates—to have ever existed. For example, H. Werner (*Neue kirchliche Zeitschrift*, May, 1911, p. 389) exclaims, "He was at the same time humble and proud, acute-minded and weak-minded, clear-sighted and blind, sober-minded and fanatical, with profound knowledge of men and no self-knowledge, clear in his insight of the present, and full of fantastic dreams of the future. His life was, as Lipsius strikingly said, 'a tragedy of fanaticism.' " Standing before this puzzle of His life-manifestation, Adolf Harnack writes: "Only one who has had a kindred experience could go to the bottom here. A prophet might perhaps attempt to lift the veil; such as we must be content to assure ourselves that the Jesus who taught self-knowledge and humility, yet gave to himself, and to himself alone, the name of the Son of God."—*Christology and Criticism*, pp. 285–86; 303–4

II. THE CHILDHOOD

Being appointed to write of Christ's humanity, Luke has given the more complete account of the birth and childhood of Christ, though Matthew, who was appointed to write of the kingliness of Christ, has, in accordance with that which concerns a king, recorded His birth, His parentage, His name, and traced the divine protection over Him. As Luke traces the genealogy from Adam—the head of the human race—so Matthew traces His genealogy from Abraham through David; and the Scriptures are careful to state that both Mary and the foster father Joseph are in the Davidic line. Since Mark declares the servanthood of Christ, there is no occasion for him to include a genealogy; and since John portrays the Deity of the Savior, there is for the eternal Logos no ancestry. The two genealogies—important per se—constitute a study in themselves.

There were three appointed events in the life of a male child in Israel —*circumcision* at the time he was eight days old (Lev. 12:3), *presentation* at the time he was forty days old (Lev. 12:4–7), and *confirmation* at twelve years of age (Ex. 34:23; 23:17)—and the male children began to be numbered at twelve years of age. In the case of the male child appointed to public service there was a recognition and consecration when the appointed service began, but not until the man was at least thirty years of age (Num. 4:3). So far as the observance of the three events is concerned, the law which required them was observed perfectly. In connection with the fourth, Christ, being thirty years of age, was set apart and consecrated by His baptism. Of this more is due to be said in the following chapter.

On the human side, "the child grew, and waxed strong in spirit, filled with wisdom; and the grace of God was upon him" (Luke 2:40), and "Jesus increased in wisdom and stature, and in favour with God and man" (Luke 2:52). Each phase of these declarations is revealing. They record the development of One far removed from that which is normal in childhood. That which would differentiate Him from all others is the fact that He never even to the least degree committed any sin. He came to maturity and to His public ministry without having wrought or even thought that which would be unworthy of God. He went to the cross as the spotless Lamb of God, holy, harmless, undefiled, and separate from sinners. The manner of His appearance in the temple at twelve years of age confirms the distinctive character of the Christ child. Yet in all His purity and sinlessness which so completely set Him apart from all others and unto God, He is said to have been "subject" to His legal parents. The entire thirty years must be judged by these meager disclosures, but they suffice, if thoughtfully contemplated, to reveal the incomparable babyhood, childhood, youth, and young manhood of the Christ of God. Mary indeed had many things to ponder and many sayings to keep in her heart.

Thus the theanthropic Person entered the human family. His advent —the importance of which is knowledge-surpassing—had been anticipated throughout the sacred Scriptures by all the prophets and seers. That expectation traces Him from the protevangelium of Genesis 3:15 to His return to the earth in glory. He is the blessing of all nations in the Abrahamic promise, the Shiloh of the tribe of Judah, the everlasting King on David's throne, and the virgin-born son foreseen by Isaiah. It is the burden of each of the two major passages which predict His birth that He should be born in the Davidic line and sit on David's throne forever (cf. Isa. 9:6-7; Luke 1:31-33). Of the two great divine purposes—one for the earth centered in Israel and one for heaven centered in the Church—Christ is the Executor and Consummator of each. As the everlasting occupant of David's throne, the whole earth shall be filled with His glory. As the Lamb whose blood of redemption was shed and who arose from the dead, He became the First-Born among many brethren, which company He is bringing unto heaven's glory. Now He became a son in a fivefold sense—the Son of Adam, the Son of Abraham, the Son of David, the Son of Mary, and the Son of God. Likewise, Christ was the fourfold expectation of Jehovah to come. On this aspect of truth Dr. C. I. Scofield has written, "(1) 'The Branch of Jehovah' (Isa. 4:2), that is, the 'Immanuel' character of Christ (Isa. 7:14) to be fully manifested to restored and converted Israel after His return in divine glory (Mt. 25:31); (2) the 'Branch of David' (Isa. 11:1; Jer. 23:5; 33:15), that is, the Messiah, 'of the seed of David according to the flesh' (Rom. 1:3), revealed in His earthly glory as King of kings, and Lord of lords; (3) Jehovah's 'Servant, the Branch' (Zech. 3:8), Messiah's humiliation and obedience unto death according to Isa. 52:13-15; 53:1-12; Phil. 2:5-8; (4) the 'man whose name is the Branch' (Zech.

6:12–13), that is, His character as Son of man, the 'last Adam,' the 'second Man' (1 Cor. 15:45–47), reigning, as Priest-King, over the earth in the dominion given to and lost by the first Adam. Matthew is the Gospel of the 'Branch of David'; Mark of 'Jehovah's Servant, the Branch'; Luke of 'the man whose name is the Branch'; John of 'the Branch of Jehovah'" (*Scofield Reference Bible,* pp. 716–17).

By His advent into the world Christ became the Fulfiller of all divine purposes and all Old Testament expectation, and the answer to the need of a lost world.

CHAPTER IV

THE BAPTISM OF CHRIST INCARNATE

THIS PARTICULAR discussion of the general theme of the life and ministry of the incarnate Son of God is centered upon one event, namely, His own baptism. In Volume VII of this work the doctrine of water or ritual baptism as related to Jews and Christians will be considered. At this point the contemplation is only of the one peculiar baptism, that of the Christ. No phase of the life of Christ on earth is more misunderstood than His baptism. This misunderstanding is evidenced by the wide variety of more or less contradictory meanings and modes assigned to it. It is obvious that, though all of these assigned meanings and modes might be untrue, not more than one of them could be true. In the light of this confusion of ideas which prevail and the dogmatic way in which theories are expressed, there is need that care be exercised to the end that this subject may be approached in an unprejudiced manner. A complete investigation cannot be introduced here, nor is a desire entertained to engender more strife among those who should, above all things, be of one mind before the unbelieving world. The general questions that need to be answered are, (1) By whom was Christ baptized? (2) For what reason was He baptized? (3) By what mode was He baptized? (4) Is Christ's baptism an example to believers of this dispensation? (5) What other baptisms were experienced by Christ?

I. THE BAPTIZER

It is no small issue to consider who is assigned the task of baptizing the theanthropic Person—one of the Godhead before whom all angels bow in unceasing adoration, the Creator of all things, for whom all things were created and by whom they consist, the everlasting Ruler of the universe, the Redeemer of a lost world, and the final Judge over the creation of God including both angels and men. Later it is revealed that He Himself baptized with the Holy Spirit and with fire. Though some may question why He should be baptized at all, He is nevertheless baptized both by water and by suffering unto death (cf. Matt. 20:

20–23 with Matt. 26:42; John 18:11). To John is the high honor given of baptizing the Savior, and John is declared to be the last of the prophets of the old order (cf. Matt. 11:13), that one who was the greatest of all born of woman (cf. Matt. 11:11), and the divinely-appointed messenger —the forerunner who was specifically sent to announce the advent of Messiah, who is Jehovah. Isaiah predicted of John, "The voice of him that crieth in the wilderness, Prepare ye the way of the LORD, make straight in the desert a highway for our God. Every valley shall be exalted, and every mountain and hill shall be made low: and the crooked shall be made straight, and the rough places plain: and the glory of the LORD shall be revealed, and all flesh shall see it together: for the mouth of the LORD hath spoken it" (40:3–5). Malachi also announced as the word of Jehovah, "Behold, I will send my messenger, and he shall prepare the way before me." This is followed by the anticipated message of John, the character of which is fully in accord with the recorded preaching of John—a comparison which should not be overlooked—for it relates John's ministry, in the main, to the merit system of Moses and not in any way to the grace system which came into effect through the death and resurrection of Christ. The appointment as Jehovah's messenger and forerunner is a responsibility far exceeding that committed to any other man. John was divinely delegated to "prepare the way of" Jehovah-Messiah (cf. Mark 1:2; Acts 19:4), and "that he [Christ] should be made manifest to Israel [and how] "therefore am I come baptizing" (John 1:31). Concerning this, the message of the angel to Zacharias the father of John regarding the birth and service of John, as recorded in Luke 1:13–17, is revealing, "But the angel said unto him, Fear not, Zacharias: for thy prayer is heard; and thy wife Elisabeth shall bear thee a son, and thou shalt call his name John. And thou shalt have joy and gladness; and many shall rejoice at his birth. For he shall be great in the sight of the Lord, and shall drink neither wine nor strong drink; and he shall be filled with the Holy Ghost, even from his mother's womb. And many of the children of Israel shall he turn to the Lord their God. And he shall go before him in the spirit and power of Elias, to turn the hearts of the fathers to the children, and the disobedient to the wisdom of the just; to make ready a people prepared for the Lord." Here it would be well to note the extended description of John's interview with the priests and Levites who were sent to inquire who John might be: "And this is the record of John, when the Jews sent priests and Levites from Jerusalem to ask him, Who art thou? And he confessed, and denied not; but confessed, I am not the

Christ. And they asked him, What then? Art thou Elias? And he saith, I am not. Art thou that prophet? And he answered, No. Then said they unto him, Who art thou? that we may give an answer to them that sent us. What sayest thou of thyself? He said, I am the voice of one crying in the wilderness, Make straight the way of the Lord, as said the prophet Esaias. And they which were sent were of the Pharisees. And they asked him, and said unto him, Why baptizest thou then, if thou be not that Christ, nor Elias, neither that prophet? John answered them, saying, I baptize with water: but there standeth one among you, whom ye know not; he it is, who coming after me is preferred before me, whose shoe's latchet I am not worthy to unloose. These things were done in Bethabara beyond Jordan, where John was baptizing" (John 1:19–28). This passage is important because of various disclosures which it records; but none more significant than that baptizing by prophets was fully recognized and established in the minds of the authorities as a right procedure, and also that the Messiah would baptize when He came. In this connection, it is needful to consider that the disciples of Messiah did also baptize. Of this fact it is written later on, "After these things came Jesus and his disciples into the land of Judæa; and there he tarried with them, and baptized" (3:22). However, in John 4:1–3 it is said that Christ did not Himself baptize. This passage reads, "When therefore the Lord knew how the Pharisees had heard that Jesus made and baptized more disciples than John, (though Jesus himself baptized not, but his disciples,) he left Judæa, and departed again into Galilee." The unfavorable reaction of the Pharisees against baptizing on the part of Christ's disciples indicates again that which was generally recognized as the Jewish law respecting the practice of baptism. It is probable that John's baptism served as a sealing of his reformation preaching. The revealing of the Messiah was accomplished when he said, "Behold the Lamb of God, which taketh away the sin of the world" (John 1:29). Likewise his unique baptism of Christ served to designate the Messiah. With all his divine appointment—of which he was duly conscious, for he said, "I am the voice of one crying in the wilderness, Make straight the way of the Lord, as said the prophet Esaias"—John shrank from the responsibility of baptizing Christ. Of this it is written, "Then cometh Jesus from Galilee to Jordan unto John, to be baptized of him. But John forbad him, saying, I have need to be baptized of thee, and comest thou to me? And Jesus answering said unto him, Suffer it to be so now: for thus it becometh us to fulfil all righteousness. Then he suffered him" (Matt. 3:13–15). The hesitancy of John and the assuring response of

Christ is well pictured by Gregory Thaumaturgus (X, 1184–8), as cited by Dr. J. W. Dale in his *Johannic Baptism* (pp. 404–5):

"How shall I touch thy undefiled head? How shall I stretch out my right hand over thee who hast stretched out the heavens as a curtain and established the earth upon the waters? How shall I stretch out my servile fingers over thy divine head? How shall I wash the spotless and the sinless? How shall I enlighten the light? How shall I offer prayer for thee who dost receive the prayers of those who know thee not? In baptizing others I baptize into thy name that they may believe upon thee coming with glory; baptizing thee of whom shall I make mention? Into whose name shall I baptize thee? Into the name of the Father? But thou hast all the Father in thyself, and thou art all in the Father. Or, into the name of the Son? But there is no other beside thee, by nature, the Son of God. Or, into the name of the Holy Ghost? But he is in everything united with thee, as of the same nature with thee, and of the same will, and of the same mind, and of the same power, and of the same honor, and with thee receives worship from all. Baptize, therefore, if thou wilt, O Lord, baptize me the Baptist. Make me, whom thou hast caused to be born, to be born again. Stretch out thy dread right hand which thou hast prepared for thyself, and crown by thy touch my head, that forerunner of thy kingdom, and crowned like a forerunner, I may preach to sinners, crying unto them: 'Behold the Lamb of God which taketh away the sins of the world. . . .' Jesus is represented as answering: 'It is necessary that I should, now, be baptized with this baptism, and, hereafter, confer upon all men the baptism of the Trinity. Lend me thy right hand, O Baptist, for the present administration. . . . Take hold of my head which the Seraphim worship. Baptize me, who am about to baptize them that believe (δι ὕδατος, καὶ πνεύματος, καὶ πυρὸς) *by* water, and Spirit, and fire; (ὕδατι) *by* water, which is able to wash away the filth of sin; (πνεύματι) *by* Spirit, which is able to make the earthy spiritual; (πυρὶ) *by* fire, consuming, by nature, the thorns of transgressions.' The Baptist having heard these things, stretching out his trembling right hand, baptized the Lord."

It should not be overlooked that John was the son of a priest, Zacharias of the course of Abia, and that his mother was a daughter directly of Aaron (Luke 1:5). John was therefore a priest in his own right, though no record exists that he was consecrated to the priestly office, and no record exists that he was not consecrated. He was rightfully a priest as well as the greatest of the Old Testament prophets, and this fact enters largely into the meaning of his baptizing ministry. It was by this so unusual, God-appointed, and God-provided priest and prophet that Christ was baptized.

II. THE NEED

Certain theories have been advanced concerning the baptism of Christ, but any theory is doomed to fail which cannot account for the central idea advanced by Christ when He said "Thus it becometh us to fulfil all righteousness" (Matt. 3:15). These theories may be mentioned briefly.

First, it is claimed that Christ received John's baptism which was one of repentance and unto the remission of sins. The truth that Christ was sinless to an infinite degree and therefore needed no repentance or remission of sin is not denied by those who make this claim. It is rather asserted that in some way not clearly defined and to some degree Christ was, in His baptism, identifying Himself with sinners, or was already substituting for them as the One who would later take their place in a sacrificial death. Earlier in this work it has been pointed out that the substitutionary redemptive work of Christ was restricted to the sufferings and death of the cross. On this theory and in defense of it, Dean Alford remarks:

> Why should our Lord, who was *without sin,* have come to *a baptism of repentance?* Because He was *made sin for us:* for which reason also He suffered the curse of the law. It became Him, being *in the likeness of sinful flesh,* to go through those appointed rites and purifications which belonged to that flesh. There is no more strangeness in His having been baptized by John, than in His keeping the Passovers. The one rite, as the other, belonged to *sinners*— and *among the transgressors He was numbered.* The prophetic words in Ps. 40:12, spoken in the person of our Lord, indicate, in the midst of sinlessness, the most profound apprehension of the sins of that nature which He took upon him. I cannot suppose the baptism to have been sought by our Lord merely *to honour John,* or as *knowing that it would be the occasion of a divine recognition* of his Messiahship, and thus pre-ordained by God: but *bona fide,* as bearing the infirmities and carrying the sorrows of mankind, and thus beginning here the triple baptism of water, fire, and blood, two parts of which were now accomplished, and of the third of which He himself speaks, Luke 12:50, and the beloved Apostle, 1 John 5:8—His baptism, as it was our Lord's *closing* act of obedience under the Law, in His hitherto concealed life of legal submission, His fulfilling all righteousness, so was His *solemn inauguration and anointing for the higher official life of mediatorial satisfaction* which was now opening upon Him. See Romans 1:3, 4. We must not forget that the *working out of perfect righteousness in our flesh* by the entire and spotless keeping of God's law (Deut. 6:25), was, in the main, *accomplished during the thirty years previous to our Lord's official ministry.—New Testament for English Readers,* I, 16, on Matt. 3:13

This interpretation of the baptism of Christ, though held by the majority of those who construe water baptism to be a symbol of Christ's burial and resurrection, has never been sustained by Scripture. The weakness of Dean Alford's contention is evidenced when he likens Christ's baptism to His participation in the Passover feast, and when he declares that both baptism and the Passover belong to sinners. Respecting the Passover, it may be said that it was only a memorial which celebrated the time when God passed over and saved His people from death in Egypt. The Passover had no direct meaning respecting the sins of future generations who might celebrate that feast. Those who in later generations partook of that feast were not relating it to their own sins or expecting God, because of that feast, to pass over their own sins. This whole contention may well be classed as one very strongly asserted but unproved theory. It should be remembered that Christ's early ministry was wholly confined to the nation Israel (cf. Matt. 10:6; 15:24; Rom. 15:8), and that the whole reality of the cross is entered and consummated only when He has been rejected by that nation. It is clear that the cross recognizes the need of the whole world as well as Israel (John 3:16; Heb. 2:9; 1 John 2:2). This theory can incorporate the fulfilling of all righteousness only in the most indirect and unsatisfactory way. What Christ did in baptism was of necessity related to His Israelitish ministry and concerns what to Israel was the fulfilling of all righteousness. There is little basis for a theory which would connect Christ's supposed identification with sinners through baptism with the fulfilling of all righteousness.

Second, it is claimed that by His baptism Christ was set apart to His Messianic ministry. In this connection it is suggested that as the kingdom in which Messiah is to reign will be ushered in by the bringing in of everlasting righteousness (cf. Dan. 9:24), there is some reference to this in Christ's words to John about fulfilling all righteousness. This theory is especially weak in that there is no real connection between these two references to righteousness, nor is there a Biblical ground upon which the theory might rest.

Third, it is also advanced as a hypothesis that Christ in His baptism was taking His supposed part with the godly remnant who responded out of Israel to the preaching of John; but, again, there is no well-defined basis for this supposition that by so doing Christ fulfilled all righteousness.

Fourth, it is pointed out that the three events—the baptism, the transfiguration, and the future seating of Christ on David's throne (cf. Matt. 3:16–17; 17:5; Ps. 2:6–7)—are signalized by a divine voice from heaven. It is believed that the voice will speak again as a divine attestation. It is likewise noted that evidently the transfiguration voice is an attestation of Christ's prophetic ministry since in all three accounts the words are added "Hear ye him." Thus the baptism is related to the priestly office and the voice that spoke is the attestation of Christ's appointment as a Priest. It is true that the exercise of the ministry of Priest did not begin until He offered Himself without spot to God, and that the final exercise of the King-Priest service, which is after the order of Melchizedek, will be manifested in the millennial reign. However, it is reasonable for Christ, having reached the appointed age of thirty years, to be consecrated as Priest. It is significant that when Christ came to be baptized it is declared, "Jesus himself began to be about thirty years of age" (Luke 3:23). Such a detail is not added without meaning, and, when reviewing the Mosaic Law, it is discovered that the male child who would enter the priesthood was not eligible to do so until he was thirty years of age (cf. Num. 4:3), and from the added fact that there was no other public ministry to be entered which prescribed its age limits it is reasonable to conclude that the baptism of Christ had to do with His consecration to the priestly office. It will be remembered that Christ was of the tribe of Judah and that, according to the Mosaic Law, no priest could naturally arise from Judah; yet none can question that Christ is a Priest, both as typified by Aaron and after the order of Melchizedek. The Epistle to the Hebrews, chapters 5 to 10, is a setting forth of the truth that Christ is a Priest. Hebrews 7:14–17 states, "For it is evident that our Lord sprang out of Juda; of which tribe Moses spake nothing concerning priesthood. And it is yet far more evident: for that after the similitude of Melchisedec there ariseth another priest, who is made, not after the law of a carnal commandment, but after the power of an endless life. For he testifieth, Thou art a priest for ever after the order of Melchisedec." Thus it is divinely acknowledged that Christ's priesthood was exceptional in character. Not only does He arise out of Judah, but He follows the similitude of Melchizedek, who was not of Aaron's line, nor was he of Israel at all. Since Christ's priesthood is so much an exception, it is reasonable to expect that the consecration will be exceptional; and it was. It was accomplished by John who not only surpassed the high priest in divine appointment, but surpassed all Old Testament prophets in authority and divine recognition. In fact, one of John's divine commissions was thus to introduce the Messiah—Israel's Prophet, Priest, and King. It only remains to emphasize the truth that, according to the Mosaic Law which God Himself decreed and which the people were taught to honor, every priest must be ordained and Christ, being a Priest, was allowed no exception in the matter of ordination. His compliance with the divinely established law constituted the fulfilling of all righteousness. "The righteousness of the law" is a phrase which means nothing else other than that the law is fulfilled to the last degree (cf. Rom. 2:26; 8:4).

It may be concluded, then, that Christ, though of the tribe of Judah and not therefore to be recognized as a Priest by any high priest, is nevertheless the consummating Priest, and that He, in compliance with the law which Jehovah established, was consecrated or ordained to the priestly office, and, in doing so, He, whose earth-life was lived under the law and who perfectly observed the law, fulfilled all righteousness in the respect that He was duly set apart to the priestly office. He who was disqualified according to the rules imposed upon the high priest as to who might be ordained to priesthood, was ordained by God's appointed priest and prophet of whom Christ Himself said, "a prophet . . . and more than a prophet," and among those born of women no greater than John had arisen (Matt. 11:9, 11). No more vital thing could be done in preparing the way of Jehovah-Messiah (cf. Isa. 40:3; John 1:23) than that the legal dedication of the Priest above all priests should be accomplished.

III. THE MODE

In this division of this subject the attempt is made to determine the mode of Christ's baptism. This is not done to induce a discussion relative to the proper mode of Christian baptism; for, as the case is conceived, there is no direct relation existing between the baptism of Christ and the baptism of a believer. A very wide difference also obtains between what is styled *John's baptism* and the baptism of the Messiah by John. Though Christ was baptized by John, it was not John's usual baptism which was one of repentance and unto the remission of sins. As a preparation for the Messiah, a baptism designed for sinners could not be required. As before intimated, all attempts to identify the Messiah with the sins of the people in His baptism are in danger of dishonoring the Lord of Glory, and without Biblical support. The penitence of a sinner is in no way the fulfilling of all righteousness. Whatever involves an absurdity must be deemed untrue. "Repentance," "fruits meet for repentance," and "remission of sins," though the basis of John's baptism, are wholly foreign to the Person of the Lord. He never sinned, therefore He neither repented nor brought forth fruits meet for repentance. Should it be asserted that Christ's baptism was only the form and not the substance, it is well to remember that no baptism exists apart from its substance. It is clear that John's baptism was not Christian baptism else the Apostle would not have rebaptized the twelve disciples of John—the only instance in the New Testament of rebaptizing (Acts 19:4–5). It is even more clear that Christ's baptism as accomplished by John is not Christian baptism, and the oft-repeated injunction to "follow Christ in baptism" is both unfounded and misleading. Christians may follow Christ in moral or spiritual issues, but not in official acts; and Christ's baptism involved no moral principle other than that it wrought out the peculiar obligation which rested upon Him. The law which engendered this obligation could never apply to a believer in the present age. The familiar injunction, however, usually means no more than that the Christian should submit to the same mode of baptism as that by which it is assumed that Christ was baptized; but by what mode was Christ baptized? This is no new question but is one which, if past controversies disclose anything, will not be determined by any amount of evidence that may be advanced. That Christ was dipped into the river Jordan is purely an inference since there is no such declaration unequivocally set forth in the Scriptures. Had there been such a declaration, more than three-fourths of the church—embracing the vast majority of the great scholars—would hardly be of an opposite mind. An interesting incident is reported by John Goff (*How Was Jesus Baptized and Why?* pp. 1–2) concerning a brilliant lawyer who assumed that Christ was dipped in the river Jordan and who was asked whether, had there been a law in John's day prohibiting dipping as baptism, he could convict John on existing evidence. He supposed that he could do so easily, but he discovered that, when the matter was brought under the acid test of indisputable proof, the evidence was less than circumstantial. Those who in all sincerity contend that Christ was dipped in the river Jordan do so upon two general lines of supposed attestation, namely, the philological evidence, and the inspired record of the baptism of Christ or exegetical evidence.

1. THE PHILOLOGICAL EVIDENCE. This line of reasoning asserts that the mode of Christ's baptism is determined by the meaning of the word βαπτίζω. This word is used about eighty times in the New Testament and at least twenty of these usages belong to situations in which there could be no physical intusposition or envelopment, and thus the dogmatic declaration that this word means 'to dip or plunge' wherever found in the New Testament is subject to doubt. A more accurate teaching is found in the fact that βαπτίζω, like its kindred word βάπτω, has both a primary and a secondary meaning. Βάπτω is used but three times—twice with its

primary meaning, 'to dip' (Luke 16:24; John 13:26), and once in its secondary meaning (Rev. 19:13, with the same situation described more definitely in Isa. 63:3). Where the secondary meaning is used, the physical dipping disappears and an object, such as Christ's garment, is connected with βάπτω if it be dyed or stained by any means. Similarly, βαπτίζω appears with a primary meaning which is 'to immerse or to submerge,' i.e., dispatch with but one motion, all of which gives no authority for the lifting out (as true also in the case of βάπτω) from the submerged state, while the secondary meaning recognizes that the object has been brought under some power or influence, or been characterized by some baptizing agent. Those who hold that ritual baptism calls for a complete envelopment in water contend that, on the ground of the primary meaning of the word βαπτίζω, Christ was thus baptized; however, the priests of the old order were, when inducted into the priestly office, sprinkled with water and anointed with oil—the latter a symbol of the Holy Spirit. So Christ, when consecrated as a Priest, was baptized with water and anointed with the Holy Spirit. The meaning of βαπτίζω being that a thoroughly changed condition is secured by the influence of the baptizing agent, so Christ by a formal baptism with water was thoroughly changed to the extent that He was constituted a Priest according to the Mosaic requirements.

It will be remembered that the present discussion is restricted to the mode of Christ's baptism. It remains to demonstrate, as far as may be possible, that Christ entered the priestly office in the manner prescribed by the Mosaic Law. According to that requirement, He was set apart by the administration of water and by the anointing of the Spirit when the Spirit descended upon Him in the form of a dove. As these two features answered the demands of the law, they constituted the fulfilling of all righteousness. Of the four early dates mentioned in the earth-life of Christ—circumcised on the eighth day; presented on the fortieth day; confirmed in the temple at twelve years of age; and consecrated, if entering the priesthood, at thirty years of age—each one is a definite compliance with the Mosaic Law. His consecration at thirty years was as much prescribed as was circumcision on the eighth day, and Christ fulfilled all righteousness by being circumcised the eighth day.

If it be true that Christ's baptism was His formal induction into the office of Priest, it only remains to discover by what mode priests of the Mosaic system were consecrated; for His baptism, if it fulfilled all righteousness, could not depart from the specified requirements of the law. Though in Exodus 28:1—29:37, Leviticus 8:1—9:24, Numbers 8:5–26 the full requirement for the entrance into the priesthood is prescribed, nearly all of those portions of Scripture apply to the problem of bringing sinful men into that holy office. None of those features was very appropriate for the sinless Son of God. In fact, only the dedication by baptism and the anointing with oil (Ex. 29:4, 7) could be applicable to Christ. With regard to the ceremonial application of water—in the Old Testament by sprinkling and not by dipping—only the thought of a formal setting apart is found in Christ's baptism, and with no reference to cleansing. As the Old Testament priest was anointed with oil as a symbol of the Holy Spirit, Christ was anointed with the Spirit Himself. It should be remembered that these contrasts and similarities are between the Old Testament priest and Christ, and that there is another and far different group of contrasts and comparisons to be seen between the Old Testament priest and the New Testament believer who is a priest unto God. It is of great importance to recognize that because it involved the unique, sinless Person—Jehovah-Messiah—who is the eternal divine Priest who came, not from Aaron's line, but from the tribe of Judah—a minister not of a fallen people, but to a fallen people —the baptism of Christ must ever be classed by itself and rated as an official act which, because of its distinctiveness, could not be compliance in every respect to a law designed for sinful men who entered the priesthood, nor a pattern for New Testament believer-priests who come after Him. No baptism before or since could be for the same purpose as was the baptism of Christ. Though a fuller discussion of the meaning of βαπτίζω is reserved for later consideration of the believer's baptism, it may be restated here that there is nothing in the meaning of the word used in the New Testament respecting Christ's baptism nor in the demands of the law which He fulfilled which necessitates the belief that Christ was dipped in water. In truth, such a baptism would have been a violation of the law.

2. THE EXEGETICAL EVIDENCE. In this particular division of the general theme of the baptism of Christ the entire baptizing ministry of John is indirectly involved; for in the midst of that ministry, with regard to its location and the features employed, Christ's baptism occurred. The facts relative to John's baptism, with which the baptism of Christ is associated, are found in the passages here listed.

Matthew 3:1–2. "In those days came John the Baptist, preaching in the wilderness of Judæa, and saying, Repent ye: for the kingdom of heaven is at hand."

Though throughout Jewish history many may have administered baptism, but one is designated *the Baptist,* and doubtless in part because of the great number who came to him for baptism and more specifically because of his mission as the one divinely appointed to baptize Christ.

Matthew 3:11. "I indeed baptize you with water unto repentance" (cf. Mark 1:7–8; Luke 3:16; John 1:33).

In this passage, as in another of those cited with it where the word also occurs, the translation of ἐν by the word *with* as indication of the instrumental baptizing agent is justified. The setting up of the Holy Spirit's relation to the believer is also a baptism which Christ as the baptizing agent accomplished. A certain group would force a rendering of ἐν πνεύματι and ἐν ὕδατι—wholly similar in form—by translating the words '*into* the Spirit' and '*into* water'; but the great majority of scholars sustain the Authorized rendering, namely, '*with*' the Spirit and '*with*' water.

Matthew 3:6. "And were baptized of him in Jordan, confessing their sins."

Mark 1:4–5. "John did baptize in the wilderness, and preach the baptism of repentance for the remission of sins. And there went out unto him all the land of Judæa, and they of Jerusalem, and were all baptized of him in the river of Jordan, confessing their sins."

Luke 3:3. "And he came into all the country about Jordan, preaching the baptism of repentance for the remission of sins."

John 3:22–23. "After these things came Jesus and his disciples into the land of Judæa; and there he tarried with them, and baptized. And John also was baptizing in Ænon near to Salim, because there was much water there: and they came, and were baptized."

John 10:40. "And went away again beyond Jordan into the place where John at first baptized; and there he abode."

Uniformly in these passages (two passages use another word) the word ἐν would be rightly rendered *at*, and with reference to locality Mark 1:5 is no exception to this interpretation. John was baptizing at the Jordan—a territorial locality—and not *into* Jordan.

Mark 1:9. "And it came to pass in those days, that Jesus came from Nazareth of Galilee, and was baptized of John in Jordan."

This one passage—the only one—seems at first sight and because the preposition is εἰς to teach that John's baptism was actually *into* Jordan. If the passage is rendered thus, it will either contradict or go beyond all other passages, for the other passages, as indicated above, treat Jordan as a specific geographical locality. The Jordan, or the river Jordan, is where John baptized, however, and not the water into which he baptized. This exceptional passage, therefore, calls for careful consideration. The sentence which this text sets forth, it will be seen, is subject to change in order, that is, the phrase, "and was baptized of John," may rightly be treated as parenthetical and introduced at the end as well as in the midst of the main declaration. Thus the reading could just as well be, "Jesus came from Nazareth of Galilee to [unto or into] the Jordan [locality] and was baptized of John." By such an arrangement, which is fully justified, this Scripture conforms to all other similar passages and does not introduce an idea which is nowhere else advanced in the New Testament. Matthew 3:13 is of particular interest on this point, which reads, "Then cometh Jesus from Galilee to [ἐπί] Jordan unto [πρός] John, to be baptized of him." Naturally, for those who are persuaded that the name *Jordan* means water and not locality and that the verb *baptize* necessitates a physical intusposition, the discussion is closed and sealed; but such closing and sealing has no sure ground on which to rest. The term *Jordan*, which includes the water, the banks, and the territory adjacent, does not in New Testament usage mean simply water, nor does the presence of the verb *to baptize* have any power to require that the term *Jordan* shall mean water. It is, however, asserted that Christ was baptized by John in the locality known as Jordan. All else about proximity to the water and the precise mode of baptism employed must be determined from other sources.

Respecting the one passage in question, Dr. Dale quotes Dr. R. Wilson, Professor of Sacred Literature, Royal College, Belfast, thus: "The preposition εἰς, with a word *supposed* to signify the baptizing element, forms the regimen of βαπτίζω, in one solitary occurrence. The unique exception to which we refer is found in Mark 1:9, 'He was baptized of John in Jordan.' On this construction great stress has been laid, as if it necessarily affirmed that our blessed Lord was dipped into the river of Israel. . . . We are not disposed, however, to surrender to our opponents the preposition εἰς in this important testimony. Supported by the authority of New Testament usage, we maintain that in numerous constructions, several of them closely parallel to the example before us, εἰς is employed where motion is not indicated by the verb with which it stands connected, and where, therefore, the rendering *into* is totally incompatible with the existing syntax. Bruder, in his *Concordance* to the Greek Testament, enumerates not fewer than *sixty-five* instances of this construction, and among them he includes the text under discussion" (*Op. cit.*, p. 380). And Dr. Dale adds that the interpretation of

Mark 1:9 as a dipping in the river Jordan involves six assumptions, which he enumerates as follows: "It has been assumed by writers, on the mere ground of the juxtaposition of words, that 'Jesus was dipped into the Jordan.' This assumption cannot be made without a handful of other assumptions: 1. The assumption, that εἰς, here, means 'into,' while, elsewhere, it means *unto*. 2. The assumption, that 'Jordan,' here, means *water*, while, elsewhere, it means *locality*. 3. The assumption, that the phrase εἰς Ἰορδάνην is complementary to βαπτίζω, which assumption is based on a previous assumption, that the phrase denotes *water*, and which assumption rests on the antecedent assumption, that proximity makes complement. 4. The assumption, that βαπτίζω is, here, used in a primary and literal sense, while, elsewhere, it is used in a secondary and figurative sense. 5. The assumption, that βαπτίζω here means *dip*, while, elsewhere, and everywhere, it has no such meaning. 6. The assumption, that Mark in relating the same transaction which is related by Matthew, gives an entirely different representation from his fellow Evangelist, while his language is capable of the most absolute unity of interpretation" (*Ibid.*, p. 384).

IV. CHRIST'S BAPTISM AND CHRISTIAN BAPTISM

To the reader who is dependent on the English translation as set forth in the Authorized Version, there is confusion engendered by the varying translations of four prepositions employed in the original text. These are:

ἐν. A word which is given a very great variety of meanings, and, as stated above, does not necessarily need to be translated by the word *in*. It is used in the New Testament 330 times when translated *at, on,* or *with*. John baptized *at* Jordan, and Christ baptized *with* the Holy Spirit. So, also, the Authorized Version uniformly translates ἐν ὕδατι by *with* water and not *in* water.

ἀπό. This preposition is given at least twenty meanings in the New Testament, and is translated 374 times by the word *from*. Jesus, when he was baptized, went up straightway "out of the water" (Matt. 3:16), which is just as well translated *up from the water*.

εἰς. A word given at least twenty-six different meanings and, in all, is translated by the word *unto* 538 times. Therefore, as in Acts 8:38, they both went "down into the water" is just as correctly rendered, *down unto the water*.

ἐκ. A word with twenty-four meanings, this preposition is translated by the word *from* 168 times. Acts 8:39 may as well read: They were come up *from* (rather than *out of*) the water. Thus any argument respecting mode of water baptism built on the prepositions is without substance. John was baptizing *at* Jordan and those baptized went down *unto* the water and came up *from* the water. The fact that translators give the prepositions meanings which imply a mode of baptism lends no support, unless it is demonstrated that a certain translation is itself equally inspired along with the Greek original.

Apart from every consideration of the mode by which Christ was baptized, it is certain that His was not Christian baptism. Assuming that Christian baptism represents crucifixion, death, burial, and resurrection, there could be no meaning in Christ enacting that which later He would accomplish in substance. To declare that He was so acting is to substitute human imagination for the absence of a Biblical intimation. Similarly, assuming that Christian baptism is a sign and seal of the presence and work of the Holy Spirit in the believer is equally as foreign to any feature of Christ's program. However, were the imagination to be employed where no Scripture directs, the fact that Christ received the Holy Spirit without measure at the time He was baptized might indicate that such was the meaning of His baptism. As before declared, Christians follow Christ in moral rather than official issues, and Christ's baptism was official. It has been pointed out that His baptism was different in its meaning and purpose than the usual baptism by John; it is equally demonstrable that Christ's baptism differs from usual Christian baptism.

V. OTHER BAPTISMS

In its secondary usage—that so largely employed in the New Testament—the word βαπτίζω means that a thorough change of condition is brought about by the power of a baptizing agency. There was a baptism *into* repentance, a baptism *into* the remission of sins, and a baptism *into* Moses. There is a baptism *into* the name of the Father, the Son, and the Holy Spirit, a baptism *into* that estate of high privilege accorded those who receive the Holy Spirit with all His benefits, and there is a baptism *into* Christ by the Holy Spirit. In the Mosaic dispensation as in the Christian there is a baptism by means of symbolic water—not *into* water, but *into* whatever may be the objective estate related to a given baptism. It is in this far-reaching secondary meaning of βαπτίζω— never to be interpreted as a momentary dipping into some enveloping physical element—that two other baptisms were experienced by Christ. These are:

1. THE BAPTISM BY THE HOLY SPIRIT. Of this baptism it is written in John 1:32–33, "And John bare record, saying, I saw the Spirit descending from heaven like a dove, and it abode upon him. And I knew him not: but he that sent me to baptize with water, the same said unto me, Upon whom thou shalt see the Spirit descending, and remaining on him, the same is he which baptizeth with the Holy Ghost."

If it be objected that in the passage it is not said that this was a baptism, it may be replied that no Scripture more clearly describes that which constitutes a complete and perfect baptism. Little, indeed, is it required that an incident so true to form should be styled a baptism in order that it may be recognized as such. On the theme of the baptism of Christ by the Holy Spirit—not to be confounded with any other Spirit baptism—Dr. J. W. Dale writes in *Christic and Patristic Baptism* (pp. 32–33):

Evidence, to excess, has been furnished for the existence of baptisms where no envelopment was to be found in fact, or could rationally be conceived. The usage, under such circumstances, being based on a similarity of condition with that produced on a class of bodies susceptible of being penetrated, pervaded, and so receiving quality from some enveloping element. Therefore this descent of the Holy Ghost and his abiding upon our Lord is called a baptism, and not because of any irrational and impossible external envelopment. That the whole being of "the Christ" was henceforth under the influence of this *anointing* the Scriptures abundantly testify: 1. By declaring through the Forerunner (John 3:34) that "the Spirit is not given by measure unto him," and therefore the farther statement, "Jesus being full of the Holy Ghost." That such a gift would have a controlling influence, we are not left to infer; but it is expressly declared by John—"He whom God hath sent speaketh the words of God, *for* God giveth not the Spirit by measure unto him." 2. This gift was as unlimited in continuance as it was in measure—"I saw the Spirit descending from heaven like a dove and it *abode* upon him" (John 1:32). 3. Under this influence he preached—"The Spirit of the Lord is upon me, because he hath anointed me to preach the gospel to the poor, . . . to preach the acceptable year of the Lord. And he began to say unto them, This day is this Scripture fulfilled in your ears" (Luke 4:18, 21); "God anointed Jesus of Nazareth with the Holy Ghost and with power" (Acts 10:38). 4. His miracles were wrought by this power—"If I by (ἐν) the Spirit of God cast out devils then the kingdom of God has come unto you" (Matt. 12:28). 5. The offering up of himself as the Lamb of God was through the same Spirit—"Who through the eternal Spirit offered himself without spot to God" (Heb. 9:14). . . . It was conclusive evidence of the pervading and controlling influence of a baptism, that the Saviour immediately after such baptism is represented as being under the full influence of the divine Spirit—"Then was Jesus led up by (ἐν) the Spirit into the wilderness" (Luke 4:1). And when he came out of the wilderness he came invested with all the singular potency of this Divine agent—"Jesus returned in the power of the Spirit" (Luke 4:14).

2. THE CUP BAPTISM. "But Jesus answered and said, Ye know not what ye ask. Are ye able to drink of the cup that I shall drink of, and to be baptized with the baptism that I am baptized with? They say unto him, We are able" (Matt. 20:22).

"But Jesus said unto them, Ye know not what ye ask: can ye drink of the cup that I drink of? and be baptized with the baptism that I am baptized with? And they said unto him, We can. And Jesus said unto them, Ye shall indeed drink of the cup that I drink of; and with the baptism that I am baptized withal shall ye be baptized" (Mark 10: 38–39).

"But I have a baptism to be baptized with; and how am I straitened till it be accomplished" (Luke 12:50)!

It is certain that this simple rhetorical usage indicates that the cup —referring properly to the bitter draught it contains—is a baptizing agent. The Savior did not imply that He was to be baptized *in* or *into* a cup, but that the cup was to baptize Him. This is not an exceptional baptism outside the range of usual Biblical baptisms. In truth it, like Christ's baptism by the Spirit, is fundamental in its character and discloses the very essence of all New Testament baptisms, namely, the bringing of the subject into a baptized estate by means of a baptizing agent, whether it be by the Holy Spirit, a cup, the cloud and the sea, or water. The baptizing agency is not the baptism any more than a hangman's rope is death. The rope may induce death, but the rope itself is not death. There is general agreement that Christ's reference to the cup by which He was to be baptized was a reference to His penal death, which cup He should drink from the hand of His Father. It is written: "Then said Jesus unto Peter, Put up thy sword into the sheath: the cup which my Father hath given me, shall I not drink it?" (John 18:11). Likewise it is recorded that He prayed, "O my Father, if it be possible, let this cup pass from me: nevertheless not as I will, but as thou wilt. . . . O my Father, if this cup may not pass away from me, except I drink it, thy will be done" (Matt. 26:39, 42; cf. Mark 14:36; Luke 22:42). Beyond the sphere of human sympathy it was impossible for another to drink of this cup, though they might themselves experience physical death. As a memorial, a cup is drunk which contains in symbol the shed blood of Christ—blood shed when He drank His cup of penal death, the Just for the unjust. The contents of that cup served to baptize the Son of God into death.

Thus in conclusion it may be observed that Christ became the subject of three baptisms:

First, as a setting-apart to His priestly office, which office anticipated His one great priestly achievement of offering Himself without spot to God. He was baptized into that office by means of symbolic water according to the mode and manner prescribed by the Law of Moses. There is no record which states that He was baptized *into* water. The baptism placed Him in the position of a priest according to the law. Into water and into the priesthood are two quite different propositions. Water is the agent and not the receiving element. Therefore the mode of Christ's baptism is not determined by a dogmatic assertion that He was momentarily dipped in water. He was baptized by means of water into the everlasting perpetuity of His priestly office. It matters little whether it be little or much water so long as water is reserved—and in accordance with all references in the Sacred Text—as the baptizing agency and is not exalted to the place of the receiving element. This must be the Biblical conception, as the text of Scripture declares that Christ was baptized into His priestly office at Jordan—a locality—and not momentarily dipped into Jordan. Of itself, the supposed dipping into Jordan could accomplish nothing as respects a thoroughly changed condition. However, water when applied by a duly qualified baptizer and in accordance with the prescribed law did become an integral factor in securing Christ's baptism into the priestly office. The Greek prepositions used cannot be made to assert that Christ was baptized both *into* water and *into* the priestly office.

Second, Christ was baptized by the Holy Spirit. The text does not state that He was baptized *in* or *into* the Holy Spirit. The Spirit was the baptizing agent and the baptism was into the estate in which Christ, with regard to His humanity, lived and served; for He wrought all His works by the power of the Spirit and to Him the Spirit was given without measure (John 3:34).

Third, Christ was baptized by a cup which contained penal death, and into the estate of death. He was not baptized *into* the cup, but *by* the cup He was baptized into the death which alone could serve as a perfect redemption, a perfect reconciliation, and a perfect propitiation.

CHAPTER V

THE TEMPTATION OF CHRIST INCARNATE

I. THREE FUNDAMENTAL FACTORS

As AN ESSENTIAL introduction to the study of the complicated theme respecting the temptation of Christ, three fundamental aspects of qualifying truth appear for consideration. These are (1) the meaning of the word πειράζω, which is usually translated *to tempt,* (2) the sense in which God may be tempted, and (3) the truth that the temptation of Christ was in the sphere of His humanity and not in the sphere of His Deity.

1. THE MEANING OF πειράζω. This word, which appears in the Sacred Text some fifty times, conveys the idea of a test or a making of trial. It has two significations: one to test with a view to proving or developing virtue, the other to solicit in the way of evil. Of the latter it may be said that such solicitation cannot come from God, but must arise either with the individual's fallen nature or Satan's instigation. James asserts a positive affirmation respecting this when he says, "Let no man say when he is tempted, I am tempted of God: for God cannot be tempted with evil, neither tempteth he any man: but every man is tempted, when he is drawn away of his own lust, and enticed" (1:13–14). As respects the former—a testing in proof of virtue—the experience of Abraham in the offering of Isaac is an example. The command came directly from God, it recognized no evil in Abraham to be corrected, and closed with the words, "Now I know that thou fearest God, seeing thou hast not withheld thy son, thine only son from me" (Gen. 22:12). The Christian is enjoined to make trial of himself to learn whether he be in the faith. He is to prove himself by testings based on the fact that Christ is in him (2 Cor. 13:5). In view of the truth that God solicits no man in the way of evil, the prayer "And lead us not into temptation, but deliver us from evil" (Matt. 6:13) must be interpreted as meaning that the one who prays thus desires to be spared from testing, but if, in the wisdom of God, testing must be endured, that he desires to be delivered from the evil of unyieldedness and unfaithfulness. The thorn in the Apostle's flesh became a testing which could not be removed. Of this he

wrote, "Ye know how through infirmity of the flesh I preached the gospel unto you at the first. And my temptation which was in my flesh ye despised not, nor rejected; but received me as an angel of God, even as Christ Jesus" (Gal. 4:13–14). James also wrote, "My brethren, count it all joy when ye fall into divers temptations. . . . Blessed is the man that endureth temptation: for when he is tried, he shall receive the crown of life, which the Lord hath promised to them that love him" (1:2, 12). Thus, likewise, the great tribulation is said by the glorified Christ to be an hour of testing which is to come upon the whole world from which the Church is to be saved (Rev. 3:10). Christians are even now in "manifold temptations" which engender heaviness of spirit (1 Pet. 1:6), and yet no temptation will be greater than they, by divine enablement, may bear. Of this it is written, "There hath no temptation taken you but such as is common to man: but God is faithful, who will not suffer you to be tempted above that ye are able; but will with the temptation also make a way to escape, that ye may be able to bear it" (1 Cor. 10:13). Saints of old were tested (cf. Heb. 11:37).

2. GOD MAY BE TESTED. At least twenty-seven incidents or references are recorded in which it is said that God has been or might be tested; but these are always to be considered in the light of the assurance that God cannot be tempted in the way of evil, nor does He so tempt any man (James 1:13–15). The divine testings extend to each Person of the blessed Trinity. Of the Father it is said with respect to the imposition of the Mosaic Law upon perfected believers, "Now therefore why tempt ye God, to put a yoke upon the neck of the disciples, which neither our fathers nor we were able to bear?" (Acts 15:10). To those who, perhaps in ignorance, teach that the Mosaic system is a rule of life for the believer already perfected in Christ, the warning which this Scripture advances should be effective. There are no elements of piety in the act of imposing the Mosaic system upon the Church; rather it is a dangerous and awful provoking of God. It is significant that, of all the wickedness in which Christians may indulge, only this one high crime against God is mentioned as the cause of His testing from believers. Thus, also, the Spirit may be tested. In this there is a similarity with the preceding, since but one incident of the Spirit's testing is recorded. This experience was brought to pass by a falsehood uttered by two early Christians, which falsehood was declared to be against the Holy Spirit. It is written: "And Peter answered unto her, Tell me whether ye sold the land for so much? And she said, Yea, for so much. Then Peter said unto her, How is it that ye have agreed together to tempt the Spirit of the

Lord? behold, the feet of them which have buried thy husband are at the door, and shall carry thee out. Then fell she down straightway at his feet, and yielded up the ghost: and the young men came in, and found her dead, and, carrying her forth, buried her by her husband" (Acts 5:8–10). Of the temptation of Christ the Son more Scripture is written —cf. Luke 4:1–13; Hebrews 2:18 and 4:15. The discussion of these important declarations will be considered in the following section.

3. CHRIST WAS TEMPTED. When declaring, as above, that the testings which came to Christ were in the sphere of His humanity and not addressed directly to His Deity, not only is the truth asserted that He, being God, could not be solicited respecting things evil, but the whole problem, which may be extended into infinity, concerned with the relations of His two natures to one another is introduced again. There is general agreement that, had Christ sinned, the lapse would have arisen wholly from His human nature; but in all the discussion respecting His impeccability the truth is too often ignored that Christ was wholly free from a sin nature and all that the sin nature generates. Some theologians, much as heathen philosophers might do, have based their speculations on the acknowledged limitations of fallen men. It is argued that no man is free from sin and, since He was a man, Christ was solicited to evil even as other men. In his discourse on the problem of Christ's personal relation to sin, Bishop Martensen writes (*Christian Dogmatics,* pp. 284–85):

The fact that the Second Adam experienced all temptations—enticements to sin, threats and tortures of body and mind—is to be explained upon the ground, not of His moral freedom only, nor of the progressiveness of His nature, but of both these combined. The propositions, *potuit non peccare,* "it was possible for Him not to sin," and *non potuit peccare,* "it was impossible for Him to sin," so far from being distinct or contrasted, may be said to include and to presuppose each other. The first, which means that sinlessness was only a possibility for Christ, implies that He experienced temptation as an actual power; for while it came upon Him from without, it must, if it were not a mere pretence, have excited some corresponding feeling within Him; through which alone He could have been really tempted. And as the contrast between the cosmical and the sacred—the natural and the spiritual—was necessary in the Second Adam in order to a twofold influence upon the will;—as the Second Adam cannot be viewed as Monotheletic, which would be in fact to consider Him Monophysite, but Duotheletic,—the same principle must have been active in Him which made the fall of the first Adam possible. The possibility of evil existed in the Second Adam; but this possibility never became active, was never realized; it served only as the dark and obscure background to show forth His perfect holiness. This was guaranteed, not by the force of virtue or innocence, which the very idea of temptation makes uncertain and doubtful, pending the trial, nor again by the force of the Divine nature as distinct from the human, or the human as distinct from the Divine, but in virtue of the indissoluble union of the divine and human natures in Him; that *bond* which might indeed be strained and shaken to the greatest apparent tension and contrast of the two natures, but which never could be broken. This is expressed in the second proposition *non potuit peccare*, "it was impossible for Him to sin." Though the temptation itself and the conflict against it were not apparent merely but real and sternly earnest, the result could never have been doubtful; for the bond between the Divine and the human natures, which may be severed in the creature, was indissoluble in Him who is the Mediator between the Father and all His creatures. This bond may be broken only when the connection of the divine with the human is merely relative and representative; never when it is essential and archetypal, as in Him, in whom the counsels of the Father were comprehended before the foundation of the world.

Dr. Martensen here, along with many theological leaders, sustains a very high regard for the theanthropic Person, but his implications are that Christ suffered those temptations which belong to a fallen nature; still, Christ could not have possessed a sin nature without having partaken of the fall, since that nature does not belong to unfallen humanity. Naturally, the only examples of this form of human existence are restricted to Adam before he fell and to Christ. If Christ had been Himself a fallen Being, He could not have been the uninvolved Kinsman-Redeemer that was demanded. Perhaps some fail at this point to realize that the saving work of Christ extends as much to the sin nature of those He saves as to their individual transgressions. Had Christ been Himself a fallen man, He would have needed to be saved and could not have saved Himself or another. If, on the other hand, He was unfallen and theanthropic in His Being, He had no solicitations to evil such as arise out of a sin nature. It is intrinsic divine holiness which is predicated of Him (Luke 1:35). It has been declared on previous pages and is reasserted here that Christ was impeccable in the *non potuit peccare* sense; that is, it was *impossible* for Him to sin. That which creates doubt in many devout minds is the obvious fact that, as illustrated by Adam, an unfallen human being is capable of sinning. Tragic indeed, in this instance, is the failure to recognize that the first Adam was unsupported in the hour of his testing, but that the Last Adam though equally possessed of an unfallen human nature was—as Dr. Martensen so well affirms— because of "the indissoluble union of the divine and human natures" unable to do what He might otherwise have done if His human nature had been left to itself, which disunion of the two natures could never occur.

Even then the case, as with Adam, differs from that of any fallen man. While the fallen man is utterly prone to sin, both the unfallen Adam and the humanity of Christ had no such impetus to sin, and the unfallen Adam might have easily avoided the thing that he did. Since this bond of union which unites Christ's two natures—for He is one Person—is so complete, the humanity of Christ could not sin. Should His humanity sin, God would sin. When the absolute Deity of Christ is recognized, there is no logic which is more inexorable than this. Though unsupported unfallen humanity might sin, a theanthropic Person even if He incorporates an unfallen human nature is incapable of sinning. The contention that Christ *could,* but *would not,* sin is far removed from the contention that Christ *could not* sin. The former either denies His Deity or else dishonors God with the calumnious averment that God is Himself capable of sinning. Again, it must be declared that Christ's human traits which did not involve moral issues could be exhibited freely. The idea might be admitted with certain reservations that He was both omnipotent and impotent, omniscient and ignorant, infinite and finite, unlimited and limited; but it could never be allowed that He was both impeccable and peccable. There are no God-dishonoring elements in human weakness, human pain, human hunger, human thirst, or human limitations with respect to various capacities—even human death may be admitted as a death undergone for others, but not for Himself.

It may be seen from the foregoing that whatever testings came to Christ were not such as find their expression in and through a sin nature. Nevertheless, He was tested and tried and that without sin. As for fallen man, his temptations may arise either from the world, or from the flesh, or from the devil; but testing which is to develop or establish virtue usually comes from God. The world had no claim on the One who could say, "I am not of the world" (John 17:14, 16), and the flesh, conceived as a fallen nature, was not even latent in the Son of God. Of Satan He said, "The prince of this world cometh, and hath nothing in me" (John 14:30). As it is possible for an unconquerable city to be attacked, so an impeccable theanthropic Person may be assailed. Christ was tempted not to prove His impeccability either to Himself or to His Father; it was for the sake of those who are called upon to trust Him. As God might be tested so Christ was tested. It is written, "But Jesus perceived their wickedness, and said, Why tempt ye me, ye hypocrites?" (Matt. 22:18; cf. Mark 12:15; Luke 20:23; John 8:6). The major passages bearing on the temptation of Christ are:

Luke 4:1–13 (cf. Matt. 4:1–11; Mark 1:12–13). And Jesus being full of the Holy Ghost returned from Jordan, and was led by the Spirit into the wilderness, being forty days tempted of the devil. And in those days he did eat nothing: and when they were ended, he afterward hungered. And the devil said unto him, If thou be the Son of God, command this stone that it be made bread. And Jesus answered him, saying, It is written, That man shall not live by bread alone, but by every word of God. And the devil, taking him up into an high mountain, shewed unto him all the kingdoms of the world in a moment of time. And the devil said unto him, All this power will I give thee, and the glory of them: for that is delivered unto me; and to whomsoever I will I give it. If thou therefore wilt worship me, all shall be thine. And Jesus answered and said unto him, Get thee behind me, Satan: for it is written, Thou shalt worship the Lord thy God, and him only shalt thou serve. And he brought him to Jerusalem, and set him on a pinnacle of the temple, and said unto him, If thou be the Son of God, cast thyself down from hence: for it is written, He shall give his angels charge over thee, to keep thee: and in their hands they shall bear thee up, lest at any time thou dash thy foot against a stone. And Jesus answering said unto him, It is said, Thou shalt not tempt the Lord thy God. And when the devil had ended all the temptation, he departed from him for a season.

In entering upon an investigation of three passages which relate to Christ's temptations, the Lucan reference and two more, it is well to be reminded once again of the truths that these temptations were outside the range of those factors in human life which are the result of the fall, and that these temptations were addressed only to His humanity. The threefold temptation of Christ which the above Scripture sets forth indicates the fact of His testing and that that which is involved is the relationship within Himself between His two natures, His relation to the Father, and His relation to the Spirit. There is also a definite unveiling of His relation to Satan. All three Synoptics declare that, following His baptism, Christ was taken by the Holy Spirit into the wilderness and that there He was tempted, or tested, by Satan. The record asserts that during this testing Satan took Christ both to a high mountain and to a pinnacle of the temple. Why Christ should be tested thus will be considered later. The point at issue here is that Christ, wholly subject to the Holy Spirit, was purposefully brought into the sphere of Satan's power. Why such a testing at all may be a problem quite beyond the range of human comprehension. It would be remiss indeed to fail to note here that, as in various other situations in the earth-life of Christ, issues were involved which belong to the realm of relationship which exists between God and the angelic spirits, concerning which human beings have no knowledge other than those intimations which the Bible discloses. The account of this testing—immeasurable in its outreach—may be considered under two general divisions, namely, (1) Christ's relation to the Holy Spirit and (2) the testing of Christ's humanity by Satan.

II. CHRIST'S RELATION TO THE HOLY SPIRIT

Though this specific theme will be introduced more fully under Pneumatology, it demands some consideration at this juncture. Again it should be restated that Christ's dependence upon the Holy Spirit was within the sphere of His humanity. As respects His Deity, there was no occasion for Him to be cast in dependence upon either the Father or the Spirit; and though He could as God have ministered to His own human needs as fully as did the Spirit, that arrangement would have moved Him from the position occupied by all believers, to whom His life is a pattern. Christians cannot call upon any such resource within themselves; so they are, as He was, cast utterly upon the enabling power of the Spirit. The New Testament asserts throughout—even from His conception through the generating power of the Spirit to His death through the same eternal Spirit—that Christ lived and wrought on a principle of dependence upon Another. No attentive student can fail to observe this truth (cf. Matt. 12:28; Mark 1:12; Luke 4:14, 18; John 3:34). The truth that Christ—and to the end that He might demonstrate the effectiveness of life that is lived wholly in reliance upon the Spirit —was Himself dependent upon the Spirit, should not be allowed to engender any failure to recognize the absolute Deity of the Savior. His own authority over the Spirit in other spheres of relationship and according to the eternal counsels of God is seen in Christ's own declaration: "If I go not away, the Comforter will not come unto you; but if I depart, I will send him unto you" (John 16:7).

III. CHRIST'S TESTING BY SATAN

In this threefold testing it is declared that Christ was driven of the Spirit into the wilderness with the express objective in view that He should there be tested by Satan. No small importance gathers about this revelation which implies that this testing did not originate with Satan, though it may be believed that all was wholly agreeable to that mighty angel. A parallel to this is found in the experience of Job (Job 1:6—2:8), in which experience Job is tested by Satan and wholly on the instigation of Jehovah (cf. Job 1:8; 2:3). The Sacred Text does not indicate that Christ acted on His own account in going into the wilderness nor does it assert that He was forced to do so against His will. He Himself was "full of the Holy Spirit" and, as any individual thus blessed, was pleased to do all the mind and will of God. Christ was, according to Luke, mature both physically and spiritually. The combat thus becomes crucial in every respect and most evidently reaches out into unrevealed spheres of relationship between Christ and the fallen angels. Speculation is of little avail on why such a testing should have been divinely ordered and executed. It certainly relates to the humanity of the Savior and its value is, so far as men are concerned, a matter of demonstrating the absolute impeccability of the Son of God. The grammatical construction sustains the thought that this testing continued unrelentingly over the entire forty days, though but three specific tests are recorded and these, evidently, occurred at the end. When Christ had fasted forty days He was hungry and that fact became the basis for the first of the three recorded testings.

Satan really originates nothing. Here, as in every instance, only the sovereign purpose of God is realized. This is not to say that Satan, like misguided man, does not imagine that he originates all that occurs in his efforts. The testing of Christ's humanity secures too much value to the believer to have originated with Satan. By three avenues of approach Satan sought to persuade the Last Adam to embrace that philosophy of independence of God which he himself seized upon soon after his creation and which he imposed with success upon the first Adam. The real issue was clear: Would the humanity of Christ yield to an appeal to act independently of God even when all the kingdoms of this *cosmos* world (cf. Matt. 4:8) are offered as a bribe—kingdoms which, in the end, would be His from the hand of His Father (cf. Ps. 2:7–9; 1 Cor. 15:24–28; Rev. 11:15; 19:16)? As a self-imposed covenant, the Son of God had said when He was about to enter the world and with respect to His humanity (evidenced by His making the address to *God* rather than to His Father): "Wherefore when he cometh into the world, he saith, Sacrifice and offering thou wouldest not, but a body hast thou prepared me: in burnt-offerings and sacrifices for sin thou hast had no pleasure. Then said I, Lo, I come (in the volume of the book it is written of me,) to do thy will, O God" (Heb. 10:5–7). Thus the avowed attitude of the Son was, even before He entered the world, to do the will of God. To do that will is the highest and greatest achievement of any creature, angel or man. He who is ever the Supreme Pattern must be to infinite perfection the example of that which is man's highest responsibility.

Considering these three testings separately it may be seen, (1) that the proposal to minister to His hunger by turning stones into bread struck at the very center of that which is distinctly human. Man is dependent upon God. It is written, "Thou openest thine hand, and satisfiest the desire of every living thing" (Ps. 145:16). For Christ to employ His divine power in creation to gratify His own human need would have been to forsake the sphere of human limitations, which sphere was the will of God for Him. Had He thus supernaturally attended upon His own human needs, He would not have been in all points tested as men are tested. Men are cast upon God with no creative power by which to secure relief. (2) The second test, already mentioned, that the kingdoms of this world would be given in exchange for the worship of the theanthropic Christ, did likewise propose that the pursuance of the divine will and plan should be abandoned in an opposing self-will; but this test reaches into angelic spheres where human comprehension may not fully enter. Comparatively, it is not difficult to think of the authority over the *cosmos* (which Satan holds under divine permission) being surrendered by Satan to Christ. All of that will be achieved in due time; but to contemplate the audacity, the insolence, and the insult to God which were involved in the suggestion that the Son of God worship a creature of His own hand who is the archenemy of God may be but feebly recognized in this world: its wickedness can only be measured in celestial realms. (3) The final testing, as recorded by Luke, was to the end that Christ, by useless exercise of divine power (for He had a claim upon this as the theanthropic Person) might do a thing for self-glory that was not included in the will of God for Him.

In all of these testings, Christ was victorious while remaining wholly in the realm of human resources. He was challenged by the words, "If thou be the Son of God." This became a clear test of Christ's humanity in that it proposed the use of powers belonging to His Deity. He conquered as man may conquer—by the Word of God, which Word is to be cherished as the revelation of the divine will to which man should be submissive. To be other than submissive is, as declared by Christ, to "tempt the Lord thy God" (Matt. 4:7).

Hebrews 4:15. "For we have not an high priest which cannot be touched with the feeling of our infirmities; but was in all points tempted like as we are, yet without sin."

Though a High Priest and in the respect that He is the archetypal

High Priest—the true High Priest regarding whom all other high priests were but shadows—Christ is, nevertheless, able to sympathize with the children of God who are likewise tested. He was Himself in all points tested as they are—sin apart—that is, apart from the testings which arise from a fallen sin nature. Earlier in this discussion it has been demonstrated that Christ could not have had a sin nature nor could He have sinned. This passage does not merely assert that Christ, tempted in all points as man is tempted, did not sin. It also declares that He experienced no temptations which a sin nature engenders. As the Kinsman-Redeemer He could not Himself be involved in the calamity from which He is appointed to redeem. He could not be the holy, spotless Lamb of God that a true redemption demands if He were possessed with the slightest taint of sin. He serves as a sympathizing and merciful High Priest and not as One who partakes of that which causes the distress. He said of Himself, "The prince of this world cometh, and hath nothing in me" (John 14:30). This declaration, according to that which follows, is a reference to His death and the fact that He was in no sense worthy of death. Death, the penalty of human sin, had no rightful claim upon Him. When He died, it was His own voluntary act of obedience to His Father's will. The point at issue in this aspect of this theme is that Christ was, in the sphere of that which is unrelated to the fall, tested in all points, which testing included the experience of human infirmity and limitations.

Hebrews 2:17–18. "Wherefore in all things it behoved him to be made like unto his brethren, that he might be a merciful and faithful high priest in things pertaining to God, to make reconciliation for the sins of the people. For in that he himself hath suffered being tempted, he is able to succour them that are tempted."

In this passage the emphasis falls on the exceeding greatness of the mercy of Christ. It is the mercy of the God of all grace who, having Himself been tested in man's sphere, is able also to help those who are tested. It is one more competency of the Savior.

It is thus demonstrated that Christ was tested in this world, and it is certain that men knew nothing of that trial which His holy character endured. The writer to the Hebrews, having presented the account of the testings of Christ, concludes the theme by saying, "For consider him that endured such contradiction of sinners against himself, lest ye be wearied and faint in your minds. Ye have not yet resisted unto blood, striving against sin" (Heb. 12:3–4). The implication is that Christ's testing called for a resistance unto blood. This may lead on to the experience which was His in the garden, into which reality no other may intrude.

He was not tested with a view to ascertaining whether He would fail, but rather to prove to those of a doubtful mind that He could not fail.

Chapter VI

THE TRANSFIGURATION OF CHRIST INCARNATE

An event marvelously spectacular—yet more meaningful than spectacular—occurred on the Mount of Transfiguration. To theologians who neglect the whole millennial age or to those who have sought to identify it as already past or to those who contend that there will be no such age in the program of God, the transfiguration is largely meaningless. Neander (*History of the Planting of the Christian Church*, I, 376), as a reason for rejecting 2 Peter as spurious, states: "But it certainly is not natural to suppose that one of the apostles should select and bring forward from the whole life of Christ of which they had been eye-witnesses, this insulated fact [2 Pet. 1:16 ff.], which was less essentially connected with that which was the central point and object of His appearance" (cited by Peters, *Theocratic Kingdom*, II, 559). Similarly, those of the Church-Kingdom or Covenant Theology are, for the moment, encouraged in their theory by the fact that in the transfiguration Old Testament saints—Moses and Elijah—are present with those disciples —Peter, James, and John—who afterward became the apostles of the Church. The assumption being that the transfiguration is a miniature of the Church in heaven, Dr. Charles Hodge, a representative of this school of theology, declares, "The transfiguration on the mount was a type and pledge of the glory of the second advent" (*Systematic Theology*, III, 796). This is but a partial recognition of that which Peter declares the transfiguration to have been, namely, a preview of the coming kingdom on earth. Unless the transfiguration is approached with the background of all that the Old Testament revelation concerning the earthly Davidic Kingdom presents, there can be no understanding of this major event in the life of Christ. The premillenarian alone is able to give this peculiar portrait its full and worthy signification and explanation. As will be seen, this manifestation of the earthly kingdom glory is far removed from being of no importance. The discussion of this theme may well be pursued now.

The word *transfigure* (μεταμορφόομαι) is used but four times in the New Testament (cf. Matt. 17:2; Mark 9:2; Rom. 12:2; 2 Cor. 3:18), and conveys a meaning which is peculiar and distinctive when contrasted with $\mu\epsilon\tau\alpha\sigma\chi\eta\mu\alpha\tau\iota\zeta\omega$, which is translated *transforming* or *transformed* (cf. 2 Cor. 11:13–14 where Satan is said to be transformed as an angel of light; so, also, the believer's body will be changed—cf. Phil. 3:21). It is evident that a thing is transformed by influences from without, while a thing is tranfigured by the outshining of a light or vitality which is resident within. Christ's essential glory was veiled while here upon the earth, but in the moment of transfiguration His intrinsic Shekinah glory was allowed to break forth. He was not merely assuming a glory or standing in the radiance of an outward glory which fell upon Him. The glory was His own, and originated in Him and emanated from Him. It is this truth which lends so much importance to the two passages wherein transfiguration is related to believers—Romans 12:2; 2 Corinthians 3:18. The believer is subject to transfiguration and not to mere transformation. The divine Presence within is as a light, and this is to have its normal outshining and will work great changes within the heart where that Nature dwells.

I. THE IMPORTANCE

The divine estimation respecting the importance of the transfiguration is suggested by the fact that it appears at length in each of the Synoptics: Matthew 16:27—17:13; Mark 9:1–13; Luke 9:27–36. The entire picture can be seen only as all three accounts are diligently compared. In all, thirty-eight verses of the Sacred Text are assigned to the description of this event; added to these are the three verses of 2 Peter 1:16–18, in which portion the divine interpretation is revealed. It is significant, also, that this great event is reported only by the Synoptic Gospels—which to a large extent are concerned with the kingdom aspects of Christ's ministry while here on earth—and that it is not recorded by John who, in the main, sets forth truth belonging to the present unforeseen age and to the Church. There is no admission to be made, however, that this distinction is not both valid and vital, when it is observed here that such discriminations are unknown to the Church-Kingdom school of interpreters. Disregarding chapter divisions which are often enough unrelated to the continuity of the context, it will be noted that each account of the transfiguration follows a declaration by Christ respecting His second advent. The record declares that He said that the Son of man should come "in the glory of his Father with the holy angels" (Mark 8:38), or "in the glory of his Father with his angels"

(Matt. 16:27), or "in his own glory, and in his Father's, and of the holy angels" (Luke 9:26). To a Jewish mind, the coming in glory was inevitably related to Daniel 7:13–14. To this revelation of His return He adds, "Verily I say unto you, There be some standing here ['there be some of them that stand here'—Mark; 'there be some standing here'—Luke], which shall not taste of death, till they see the Son of man coming in his kingdom" (Matt. 16:28—"till they have seen the kingdom of God come with power"—Mark 9:1; "till they see the kingdom of God"—Luke 9:27). The rapture of the Church could not fulfill the promises concerning the second advent of Christ to the earth. In the Synoptics, as in Daniel, that coming is to the earth with power and great glory. It is related, not to heaven, but to that kingdom which is to be set up on the earth at the appearing of the Son of man. Though approximately a week intervenes, all the Evangelists are careful to relate the transfiguration with the promise that some of the twelve—Peter, James, and John were later chosen—would not taste of death until they should see the Son of man coming in His kingdom. All of the twelve eventually saw death in their generation, and fully seventy generations have followed and yet the actual coming is deferred. It is evident, therefore, that this promise regarding some of them was fulfilled in their own day and generation. It is evident also that Peter—chief of the favored three on the Mount—relates the transfiguration to this promise; that is, the transfiguration was, according to Peter, the fulfillment of the promise. The transfiguration is not the final and actual appearing of Christ in the glory of His Father and of the holy angels, but is a preview which presented it as a thing to be seen and to which "eyewitnesses" could bear testimony. It was a momentary enactment of that which shall constitute both the kingdom and its glory when it is set up on the earth. The presence of the angels and the stupendous world-transforming events which accompany the actual coming of Christ are not included in the preview; but such elements as were required to accomplish the divine purpose in the transfiguration were present.

II. THE REASON

The entire transfiguration occurrence as a feature of the life of Christ calls for some explanation about why such a peculiar innovation should have been introduced into a program which otherwise, apart from miracles, was characterized by conditions which were within the range of human activities. The premillennialist alone has a worthy solution to this problem. The answer may be considered in two parts, namely, (1) the immediate need and (2) the agelong need.

1. THE IMMEDIATE NEED. Two important passages which contain prohibitions serve to express the immediate need of the transfiguration; these are Matthew 16:20 and 17:9, and these read after this manner: "Then charged he his disciples that they should tell no man that he was Jesus the Christ. . . . And as they came down from the mountain, Jesus charged them, saying, Tell the vision to no man, until the Son of man be risen again from the dead." It will be remembered that the cognomen *The Christ* is the New Testament equivalent to the Old Testament *Messiah*. That is, when in the New Testament the Messianic features of Christ's ministry are in view they will be related to Him under the designation of *Christ*—not of *Jesus,* which term speaks of His Saviorhood, and not of *Lord,* which asserts His essential Deity. Immediately preceding the giving of the charge that no man should be told that He is the Christ is the peculiar first announcement of the Church and the giving of the keys of the kingdom of heaven to Peter. Up to this time the disciples, along with John and Christ, have been presenting the messianic message respecting the King and His kingdom, and that as "at hand" in the Person of the King (Matt. 3:1–2; 4:17; 10:5–42). Because of the execution of John the Baptist and the evident unwillingness of the people—especially the rulers—to receive their Messiah (cf. Matt. 11:20–26; 16:13–14), the kingdom message is concluded; yet the ground of redemption—the new theme of infinite grace —is not established, nor could it be, until His blood was shed. Since the rejection of Christ had been effected and divinely recognized, there is no longer an offer to be made regarding His Messiahship until His work of redemption is accomplished. On this point Dr. C. I. Scofield may well be quoted: "The disciples had been proclaiming Jesus as the Christ, i.e., the covenanted King of a kingdom promised to the Jews, and 'at hand.' The church, on the contrary, must be built upon testimony to Him as crucified, risen from the dead, ascended, and made 'Head over all things to the church' (Eph. 1:20–23). The former testimony was ended, the new testimony was not yet ready, because the blood of the new covenant had not yet been shed, but our Lord begins to speak of His death and resurrection (Matt. 16:21). It is a turning point of immense significance" (*Scofield Reference Bible,* p. 1022). It is significant that Christ went on directly after Matthew 16:20 to say, "From that time forth began Jesus to shew unto his disciples, how that he must go unto Jerusalem, and suffer many things of the elders and

chief priests and scribes, and be killed, and be raised again the third day" (16:21). In the light of the postponement of the kingdom, which kingdom constituted the Jewish hope and which was to that time the only thought of His disciples (cf. Mark 9:10; Acts 1:6–7), it was essential to verify the promise of the kingdom and thus give full assurance of its final realization; and that is precisely the thing which the transfiguration accomplished. Three eyewitnesses were chosen to see the Son of man coming in the glory of His kingdom (Matt. 17:1). To Peter, James, and John—two of whom were appointed writers of the New Testament text—and later to Paul in Arabia, the important information respecting the certainty of the coming of the kingdom must be given, that which later would be comprehended in its relation to the new order of grace. The disciples did not understand the meaning of the transfiguration at the time of it, but its assurance served them well in solving the problems which arose with the inauguration of the divine program for the outcalling of the Church (cf. Acts 15:13–18; 2 Pet. 1:16–17). By the statement that He should no longer be proclaimed in His Messianic character, the Lord not only withdrew the whole plan of kingdom proclamation which had engaged Himself, the disciples, and John up to that hour, but He was manifesting Himself as one about to be crucified. If any basis should remain upon which a kingdom hope—so vital in every Jewish covenant and promise—might rest, it called for a vivid demonstration which in the transition days that were to follow would serve as evidence that the unchangeable promises for Israel could not, and therefore would not, be broken. Apart from this demonstration, it would have been natural—well illustrated by the present misunderstandings of Church-Kingdom theologians—for the disciples to have concluded that God had broken His covenants with Israel and that their national hope was to be abandoned. Thus the transfiguration serves to preserve the Jewish anticipation as the divine purpose, even though it be postponed for an age. That the transfiguration had the ultimate effect upon the disciples intended is seen from Peter's statement (2 Pet. 1:16–18). Closely allied to the prohibition of Matthew 16:20—that the Messianic message should no longer be preached—is the prohibition of Matthew 17:9, which declares, "And as they came down from the mountain, Jesus charged them, saying, Tell the vision to no man, until the Son of man be risen again from the dead." And to this Mark adds, "And they kept that saying with themselves, questioning one with another what the rising from the dead should mean" (9:10). The fact that they reasoned about what His reference to His resurrection might mean gives evidence of their unpreparedness for all that was so soon to come to pass. As before intimated, the doctrinal force of the transfiguration could not be really grasped until after His death and resurrection; hence the mandate that no report regarding the transfiguration should be made until He was risen from the dead. To have published the transfiguration event before His death and resurrection would have been, since it proclaimed the kingdom, tantamount to a continuation of the kingdom message, which, as has been seen, was of necessity withdrawn.

2. THE AGELONG NEED. Whatever may have been required to save the disciples from the conviction that God had abrogated His entire program of an earthly kingdom to fulfill which Christ was born (cf. Isa. 9:6-7; Luke 1:31-33), the same need extends to all generations of the Church to the end that they too may be intelligent in their interpretation of the present age in its relation to the immutable earthly purpose of God. The conclusion reached at the first council of the Church (Acts 15:13-18) and the order of truth set forth in the Epistle to the Romans (cf. chapters 9-11 as an explanation by the Apostle of the relation of Israel's unchangeable covenants to the present order of grace which chapters 1-8 set forth) go to demonstrate how perfectly the early Church understood the truth which the transfiguration announced. It was the failure of Reformers to return to the conclusions of the early Church which has made possible various forms of unscriptural theology.

III. THE REALITY

There is slight need to give space to the consideration of the unbelieving theory that the transfiguration was only a vision or dream. Luke does state that the three disciples were "heavy with sleep," but he goes on to say that it was "when they were awake" that they saw that which is recorded (Luke 9:32). The Sacred Text presents the event as a historic fact. These men were in an upright position and from that they fell on their faces in the presence of the glory. It would be strange indeed for all three of these men to dream identically the same thing and for Peter to speak for the others while in a dream. Of the transfiguration John testified, "And we beheld his glory" (John 1:14), so also Peter refers to that glory as "the excellent glory" (2 Pet. 1:16-18). Peter describes the three as "eyewitnesses of his majesty." All of this speaks not of dreams, but of a reality. The Scriptures declare, "And he was transfigured before them" (Mark 9:2).

IV. A REPRESENTATION OF THE KINGDOM

It has been assumed by those who confound the kingdom with the Church that the transfiguration was an anticipation of heaven. It is true that there shall be great glory in heaven and that Christ will be the center of that glory. It was thus that John—though he had seen Him in the glory of the transfiguration and of His appearances after His resurrection—saw Him in His heavenly glory and there, too, fell at His feet as dead (Rev. 1:17). As already indicated, the Scriptures declare that the transfiguration was a setting forth of the coming of the Son of man in His kingdom. That coming is everywhere said to be in surpassing glory (Dan. 7:13–14; Matt. 24:30; 2 Thess. 1:7–9). It is the earthly glory of the King.

As a general treatise on the transfiguration, George N. H. Peters has written conclusively and at length as follows:

The transfiguration, following the announcement that "some" should, before their death, see "the Son of man Coming in His Kingdom," is *a representation of the Kingdom* in some of its aspects, viz., *in the glory of "the Christ" or King, in the presence of* (who also "appeared in glory," Luke 9:31) *the translated and dead saints, and in the witnessing of that glory by mortal men.* It was a temporary display, an outward manifestation or revealing of the majesty and glory *that belongs* to Jesus when He comes *at the Second Advent in His Kingdom* with His saints to reign over the nations. That this is the correct idea appertaining to this astonishing transaction is evident by regarding Peter's reference to it. He (2 Pet. 1:16–18) says: *"We have not followed cunningly devised fables"* (as so many now allege) *"when we made known unto you the power and coming of our Lord Jesus Christ, but were eye-witnesses of His Majesty,"* etc. Notice that he calls this transfiguration scene, *"the coming of the Lord Jesus Christ,"* thus identifying it fully with Matt. 16:27, 28. This is unquestionably, then, linking it with the still future Advent as a striking exhibition of the glory that shall be revealed—which is confirmed by Peter introducing this allusion to prove that Christ would thus again come, and by his uniting such a Coming with (ch. 1:11) *"the everlasting Kingdom of our Lord and Saviour Jesus Christ,"* and with His Coming, the new heaven and new earth (ch. 3:4, 13) of prophetic promise. (See also the references to this Coming in first Epistle.) Let us survey these several aspects. First and supreme stands forth the transfiguration of Jesus, changed in form, so that *"His face did shine as the sun and His raiment was white as the light"* (Matthew); *"His raiment became shining, exceeding white as snow, so as no fuller on earth can white them"* (Mark); *"the fashion of His countenance was altered, and His raiment was white and glistening"* (Luke). Here is *the Theocratic King* arrayed in light and glory, His face shining with brightness like that of the sun and His garments dazzling in their whiteness. Thus (comp. Rev. 1:13–16, etc.)

will *the Mighty Christ appear* when He comes to re-establish the Theocracy. Next we have *"two men"* (Luke 9:30), Moses and Elias, who also appeared *"in glory."* The Coming of Christ in His Kingdom is usually *associated* with that of the saints, His brethren, who are *co-heirs* with Him in the same glory. Hence, to give a representation of His Coming—His appearance when Coming—in His Kingdom it was *eminently suitable to have*—to fill out the picture—*the saints, glorified, also represented.* This is done; and in view of the fact that at His Second Advent these are made up of two parties, viz., *the dead* saints and *the living saints translated,* these two, Moses and Elias, are *purposely chosen as a correct exhibition* of the two parties—forming one class— who shall *then appear "in glory" with Christ.* Moses represents the body of saints who have died, but who will also be glorified with Christ; and as he was in converse with the glorified Saviour, so will they also be in nearness to Him. Moses and Elias both appearing "in glory," seems to indicate the same glorification of body. Elias represents another body, who, like himself, shall not fall "asleep," but shall be translated without experiencing the power of death. These two, the dead and the living, who shall be glorified at the Coming of Jesus, are graphically portrayed in 1 Cor. 15:51, 52, and 1 Thess. 4:15–17. These not only *see* His glory, but *partake* of the same, 1 Jno. 3:2; Phil. 3:21, etc., for of them it is said: *"When Christ"* (notice, as "Christ"), *"who is our life, shall appear, then shall ye also appear with Him in glory,"* Col. 3:4. But in addition to these, we have, to meet the prophetic announcements and to fill out the representation, *three persons,* Peter, James and John, *unglorified, mortal men living on the earth,* who see this glorified Christ and His glorified associates, and are so deeply impressed, so delighted with *the exceeding glory* revealed, that through the spokesman Peter, the emphatic declaration is made: *"Lord, it is good for us to be here."* Thus, if willing to receive it, *will it be* at the Second Advent, *when* Christ, "The Christ," comes in His glory and *with* His brethren gathered and glorified, *then* shall the spared Jewish nation and Gentiles, as prediction after prediction in glorious language portrays, *rejoice and exult* in the marvellous glory that shall be manifested. Jesus *personally* appears in His Kingly aspect; the saints *personally* are present in their glory; the disciples *personally* behold and admire the astonishing splendor and "majesty" of the scene. Jesus is here, "the Coming One" (a phrase well understood by the Jews), as He will exhibit Himself "in His own Kingdom;" the saints form "the first-fruits," who, as the predicted "kings and priests," reign with Christ in His Kingdom; and the mortal men are the servants or subjects (as even the tender of the three tents indicates) who gladly receive this glory, and are willing to abide under its radiance. The conversation respecting the approaching death at Jerusalem indicates that this was a temporary assumption of glory, in order to be, if we may so express it, a counterpoise to that which virtually—to the Jews—seemed to end the fondly anticipated Christship of Jesus, giving a *most direct proof* that the covenant and prophets would *yet be fulfilled.* The voice of the Father, lovingly acknowledging (having previously in answer to prayer brought about this supernatural change in David's Son) the Christship of Jesus and the power thus committed unto Him, *binds the whole together* into *an earnest, actual reception of glory,* which, thus represented, shall characterize David's Son and Lord when He comes to restore the fallen throne and Kingdom, and reigns indeed and in truth *the manifested Christ*. The presence of the Father and some kind of avowal, or, confession, or acquiescence is requisite to meet the requirements of prediction concerning the Coming of the Messiah in His Kingdom (as e.g. Dan. 7; Ps. 2, etc.), and *thus perfect* the representation of *the real Theocratic* position of Jesus. Surely, when considering *how many* particulars this transfiguration meets, *how* it demonstrates in the most forcible manner *"The Christ;" how* it supplies additional evidence of the ultimate manner of procedure in the Redemptive scheme, *it is folly* to ascribe all this, compressed into a few brief sentences, to the natural descriptive powers of "uneducated and ignorant" men, or to make it out a trivial, unimportant affair not worthy of our special attention. Viewed, as we have done, in the light of the great, leading doctrine of the Kingdom, it stands forth, *pre-eminently*, as *a Divine confirmation of the Theocratic Kingship of Jesus, of the glory of His saints, and of the happiness of the nations* who shall witness it—a fact *so striking and corroborative* of the ultimate Redemption of saints and of the race, that Peter seizes upon it as *a grand proof* that Jesus shall come unto so great Salvation.—*Theocratic Kingdom,* II, 559–61

V. THE DIVINE ATTESTATION

It remains to be indicated that, though much overlooked, there is far-reaching significance in the words—reported diligently by each of the three Evangelists—"Hear ye him." Apart from the divine witness or response recorded in John 12:28, there are three divine attestations of the Christ. Space has been given earlier to the evidence that the baptism of Christ served as a setting apart of the Lord to the priestly office, and in this He was acknowledged from heaven to be well-pleasing to His Father. At the return of the King and when He is by His Father seated upon David's throne in Zion (Jerusalem—cf. Ps. 2:6), it is suggested that there will then be the same divine attestation of the King, "Thou art my Son; this day have I begotten thee" (Ps. 2:7). Thus, also, in the transfiguration He is divinely recognized as Jehovah's Prophet. Such is the significance of the words *Hear ye Him*. In the very transfiguration itself the Lord was speaking prophetically of His future coming in glory. Such an injunction gathers up all He had ever said before and all that He would later say on earth (cf. Matt. 23:38—25:46) or from the glory, and as such addressed to all peoples in every generation.

In concluding this contemplation of the transfiguration, let it be observed again that there is only one primary meaning to it. It portrays the power and coming of Christ in His kingdom, it presents specifically the features and classifications of men in the kingdom, and is in no way related, according to the Sacred Text, to the Church or to the glory which is of heaven. The Church will share with Christ in the earthly kingdom glory, as represented by Moses and Elijah; but this should not be confused with the surpassing glory which belongs to the Bride in the splendor of heaven.

CHAPTER VII

THE TEACHINGS OF CHRIST INCARNATE

THROUGHOUT THE Bible the prophet may win his title either by fore-telling or by forthtelling. Christ was in both respects a Prophet. He was the One of whom Moses spake (cf. Deut. 18:15, 18–19; John 1:21), and none ever answered more completely to all that belongs to the perfect service of the prophet than did the Christ of God. He taught and ministered the Word of God accompanying it with His mighty works, and He also gave the most direct and determining predictions of any prophet who ever walked on the earth. In truth, the predictions of Christ should be studied closely by every student of Eschatology, remembering that these are the infallible words of the Son of God. It is also important to observe that the merest fraction of all that Christ said in three and a half years has been recorded in the Gospels; for that recorded may be read in as many hours as there were years of His ministry. Of this John writes, "And there are also many other things which Jesus did, the which, if they should be written every one, I suppose that even the world itself could not contain the books that should be written" (John 21:25). However, that which is presented in the Sacred Text has been selected by the Holy Spirit with that divine wisdom and perfection which characterizes all the works of God. These chosen records serve to tell all that it is God's purpose to disclose to succeeding generations and are, therefore, all that is needed for a right understanding of every aspect of the truth which belongs to the sphere of the four Gospels. Matthew, guided by the Spirit, has selected such records as present Christ as the King of the Jews. Mark, thus guided, has selected such records as present Christ as Jehovah's Servant. Luke, in turn, has been led to present Christ in His humanity, while John, by the same divine Spirit, portrays Christ in His essential Deity. It is probable that no uninspired writer having the story to tell that presented itself at the close of Christ's ministry—including His supernatural birth, His childhood, His teachings, His mighty works, His death, and His resurrection—could have compressed his message into the limits which are claimed by the four Writers. In this there is evidence of the

95

working of the divine hand as the Author of these marvelous and price-less documents. While much vital truth is found in those snatches of conversation which are recorded and in the brief sayings reported in the later portions of the New Testament (cf. Acts 20:35; 1 Thess. 4:15–17; 1 John 1:5) and particularly in the post-ascension declarations reported in the Revelation—chapters 1–3 and 22—the indicative teachings of Christ are found in three major discourses—the Sermon on the Mount, the Olivet Discourse, and the Upper Room Discourse. In the contemplation of the full prophetic ministry of Christ, the plan to be pursued is to consider (1) the three major discourses separately, (2) the parables, (3) the special teachings, and (4) the conversations.

I. THE MAJOR DISCOURSES

Before attempting an examination of these discourses separately, it may be well to observe that they present the widest possible latitude in subject matter. This fact has not only been greatly overlooked, but can be accounted for only when dispensational distinctions are recognized. If critical scholars assume it possible to claim two Isaiahs on the evidence afforded in the difference in style and subject matter which the two parts of Isaiah's writing set forth, there would be by far more conclusive proof of at least three Christs. It seems not to occur to a certain group of theologians that these discourses not only introduce principles which, from a doctrinal standpoint, are irreconcilable, but also happen to be addressed to classes which are differently related to God and to Christ. No proof of this assertion respecting the varied character of the discourses is needed other than the suggestion that they be given attentive study by placing them in comparison to, or over against, each other. If such a study has been pursued actually and to a reasonable degree of completeness, the distinctions which will be advanced in this thesis would be received as true. These discourses represent the doctrine which Christ taught, and it will be found that every major division of Systematic Theology is not only represented, but, more frequently than is generally realized, a final word is spoken by the Son of God. That so much of His teaching is couched in a narrative form and simplified to the last degree has misled some into supposing that Christ did not teach doctrine, that the presentation of doctrine was left for the later writers of the New Testament—especially Paul. Christ's utterances in doctrine were often presented in germ form and these were extended into wider fields by the later writers. However, it becomes the serious-minded student to investigate most diligently the actual teachings of the Son of God. It is the intention of this thesis to attempt a comprehensive scrutiny of that which is involved.

1. THE SERMON ON THE MOUNT. A rather extended consideration of this discourse has been previously introduced under Ecclesiology and to this the student is again directed. Howbeit, when attempting as in this instance to set forth the general theme of the teachings of Christ, the effort must be incomplete to an inadmissible degree should no attention be given at this point to this great discourse. The treatment of this discourse by writers of the past and present often reveals the extent of their comprehension of the present divine economy under grace. Apparently, the root difficulty is the failure to recognize what is rightfully a primary and what is rightfully a secondary application of this teaching. When the primary application is given to this Scripture, it is usually on the supposition that the Church is the kingdom and therefore passages related to the kingdom are addressed to her. Let it be dogmatically asserted at this point that those who hold such views either have failed to recognize the hopeless, blasting character of the law which this discourse announces and from which the Christian has been saved (Rom. 6:14; Gal. 5:1), or they have failed to comprehend the present position and perfection in Christ which is the estate of every believer. Apparently the two great systems—law and grace—become so confused that there could be no order of thinking possible. Distortions of the divine revelation are due, it would seem, to a slavish adherence to traditional interpretation and not to any unbiased personal investigation into the problems that are involved. Accompanying this inattention to the exact character of doctrine is, too often, the blind assumption that the student who does observe the patent character of this discourse and who therefore cannot give it a primary application to the Church is striking hands in agreement with the destructive critic who boldly rejects Scripture altogether. To give this discourse a primary application to the Church means that it is made to be, word for word, the rule of life prescribed for the child of God under grace. A secondary application to the Church means that lessons and principles may be drawn from it, but that, as a rule of life, it is addressed to the Jew before the cross and to the Jew in the coming kingdom, and is therefore not now in effect. At this point it cannot be too definitely emphasized that this entire discourse presents a complete rule of conduct and is not subject to that destructive method of interpretation which accepts one portion of it while rejecting another portion of it. If the Christian believes he is saved from hell fire through

the measureless grace of God, he will recognize that he has no relation to those warnings—three times uttered (Matt. 5:22, 29–30)—concerned with the danger of hell fire; but he must also observe that he has no primary relation to a system in any of its parts which could at any place or under any circumstances expose him to the danger of hell fire. If there are some portions of this discourse which are more gracious in character, these, it will be seen, are found also in the grace system, and it is not necessary for one to assume the inconsistent position which presumes to select or reject at will from that which, being a unit in itself, stands or falls together. It is precisely this impossible freedom to choose one portion and reject another which has kept a great company of men from coming to a clear understanding of the most elementary distinctions between the two systems—law and grace—as governing principles in daily life.

The Bible provides three complete and wholly independent rules for human conduct—one for the past age (there was no need of recording such rules as held good for people who lived before the Bible was written) which is known as the Mosaic Law and is crystallized in the Decalogue; one for the future age of the kingdom which is crystallized in the Sermon on the Mount; and one for the present age which appears in the Gospel by John, the Acts, and the Epistles of the New Testament. The Bible is God's one Book for all ages, and it should be no more difficult to recognize that there are portions which belong to a future age than it is to recognize that there are portions which belong to a completed past age. A moment's reflection would convince a candid mind that there were age-transforming events which serve as a cleavage between the conditions which obtained under the Mosaic system and those which obtain in the present age. "The law was given by Moses, but grace and truth came by Jesus Christ" (and not by His birth, but by His death). Relationship to God could not be the same for His saints after Christ's death, His resurrection, His ascension, the advent of the Holy Spirit, the placing of Jews along with Gentiles under sin, and the inauguration of a new system by which the chief of sinners may be justified forever through justice—who does no more to that end than to believe in Jesus—as it was before. Nor could it be the same in a coming age after the removal of the Church to heaven, the glorious appearing of Christ to reign on the earth, the judgment and restoration of Israel, the judgment of the nations with the termination of man-made institutions, and the binding of Satan—as it has been in this age. All this is obvious, yet there are those who shrink from such distinctions under the impression that being deprived of the law's curse and of the kingdom's danger of hell fire they are losing some priceless treasure. Neither the curse nor the hell fire is desired, but there are features of these systems which are more attractive and these are claimed while the undesirable is rejected. It may well be restated that none of these attractive elements are lost, for they are incorporated into the grace system and belong to those who are once-for-all perfected in Christ Jesus.

It therefore stands as well founded that the Sermon on the Mount both by its setting in the context and by its doctrinal character—which assertions will yet more fully be demonstrated as true—belongs for its primary application to the future kingdom age. It was addressed to the people before Him and concerned the requisite preparation on their part for admission into the kingdom of heaven then being published as "at hand." It likewise declared the manner of life that would be demanded within the kingdom when once it is entered. This attempted analysis of this discourse may be advanced under three general divisions —(1) its setting, (2) its distinctive character, and (3) the delay in its application.

a. SETTING. As the Old Testament closes with the predictions regarding Israel's coming Messiah-King unrealized (Mal. 4:1–6), Matthew's Gospel, as the introduction to the New Testament and the bond of connection between the Testaments, opens with the announcement of the presence of the Messiah among His people. All prophesied requirements are met by Him. He is of the tribe of Judah, of the house of David, born of a virgin in Bethlehem of Judea. His coming is in "the fulness of the time," that is, at God's appointed time. His predicted forerunner preceded Him, and the kingdom described in the Old Testament by the prophets and foreseen throughout the Scriptures as Israel's hope is announced as "at hand"—subject, however, to the choice of the people, whether or not they would receive their King. In this matter of choice there is a strong contrast set up when compared with His final advent, when the kingdom will be ushered in with no reference to human determination, though He will have wrought in the hearts of His earthly people not only to receive Him as Joseph's brethren received Joseph in Egypt, but also to enter their land, the land of promise, and their kingdom with everlasting joy and gladness. The important fact to be noted by all who would comprehend the Synoptic Gospels, and Matthew in particular, is that the kingdom was offered to Israel at the first advent, with the latitude granted to receive or reject it. Had it been in the "determinate counsel" of God (Acts 2:23) for that nation to enter then her covenanted kingdom, they would have done so (and as they yet will do under the sovereign hand of Jehovah). The "determinate counsel" concerning the first advent was rather that He should be rejected and put to death and that the kingdom should be deferred until the unforeseen intercalary age of the Church should run its course. Those who do not discern the Israelitish kingdom purpose or who suppose that the Old Testament hope is realized in the Church are, because of insuperable problems which their theory engenders, not much given to exposition of Matthew's Gospel, nor can they be rated as safe expositors of either Testament.

The Gospel by Matthew opens with an introduction of the Christ, first, as Son of David and, second, as Son of Abraham. Though this is the reverse of what would be the natural order, it conforms to the plan of Matthew's Gospel which first presents the King as the Son of David, the consummator of the Davidic Covenant, Israel's Messiah, and later turns to the world-wide blessings which are related to the death and resurrection of Christ as the fulfiller of the Abrahamic Covenant expectation. In this Gospel Christ's birth as the fulfillment of much prophecy is recorded, He is baptized at thirty years of age, He is filled with the Spirit without measure, His humanity is tested by Satan, and He Himself takes up, with the disciples whom He has chosen, the message of His forerunner John—"Repent: for the kingdom of heaven is at hand" (cf. Matt. 3:1–2; 4:17; 10:5–7). He suffers His disciples to preach this message to none but Israel. This prohibition is of vital importance, since in all His instructions respecting kingdom preaching (cf. Matt. 10) this direction stands first. It is written: "These twelve Jesus sent forth, and commanded them, saying, Go not into the way of the Gentiles, and into any city of the Samaritans enter ye not: but go rather to the lost sheep of the house of Israel. And as ye go, preach, saying, The kingdom of heaven is at hand" (Matt. 10:5–7). After this, restricting His own ministry for the time being to that one nation, He said, "I am not sent but unto the lost sheep of the house of Israel" (15:24). The Apostle reveals his own clear understanding of this specific Israelitish ministry which was to be followed by the age of grace when he said, "Now I say that Jesus Christ was a minister of the circumcision for the truth of God, to confirm the promises made unto the fathers: and that the Gentiles might glorify God for his mercy" (Rom. 15:8–9). Apart from a recognition of a dispensational distinction at this point, there can be little understanding of these imperative discriminations. It is here that the student should note that, as there was for a time a restricted Israelitish purpose in the ministry of Christ, there was, at the same time, a peculiar and appropriate Israelitish message which John, Christ, and His disciples declared. This message, if given any worthy consideration, would not be confused with a world-wide proclamation of saving grace which became possible and exclusively authoritative by divine provision through the death and resurrection of Christ. It is strange, indeed, that men who have won honors as theologians of the first magnitude do not see the difference between the proclamation of an earthly kingdom addressed to one elect nation to be established on legal grounds, and the proclamation of a grace message which concerns only individuals with Jews and Gentiles, on an equal footing, under sin and offers in sovereign grace to the one who believes on Christ that he will be made meet to be a partaker of the inheritance of the saints in light. It is a serious doctrinal bondage so to be committed to a one-covenant theory with its supposed one divine purpose that these immeasurable dissimilarities must be obliterated in meaningless generalities.

During His three and a half years of ministry on earth Christ had in view the three major ages already mentioned—the Mosaic age which closed with His death; the future kingdom age which was the reasonable hope of the instructed Jew but which, being postponed, will begin with His second advent; and the present unforeseen age which began with His death and will end with His return. Christ lived under the Mosaic system and therefore was Himself conformed to it and upheld its requirements. He proclaimed the kingdom age as "at hand" and gave instructions on its character and the terms of admission into it. Likewise, while His rejection as King grew in force, He anticipated the present age and gave explicit teaching about its relationships and doctrines. The accuracy of this brief analysis of the whole ministry of Christ need not be further defended here.

With reference to the setting, then, it is to be seen that the Sermon on the Mount was given in the midst and as a feature of the kingdom proclamation which first occupied the ministry of Christ on earth. It constituted the authoritative edict of the King relative to the character of the kingdom, its requirements, and the conditions of admission into it. It had to be restricted to Israel for it belonged to them alone, and it must be legal in character—though greatly advanced as such over the Mosaic system (Matt. 5:21–48)—for prediction was given by Moses respecting the legal character of that kingdom when he said, "And thou shalt return and obey the voice of the LORD, and do all his commandments which I command thee this day" (Deut. 30:8; cf. Jer. 31:31–34). The subject matter contained in the Sermon on the Mount not only sustains the contention that it is legal in character, but also asserts that it pertains to the kingdom as the surrounding context so clearly relates it. With all this in view, namely, (1) that Christ's early ministry was itself restricted to Israel and their covenanted kingdom, (2) that its character is legal and accords with the predictions in this respect, (3) that by its own subject matter it relates itself to the kingdom, and (4) that that which goes before as well as that which follows this sermon in the context is in every particular of the kingdom, it would be exceedingly difficult to relate this great rule of life to any other age than that of the Messianic reign of Christ on the earth. This discourse is no more related to the Church than the Messianic, Davidic, earthly kingdom is related to the Church, and those who apply it to the Church seem little aware of the problems which are involved. Some of these problems will be considered in connection with that which follows.

b. DISTINCTIVE CHARACTER. Though treated at length under Ecclesiology, the analysis of this discourse constitutes a theme of such surpassing importance that it should be considered here somewhat fully. It is a formal declaration—unlike so many of Christ's teachings which were broken into by conversation. Nothing is gained by the modern notion that this is a compilation of "single sayings which Jesus spoke at various occasions to different people," and that "these sayings were connected with each other to form a continuous discourse partly by Matthew, partly by the author of his source" (Martin Dibelius, *The Sermon on the Mount*, p. 105). By so much the plain assertion that Christ spoke all these words on one occasion is discredited and the accumulative force of the message is assigned to Matthew rather than to Christ. It was addressed to His disciples, evidently as detailed instruction to those who were then serving as preachers of the kingdom message. The address closes with the words, "And it came to pass, when Jesus had ended these sayings, the people were astonished at his doctrine: for he taught them as one having authority, and not as the scribes" (Matt. 7:28–29), which indicates that the multitude were present and heard, though it was spoken to His disciples (5:1). Though these disciples were soon to be brought into the Church and into this new age, the address to them, like the offer of the kingdom to Israel, was in good faith. Well did Christ know that these men would not enter the kingdom, but that they would be saved into the Church when His rejection was complete. Well did He know, also, that the kingdom itself would be refused and delayed until His second advent. There is no small advantage in keeping in mind the fact that this was the address of a Teacher to teachers, that it was to His disciples. On the general character of the address and its application, Dr. C. I. Scofield writes:

Having announced the kingdom of heaven as "at hand," the King, in Mt. 5.–7., declares the *principles* of the kingdom. The Sermon on the Mount has a twofold application: (1) Literally to the kingdom. In this sense it gives the divine constitution for the righteous government of the earth. Whenever the kingdom of heaven is established on earth it will be according to that constitution, which may be regarded as an explanation of the word "righteousness" as used by the prophets in describing the kingdom (e.g. Isa. 11:4, 5; 32:1; Dan. 9:24). In this sense the Sermon on the Mount is pure law, and transfers the offence from the overt act to the motive (Mt. 5:21, 22, 27, 28). Here lies the deeper reason why the Jews rejected the kingdom. They had reduced "righteousness" to mere ceremonialism, and the Old Testament idea of the kingdom to a mere affair of outward splendour and power. They were never rebuked for expecting a visible and powerful kingdom, but the words of the prophets should have prepared them to expect also that only the poor in spirit and the meek could share in it (e.g. Isa. 11:4). The seventy-second Psalm, which was universally received by them as a description of the kingdom, was full of this. For these reasons the Sermon on the Mount in its primary application gives neither the privilege nor the duty of the Church. These are found in the Epistles. Under the law of the kingdom, for example, no one may hope for forgiveness who has not first forgiven (Mt. 6:12, 14, 15). Under grace the Christian is exhorted to forgive because he is already forgiven (Eph. 4:30–32). (2) But there is a beautiful moral application to the Christian. It always remains true that the poor in spirit, rather than the proud, are blessed, and those who mourn because of their sins, and who are meek in the consciousness of them, will hunger and thirst after righteousness, and hungering will be filled. The merciful *are* "blessed," the pure in heart do "see God." These principles fundamentally reappear in the teaching of the Epistles.—*Scofield Reference Bible,* pp. 999–1000

Matthew 5:3–12. This sermon opens with a proclamation of the blessedness of those who in personal merit meet certain requirements. To the poor in spirit there is promise of the kingdom of heaven—the Davidic, Messianic, earthly, millennial kingdom. The agencies of human authority will not then prevail in that kingdom. A vast change will have come over this world when the humble in spirit will be honored by the possession of the kingdom. Through Isaiah Jehovah anticipated this priceless characteristic when He said, "For all those things hath mine hand made, and all those things have been, saith the LORD: but to this man will I look, even to him that is poor and of a contrite spirit, and trembleth at my word" (66:2). Those that mourn shall be comforted. Doubtless this is a constant provision throughout that glorious age, but it is especially true that Israel when saved into that kingdom will be saved from that mourning which is theirs in the tribulation. The King Himself at His second advent will "comfort all that mourn." He will "appoint unto them that mourn in Zion, to give unto them beauty for ashes, the oil of joy for mourning, the garment of praise for the spirit of heaviness" (Isa. 61:2-3). This mourning is described by Christ when in relation to His return He said, "And then shall appear the sign of the Son of man in heaven: and then shall all the tribes of the earth mourn, and they shall see the Son of man coming in the clouds of heaven with power and great glory" (Matt. 24:30). Of the meek, Christ said that they shall "inherit the earth." This, again, is far removed from earth conditions of today. The meek and poor in spirit arise to honor and to authority over men, but such a reward does not concern the Christian who has no right or citizenship on the earth. It would be thought-provoking if Christians who repeat the Decalogue and the Beatitudes with application to themselves should be required to designate "the land which the LORD thy God giveth thee" (Ex. 20:12) or to defend their title to the earth. An instructed believer is not looking for long life; he is waiting for his Lord from heaven. He is not looking for a land or a place in the earth; his citizenship is in heaven. The Jew alone can respond to the promise of Psalm 37:3 which reads, "Trust in the LORD, and do good; so shalt thou dwell in the land, and verily thou shalt be fed." The meek among Israel shall inherit the earth. Hunger and thirst after righteousness shall be the experience of those in the kingdom upon whose hearts Jehovah has written His law (cf. Deut. 30:6; Jer. 31:33) and that hunger and thirst shall be satisfied. This is the promised tranquillity of the children of the King. The proclamation that the merciful shall obtain mercy introduces one of the strongest contrasts between the governing principles of law and grace, and the persistent determination to retain this portion of this discourse as applicable to the Christian has, next to Matthew 6:12, wrought more confusion among believers than almost any other misapplied Scripture. The declaration that the merciful shall obtain mercy requires no labored adjustment to make it seem to fit into the grace relationship to God. It cannot be thus fitted in. It belongs to an age when the beatitude which is clearly stated will be perfectly true. Wide, indeed, is the difference between the conception of individual meritorious mercy and the words about mercy addressed to the Christian of this age: "But God, who is rich in mercy, for his great love wherewith he loved us, even when we were dead in sins" (Eph. 2:4–5). Unmerited and limitless mercy shall yet be the portion of the nation Israel in the day of their salvation (Ps. 103:8–11). It is true that the pure in heart always see God; and since peace and righteousness are the essential features of life in the kingdom, those who promote peace and those who are persecuted—before or in the kingdom—for righteousness' sake shall be rewarded. Record of that reward due is kept in heaven (cf. Mal. 3:16–17).

Matthew 5:13–16. The second section of this address represents the saints of the kingdom and those worthy to enter it as "the salt of the earth" and "the light of the world." All of this is revealing since it intimates the responsibility men are to assume in that coming age. None will deny that believers of this dispensation have similar obligations, but the mere paralleling of truth does not place Christians in Israel's kingdom, nor does it place inside the Church Israel as a nation.

Matthew 5:17–48. The next section should be classed as one of the most determining portions in this great discourse. It discloses Christ's own upholding of the law then in effect, and presents the legal aspect of the kingdom requirements in their clearest light. This portion should be pondered with utmost care and its drastic features taken seriously. To those who comprehend but little of that "grace and truth" which came by Jesus Christ, who have had no other thought of themselves than that they are under law, obligation to these requirements is not, naturally, disturbed by the assumption of this "yoke of bondage," and those of such a legal mind will easily discredit as destructive critics any who consider that through grace they are under no obligation to these and other legal requirements. Pure doctrine cannot be guaranteed by following tradition whether it be of Protestantism or of Rome, nor are mere habits of interpretation a safe guide. All of these legal utterances of Christ's were in full divine force when they were spoken, but the child of God of this age has been saved from the entire merit system. The believer is delivered from and dead to the law (Rom. 7:4, 6). The Apostle when defending the positions and privileges of grace not only asserted that the law is "done away" (2 Cor. 3:11; Gal. 3:23–25), but he declares that the Christian is not under law (Rom. 6:14). To contend that Christians are under law obligation simply because Christ enforced it upon Jews, to whom it alone belonged and that before His death, is to contradict directly the grace teaching regarding freedom from the law—as cited above. This division of this discourse opens with the assurance that He had come to fulfill both "the law and the prophets," that is, He fills all the place assigned Him in the Old Testament. E. Schuyler English in his book *Studies in the Gospel According to Matthew* (p. 50) states, "Think not that He came to destroy the law. He was made under the law (Gal. 4:4); He lived in obedience to the law (1 Pet. 2:21); He fulfilled the types of the law (Heb. 9:11–28); He bore for us the curse of the law (Gal. 3:13); and He redeemed us from the position of servants of the law to that of sons of God (Gal. 4:5)." It is evident from Deuteronomy 30:8, which reads, "And thou shalt return and obey the voice of the LORD, and do all his commandments which I command thee this day," that the kingdom rule is the Mosaic system which, as Christ indicated (Matt. 5:21–44), has now been extended to realms vastly more demanding; and the standing of men will be measured by their personal adherence to the law that then reigns. It is no small feature of the kingdom that some shall be called "great" (Matt. 5:19; 11:11). The declaration regarding human greatness is followed by the words, "For I say unto you, That except your righteousness shall exceed the righteousness of the scribes and Pharisees, ye shall in no case enter into the kingdom of heaven" (5:20), and here it is certain only personal rectitude is in view. No reference, here or elsewhere in this sermon, is made to imputed righteousness. The kingdom saints' righteousness under Messiah's reign will exceed the righteousness of the scribes and Pharisees. Indeed, such personal quality and merit are demanded for entrance into that kingdom at all. Many Jews will be judged unworthy to enter the kingdom, and those who will be judged will include Jews of the past dispensation who are raised to this judgment (cf. Dan. 12:1–3) as well as the last generation living who will enter that judgment. A reminder at this point may be in order, which asserts again that the believer is provided in this age with righteousness which is a gift from God made possible through the sweet savor aspect of Christ's death and on the ground of the believer's position in Christ. Of the Christian it is said, "But after that the kindness and love of God our Saviour toward man appeared, not by works of righteousness which we have done, but according to his mercy he saved us, by the washing of regeneration, and renewing of the Holy Ghost" (Titus 3:4–5). Such wide differences should not go unheeded as, too often, they do. Still continuing the emphasis which He placed upon the law, Christ goes on to state that the kingdom law, while introducing no new subjects of regulation, does, nevertheless, extend the obligation beyond the act to the motive. The phrase "Ye have heard that it hath been said" —the Mosaic declaration—is followed by the phrase, "But I say unto you"—the kingdom demand. Thus throughout Matthew 5:21–44 the contrasts are drawn. The scribes and Pharisees attended upon the law in their age, but a greater or more perfect righteousness than theirs will be demanded of those who enter the kingdom. The former prohibition against murder with its extreme penalty is advanced to apply to those who are angry without a cause. The one who says, "Thou fool," shall be in danger of hell fire. The most exacting demand rests upon the one who does not agree with his adversary quickly. The penalty is no less than that he be cast into prison and that without relief or mercy. The judgment which should fall upon the adulterer is imposed without grace upon the one who casts a lustful glance. The offending member is to be sacrificed lest one be cast into hell fire. Divorce will be restricted to the one cause of unfaithfulness. Communications shall be free from every oath. The other cheek must be turned when smitten. The cloak must be given to the one who by law takes away the coat. A second mile is to be added. Gifts are to be made to all who ask, and none are to turn from those who would borrow. Enemies are to be loved, those that curse are to be blessed, good is to be done to those that hate, and prayer offered for those who persecute. All this is required since it represents the character of the Father. A moment's reflection will convince the mind that such a standard as this belongs to another social order than the present one. It is designed for a day when the King reigns upon His earthly throne and when Satan is in the abyss. Of the reign of the King, Isaiah writes, "And the spirit of the LORD shall rest upon him, the spirit of wisdom and understanding, the spirit of counsel and might, the spirit of knowledge and of the fear of the LORD; and shall make him of quick understanding in the fear of the LORD: and he shall not judge after the sight of his eyes, neither reprove after the hearing of his ears: but with righteousness shall he judge the poor, and reprove with equity for the meek of the earth: and he shall smite the earth with the rod of his mouth, and with the breath of his lips shall he slay the wicked. And righteousness shall be the girdle of his loins, and faithfulness the girdle of his reins" (11:2–5). The undiscerning may feel it their duty to uphold and place such requirements upon those who are forever perfected in Christ, but this would be due to the failure to understand what it means to be in Christ and perfected forever. Even those who apply these requirements in sincerity to themselves and to others utterly fall short of the fulfillment of them. The present superabounding grace of God does not merely forgive the one who breaks the law; it saves one from any obligation to a merit system and enjoins him to walk worthy of the position which is his in Christ Jesus. What, then, does the Apostle mean when he said, "Stand fast therefore in the liberty wherewith Christ hath made us free, and be not entangled again with the yoke of bondage" (Gal. 5:1; cf. Acts 15:10; Col. 2:8)? Who but the most prejudiced Arminian can incorporate into his scheme of doctrine the threefold warning against hell fire which is found in this portion of Matthew? The believer "cometh not into judgment" (John 5:24, R.V.); "they shall never perish" (John 10:28); "there is therefore now no condemnation to them which are in Christ Jesus" (Rom. 8:1). If the warnings respecting hell fire do not fit into the grace system—and they do not—it is because the entire kingdom program of relationship and conduct is far removed from that which belongs to grace. The kingdom rule of life is an extension of the Mosaic system in the direction of a more drastic law; it is not the modification of law in the direction of grace. To say as some have done that they accept the Sermon on the Mount as the rule of their lives but omit those portions which threaten hell fire, is to disregard the revealed truth respecting the law, namely, that the one who assumes the least portion of it is a debtor to do the whole law (cf. Gal. 5:3; James 2:10).

Matthew 6:1–18. This, the next section of this Sermon, concerns the mere outward pretense in the giving of alms, of prayer, and of fasting. It is in the midst of this portion respecting prayer that the so-called "Lord's Prayer" is introduced, which prayer at once becomes a most difficult portion of this address for many to release to the kingdom system. In fact, like Matthew 5:20 which proclaims the terms of admission into the kingdom for the Jew, the "Lord's Prayer" is the divinely prescribed petition for the coming of that kingdom on the earth. "Thy kingdom come. Thy will be done in earth, as it is in heaven." It is probable that of the many who repeat these words but few have pondered their far-reaching significance. Not every mind can grasp so vast a theme; and it may not, when repeated, express a personal desire that arises within the individual's own conception of need. Especially is this true of those who have no understanding of that which is meant in the Scripture by the word *kingdom*. The kingdom will come and the Father's will be done on earth as it is in heaven, but only by virtue of the returning Messiah. The point of difficulty in the prayer, however, is not the petition in behalf of the earthly kingdom, which kingdom will come with the second advent and was "at hand" when the prayer was given to the disciples, but it is the one petition, "And forgive us our debts, as we forgive our debtors." This being the only portion of the prayer which is taken up by Christ for special elucidation, it evidently, in His mind, called for such remarks as might keep it from misunderstanding. As it is—in spite of the clarifying comment which the Lord added—there is much disregard for all that He emphasized and a determination to bend this legal condition into some conformity with grace. His comment is as follows, "For if ye forgive men their trespasses, your heavenly Father will also forgive you: but if ye forgive not men their trespasses, neither will your Father forgive your trespasses" (6:14–15). It cannot but be recognized that this one petition—meaning what Christ insists it means—is directly opposed in principle to the grace ideal as set forth in Ephesians 4:32, which declares, "And be ye kind one to another, tenderhearted, forgiving one another, even as God for Christ's sake hath forgiven you." Such is also the restatement found in Colossians 3:13, "Forbearing one another, and forgiving one another, if any man have a quarrel against any: even as Christ forgave you, so also do ye." The truth that God is "rich in mercy" even when we were "dead in sins" is one truth concerning which the child of God should be jealous with a great passion of soul. On that truth his only hope depends. Sad, indeed, is the spectacle when Christians assume that the Sermon on the Mount represents the high calling of the Church and attempt to modify the character of sovereign grace to the end that it may conform to a merit system. When it is recognized that this petition and this entire prayer is not only embedded in the kingdom manifesto but is itself a plea for the kingdom to come, difficulties are removed. Added to the conclusive character of the prayer is the fact that it is not "in the name" of Christ. Prayer for the Christian is upon a new and infinitely higher basis than any could be in any other age or relationship. In His last words to His disciples, Christ opened to them the new ground of prayer which is in His name (John 14:14), and declared that hitherto prayer had not been offered in that name (John 16:24). Again the child of God may well be jealous with a great passion respecting this new and marvelous approach to God in prayer. When the Lord said "Hitherto have ye asked nothing in my name," He contemplated all previous prayers—including the "Lord's Prayer"—as in no way to be compared with that new ground of prayer then opened unto believers.

Matthew 6:19–24. Devotion to God is the theme discussed in this division of the discourse. Treasures may be laid up in heaven in the sense that the record of faithfulness is preserved in heaven (cf. Mal. 3:16). In this there is something similar to the grace relationship.

Matthew 6:25–34. What is deeply devotional follows, surpassing anything found in the Old Testament presentation of the Mosaic system. To those who feel that Matthew 6:19–34 presents truth so rich and helpful that it must be claimed for their own portion as Christians, it may be restated that all Scripture is profitable, and accordingly this material, though also directly taught under grace, may be employed on the basis of a secondary application. It yet remains that these truths belong to the address in which they are found. It is not right or commendable for believers to claim Israel's richest blessings, but refuse her penalties and curses.

Matthew 7:1–6. Nothing more drastically legal or based on human merit will be found than the teachings in this portion of this Sermon. Here it is written, "Judge not, that ye be not judged. For with what judgment ye judge, ye shall be judged: and with what measure ye mete, it shall be measured to you again" (vss. 1–2). With this there is a scathing rebuke for those who assume to judge others when self-judgment has been neglected.

Matthew 7:7–11. Christ here returns again to the subject of prayer, with the assurance that prayer will be answered, that God is in infinite goodness more willing to give good gifts to them that ask Him than earthly parents are to give good gifts to their children.

Matthew 7:12–14. In this section those among Israel are reminded that to enter the kingdom a surpassing righteousness is required. The time of entering and of judgment is "in that [prophesied] day." The common ethics of moral men is proclaimed in the so-called "Golden Rule," which rises no higher than what is human self-interest. This rule is a standard for "just men" of the Old Testament order. By such faithfulness, measured by one's own self-interest, entrance would be made into the "strait gate." There is a "wide gate" that leads to destruction and a strait and narrow way that leads to life. Here "life" is not presented as a present possession of the Jew, as it is now of the Christian (cf. John 3:36; 10:28; Rom. 6:23; 1 John 5:12), but it is presented as an expectation, an inheritance, that is to be bestowed (cf. Luke 10:25–28; 18:18). Life, in its kingdom aspect, is at the end of the path which leads unto it. The nation Israel, to whom these words are spoken, are to come up for a final judgment when some will enter the kingdom and some will not (cf. Ezek. 20:33–44; Matt. 24:37—25: 30). "The strait and narrow way" is an outworking of personal merit and righteousness and is far removed from salvation, which provides a perfect and eternal justification based on an acceptance in the Beloved. The Christian has been saved by an act of faith and not by relentless persevering in a narrow path. Luke reports this same saying of Christ's —perhaps upon another occasion—when he records Christ as saying,

"Strive to enter in at the strait gate" (Luke 13:24), and the word here rendered *strive* is ἀγωνίζομαι, which could well be translated *agonize*. There is no rest here in the finished work of Christ (cf. Heb. 4:9); all is personal merit as the basis of hope for entrance into the kingdom of heaven.

Matthew 7:15–20, 21–29. This portion presents two warnings and with these the discourse ends. The first is against false prophets and unveils the method by which they may be detected. The second is against mere professors who render lip service, who say "Lord, Lord," but do not the will of the Father. Merely to call on the name of the Lord (cf. Rom. 10:13) or to have done wonderful works in that name will not suffice. The same drastic demand is again stated by Christ and in connection with the same situation in the parable of the ten virgins. Of those shut out of the marriage feast (note R.V. on Matt. 25:10) the Lord will say, "Verily I say unto you, I know you not" (25:12). The life that is given over to the keeping of those sayings of Christ—set forth in this Sermon and when the kingdom objective is before Israel, whether in the days of Christ's ministry on earth or when the King returns—is building on a rock; but this is purely a matter of individual merit. It is "he that doeth" and not "he that believeth." The people heard this address and were astonished at His doctrine, for He taught them as one having authority and not as the scribes. This authority was that of the sovereign God and King. It breathed in every portion of the address. "I say unto you" above and in the place of the Law of Moses was that which no other would assume to declare. The Originator of all things—greater than Moses and the Author of all that Moses said —had no occasion to refer to any other than Himself. What He proclaimed would transpire simply because He said so. No man ever spoke as this Man spoke.

The conclusion growing out of this analysis of this discourse is that it is the direct and official pronouncement of the King Himself of that manner of life which will be the ground for admission into the kingdom of heaven and the manner of life to be lived in the kingdom. It relates itself backward to the Mosaic Law and the prophets and not forward into the then unknown spheres of sovereign grace. When considered with this interpretation in mind, this Sermon is full of meaning and free from insuperable problems. It will be borne in mind, however, that there is no divine objective in the present age unto the setting up of that earthly kingdom. The offer of the kingdom, together with all situations and teachings related to it, was withdrawn for this age and will be renewed when the Church has been removed and the King is about to return in power and great glory.

Having presented this somewhat limited summarization of the Sermon on the Mount, it remains to investigate that which is excluded from this discourse. It is in this connection that the inattention of many is revealed. It will be discovered that the most vital elements of the believer's relation to the Persons of the Godhead—such relationships as are set forth in the Upper Room Discourse—are all wanting in this address; but the disappointing feature is disclosed when so many embrace a system demanding supermerit requirements and seem not to recognize that the priceless things pertaining to both a perfect standing and eternal security in Christ are omitted. A dominating jealousy for those things on which Christian reality depends would at least be reasonable and natural.

There is in the Sermon on the Mount a recognition of the Father and the Messiah-Son, but no reference will be found to the Holy Spirit whose indwelling and limitless ministry is so great a factor in this age of the Church. There is no reference to the death of Christ with its redemption, reconciliation, and propitiation values. There is no regeneration and no mention of the faith principle as a way into the saving grace of God. There is a reference to faith as a life principle (Matt. 6:25–34), but this is in no way related to salvation from sin. The great truth of a New Creation procured and secured through the resurrection of Christ is wholly wanting in this address. The phrase *in Christ* with its infinite meaning relative to positions and possessions is not present, nor is even one of those positions or possessions hinted at throughout its more than one hundred verses. No enabling power whereby these great demands both in character and conduct may be realized is intimated. It represents a human responsibility. The great word *justification* could not possibly be introduced nor that imputed righteousness upon which justification is founded. How far removed is a mere man-wrought righteousness which exceeds the righteousness of the scribes and the Pharisees (Matt. 5:20) from the "gift of righteousness" bestowed on those who receive "abundance of grace" (Rom. 5:17)! And how great is the difference between those who hunger and thirst after righteousness (Matt. 5:6) and those who are "made the righteousness of God in him" (2 Cor. 5:21)! Thus, also, great is the difference between those who are in danger of hell fire (Matt. 5:22, 29–30) and those who are justified on a principle of perfect divine justice who have done no more than believe in Jesus—even the ungodly (Rom. 3:26; 4:5). Thus, again, note should be made of the divergence between those who obtain mercy by being merciful (Matt. 5:7) and those who have found everlasting mercy even when dead in sins (Eph. 2:4–5), likewise between those who hope to be forgiven on the ground of their own forgiveness of others (Matt. 6:12–15) and those who for Christ's sake have been forgiven (Eph. 4:32; Col. 3:13). And, yet again, consideration must be given to a distinction between those who follow a course—strait and narrow—with the goal in view that they may find life at the end of that path (Matt. 7:14) and those to whom eternal life has been given as a present possession (John 3:36; Rom. 6:23; 1 John 5:11–12). Finally, far removed is a situation in which some hear the Lord say, "I never knew you: depart from me, ye that work iniquity" (Matt. 7:23) and an assurance that one trusting in Christ "shall never perish" (John 10:28; Rom. 8:1). With these and many other contrasts in view, agreement cannot be accorded Professor Martin Dibelius in his book *The Sermon on the Mount* wherein he says, "The Sermon on the Mount is not the only program of Christian conduct in the New Testament. The New Testament contains many other sayings of the same kind, especially the instructions for the disciples, the well-known similes and parables and the admonitions found in the Epistles. But the Sermon on the Mount overshadows all of these and thus has special symbolic value as the great proclamation of the new righteousness" (pp. 105–6). Apparently Professor Dibelius does not lack in the matter of appreciation of the high moral standards set forth in the Sermon on the Mount; he does lack, however, the understanding of that which enters into the whole divine undertaking of saving grace, nor does the Professor, as many a theologian in his class, distinguish between the earthly Jewish purpose of God which is consummated in the Davidic, Messianic kingdom of heaven and the heavenly purpose of God which is consummated in the Church and her destiny in heaven.

c. DELAY IN ITS APPLICATION. Nothing new is introduced under this division of the discussion. It has been repeatedly demonstrated in previous pages that as certainly as the kingdom itself was postponed, so certainly all that appertains to it was postponed until the present unforeseen intercalary age has run its course. The rule of life looking to and governing in that kingdom was, with respect to its application, postponed. All that enters into the general fact of the kingdom's delay, as well as the objections raised against this doctrine, has been considered at length under Ecclesiology. Suffice it to say that the kingdom requirements presuppose the kingdom as present. The social order in the earth which the kingdom prescribes must be such as will make possible this supermanner of life. The King Himself must be present and reigning, Satan must be bound, the law of God must be written in the heart, and all Israel must know the Lord from the least unto the greatest (Jer. 31:31–34).

2. THE OLIVET DISCOURSE. The second major discourse delivered by Christ was spoken but two days before His crucifixion. This limit of time is clearly indicated by the words which follow immediately after the address, "And it came to pass, when Jesus had finished all these sayings, he said unto his disciples, Ye know that after two days is the feast of the passover, and the Son of man is betrayed to be crucified" (Matt. 26:1–2). This discourse, like that known as the Sermon on the Mount, is addressed to Israel. Christ's lament over Jerusalem is the divinely arranged introduction to it. That lament is recorded thus, "O Jerusalem, Jerusalem, thou that killest the prophets, and stonest them which are sent unto thee, how often would I have gathered thy children together, even as a hen gathereth her chickens under her wings, and ye would not! Behold, your house is left unto you desolate. For I say unto you, Ye shall not see me henceforth, till ye shall say, Blessed is he that cometh in the name of the Lord" (Matt. 23:37–39). This portion, in turn, has been preceded by drastic condemnation of the scribes and Pharisees (Matt. 23:1–36). As in the Sermon on the Mount, this major address is given to the disciples "privately," and these twelve are here treated as Jews and as representatives of that nation. They are spoken to as though they, like all Jews before them, would share in the events described in this discourse. The address is of the nature of a farewell to the nation Israel. Its purpose is not to condemn that people nor to instruct those then living, beyond the preparation of writers who would prepare the New Testament text, but to instruct those who live in the end time—with which it deals—when these disclosures and instructions will apply. It is reasonable to believe that God who provided these teachings will bring them to the attention of those, in their day of trial, to whom they belong. Jews in the tribulation will profit exceedingly by these words, and recognize them as the words of their Messiah-King. The King speaks, but quite without the use of the first person pronoun. He rather uses the third person form and refers to Himself as "the Christ, the bridegroom, the Son of man, and the king." Few portions of the New Testament place recorded events in a more complete chronological order than this address. This fact is an essential truth which determines much in the right interpretation. That which belongs to the

age of the Church is but provisionally referred to in a section which may
be classed as an introductory portion. The discourse proper, it will be
seen, begins with a description of the great tribulation and provides
exhortations and warnings to Israelites of that time. The discourse concludes with a recital of the judgments which fall first upon Israel and
then upon the nations. These judgments are determined by the King
Himself and occur when the tribulation is over and when the King has
returned to the earth. As the Church is not directly seen as present in
Matthew's Gospel, excepting as her presence is implied in chapter 13,
and is anticipated in 16:18, so—and even more emphatically—the
Church is not seen even remotely in this farewell discourse to Israel. Two
days later in the Upper Room Discourse—that to be considered later—
the Lord gave His farewell message to the disciples not as Jews, but as
those who were clean through the Word (John 13:10; 15:3), and who
were no longer to be classed as under the Mosaic Law (15:25).

The wide difference which obtains between the Olivet Discourse and
the Sermon on the Mount hardly needs elucidation. Though both were
spoken by the Messiah to the nation Israel, they have almost nothing in
common. One presents the responsibility of the individual Jew respecting entrance into and life within the Messianic kingdom. The other directs and warns the whole nation about its sufferings in the tribulation
and gives most explicit directions and predictions relative to the place
that nation must occupy in the most eventful days the world will see,
namely, the seventieth week as foretold by Daniel (cf. Dan. 9:25–27;
Matt. 24:15). Those days of unsurpassed tribulation are determined
for the future and with them the final disposition of all Gentile governments and institutions. Israel, too, must be judged and the earth be
changed from the present man-governed, Satan-ruled, *cosmos* world
into the kingdom of heaven, and righteousness and peace cover the
earth as waters cover the sea. It is both reasonable and much to be ap-
preciated that Christ should give before His departure these explicit
instructions to His beloved nation concerning such incomparable days.
To those who have no understanding of and, therefore, no interest
in these great predictions, this address can mean no more than aimless
and useless remarks on the part of the Savior. However, the worthy
student will enter into the contemplation of these far-reaching declarations with utmost attention.

It would hardly seem necessary, in the light of all that has been presented under Eschatology, to restate the truth that in the order of events
—all clearly arranged by the Holy Spirit and to be observed by careful

students—the Church is removed from the earth before Daniel's seventieth week begins, and that the Church is not therefore on the earth or to be seen in any of these situations.

It is probable that no body of prediction in the entire Bible is more definite or more interrelated with all the field of Biblical prophecy than this address. Almost every separate declaration may be taken as a starting point from which much prediction may be traced in its order. It could not be otherwise, since this is the consummating foretelling on the part of the Messiah-King and near the hour of His departure from this world. As often stated before in this work, God has a twofold purpose, namely, that for the earth which is centered in His earthly people and that for heaven which is centered in His heavenly people. It is therefore to be expected that Christ, who is the Consummator of each, should deliver two farewell messages—one for each of these groups of people. This is exactly the order of truth found in the Gospels. In this connection it will be seen that there is no intermingling of the truth which comprises these two farewell discourses. That addressed to Israel —now to be considered—is wholly apart from any reference to the Church, and that addressed to the Church—to be considered in the next division of this Chapter—is wholly apart from any complication with Israel or her kingdom. The analysis of the Olivet Discourse may be undertaken after the following manner:

Matthew 23:37-39. "O Jerusalem, Jerusalem, thou that killest the prophets, and stonest them which are sent unto thee, how often would I have gathered thy children together, even as a hen gathereth her chickens under her wings, and ye would not! Behold, your house is left unto you desolate. For I say unto you, Ye shall not see me henceforth, till ye shall say, Blessed is he that cometh in the name of the Lord."

From the viewpoint of its inclusiveness, there are few more extended prophetic declarations than this. It may be reduced to a few meaningful phrases—"Jerusalem," "I would have gathered thy children together," "Ye would not," "Your house is left unto you desolate," "Ye shall not see me . . . , till ye shall say, Blessed is he that cometh in the name of the Lord." The address is to Jerusalem's children, which, in this instance, is a representation of the nation Israel. As before indicated, the entire discourse from Matthew 24:4 on (but for this opening portion— 23:37-39), though immediately spoken to His disciples who are still classed as Jews and represented a people who will pass through the experiences described in this address, is directed toward the entire nation and especially to those who will endure the trials depicted therein.

The phrase, "I would have gathered thy children together," not only discloses that He speaks to Israel, but refers to the fulfillment of much prophecy respecting the final regathering of Israel into their own land. In the accomplishment of His kingdom purpose, Christ is to regather Israel. This was indicated in His kingdom messages delivered during His first advent. The purpose will be executed perfectly at His second advent. Later on in this same address, He declares—and in relation to His second advent—"And he shall send his angels with a great sound of a trumpet, and they shall gather together his elect from the four winds, from one end of heaven to the other" (24:31). Of this same event, Jeremiah said, "Therefore, behold, the days come, saith the LORD, that they shall no more say, The LORD liveth, which brought up the children of Israel out of the land of Egypt; but, The LORD liveth, which brought up and which led the seed of the house of Israel out of the north country, and from all countries whither I had driven them; and they shall dwell in their own land" (Jer. 23:7–8). That Israel "would not" is Christ's own identification of their rejection of the King and His kingdom. And this declaration places the responsibility upon the nation. Later, and in harmony with this announcement respecting His rejection, they said, "His blood be on us, and on our children" (Matt. 27:25). "Your house" is a reference to the house of Israel which became centered in the kingly line of David. In Acts 15:16 this entity is termed "the tabernacle of David." The passage reads, "After this I will return, and will build again the tabernacle of David, which is fallen down; and I will build again the ruins thereof, and I will set it up." The term "desolate" is one of several words used to describe Israel's situation in the world throughout this age (cf. "scattered and peeled"—Isa. 18:2, 7; James 1:1; 1 Pet. 1:1; "cast away," in the sense of abandoned for a period of time—Rom. 11:15; "broken off"—Rom. 11:17; afflicted with "blindness"—cf. Isa. 6:9; Rom. 11:25; "hated"—Matt. 24:9). "Ye shall not see me" is an assertion which anticipates His total absence, respecting His peculiar relation to Israel "till" He returns, at which time "every eye shall see him" (Rev. 1:7), "and they shall see the Son of man coming in the clouds of heaven with power and great glory" (Matt. 24:30). Israel will then say, "Blessed is he that cometh in the name of the Lord." How great is the faithfulness of Jehovah to Israel! Isaiah records Jehovah's message to that people as it will be at their final restoration: "For Zion's sake will I not hold my peace, and for Jerusalem's sake I will not rest, until the righteousness thereof go forth as brightness, and the salvation thereof as a lamp that burneth. And the Gentiles shall see thy righteousness, and all kings thy glory: and thou shalt be called by a new name, which the mouth of the LORD shall name. Thou shalt also be a crown of glory in the hand of the LORD, and a royal diadem in the hand of thy God. Thou shalt no more be termed Forsaken; neither shall thy land any more be termed Desolate: but thou shalt be called Hephzi-bah, and thy land Beulah: for the LORD delighteth in thee, and thy land shall be married. For as a young man marrieth a virgin, so shall thy sons marry thee: and as the bridegroom rejoiceth over the bride, so shall thy God rejoice over thee. I have set watchmen upon thy walls, O Jerusalem, which shall never hold their peace day nor night: ye that make mention of the LORD, keep not silence, and give him no rest, till he establish, and till he make Jerusalem a praise in the earth" (Isa. 62:1-7).

Matthew 24:1-3. "And Jesus went out, and departed from the temple: and his disciples came to him for to shew him the buildings of the temple. And Jesus said unto them, See ye not all these things? verily I say unto you, There shall not be left here one stone upon another, that shall not be thrown down. And as he sat upon the mount of Olives, the disciples came unto him privately, saying, Tell us, when shall these things be? and what shall be the sign of thy coming, and of the end of the world?"

A brief interlude is set forth in these verses which has to do with a fulfilled prophecy, namely, the destruction of Jerusalem. The disciples have called Christ's attention to the size and costliness of the Temple. Possibly He had not exhibited the usual Jewish admiration and amazement at the character of the stones (cf. Mark 13:1; Luke 21:5). Little did His disciples realize that He to whom they spoke had called every material thing into existence by the word of His power. These stones, however, Christ predicted would be thrown down. The same had been foretold before (cf. Jer. 9:11; 26:18; Mic. 3:12). This statement regarding the destruction of the temple, which statement was to the Jew most pessimistic to the last degree, prompted the disciples to ask three questions, the answers to which enter largely into this discourse. They inquired, "Tell us, when shall these things be? and what shall be the sign of thy coming, and of the end of the world?" (vs. 3). The answer to the first of these questions respecting the destruction of Jerusalem is not included in Matthew's account, but is recorded in Luke 21:20-24 as follows, "And when ye shall see Jerusalem compassed with armies, then know that the desolation thereof is nigh. Then let them which are in Judæa flee to the mountains; and let them which are in the midst of it depart out; and let not them that are in the countries enter thereinto. For those be the days of vengeance, that all things which are written may be fulfilled. But woe unto them that are with child, and to them that give suck, in those days! for there shall be great distress in the land, and wrath upon this people. And they shall fall by the edge of the sword, and shall be led away captive into all nations: and Jerusalem shall be trodden down of the Gentiles, until the times of the Gentiles be fulfilled." That all of this was accomplished by Titus in the year 70 A.D. is well known. There is need of warning, however, lest some phraseology in Luke's account be confused with the same phraseology in Matthew's account (cf. 24:16–20) and it be assumed on the basis of this similarity that the two accounts are parallel. In Luke's account Christ is describing conditions and giving directions to the Jews about the time when the destruction of Jerusalem would be impending; Matthew's account records the conditions and timely instructions to the Jews that will be in order when the tribulation comes and the King is about to return. A careful comparison of these two Scriptures will vindicate this assertion. It is at this point that the erroneous theory got its inception that the coming of Christ was fulfilled in the destruction of Jerusalem. The second and third questions, namely, "What shall be the sign of thy coming, and [the sign] of the end of the world [age]?" are answered by Christ in their reverse order. The disciples knew nothing of the order of events. This order Christ corrected by answering the last of these two questions first, and the first question relating to the sign of His coming He answered last.

It is needful to pause here for a consideration of what age is in view when they ask for a sign of its ending. As indicated above, it is probable that the word *sign* should be supplied in this question. The term *world* is a translation of the word αἰών which means *age*, or a period of time. Their question was about the sign of the age in which they were living. Though some foreshadowing had been given by Christ, as recorded in Matthew, chapter 13, the disciples knew nothing of the present Church age (cf. Acts 1:6–7) and therefore could have known nothing of its end. They were living in the Mosaic age, the latter part of which Daniel had predicted would continue for 490 years. He predicted also that the last seven years of that period—Daniel's seventieth week—would be the time of the greatest human upheaval, including the great tribulation and the presence of the man of sin whom Christ styled "the abomination of desolation, spoken of by Daniel the prophet" (Matt. 24:15; cf. Dan. 9:26–27). In other words, the great tribulation and the man of sin belong to the Mosaic age that is past and are wholly unrelated to the present age of the Church. The man of sin will not "stand in the holy place" at the end of the Church age; it is at the end of that age then in effect when the disciples asked this question. The man of sin will stand in the holy place during the tribulation (Matt. 24:15; 2 Thess. 2:3–4).

Matthew 24:4–8. "And Jesus answered and said unto them, Take heed that no man deceive you. For many shall come in my name, saying, I am Christ; and shall deceive many. And ye shall hear of wars and rumours of wars: see that ye be not troubled: for all these things must come to pass, but the end is not yet. For nation shall rise against nation, and kingdom against kingdom: and there shall be famines, and pestilences, and earthquakes, in divers places. All these are the beginning of sorrows."

Before answering the question about the sign of the end of the age, Christ gives a general comment on the intervening time before the Jewish age will come to its defined ending. At this point, for the disciples and all others there is need for special attention to these words of Christ lest deceptions arise. In spite of many false christs and of wars, etc., instructed saints are not to be deceived. These events—false christs, wars, famines, pestilences, and earthquakes—do not constitute a sign of the end of the Jewish age. This is the purport of Christ's words—"but the end is not yet," or more literally, *but not yet is the end.* Nations rise against nations and kingdoms against kingdoms. As always, famines and pestilences follow. None of these are ever to constitute the sign of the end of the Jewish age, though they may and do have real significance regarding this age in which they occur. They are the characteristics of the unforeseen intervening or intercalary age. These age-characteristics are by Christ likened to "the beginning of sorrows." The word *sorrows* is better rendered *travail,* which means labor at childbirth, anguish, or distress. It is true of birth pains that they grow more intense as the birth itself is approached. These conditions, then, which belong to this age, though they may increase in intensity, are the preliminary pains and to be distinguished from the excruciating pain of the birth itself. The birth pain itself serves to illustrate the tribulation and the accelerating characteristics of this age illustrate the "beginning of sorrows." The important truth disclosed by Christ is that the "beginning of sorrows" is not the sorrow itself which belongs to Israel's experience and to their former age and in which the abomination of desolation, or the desolater, appears.

Matthew 24:9–28: Then shall they deliver you up to be afflicted, and shall kill you: and ye shall be hated of all nations for my name's sake. And then shall many be offended, and shall betray one another, and shall hate one another. And many false prophets shall rise, and shall deceive many. And because iniquity shall abound, the love of many shall wax cold. But he that shall endure unto the end, the same shall be saved. And this gospel of the kingdom shall be preached in all the world for a witness unto all nations; and then shall the end come. When ye therefore shall see the abomination of desolation, spoken of by Daniel the prophet, stand in the holy place, (whoso readeth, let him understand:) then let them which be in Judæa flee into the mountains: let him which is on the housetop not come down to take any thing out of his house: neither let him which is in the field return back to take his clothes. And woe unto them that are with child, and to them that give suck in those days! But pray ye that your flight be not in the winter, neither on the sabbath day: for then shall be great tribulation, such as was not since the beginning of the world to this time, no, nor ever shall be. And except those days should be shortened, there should no flesh be saved: but for the elect's sake those days shall be shortened. Then if any man shall say unto you, Lo, here is Christ, or there; believe it not. For there shall arise false Christs, and false prophets, and shall shew great signs and wonders; insomuch that, if it were possible, they shall deceive the very elect. Behold, I have told you before. Wherefore if they shall say unto you, Behold, he is in the desert; go not forth: behold, he is in the secret chambers; believe it not. For as the lightning cometh out of the east, and shineth even unto the west; so shall also the coming of the Son of man be. For wheresoever the carcase is, there will the eagles be gathered together.

This extended Scripture presents Christ's own message to Israel regarding the great tribulation. As verse 8 with its reference to travail closes His brief picture of this present intervening age, verse 9, opening as it does with the word *then,* marks the time of the agony and pain of the birth. This time-word occurs throughout this context and serves to date all that is predicted within the bounds of this unprecedented trial on the earth. It is the same time as is referred to in verse 21: "For then shall be great tribulation." This same context, it will be seen, is followed by another time-expression in verse 29, "Immediately after the tribulation of those days." Thus the boundaries of this context are determined. The student will bear in mind the truth that the tribulation period is described in various passages in both Testaments. Three distinct divine purposes may be discovered in this tribulation time. The passages here referred to are of great importance, but cannot be quoted in full. First, it is the time of "Jacob's trouble." Special and final judgments upon the chosen people, which have long been foretold, will end their agelong afflictions (Jer. 25:29–38; 30:4–7; Ezek. 30:3; Dan. 12:1; Amos 5:18–20; Obad. 1:15–21; Zeph. 1:7–18; Zech. 12:1–14; 14:1–3; Mal. 4:1–4; Matt. 24:9–31; Rev. 7:13–14). Second, this period will be a time when judgment will fall on the Gentile nations and the sin of the whole earth (Job 21:30; Ps. 2:5; Isa. 2:10–22; 13:9–16; 24:21–23; 26:20–21; 34:1–9; 63:1–6; 66:15–24; Jer. 25:29–38; Ezek. 30:3; Joel 3:9–21; Zech. 12:1–14; Matt. 25:31–46; 2 Thess. 2:3–12; Rev. 3:10; 11:1—18:24). Third, this time is also characterized by the appearance and reign of the man of sin whose career, like the period in which he appears, cannot begin until the divine restraint is removed (2 Thess. 2:6–10) and will end with the return of Christ and His coming in "power and great glory" (2 Thess. 2:8). This world-ruler is the fitting manifestation of the last efforts of Satan under his present freedom in his opposition against God and his attempted self-exaltation above the Most High. What God has been pleased to reveal respecting this time of trial will be comprehended only as these and similar Scriptures are considered with marked attention. This is the student's reasonable task. Indeed, there is great solemnity in the words of Christ on this important theme.

This portion of the Olivet Discourse opens with specific counsel to Israel respecting their lot in this time of their affliction. That Israel is addressed alone in this context is determined with certainty in verse 9. That people alone will be hated of all nations, and, though the world cannot analyze its own passions, this hatred is their resentment against a divinely chosen race, which resentment has continued as a heritage from the earliest days of Israel's history. That hatred is literally "for my name's sake"; for His name has been upon that people from their beginning. They are to be delivered up, afflicted, killed, and hated. This will result in many of Israel being offended, who will then betray one another. These are to be misled by false prophets and the abounding of iniquity, which will diminish the love of many. In this time, however, salvation is assured at the end of the trial. The reference to salvation is to that promised to Israel in Romans 11:26–27, "And so all Israel shall be saved: as it is written, There shall come out of Sion the Deliverer, and shall turn away ungodliness from Jacob: for this is my covenant unto them, when I shall take away their sins." There is no reference here to a believer's salvation by grace through faith, which salvation obtains in the present age. Were it such it would read, *He that is saved shall endure unto the end.* The assurance is that the end of the age will come when "this gospel of the kingdom" has been preached as a witness in all the inhabited earth. Immeasurable confusion has followed the attempted application of this verse to present world conditions. The believers of this age have a commission to evangelize every nation and this should be repeated with every new generation, but the coming of Christ to receive His Bride has never been made to await some total world-wide evangelization. That referred to in this passage is distinctly the gospel of the kingdom, which occupied the early ministry of Christ and, to that moment, was the only gospel known to the disciples. This gospel will be preached again by the 144,000 sealed ones of Revelation 7:1–8 and such other witnesses as God may elect for that service during the tribulation period. It is reasonable that the message which prepared for His Messianic kingdom in the first days before the Messiah and His kingdom were rejected should be renewed and preached before His second advent, when that kingdom will be set up by the power of God and without rejection of the King. There is no need to return at this point to a rediscussion of the difference that obtains between the gospel of the kingdom which announces once more that the King is at hand, and the gospel of the grace of God which offers eternal salvation in glory to individual Jews and Gentiles and on the one condition of faith in Christ. It is reprehensible to take this verse out of its setting as embedded in the Lord's own description of the tribulation and from it draw a conclusion that Christ cannot come for the Church until the present gospel is preached in all the world. When this testimony of the kingdom is completed Christ declares that the end will come. Reference is to the end of the Jewish age and a deferred portion of that age. Of this end the disciples inquired. Having declared the program of kingdom preaching, Christ goes on to reveal the sign of the end of the age. This is stated in verse 15, and is none other than the long-predicted appearance of the man of sin in the restored Jewish temple. Christ Himself looked backward to Daniel's prophecy regarding this desolater (Dan. 9:26–27). Later the Apostle Paul describes the same event thus, "Let no man deceive you by any means: for that day shall not come, except there come a falling away first, and that man of sin be revealed, the son of perdition; who opposeth and exalteth himself above all that is called God, or that is worshipped; so that he as God sitteth in the temple of God, shewing himself that he is God" (2 Thess. 2:3–4). The temple will be the place provided by the unbelieving Jews, when they will have been given freedom for seven years by the man of sin and that to worship as they desire in their own land. This covenant is broken in the midst of the seven years (cf. Daniel's predictions and those of John in the Revelation). The presence of the desolater in the holy place is the identification given of him throughout the Word of God. It is his assumption to be God (cf. Ezek. 28:1–10). Since his appearance in the holy place commands so conspicuous a place in the prophetic Scriptures, it is not strange that Christ gives to it the character of a sign to the nation Israel of the end of that deferred portion of their own age.

Following the revelation of the sign of the end of the age, Christ gives specific instructions concerning the immediate action of all who observe this sign. These directions, as before said, though similar to those given in Luke respecting the destruction of Jerusalem, are nevertheless quite different, being adapted in each case to the impending crisis. One particular instruction in the Matthew account should be noted, namely, "But pray ye that your flight be not in the winter, neither on the sabbath day" (24:20). In this verse evidence is found that the Jewish age is restored, since the Sabbath is again in effect. This is conclusive to one who has investigated the distinctions which obtain between the Sabbath for Israel and the New Creation Lord's day for His Church. Likewise, in this verse is an injunction to offer the prayer that flight should not be in the winter nor on a Sabbath day. These are strange petitions as viewed in their relation to the present age. No one assumes to offer this prayer—even the most confused antidispensationalist. Over against this is the fact that these same individuals are offended if it be intimated that one of this age is not appointed to pray, "And forgive us our debts, as we forgive our debtors."

The declaration of verses 21 and 22, like Daniel 12:1, should silence posttribulationists who in defense of their theory that the Church goes through the great tribulation seek to soften the character of those excruciating days. To claim, as some have, that the terror of this period is "overdrawn" is to challenge Christ Himself—sustained by the Holy Spirit through Daniel—that never in the past nor yet in the future will any human experience equal that of those days, for suffering upon Israel and the world. For Israel, God's elect, those days are to be shortened else no flesh could be saved. God has two elect peoples—that of Israel and that of the Church. This Scripture, like its entire context, relates to elect Israel.

In verses 23–28 instructions are again renewed and especially with reference to the detecting of the claims of false christs. Though such may come by the desert—as John the Baptist—or in the secret chamber, shrouded in occult mysteries, none can duplicate the manner of the actual return of Christ, which will be as lightning coming out of the east and shining even unto the west. The coming of Christ as described in Revelation 19:11–16 (cf. Ps. 2:7–9; Isa. 63:1–6; 2 Thess. 1:7–10) is accompanied by a great slaughter and the birds of the heavens are invited to be filled with the flesh of man and beast. It is probable that Matthew 24:28—"For wheresoever the carcase is, there will the eagles be gathered together"—makes reference to this feature of Christ's return as described in Revelation 19:17–21.

Matthew 24:29–31. "Immediately after the tribulation of those days shall the sun be darkened, and the moon shall not give her light, and the stars shall fall from heaven, and the powers of the heavens shall be shaken: and then shall appear the sign of the Son of man in heaven: and then shall all the tribes of the earth mourn, and they shall see the Son of man coming in the clouds of heaven with power and great glory. And he shall send his angels with a great sound of a trumpet, and they shall gather together his elect from the four winds, from one end of heaven to the other."

No more explicit division of time could be indicated than is expressed by the words with which this section of this address opens—"Immediately after the tribulation of those days." Since the coming of Christ terminates the tribulation and is brought to pass by Christ's own destruction of the man of sin (cf. 2 Thess. 2:8), the crushing of the armies who represent the nations of the earth (Ps. 2:7–9; Isa. 63:1–6; 2 Thess. 1:7–10; Rev. 19:11–21), the judgment of Israel (Ezek. 20:33–44; Matt. 24:37—25:30), and the judgment of the nations (Matt. 25:31–46), it is probable that the phrase "the tribulation of those days" refers to the particular anguish and trial of Israel as having been consummated rather than that all these events named above and which fall in Daniel's seventieth week are completed. At this point, at whatsoever moment it occurs, there is the convulsion of nature which reaches to the stars of the heavens. It is then that "the sign of the Son of man" shall appear. It will be remembered this serves to answer the second, which in this revised order, is the last of the questions of verse 3 to be answered. There is no disclosure of what that sign will be. Men have advanced their conjectures, but Christ did not tell the nature of the sign and His silence may well be respected. He does say, however, that there shall be a sign and that it will appear. It will be such that all will recognize its significance, especially Israel; for when it is seen by them all their tribes—meaning the whole house of Israel (cf. Matt. 23:39)—shall mourn. They behold the One whom they have rejected coming in the clouds of heaven with power and great glory. It is then that they recognize their Messiah. As the brethren of Joseph fell before him when his identity was revealed to them, in like manner will Israel acknowledge their Messiah. The sign will be worthy as one of the greatest of all divine manifestations and its effect complete. Some believe that this sign will be a mighty display of the agelong symbol of the cross. It is noteworthy that Zechariah, when speaking of Christ's return, declares, "And I will pour upon the house of David, and upon the inhabitants of Jerusalem, the spirit of grace and of supplications: and they shall look upon me whom they have pierced, and they shall mourn for him, as one mourneth for his only son, and shall be in bitterness for him, as one that is in bitterness for his firstborn" (12:10). The designation, "the tribes of the earth," belongs, in Scripture usage, only to Israel, but by Zechariah these same people are said to be "the house of David." Thus added evidence is presented that in the Olivet Discourse it is Israel that is addressed. At this same time, also, Israel shall be regathered for the final time into their own land. Of this regathering the prophets have spoken, and that event cannot fail since the mouth of Jehovah has spoken it. However, that regathering is supernatural. It is here said to be achieved by angelic ministration. Great and marvelous was the display of divine power when He brought the children of Israel out of Egypt. To this stupendous event Jehovah has often turned when seeking to impress His people with His might. He said, "I am the LORD thy God, which brought thee out of the land of Egypt." Jeremiah by the Spirit asserts that the final regathering of Israel into their own land will be a greater display of divine power than their deliverence from Egypt, so great, indeed, that there will be no remembrance of the Egyptian deliverance as compared with this last regathering. Jeremiah says, "Therefore, behold, the days come, saith the LORD, that they shall no more say, The LORD liveth, which brought up the children of Israel out of the land of Egypt; but, The LORD liveth, which brought up and which led the seed of the house of Israel out of the north country, and from all countries whither I had driven them; and they shall dwell in their own land" (23:7–8).

Matthew 24:32–36. "Now learn a parable of the fig tree; When his branch is yet tender, and putteth forth leaves, ye know that summer is nigh: so likewise ye, when ye shall see all these things, know that it is near, even at the doors. Verily I say unto you, This generation shall not pass, till all these things be fulfilled. Heaven and earth shall pass away, but my words shall not pass away. But of that day and hour knoweth no man, no, not the angels of heaven, but my Father only."

Having declared the *manner* of His coming, Christ now turns to the *certainty* of His coming. The fig tree provides an illustration. Summer is evidently nigh when its tender leaves appear. It is doubtless true that the fig tree represents in other Scriptures the nation Israel (cf. Matt. 21:18-20), but there is no occasion for this meaning to be sought in the present use of that symbol. When the things of which Christ had just spoken, including even the beginnings of travail, begin to come to pass, it may be accepted as certain that He is nigh, even at the doors. When that hour has arrived, these words will be of the greatest value and blessing to those to whom they are addressed, and that people, Israel, shall not pass until all these things which concern them shall be fulfilled; even heaven and earth may pass away—and they will—but Christ's promise to Israel thus made shall not pass away. The word γενεά, translated *generation,* is a reference to the whole race or stock of Israel and is not here restricted to a people then living on the earth. Dean Alford's comment on this portion of Scripture is clarifying:

As regards the parable,—there is a reference to the *withered fig-tree which the Lord cursed:* and as that, in its judicial unfruitfulness, emblematized the Jewish people, so here the putting forth of the fig-tree from its state of winter dryness, symbolizes the *future reviviscence* of that race, which the Lord (ver. 34) declares shall not pass away till all be fulfilled. That this is the true meaning of that verse, must appear, when we recollect that it forms the conclusion of this parable, and is itself joined, by *this generation* passing away, to the verse following. We cannot, in seeking for its ultimate fulfilment, *go back* to the taking of Jerusalem and make the words apply to it. As this is one of the points on which the rationalizing interpreters lay most stress to shew that the prophecy has *failed,* I have taken pains to shew, in my *Greek Testament,* that the word here rendered **generation** has the meaning of *a race or family of people.* In all the places there cited, the word necessarily bears that signification: having it is true a more pregnant meaning, implying that the character of one generation *stamps itself upon the race,* as here in this verse also. The continued use of **pass away** (the word is the same in verses 34, 35) should have saved the Commentators from the blunder of imagining that the then living generation was meant, seeing that the prophecy is by the next verse carried on to the end of all things: and that, as matter of fact, the Apostles and ancient Christians *did continue to expect the Lord's coming, after that generation had passed away.* But, as Stier well remarks, "there are men foolish enough now to say, heaven and earth will never pass away, but the words of Christ pass away in course of time—; of this, however, we wait the proof."— *New Testament for English Readers,* I, 169

Dr. C. I. Scofield writes on Matthew 24:34: "Greek, *genea,* the primary definition of which is, 'race, kind, family, stock, breed.' (So all lexicons.) That the word is used in this sense here is sure because none of 'these things,' i.e. the world-wide preaching of the kingdom, the great tribulation, the return of the Lord in visible glory, and the re-gathering of the elect, occurred at the destruction of Jerusalem by Titus, A.D. 70. The promise is, therefore, that the generation—nation, or family of Israel—will be preserved unto 'these things'; a promise wonderfully fulfilled to this day" (*Op. cit.*, p. 1034).

Over against the certainty of Christ's return is the uncertainty about the *time* of His coming. Of that day and hour no man knows, nor do the angels know. All of this, it must be remembered, bears upon the glorious return of Christ to the earth and therefore concerns Israel alone, who will then be on the earth and about to enter their earthly kingdom. The element of uncertainty on the time of Christ's return is also indicated in those Scriptures which promise His earlier coming into the air to receive His Bride, the Church, in which Scriptures the believers in each generation have been told to *wait* for their Lord (cf. Rom. 8:19; 1 Thess. 1:10; James 5:7). Thus it should be noted that the uncertainty of the time characterizes each of these events; but that truth does not serve to constitute the events to be one and the same. The Church *waits* for her Bridegroom and her rapture into heaven, while Israel will in the day of Christ's near return in glory *watch* for that glorious return of her Messiah and the realization of her earthly kingdom.

Matthew 24:37—25:13: But as the days of Noe were, so shall also the com-ing of the Son of man be. For as in the days that were before the flood they were eating and drinking, marrying and giving in marriage, until the day that Noe entered into the ark, and knew not until the flood came, and took them all away; so shall also the coming of the Son of man be. Then shall two be in the field; the one shall be taken, and the other left. Two women shall be grind-ing at the mill; the one shall be taken, and the other left. Watch therefore: for ye know not what hour your Lord doth come. But know this, that if the good-man of the house had known in what watch the thief would come, he would have watched, and would not have suffered his house to be broken up. There-fore be ye also ready: for in such an hour as ye think not the Son of man cometh. Who then is a faithful and wise servant, whom his lord hath made ruler over his household, to give them meat in due season? Blessed is that servant, whom his lord when he cometh shall find so doing. Verily I say unto you, That he shall make him ruler over all his goods. But and if that evil servant shall say in his heart, My lord delayeth his coming; and shall begin to smite his fellowservants, and to eat and drink with the drunken; the lord of that servant shall come in a day when he looketh not for him, and in an hour that he is not aware of, and shall cut him asunder, and appoint him his portion with the hypocrites: there shall be weeping and gnashing of teeth. Then shall the kingdom of heaven be likened unto ten virgins, which took their lamps, and went forth to meet the bridegroom. And five of them were wise, and five were foolish. They that were foolish took their lamps, and took no oil with them: but the wise took oil in their vessels with their lamps. While the bridegroom tarried, they all slumbered and slept. And at midnight there was a cry made, Behold, the bridegroom cometh; go ye out to meet him. Then all those virgins arose, and trimmed their lamps. And the foolish said unto the wise, Give us of your oil; for our lamps are gone out. But the wise answered, saying, Not so; lest there be not enough for us and you: but go ye rather to them that sell, and buy for yourselves. And while they went to buy, the bridegroom came; and they that were ready went in with him to the marriage: and the door was shut. Afterward came also the other virgins, saying, Lord, Lord, open to us. But he answered and said, Verily I say unto you, I know you not. Watch therefore, for ye know neither the day nor the hour wherein the Son of man cometh.

While it is approached from several angles, the one objective of this extended section is the exhortation to Israel to be prepared for the coming of their Messiah-King. In the parable of the good and evil servants, He is likened to the lord of the household (24:45–51). In the parable of the ten virgins, He is the Bridegroom—not that Israel is the Bride and He their Bridegroom; but having been previously married in heaven (Rev. 19:7–8) He is returning with His Bride to His earthly reign. He will thus be greeted as the Bridegroom. In but one instance, the point at issue and which carries its own warning, is it true that some were unprepared for the return of their King. In Matthew 24:37–39 history is cited as an example of unpreparedness. As in the days of Noah, so shall it be when Christ returns. Efforts have been made by some expositors to demonstrate that this passage teaches that the wickedness on the part of the antediluvian people will be duplicated in the days before Christ's return. There is much Scripture which avers that there was wickedness before the flood and that there will be wickedness before the Messiah comes, but this passage brings no charge of wickedness against the antediluvians other than unpreparedness and unbelieving in the face of the warnings that were given unto them. In the same manner and to the same purpose Matthew 24:40–42 is a declaration of the truth that, due to unpreparedness, where two may be together—in the field or grinding at the mill—one shall be taken and the other left. Again a parallel between the experience of people at the time of the rapture and this experience of Israel is set up, but with the strongest contrasts. In the instance of the Church in her rapture, those who are truly saved are without exception taken into heaven and the unsaved who were only professors outwardly are left for the impending judgments which follow on the earth. The notion which contends that there will be but a partial rapture including only the most spiritual believers and that unfaithful

Christians will remain behind for the supposed discipline of the tribulation is an immeasurable dishonor to the grace of God. God has His own way of dealing with unfaithful believers; but no one saved by Christ and standing in the merit of Christ—as all believers stand—will be left behind for a supposed Protestant purgatory. Those who hold such beliefs fail to realize that those who are saved at all are perfectly saved in and through Christ. If Christians are to be admitted or rejected in the matter of entering heaven's glory on the basis of their personal worthiness, they all, without exception, would be rejected. Salvation by grace is not a scheme by which only good people go to heaven. Anyone can devise a plan by which good people might go to heaven—if there were such in the world; it is different, indeed, to devise a plan by which meritless and hell-deserving sinners—such as all are—are taken into heaven. God has executed that plan at infinite cost and all who believe are forever free from condemnation and judgment. Over against all this and according to the passage under consideration, those taken are taken in judgment and those left enter the kingdom blessings. In the light of this truth, the Jew of that day is told to "watch therefore: for ye know not what hour your Lord doth come." This is not an instruction to a Jew within the present age of grace; such are shut up to the gospel of divine grace. It is a word to Jews living in a period which may be defined with respect to its time and circumstances as "when ye shall see all these things, know that it is near, even at the doors" (24:33). Again, the same truth regarding preparedness is enforced by the illustration (24:43–44) that the "goodman" of the house would not have suffered his house to be broken up by the thief had he known the hour the thief would come. This in turn is followed by the appeal, "Therefore be ye also ready: for in such an hour as ye think not the Son of man cometh" (vs. 44). In 24:45–51 preparedness is likewise enjoined, and the parable of the good servant who at the coming of his master is found acting with faithfulness and the evil servant with unfaithfulness urges the same obligation upon Israel to watch and be ready. The lord of the evil servant comes at an unexpected time. The penalty is stated clearly, "The lord of that servant shall come in a day when he looketh not for him, and in an hour that he is not aware of, and shall cut him asunder, and appoint him his portion with the hypocrites: there shall be weeping and gnashing of teeth" (vss. 50–51). The Jews are, in their relation to Jehovah, servants. On none, Jew or Gentile, in this age who have believed upon Christ could such judgments be imposed. This is the sentence which awaits the unfaithful and unprepared among Israel.

Continuing the same theme of the need of watching (cf. 25:13), the nation in the hour of her judgments at the return of Christ in glory and when the earthly kingdom is about to be set up, is likened to ten virgins of whom five were wise and five were foolish. The wisdom of the wise is displayed in the fact that they took oil, the symbol of spirituality, in their lamps, while the unwisdom of the unwise is seen in the fact that they had not sufficient oil. This parable has been subject to a great variety of interpretations. It is resorted to by those who seek to divide the children of God into two divisions with reference to their relation and standing before God. There is, however, but one Body of believers (Eph. 4:4). The time when this parable will be fulfilled is at the glorious coming of Christ to earth and therefore it could have no reference to the Church. The place is on the earth. The King is returning from heaven to earth with His Bride, to whom He has been married in heaven and after the marriage supper of the Lamb has been celebrated in heaven. Of the marriage supper in heaven it is written, "Let us be glad and rejoice, and give honour to him: for the marriage of the Lamb is come, and his wife hath made herself ready. And to her was granted that she should be arrayed in fine linen, clean and white: for the fine linen is the righteousness of saints" (Rev. 19:7–8). And, in perfect chronological order, the King is seen to return to earth following the marriage supper (cf. Rev. 19:11–16). Of this return to the earth Christ declared as recorded in Luke 12:35–36, "Let your loins be girded about, and your lights burning; and ye yourselves like unto men that wait for their lord, when he will return from the wedding; that when he cometh and knocketh, they may open unto him immediately." The same figure of the lights burning is used here in Matthew and also the same theme of preparedness for the King's return. From this passage it is certain that Christ is coming from and not to His wedding. Israel on earth awaits the return of the Bridegroom with the Bride (cf. Rev. 19:11–16). Some old manuscripts add to Matthew 25:1 what is certainly sustained throughout the prophetic Scriptures, namely, that the virgins (Israel) go forth to meet the bridegroom "and the bride." The reception on earth is characterized by the marriage feast, admission to which is, for the Jew on earth, equivalent to entrance into the Messianic kingdom. The A.V. text of 25:10 requires revision to the extent of the addition to the word *feast* after "marriage" (note R.V. and all modern correct translations). This is an important change in rendering and precludes the error—so long drawn from the Authorized Version text—that Christ is coming, according to this parable, *to* His wedding, when, as cited above, it is asserted in Luke 12:35–36 that He is returning *from* His wedding. The objective in this parable is once more to stress the need of that form of watching which is fully prepared for the Messiah. Again, those excluded could not represent the true believer in this age of grace. Of such Christ could never say, "I know you not" (25:12). Describing this same situation and time Christ said, "Not every one that saith unto me, Lord, Lord, shall enter into the kingdom of heaven; but he that doeth the will of my Father which is in heaven. Many will say to me in that day, Lord, Lord, have we not prophesied in thy name? and in thy name have cast out devils? and in thy name done many wonderful works? And then will I profess unto them, I never knew you: depart from me, ye that work iniquity" (Matt. 7:21–23). So important, indeed, is this millennial scene in the King's palace (cf. Ezek. 40:1— 48:35), that the enrollment of those present is given in the Book of Psalms. There it is written, "All thy garments smell of myrrh, and aloes, and cassia, out of the ivory palaces, whereby they have made thee glad. Kings' daughters were among thy honourable women: upon thy right hand did stand the queen in gold of Ophir. Hearken, O daughter, and consider, and incline thine ear; forget also thine own people, and thy father's house; so shall the king greatly desire thy beauty: for he is thy Lord; and worship thou him. And the daughter of Tyre shall be there with a gift; even the rich among the people shall intreat thy favour. The king's daughter is all glorious within: her clothing is of wrought gold. She shall be brought unto the king in raiment of needlework: the virgins her companions that follow her shall be brought unto thee. With gladness and rejoicing shall they be brought: they shall enter into the king's palace" (Ps. 45:8–15). In this vivid description of the palace and those present are named (1) the King in garments which smell of myrrh, aloes, and cassia; (2) king's daughters among the honorable women who are present; above all (3) the queen who stands at His right side in the gold of Ophir. The queen is the Church, the Bride of the Lamb (cf. Rev. 19:8–9). An address is given to the queen in verses 10 and 11 under the title of *daughter*. This address is renewed again in verses 13 and 14 where it may well be read, *the daughter who is the King's* (bride). (4) The virgins follow the Bride, but the virgins are not the Bride. The virgins shall enter into the King's palace, but some, according to the parable of Matthew 25:1–13, who started out to meet the Bridegroom and His Bride, do not enter for want of that form of preparedness which is enjoined. Thus, again, it is revealed that, at the glorious appearing of Christ, Israel shall be judged and many who have chosen the broad way which leads unto death cannot enter the kingdom, while some who have chosen the strait and narrow way which leads unto life shall enter therein (cf. Matt. 7:13–14; 19:28–29). It is concluded, then, that, as Matthew's Gospel is addressed so largely to Israel—and the Olivet Discourse in particular—and since there is no message in this address related to Gentiles until 25:31, and even 25:31–46 is recorded there for Israel's advantage, the very extensive theme of the future judgment of Israel is in view throughout this section, namely, 24:37—25:30. It is also concluded that the parable of the virgins represents the judgment of Israel only. They are the servants who follow the Bride and who enter the palace, but Israel is not the Bride.

Matthew 25:14–30. This extended parable need not be quoted in full. The lesson respecting the talents is, as in the case of other portions of this discourse, concerned with Israel's relation to her returning King. For that return they are to watch and be ready that they may satisfy His demands. The previous reference to the days of Noah, the impending division of two working together, the "goodman" of the house, the good and evil servants, and the virgins, all aim to stress the one admonition to *watch* for the Messiah's return. So great an emphasis upon this one injunction must not be overlooked. In the parable of the ten virgins and similarly in that of the good and evil servants there is represented the element of moral and spiritual values—such works as are required for admission into the kingdom (cf. Matt. 5:1—7:29; 19:28–30; Luke 3:8–14). The good servant is found by the returning King to be attending to the household and the wise virgins had oil in their lamps. No new feature is introduced when in the present portion recognition is promised to those who have used in a profitable way the talents committed unto them. No part of the Scriptures related directly to Israel presents more forcefully the need of individual merit as the basis of acceptance with God than this parable of the talents. Far removed, indeed, from the way of divine grace bestowed freely upon meritless sinners is the verdict against the one-talent man who made no use of that committed unto him (cf. 24:50–51). Of the one-talent man it is written, "Thou oughtest therefore to have put my money to the exchangers, and then at my coming I should have received mine own with usury. Take therefore the talent from him, and give it unto him which hath ten talents. For unto every one that hath shall be given, and he shall have abundance: but from him that hath not shall be taken away even that which he hath. And cast ye the unprofitable servant into outer darkness: there shall be weeping and gnashing of teeth" (25:27–30).

A marked change in theme is reached at the end of the parable of the talents. Christ then turns to Gentile judgments. The entire discourse up to this point has concerned a well-defined people to whom certain responsibilities of merit have been entrusted, and these people are to be judged on the basis of their discharge of these responsibilities by the returning Messiah. The first demand upon them is that they be found watching with that faithfulness which is required of them. That this people thus addressed is Israel is clearly demonstrated throughout. As before indicated, this discourse is the final message of the Messiah to His earthly people, who are related to God on the basis of merit (cf. Ex. 19:4–8). The fact that the Lord at this point turns in this address to truth respecting Gentiles indicates that in the previous portion He has been contemplating only those who are not Gentiles, namely, Israel.

Matthew 25:31–46: When the Son of man shall come in his glory, and all the holy angels with him, then shall he sit upon the throne of his glory: and before him shall be gathered all nations: and he shall separate them one from another, as a shepherd divideth his sheep from the goats: and he shall set the sheep on his right hand, but the goats on the left. Then shall the King say unto them on his right hand, Come, ye blessed of my Father, inherit the kingdom prepared for you from the foundation of the world: for I was an hungred, and ye gave me meat: I was thirsty, and ye gave me drink: I was a stranger, and ye took me in: naked, and ye clothed me: I was sick, and ye visited me: I was in prison, and ye came unto me. Then shall the righteous answer him, saying, Lord, when saw we thee an hungred, and fed thee? or thirsty, and gave thee drink? When saw we thee a stranger, and took thee in? or naked, and clothed thee? Or when saw we thee sick, or in prison, and came unto thee? And the King shall answer and say unto them, Verily I say unto you, Inasmuch as ye have done it unto one of the least of these my brethren, ye have done it unto me. Then shall he say also unto them on the left hand, Depart from me, ye cursed, into everlasting fire, prepared for the devil and his angels: for I was an hungred, and ye gave me no meat: I was thirsty, and ye gave me no drink: I was a stranger, and ye took me not in: naked, and ye clothed me not: sick, and in prison, and ye visited me not. Then shall they also answer him, saying, Lord, when saw we thee an hungred, or athirst, or a stranger, or naked, or sick, or in prison, and did not minister unto thee? Then shall he answer them, saying, Verily I say unto you, Inasmuch as ye did it not to one of the least of these, ye did it not to me. And these shall go away into everlasting punishment, but the righteous into life eternal.

As noted above, this discourse makes an abrupt change in its theme beginning at 25:31. It is still the judgments to be executed when Messiah returns; but the shift is from the judgment of the nation Israel to the judgment of the nations. In each case the judgment is closely related to the glorious appearing of Christ. Israel's judgments as recorded in

24:37—25:30 are preceded by the coming of Christ with power and great glory (24:29–31), and the description of the judgment of the nations opens with the words, "When the Son of man shall come in his glory, and all the holy angels with him, then shall he sit upon the throne of his glory: and before him shall be gathered all nations: and he shall separate them one from another, as a shepherd divideth his sheep from the goats" (vss. 31–32). Thus it is disclosed that both of these judgments follow at once upon His return to the earth. If an order exists, it will likely be in conformity to the order in which these are described in this address. There is little need to call the attention of those who are faithful to the meaning of the Sacred Text to the wide difference between the judgment of the nations and the judgment of the great white throne (Rev. 20:11–15); yet many have failed to note these distinctions and suppose that the two are varied descriptions of one great judgment day. One is at the beginning of the thousand-year reign of Christ, the other is at its end. One concerns living nations, the other concerns the wicked dead of all human history; one divides the nations sending some into the kingdom and others into the lake of fire, while the other consigns all before the bar to the lake of fire.

According to the order of events in Biblical prophecy, the King will, on His return, first receive the nations from His Father. He then, by Himself, conquers them in the midst of their open rebellion. This is the prophetic picture presented in Psalm 2. This portion reads thus, "Why do the heathen rage, and the people imagine a vain thing? The kings of the earth set themselves, and the rulers take counsel together, against the Lord, and against his anointed, saying, Let us break their bands asunder, and cast away their cords from us. He that sitteth in the heavens shall laugh: the Lord shall have them in derision. Then shall he speak unto them in his wrath, and vex them in his sore displeasure. Yet have I set my king upon my holy hill of Zion. I will declare the decree: the Lord hath said unto me, Thou art my Son; this day have I begotten thee. Ask of me, and I shall give thee the heathen for thine inheritance, and the uttermost parts of the earth for thy possession. Thou shalt break them with a rod of iron; thou shalt dash them in pieces like a potter's vessel" (vss. 1–9). The opening section (vss. 1–3) presents a description of the attitude of the nations—the word *heathen* in the Old Testament Authorized Version is equivalent to the word *Gentiles* in the New Testament—toward Jehovah and His Messiah. The kings of the earth and the rulers are leading the people in this rebellion. In another Scripture—Revelation 16:13–14—wherein this same situation is again described, it is said that these kings are demon-possessed. The attitude of Jehovah is described in verses 4 and 5, and the declaration of Jehovah is recorded in verse 6. In this He states, "Yet have I set my king upon my holy hill of Zion." According to Old Testament usage, the holy hill is the throne site and Zion is Jerusalem. The throne is David's, upon which Messiah must reign and that from Jerusalem. All Scripture harmonizes with this great expectation. In verses 7, 8, and 9 the Messiah-King speaks. He declares the decree that Jehovah has acknowledged Him as King over all; so, also, Jehovah has said to Him, *Ask of me, and I shall give thee these raging nations.* This is not the first time the Father has given a portion of humanity to the Son. Christ designates the believers as them "which thou gavest me out of the world." However, the method by which these nations are to be conquered by the King is too often thought to be a peaceful missionary conquest; on the contrary, He breaks them with a rod of iron and dashes them in pieces like a potter's vessel. This violent subduing of the nations by the returning King is many times pictured in the predictions of God's Word. None of these is more vividly stated than Isaiah 63:1–6, which reads, "Who is this that cometh from Edom, with dyed garments from Bozrah? this that is glorious in his apparel, travelling in the greatness of his strength? I that speak in righteousness, mighty to save. Wherefore art thou red in thine apparel, and thy garments like him that treadeth in the winefat? I have trodden the winepress alone; and of the people there was none with me: for I will tread them in mine anger, and trample them in my fury; and their blood shall be sprinkled upon my garments, and I will stain all my raiment. For the day of vengeance is in mine heart, and the year of my redeemed is come. And I looked, and there was none to help; and I wondered that there was none to uphold: therefore mine own arm brought salvation unto me; and my fury, it upheld me. And I will tread down the people in mine anger, and make them drunk in my fury, and I will bring down their strength to the earth." In this connection attention should be given to 2 Thessalonians 1:7–10 and to Revelation 19:11–21. One verse (15) of the latter passage relates itself to both the Second Psalm and to Isaiah 63:1–6. That verse asserts, "And out of his mouth goeth a sharp sword, that with it he should smite the nations: and he shall rule them with a rod of iron: and he treadeth the winepress of the fierceness and wrath of Almighty God."

This violent subjugation of the nations by the returning King forms the preparation for appreciation of the description of the scene presented in Matthew 25:31–46. In that scene these very raging nations with their demon-driven kings and rulers are now standing in awful silence before the King, who is seated upon the throne of His glory. All resistance has been defeated and dissolved. The weapons of warfare, so much depended upon, are abandoned. All stand in solemn silence awaiting the verdict of the King. At His command, those indicated as *sheep* nations are required to move to His right side, and those indicated as *goat* nations are directed to His left side. There is no hesitating or faltering. They have but one fear, that they might displease the Monarch who has conquered them. No picture could more perfectly describe the complete defeat and subjugation of these nations who so short a time before were defying Jehovah and His Messiah, saying, "Let us break their bands asunder, and cast away their cords from us." The one question that now obtains in their minds is what disposition the King will make of them. To those on His right He says, "Come, ye blessed of my Father, inherit the kingdom prepared for you from the foundation of the world." It is at this point that misinterpretations may enter with endless confusion of ideas. There is no reason why the word *kingdom* should be given any other meaning in this passage than has been assigned to it throughout the Gospel by Matthew. The kingdom is Israel's earthly, Messianic, millennial kingdom into which, by the authority of a large body of Old Testament prediction, Gentiles are to enter and sustain the subordinate place which is assigned to them (cf. Ps. 72:8–11; Isa. 14:1–2; 60:3, 5, 12; 62:2). The reason assigned by Christ for the admission of these sheep nations into the kingdom is altogether explicit. In them has been wrought out one thing which secures the divine approval and blessing. It is not a matter of bestowing divine grace, but rather of commending pure merit. They have provided food, drink, shelter, clothing, and comfort for the King. The remarkable feature of this is that they themselves do not identify any such service as having been wrought by them. The first word to break their awful silence is *When?* In like manner, those on the left hand are dismissed into the lake of fire prepared for the devil and his angels, and for the announced reason that they have not provided food, drink, shelter, clothing, and comfort for the King. They, in turn, are equally unconscious of this omission on their part and they, too, break their silence by the inquiry *When?* All of this creates a challenge to the thoughtful student. Is there an issue in the world so vast in its import that it determines the destiny of nations and yet it is wholly unrealized and unrecognized by those nations who will stand before the King?

Such a problem is set up in this context by the King Himself and will not be overlooked by candid minds. It makes no difference at this point what method of interpretation is employed. The problem as thus stated is up for solution by every school of interpretation. Those who assume that this scene is the judgment of the saved and unsaved at the end of the world find it most difficult to identify a third group whom the King styles "my brethren." If the sheep nations are the saved people of all generations, who are these "brethren"? If the "brethren" are the saved ones who constitute the Church, who are the sheep nations? How could the Church ever be thus thrown back upon an unmitigated merit basis of acceptance with God when they have already been accepted in the Beloved? How could the Church be entering the kingdom as subjects of the King when she is sitting with Him on His throne and reigning with Him? Similarly, the Church has never been cast upon the bounty of the *cosmos* for her physical sustenance and comfort. To her it has been promised and fulfilled that "my God shall supply all your need according to his riches in glory by Christ Jesus" (Phil. 4:19). Any interpretation that would bring the Church into this scene either as the "brethren" or as the sheep nations is impossible from every consideration.

The King's own reply to the query *When?* is the answer that should satisfy the student of the text as it will satisfy the nations that stand before Him. Whatever these multitudes are able to understand can be understood by the average person of today if he will approach the subject with unprejudiced consideration of all that is involved. The King will say, "Inasmuch as ye have done it unto one of the least of these my brethren, ye have done it unto me." Who, then, are these who are classed as "my brethren"? Upon a covenant theology which recognizes but two classes of men in the future estate—the saved and the lost—and but two places—heaven and hell—there has been an insuperable problem imposed in accounting for the third group who are identified by the King as "my brethren." It is assumed by these theologians that the saved of all ages are on the right hand and the lost are on the left hand. Beyond these, according to their teaching, there could be no others; yet the King indicates a third class. There are two groups who may be identified as Christ's brethren. (1) Christians are joint heirs with Christ (Rom. 8:17), and they are the "many brethren" to whom He is revealed as the First-Born (Rom. 8:29). However, as already indicated, Christians answer to none of the features set forth in this description. On the other hand, (2) Israel in her age did stand and must yet stand upon a merit basis, and in this age she is cast upon the bounty of the *cosmos* world. Those who, in the coming tribulation, will have suffered for Christ's sake (Matt. 24:9) are His brethren after the flesh. The kingdom which is in view belongs to Israel, and it is fitting to observe that, since certain Gentile peoples are to inherit a place in Israel's kingdom, they should be such as have by a previous demonstration exercised a sympathy for Israel, the elect nation before God. There is no mere accident in the fact that the two words *blessed* and *cursed* appear in the Abrahamic covenant respecting the attitude of Gentiles toward Abraham's seed according to the flesh (Gen. 12:1–3), and that these words appear again when Gentiles are being brought into judgment respecting their treatment of God's elect people. In Genesis it is written, "I will bless them that bless thee," and in the description of the judgment of the nations it is said, "Come, ye blessed of my Father." In Genesis it is said, "I will curse him that curseth thee," while in this same judgment it is said, "Depart from me, ye cursed, into everlasting fire." But why? Only because *ye did it*, or *ye did it not unto one of the least of these my brethren*. Existing without attention to the Word of God, the nations have never realized the favored place Israel holds in the love and purpose of God. Nor do they accept this truth when it is presented to them. To no other people has Jehovah said, "For thou art an holy people unto the LORD thy God: the LORD thy God hath chosen thee to be a special people unto himself, above all people that are upon the face of the earth. The LORD did not set his love upon you, nor choose you, because ye were more in number than any people; for ye were the fewest of all people: but because the LORD loved you, and because he would keep the oath which he had sworn unto your fathers, hath the LORD brought you out with a mighty hand, and redeemed you out of the house of bondmen, from the hand of Pharaoh king of Egypt" (Deut. 7:6–8). It is to these same people that He said, "I have loved thee with an everlasting love" (Jer. 31:3). They are kept by Him as the apple of His eye and are graven upon the palms of His hands. Respecting the immutable character of Jehovah's devotion to Israel, it is written, "For the gifts and calling of God are without repentance" (Rom. 11:29). All this is true whether conceded by the nations or not. Warnings and counsels have been given them. What more direct or emphatic word could be uttered than is found in the closing portion of the Second Psalm? It reads, "Be wise now therefore, O ye kings: be instructed, ye judges of the earth. Serve the LORD with fear, and rejoice with trembling. Kiss the Son, lest he be angry, and ye perish from the way, when his wrath is kindled but a little. Blessed are all they that put their trust in him" (vss. 10–12). Falling as it does at the end of the great tribulation, the judgment of the nations concerns that one generation that will have afflicted Israel during the time of Jacob's trouble. With all the present sufferings of Israel at the hand of certain Gentile peoples, there is still no situation in the world today which would serve as a basis upon which the nations might be judged as they will be judged in that coming day. To some, these verdicts upon the nations seem extreme, especially that pronounced upon those on His left hand. It is probable, however, that their departure to the lake of fire is that which belongs to them because of their lost estate and that the actual casting of them into the lake of fire is deferred until the hour described in Revelation 20:11–15 (cf. Matt. 13:30). The place to be taken in the kingdom by the sheep nations is prepared and designed for them from the foundation of the world, which indicates a definite election under the sovereignty of God. What He has determined and declared can never fail.

In conclusion it may be well to restate that this is the Messiah-King's farewell message to Israel. In its early portions is recorded His own description of the great tribulation. Its severity is asserted and the sign of the end of the deferred portion of the Jewish age is disclosed. Following this is the description of the King's return as set forth by the King Himself. To this He adds long and faithful warnings to that people to the end that they may be prepared in the day when they "see all these things" begin to come to pass. Israel must be judged on the basis of faithfulness and right conduct and in the matter of watching. The nation must be judged also as a vindication of Jehovah's sovereign right and purpose to exalt one elect nation above all the nations of the earth, and in the demonstration of His resentment at the sufferings which the nations will have imposed upon that people beloved and cherished of God.

3. THE UPPER ROOM DISCOURSE. The third and last of Christ's major discourses is recorded in John, chapters 13 to 17, and though given to His disciples, as are the other two, this is even more distinctive in character and purpose than the two already considered. The attentive and discerning student must become aware upon consideration of this portion that he is confronted at once with that form of doctrine which belongs only to the Church in the present age, and that it, unlike the Sermon on the Mount or the Olivet Discourse which look backward to the Old Testament setting, looks forward into the following

portions of the New Testament, which was then unwritten. This address—termed a conversation by some—is the seed plot of all grace
teachings, and it is asserted here that in no portion of the Scriptures
that which may be termed uncomplicated Christian doctrine is more
clearly announced. In view of the habit of some theologians calling
all Biblical doctrine *Christian,* it is pointed out again that in this work
on theology that which is Christian in character is distinguished from
Judaism and is confined to God's purpose in the present age, namely,
the outcalling from both Jews and Gentiles of those who having been
transformed through redeeming grace are the Body and Bride of Christ.
The truth related to the Church, this heavenly people, is found in the
latter portions of the New Testament, or, more definitely, all that follows the Synoptic Gospels. Since this heavenly company is to be distinguished from all other peoples of the earth by differences which are
immeasurable, it is to be expected that there will be a body of revelation specifically addressed to and designed for them. There is such a
body of truth and its first pronouncement was made by Christ Himself
in the upper room. The Upper Room Discourse is, therefore, the voice
of Christ and is the foundation of that which constitutes the positions,
possessions, and privileges of the Christian. Again attention is called
to the great difference which obtains between the three major discourses
of Christ—so great, indeed, that they would hardly be attributed to the
same speaker; but the Sermon on the Mount and the Olivet Discourse,
since related directly or indirectly to the oncoming Messianic kingdom,
have that much in common. Over against this, it will be seen that there
is no bond of truth whatsoever between the two discourses already considered and the Upper Room Discourse. These far-reaching declarations should be attested by every student; and it is confidently believed
that to identify the varied character of these discourses is to reach the
foundation of a right understanding of the Sacred Text. Especially is
it true that to comprehend the exact teachings of Christ in the upper
room is to become aware of that which is purely Christian in its character. Likewise, attention is again called to the transition that evidently took place in the two or three days that intervened between the
giving of the Olivet Discourse, which was addressed to the disciples as
representative men of Judaism, and the Upper Room Discourse, which
contemplates these same men as no longer in Jewish law (cf. John 15:
25) but as *clean* through the Word spoken unto them (John 13:10;
15:3); and no greater transformation could be indicated than is asserted by Christ when He said of these men, "They are not of the world

[*cosmos*], even as I am not of the world" (John 17:14, 16) and these are now sent into the world (*cosmos*) as the Father sent the Son into the world (John 17:18). They are now vitally related to Christ as is indicated by the words, "Ye in me, and I in you" (John 14:20). They now form a new unity comparable only to that which exists between the Father and the Son. Of this unity Christ said, "That they all may be one; as thou, Father, art in me, and I in thee, that they also may be one in us: that the world may believe that thou hast sent me. And the glory which thou gavest me I have given them; that they may be one, even as we are one: I in them, and thou in me, that they may be made perfect in one; and that the world may know that thou hast sent me, and hast loved them, as thou hast loved me" (John 17:21–23). To these same men the entire new body of doctrine was delivered and from that time forth they found their relationship in the Headship of the One who died for them and in whom they were raised to newness of life. This discourse is clearly dated with reference to its application. It was to go into effect only after His death, His resurrection, His ascension and after the descent of the Spirit on Pentecost (cf. John 13:19; 14:20, 25; 16:8, 13). In other words, these age-transforming events are required before this age could be inaugurated. These men must await the outworking of the plan of God. It was said by Christ to them that they would come into the knowledge of the truth and know their relationship when the Spirit came (cf. John 13:7; 16:12–15; 17:13–14, 16). No such doctrine had ever been introduced into the world before. It is foreign to those Scriptures which went before. There are at least seven main doctrines presented in this discourse. These are not approached in a systematic and orderly teaching. The method is more a natural conversation such as doubtless had characterized His instructions to these men in the preceding three years. The informality of it is demonstrated by the fact that Christ returned to certain subjects several times. He refers to prayer three times and to the Holy Spirit's new ministry in the world at least five times. This discourse has by expositors generally been extended to include the High Priestly Prayer as recorded in John, chapter 17. Verse 13 of that prayer so relates the prayer to the discourse; it reads, "And now come I to thee; and these things I speak in the world, that they might have my joy fulfilled in themselves." A complete exposition of all that that discourse presents cannot be entered into here. As before observed, it embraces the very foundation of all that belongs to Christian life and service and its fuller consideration must be assigned to other divisions of this work on theology. It will also be noted that there is little reference in this portion of Scripture to the way of salvation and the ground upon which it rests. The first twelve chapters of John declare the gospel of divine grace for the unsaved. Beginning with chapter 13, truth is presented which applies only to those who are saved; even John 16:7-11, though defining the Spirit's work for the unsaved, is not a message to them, but is a message of immeasurable value to the believer in directing his testimony and soul-winning activities. The major themes which are included in this discourse and which are so vital to Christian life and service are: (a) a new relationship to God through Christ, (b) cleansing unto unbroken fellowship, (c) abiding in Christ for fruit bearing, (d) a new relationship to the Holy Spirit, (e) a new relationship between believers, (f) a new ground of prayer, and (g) a new hope.

a. A NEW RELATIONSHIP TO GOD. In the Epistles—notably Romans —the supreme act of God which consummates all His mighty undertakings in the believer's salvation is justification, and justification, which is God's acknowledgment of the believer's perfection being in Christ, is made righteously possible only because of the truth that the saved one has been so vitally and eternally joined to Christ that he partakes actually and fully of what Christ is. Christ, be it said, is the righteousness of God. To be in Christ, then, is the greatest reality that can ever characterize a human being. As the race is fallen because of its place in the federal headship of fallen Adam, so the believer is righteous, having been transferred or translated out of that fallen estate into the Last Adam who is Himself the embodiment of God's righteousness. As certainly, then, as man, because of physical birth, is a partaker of that which Adam became through the fall, so certainly the believer, because of the new birth and his union to Christ through the baptism of the Spirit, partakes of that which Christ is, even the righteousness of God. In an earlier discussion this greatest of realities has been considered more completely and this, it is hoped, remains in the mind of the student. Justification, then, does not make the believer righteous; it is the divine acknowledgment or proclamation of the fact that the believer is righteous. The formula already enunciated stands, namely, *The believer is righteous because he is in Christ, and he is justified because he is righteous.* God could not be just Himself and do otherwise than to justify the one who, being in Christ, is made the righteousness of God. What is declared to be a New Creation is that entity which is formed by the union of the resurrected Christ with those who are in Him. The term *Church* is applied to the Body and Bride of Christ. It represents the company of believers apart from or in distinction to the Head and Bridegroom; but the New Creation permits no such division. It incorporates the resurrected Christ and all that are in Him. Of the New Creation it is written, "Therefore if any man be in Christ, he is a new creature: old things are passed away; behold, all things are become new" (2 Cor. 5:17); "For ye are all the children of God by faith in Christ Jesus. For as many of you as have been baptized into Christ have put on Christ. There is neither Jew nor Greek, there is neither bond nor free, there is neither male nor female: for ye are all one in Christ Jesus" (Gal. 3:26–28); "For in Christ Jesus neither circumcision availeth any thing, nor uncircumcision, but a new creature" (6:15). A misleading error arises when it is assumed that all of this was equally true of Old Testament saints in their day. There could have been no perfected saints with regard to their standing until there was a resurrected Christ who might be the source of their imputed righteousness. On the other hand, there is no such thing as a Christian in the present age who is not thus perfected because of being in Christ; therefore, there is no such thing as a Christian who is not justified forever.

It is such knowledge-surpassing truth as this which advances the New Testament revelation over that of the Old Testament. It must be obvious to the most casual observer that no such relationship is contemplated in the Old Testament, the Synoptics, or even in John's Gospel until the record is given of this Upper Room Discourse. As before stated, the first twelve chapters of John—apart from the record of Christ's reasoning with the Jews—present the gospel of salvation by grace, and it is not until the record of the Upper Room Discourse that the word appears in the entire Sacred Text that the believer is *in Christ*. The first reference to this organic, vital union between Christ and the believer occurs in John 14:20, which reads, "At that day ye shall know that I am in my Father, and ye in me, and I in you." Even the knowledge of this marvelous union is deferred until "that day," which day, according to the context, is the Day of Pentecost, the day of the advent of the Spirit into the world. No deeper revelation respecting relationship has been made than is set forth by these seven words, "Ye in me, and I in you." Well has it been said that the entire grace revelation is compressed into this twofold relationship. These are immeasurable undertakings on the part of the Holy Spirit. To be in Christ is a relationship wrought by the baptism of the Spirit; to have Christ indwelling is a relationship wrought by the regenerating power of the Spirit. This vital union with Christ is announced not alone to Jews who were His disciples, but to all that the Father hath given to the Son; and for the first time in human history this stupendous reality has come into actual existence. This truth concerning vital union to Christ and all it secures is again emphasized by Christ in John 15:2, where the branch is said to be in Christ (cf. John 17:21–23). Likewise, it is stated by Christ that the believer is removed out of the *cosmos* system and is now as unrelated to that system as Christ Himself. He declares, "If the world hate you, ye know that it hated me before it hated you. If ye were of the world, the world would love his own: but because ye are not of the world, but I have chosen you out of the world, therefore the world hateth you" (15:18–19); "These things I have spoken unto you, that in me ye might have peace. In the world ye shall have tribulation: but be of good cheer; I have overcome the world" (16:33); "I have given them thy word; and the world hath hated them, because they are not of the world, even as I am not of the world. . . . As thou hast sent me into the world, even so have I also sent them into the world" (17:14, 18). No such relationship to God was ever predicated of Israel (cf. Rom. 9:4–5), and certainly not of the Gentiles (cf. Eph. 2:11–12). A most significant inclusion in this prayer is recorded in 17:20, "Neither pray I for these alone, but for them also which shall believe on me through their word." It is thus assured to those who have believed through the word of the disciples that they are equally partakers of all that this immeasurable prayer discloses; but it is just as significant also that Christ did not pray for the saints of the Jewish dispensation. If it be claimed that since they were dead there would be no occasion to pray for them, it may be asserted that there was a whole generation then living under Judaism and these were as much entitled to a share in His prayers as was any previous generation. He did not pray for saints that were then in Judaism. He prayed for those who would believe, and the Old Testament saints were not related to God on the sole basis of belief in a Savior. The designation is clearly restricted to those of this age who are saved by grace alone. From this prayer the conclusions must be drawn that an entirely new divine undertaking has been introduced into the world, its objective being the outcalling of a company of saints each one of which company will have been perfected forever, being in Christ, and that each has attained to that exalted position by the one act of believing on Christ. So far as previous human relations to God are concerned, this is wholly new—even for the disciples themselves—and with the introduction of this truth as presented in this discourse the way is paved for its larger development in the Epistles of the New

Testament. Even those Scriptures, already considered, which deal with the oncoming millennial age, give no hint that anything relating to the New Creation will then be on earth. In the same connection, attention should be given to the title by which believers are identified by the Son when He is speaking to His Father. Within that innermost fellowship, by what name will they be designated? It is probable that when speaking to His own about themselves the Lord might adapt His language to their restricted conceptions; but when speaking to the Father about believers He identifies them by the title which obtains in the highest heavenly association—the term common to Father and Son from all eternity, since their identity has been determined and they have been chosen in Himself from before the foundation of the world (cf. Eph. 1:4). If this appellation is to any degree a description of their character or position, it will refer to the most exalted feature of this divine undertaking. In this prayer the Savior refers to believers seven times, but under only one cognomen, and therefore this title must be contemplated as being the highest of all designations assigned to them in heaven or on earth. He speaks of them, though in varied forms, as those "which thou gavest me out of the world." Since no such classification has ever been suggested for any people on earth before and since it is wholly foreign to all later groups who are anticipated in prophecy, it is to be accepted that the present age, concerning which the Lord is speaking in this discourse, is not only heaven-high with respect to its divine purpose, but contemplates a heavenly people who are, by divine exaltation and transformation, wholly different from all peoples that have been or ever will be on the earth.

b. CLEANSING UNTO UNBROKEN FELLOWSHIP. In the order of Christ's own approach to the themes which this discourse sets forth, this one respecting the cleansing of the believer unto unbroken fellowship with the Father and the Son is the opening theme. There should be no confusing of this doctrine with that of the salvation of the lost, which doctrine asserts that there is a complete removal of all condemnation for time and eternity from the one who believes. As it has been often stated, those who are in view in this discourse are considered as clean through the Word spoken to them and accepted as being in Christ. But, since sin continues to some degree in the Christian, there is needed a constant removal of defilement. This is not a renewal of salvation, but is rather a cleansing to the end that fellowship with the Father and with the Son may be unhindered. Writing of this cleansing, the Apostle John states in his first Epistle, "This then is the message which we have heard

of him, and declare unto you, that God is light, and in him is no darkness at all. If we say that we have fellowship with him, and walk in darkness, we lie, and do not the truth: but if we walk in the light, as he is
in the light, we have fellowship one with another, and the blood of Jesus
Christ his Son cleanseth us from all sin" (1:5–7). The point now to be
considered is that this message about the blood of Jesus Christ, His Son,
cleansing from all sin is a message which John declares "we have heard
of him." It is probable that the Lord spoke often to His disciples on
this theme, but it is noteworthy that He placed it first in the order of
truth considered while in the upper room. It is possible that John in
saying that this truth was heard directly from Christ was looking back
to this upper room teaching. Having loved His own which were in the
cosmos with an everlasting love, and knowing the truth that He came
from God and was about to return to God, Christ laid aside His outer
garments, girded Himself with a towel—the insignia of a servant—and,
having poured water into a basin, began to wash the disciples' feet and
to wipe them with the towel wherewith He was girded. The contrast
is strong, indeed, between this that might be termed a miniature of a
larger scene and the actuality—when He arose from the heavenly fellowship and girded Himself with humanity and by the shedding of His
blood provided a perfect salvation and cleansing for all who believe.
The larger picture is likened to a whole bath, such as the priest of old
received when inducted into the priestly office; the smaller picture is
likened to that partial bathing which the priest needed for himself at
the brazen laver before every temple service. It was a partial bathing
which Christ wrought in the upper room, that is, a bathing of those
whom He declared were clean. The Old Testament priest is a type of
the New Testament Christian. The Christian has received the whole
washing of regeneration through the Word, but is ever in need of cleansing from the defilement gained through contact with the world. It is
the blood of Jesus Christ, God's Son, which goes on cleansing from all
sin (1 John 1:7), and "if we confess our sins, he is faithful and just to
forgive us our sins, and to cleanse us from all unrighteousness" (1 John
1:9). This is the basic truth which Christ was demonstrating by bathing the disciples' feet. He did point out one application of the deed in
the need of humility and service among the disciples one for the other;
but He also said to Peter, "What I do thou knowest not now; but thou
shalt know hereafter." Plain, indeed, is the implication in these words
that there was a deeper meaning to His act of washing than could be
understood at the time. It will be remembered that Peter, like the rest

of the disciples, did not realize that Christ was going to die, nor could they then know anything which was based on His death. This they could and would know after His death had taken place. It is the blood of Jesus Christ, God's Son, which cleanseth from all sin that was represented in that symbolic bathing of the disciples' feet. This could not be explained to them until the blood was actually shed. The conversation with Simon Peter is illuminating to all believers, as it was to Peter. The question, "Lord, dost thou wash my feet?" is his recognition of the inconsistency of the act in view of that in his heart to which he had but recently made confession when he said, "Thou art the Christ, the Son of the living God" (Matt. 16:16). It was far from reasonable to Peter that Christ should wash his feet. Having been told that the washing had in it a hidden meaning, Peter declares, "Thou shalt never wash my feet." This protest secured the words from Christ which reveal the meaning of this specific cleansing, "If I wash thee not, thou hast no part with me." Two words in this saying of Christ's need to be understood. The word *wash*—νίπτω, used eight times in this context, refers to a partial bathing only, such as Christ was undertaking. The words *no part* (οὐκ μέρος), meaning no normal fellowship, evidently reached Peter's innermost heart as indicated by the entire change of attitude when he said, "Lord, not my feet only, but also my hands and my head." To this the Lord replied, "He that is washed needeth not save to wash his feet, but is clean every whit: and ye are clean, but not all" (John 13:10). In this verse the word *washed* is λούω and indicates a full bath. It is a thing already completed in the past—such as is accomplished for believers when they are saved. For such a bath there is no further need, save in case of the defilement of sin in the believer's life. Not only must the sin be cleansed if fellowship is to be enjoyed, but Christ alone is able to cleanse. It is possible for one disciple to serve another in humility, and that is the application which, for the moment, Christ gave to His act and example. It would seem unnecessary to point out that all that is indicated by the washing of the disciples' feet is wholly new so far as the Old Testament and Judaism are concerned. There was remedy for the sins of saints of Old Testament times in the sacrifices. For the Christian there is cure for sin constantly and instantly on a basis of faith in Christ's blood, which cure is secured by confession of sin. This doctrine is new.

c. ABIDING IN CHRIST FOR FRUIT BEARING. What is known as a spiritual life (1 Cor. 2:15) is the result or product of the unhindered energy of the indwelling Spirit (Phil. 2:13), who undertakes in connection with two major realities, namely, the suppression of evil in the life and the expression of that which is good. Though of great value in itself, a life is not spiritual in the fullest sense when only evil is overcome. Such an achievement is negative. The positive output of divine virtues sustained by divine enablement is required as well. A believer should not measure his spirituality by reckoning only the evil things which he does not do; the spiritual life is better measured by the God-honoring things which he does do. In the preceding division of this thesis the removal of defilement has been in view and that discussion could have been extended to the control of those tendencies in life which engender evil conduct. In the present section, fruit bearing, effectual prayer, and celestial joy are set forth as the result of abiding in Christ. The truth presented in the former division as disclosed in John 13:1-10 represents a negative aspect of spirituality, while the truth set forth in the figure of the vine and the branches presents a positive spirituality. As an illustration of a spiritual reality, the figure of the vine and the branches is easily misunderstood. Arminians have read into this figure the notion that it represents a saved or unsaved estate, that is, that one is saved so long as he abides in Christ and lost whenever he ceases to abide. Little, indeed, do they realize what is involved when the believer is joined to the Lord and thus in Christ. The idea that a believer is lost when he ceases to be fruitful is hardly the teaching of this parable. At the very opening of this passage a branch in Him which does not bear fruit is designated, thus indicating that there is such a thing as a branch in Him which is not fruitful; and human experience—even that of a saved Arminian—demonstrates this to be possible. This thought of abiding in Christ does not suggest the idea of remaining in a saved state, but it does indicate unbroken communion with Christ on the part of the one who through infinite grace has entered into an unchangeable union with Christ. This truth is established fully by Christ Himself as recorded in John 15:10, "If ye keep my commandments, ye shall abide in my love; even as I have kept my Father's commandments, and abide in his love." It is certain that Christ's abiding in the Father was not to the end that He might remain saved, but that unbroken fellowship between them might be realized. He did always the will of His Father and thus abode in the Father's love. It was no attempt to maintain His sonship relation. Thus the obedient believer will abide in Christ's love and there will be an unhindered inflow of spiritual vitality from Christ which, like the sap of the vine, will result in fruitfulness. In verse 2 it is said that those in Him who do not bear fruit are lifted up out of their place. The Father reserves the right to remove such into heaven. At this point the Arminian protests that the branch, if it is not fruitful, has no right to go to heaven, not recognizing the basic truth that no person will ever enter heaven on the ground of his own merit, but, if he enters at all, it will be on the basis of the imputed merit of the Son of God. God knows how to deal righteously and perfectly with unfruitful branches, and who among all Christians is able to assert in truth that he is fruitful to the degree which is wholly pleasing to God? Not every believer who dies is removed because of unfruitfulness. God reserves this form of correction to Himself and is faithful to the extent of giving full warning about that which might occur. Those branches in Christ which bear fruit are pruned that they may bear more fruit. Thus each class in Christ—the unfruitful and the fruitful—are said to be under the immediate care of the Father, who is the Husbandman. Wholly within the sphere of his public testimony the believer may, by not being adjusted to the will of Christ, be "cast forth as a branch" and be "withered." His profession is rejected by his fellow men and his spiritual vitality is diminished. This figure which represents the disapproval of men is very strong. It is, nevertheless, true that men repudiate the pretense of the believer whose daily life becomes an abhorrent thing in their eyes. Such, indeed, is the justification by works to which James refers when he writes, "Even so faith, if it hath not works, is dead, being alone. Yea, a man may say, Thou hast faith, and I have works: shew me thy faith without thy works, and I will shew thee my faith by my works. . . . Was not Abraham our father justified by works, when he had offered Isaac his son upon the altar? Seest thou how faith wrought with his works, and by works was faith made perfect? And the scripture was fulfilled which saith, Abraham believed God, and it was imputed unto him for righteousness: and he was called the Friend of God. Ye see then how that by works a man is justified, and not by faith only" (James 2:17–18, 21–24). It is true that only faith will justify before God (cf. Rom. 5:1), and that only works will justify before men; thus it is justification by faith before God which crowns the whole present divine undertaking in salvation by grace. Incidentally, instructions on how a branch may be fruitful to the glory of God are included, but the objective in view in the figure of the vine and its branches is to show the possibility of bearing fruit. A fruitful life is that which brings honor and glory to God, and that which is profitable. There is little need for the utterly new character of this body of truth to be pointed out. No saint of old, under any circumstances, ever sustained a perfected position in Christ, and apart from this perfected position there could be no rightful use of this figure. The saints of old had no vital union to Christ, hence they could sustain no vital communion with Christ.

d. A NEW RELATIONSHIP TO THE HOLY SPIRIT. If a dominating theme is to be found in this discourse, it is Christ's announcement of the coming of the Holy Spirit into the world to continue the Former's ministry as Παράκλητος throughout this age. For three and one-half years Christ had been the All-Sufficient One to the disciples. He was about to withdraw, but they are not to be left unattended. Another Παράκλητος was to come as He did come on the Day of Pentecost. The new Advocate was to be to men more than the bodily presence of Christ had been. It was better that Christ should go away and that the Spirit should come. That the present provision in which the Third Person indwells every believer is advantageous needs but a moment's reflection. The Christ of the three and one-half years was not in all places at the same time. When Lazarus was ill, Christ was removed from the Bethany home by a two-day journey. Under the present relationship between the Holy Spirit and the believer, there is never a separation, nor is there occasion to share Him with others or to await available moments of contact. He the indwelling Spirit is the priceless heritage of every Christian in every moment of the Christian's life. The fact that Christ was looking on in this discourse to a time and condition that was to be made possible through His death, His resurrection, His ascension, and the advent of the Spirit on the Day of Pentecost is especially emphasized by the words, "And when he is come," which words are spoken both in connection with the Spirit's ministry to the unsaved (cf. 16:8) and His ministry of teaching to the saved (cf. 16:13). It is theologically correct to state that the Spirit is sent into the world both by the Father (cf. 14:16, 26) and by the Son (cf. 16:7). This passage respecting the Holy Spirit records the central truth relative to the Person and work of the Spirit in this age.

John 14:16–17. "And I will pray the Father, and he shall give you another Comforter, that he may abide with you for ever; even the Spirit of truth; whom the world cannot receive, because it seeth him not, neither knoweth him: but ye know him; for he dwelleth with you, and shall be in you."

The promise of Christ—"I will pray the Father, and he shall give you another Comforter" (Παράκλητος)—may well be set over against Christ's word recorded in Luke 11:13, "If ye then, being evil, know how to give good gifts unto your children: how much more shall your heavenly Father give the Holy Spirit to them that ask him?" This assurance was uttered early in Christ's ministry and, being so great an innovation over the relationships provided in Old Testament times to which the disciples were alone accustomed, evidently was never entered into by them. After His ministry is well concluded and before He departs out of this world, He declares that He will pray the Father and for the very presence of the Spirit for which they had failed to pray. The provisions included in Christ's prayer are more extensive and anticipate at least two age-characterizing realities: (1) That the Spirit should be given as an indwelling Person to each of the eleven men present. They, according to Old Testament usage, had been accustomed to think of the Spirit as bestowed only for very specific purposes by the sovereign will of God. That the Spirit might be given to all men of faith and without exception was wholly new to them. Thus was introduced one of the greatest features of the new dispensation that was then coming into view—a feature too often overlooked by theologians, that the Spirit is given to all believers from the least of them to the greatest of them. Though emphasized constantly in the Epistles, this fact of the indwelling Spirit is here announced by Christ for the first time. (2) The second age-characterizing feature is the truth that the indwelling of the Spirit in the child of God is an unchangeable fact. Christ prayed that the Spirit might abide with believers forever, and that prayer is answered as definitely and certainly as the prayer that the Spirit should come at all. Thus it is assured that the Spirit indwells and that He abides in the heart forever. This same truth John again asserts in his first Epistle, "But the anointing which ye have received of him abideth in you" (1 John 2:27). This truth, it will be observed, determines much in the doctrine of the security of those who are saved. The Christian may grieve the Spirit, but he will never grieve Him away; he may quench the Spirit (in the sense that the Spirit is suppressed), but the Spirit will never leave the heart into which He has come to abide.

John 16:7-11. "Nevertheless I tell you the truth; It is expedient for you that I go away: for if I go not away, the Comforter will not come unto you; but if I depart, I will send him unto you. And when he is come, he will reprove the world of sin, and of righteousness, and of judgment: of sin, because they believe not on me; of righteousness, because I go to my Father, and ye see me no more; of judgment, because the prince of this world is judged."

Twice in this discourse Christ refers to the world (*cosmos*) in its relation to the Holy Spirit. In the portion just considered He is reported as saying of the Spirit, "Whom the world cannot receive, because it seeth him not, neither knoweth him." In the passage now being contemplated it is said that the Spirit upon coming into the world would enlighten ($\dot{\epsilon}\lambda\dot{\epsilon}\gamma\chi\omega$), not respecting every possible subject, but those of sin, of righteousness, and of judgment. These are the great themes of the gospel of God's grace, which three themes are each in turn beyond the natural understanding of the unregenerate man and therefore must be especially and supernaturally revealed to him. As has just been asserted, the unsaved do not see or know the Spirit. The Apostle Paul says, "But the natural man receiveth not the things of the Spirit of God: for they are foolishness unto him: neither can he know them, because they are spiritually discerned" (1 Cor. 2:14). And, again, "But if our gospel be hid, it is hid to them that are lost: in whom the god of this world hath blinded the minds of them which believe not, lest the light of the glorious gospel of Christ, who is the image of God, should shine unto them" (2 Cor. 4:3-4). The Arminian notion that men everywhere are able, because of a supposed common grace, to believe on Christ and thus to receive Him as Savior is rebuked by these and other Scriptures. No unregenerate person can make an intelligent acceptance of Christ as Savior until this preliminary work of the Spirit is wrought in the heart. It is most arresting, and should claim the attention of all who undertake a soul-winning ministry, that Christ introduces this specific theme in His teaching regarding the work of the Spirit in this age. The passage is not addressed to unregenerate men; it concerns only the saved and serves to bring to their attention a vital divine provision apart from which no really successful soul-saving ministry can be pursued. A preliminary work must be wrought in the heart of those who are unsaved before they can enter, by their own choice, into any saving relationship with Christ. That preliminary work is not a part of their salvation, but is rather an indispensable preparation for it. So, also, the Apostle writes, "moreover whom he did predestinate, them he also called" (Rom. 8:30), and Christ announced that "no man can come unto me, except the Father which hath sent me draw him" (John 6:44). This specific enlightening work of the Spirit within the unsaved is governed wholly by divine sovereignty and is the means by which God calls out His elect people. That company is determined, not by a supposed limited redemption in which Christ is said to die only for those who are to be saved, but by this sovereign, efficacious call. This work of the Spirit within the unsaved is limited to conviction on three topics, namely, those "of sin, because they believe not on me; of righteousness, because

I go to my Father, and ye see me no more; of judgment, because the prince of this world is judged." Respecting sin it is to be noted that the Spirit does not remind the unsaved of all their sins, a totality which Christ has borne, but He rather brings to their consciousness the one new sin, and that which alone secures condemnation. Of this same distinction, Christ said, "He that believeth on him is not condemned: but he that believeth not is condemned already, because he hath not believed in the name of the only begotten Son of God" (John 3:18). It would be difficult indeed either by sermon or appeal to make an unregenerate person realize the full condemning power of unbelief toward Christ as Savior; yet this very understanding is essential if a real decision is to be made by the unsaved. In like manner, the unsaved must come to realize that their only ground of acceptance with God is in the unseen Savior, now at the right hand of God on high. Sermons and appeals cannot create this understanding in the heart; yet such an understanding is essential if the blinding of Satan is to be overcome. And in the third instance, the Spirit will enlighten respecting judgment. This is no reference to a judgment to come, but rather it recognizes a judgment which is past. It is that judgment which belonged to the sinner, and which fell upon the Lord Jesus Christ as the sinner's Substitute. Again, sermons and appeals seem in vain when depended upon to create an understanding in the mind of the Satan-blinded, unregenerate person respecting these immeasurable values already wrought for him. Thus the unsaved persons, according to the divine plan and provision, will not only come into the possession of the understanding of realities which are essential to a right choice, but they are thus provided with something to believe respecting Christ and His saving work for them. All soul-saving ministry is confronted with this human inability caused by Satan's blinding of the mind (2 Cor. 4:3–4), and such servants of God as evangelists would do well to pause for adjustment to these revelations. Both sermon and methods should be conformed to this great reality. The supreme import of this truth is seen in the fact that Christ introduced it into the Upper Room Discourse.

John 16:12–15. "I have yet many things to say unto you, but ye cannot bear them now. Howbeit when he, the Spirit of truth, is come, he will guide you into all truth: for he shall not speak of himself; but whatsoever he shall hear, that shall he speak: and he will shew you things to come. He shall glorify me: for he shall receive of mine, and shall shew it unto you. All things that the Father hath are mine: therefore said I, that he shall take of mine, and shall shew it unto you."

As the preceding passage—dated regarding the time of its application by the words "when he is come"—disclosed the work of the Spirit in bringing truth to the unsaved, this portion—bearing the same time indication, and following immediately in the context—describes the work of the Spirit in bringing truth to the saved. It is true that Christ's provision for the writing of the New Testament is indicated in this Scripture, but neither Luke who wrote his Gospel and the Acts nor Paul who wrote the larger portion of the Epistles was present when these words were spoken. It is also clear from John 17:20 that Christ has in mind all believers of this age. The disciples had been with Him in closest intimacy as learners for three and one-half years. They had heard all His preaching and teaching and had conversed with Him as only those may who have lived together for a term of years. Their introduction to the truth was extended, though so largely pursuant to His kingdom expectation; despite all this, the Lord declares that He yet has many things to say unto them. Such, in general, is the challenge which ever confronts each child of God. Regardless of high attainments in the knowledge of God's Word, it is true that He still has many things to disclose. It will be remembered that up to that time these disciples did not believe that Christ would die or rise again from the dead. Therefore they could not receive any teaching which was based on either His death or resurrection. When all doctrine which is related to Christ's death or His resurrection is eliminated, there is comparatively little left of that which is in the most exact sense Christian. As the Synoptic Gospels disclose, Christ had been occupied largely with those features which belong to Israel's earthly kingdom. With that body of truth the disciples, like all instructed Jews, were familiar. Not believing He would die or be raised from the dead, it was imperative that they see Him die and greet Him in resurrection. Not only did they thus become aware of His death and resurrection, but they, by the Spirit, began at once to understand something of the meaning of these age-transforming events. Not long before Christ's death Peter rebuked Christ for predicting His death; yet it was this same Peter who but fifty days after the resurrection preached the greatest sermon—from the angle of results—ever preached by a man, and he based that sermon on the death and resurrection of Christ. Thus it is made evident that Peter advanced rapidly in the knowledge of the truth when taught by the Spirit. It is this possible advancement in the truth which Christ is presenting to these disciples and to all believers, that is set forth in the passage under consideration. It is here recorded that a new arrangement would be set up by the coming of the Spirit. Not only would the Spirit indwell each believer as assured in 14:16–17, and decline to speak from Himself as the originator of the message, but He would hear the message which Another would speak and would show it unto the one in whom He abides and whom He serves. The identification of the One who thus originates the message points to none other than Christ, who said "I have yet many things to say unto you." It is revealed, then, that in the process of divine instruction Christ originates and sends the message that the individual Christian needs, and this is heard by the Spirit and from Christ conveyed to the mind and heart by the indwelling Holy Spirit. The Spirit may choose to employ a human teacher or a printed page or any other means by which He can bring the message to the attention of the believer for whom it is intended. Christ's unfolding of this new divine arrangement, as set forth in this context, is momentous in its import to the Christian. By this procedure he may make uninterrupted and measureless progress in the knowledge of the truth of God. The outstanding features of this method of divine instruction are, as named above, first, that the Spirit is ever present in the least of those who are saved; second, the Savior Himself is the Teacher who devises the lesson which the pupil requires, and announces for each one the next truth He would have comprehended; and, third, the Spirit, from His incomparable position of advantage as the indwelling Person, hears this truth and passes it on to the Christian's mind and heart. Most consequential is the fact of the Spirit's position as Indweller, which gives Him command of the very springs of human understanding. In fact, He is there in a position to create understanding. It is significant that, as indicated above, He works thus in the inner consciousness of the unsaved by enlightening them, and also teaches from within those who are saved and who are adjusted to Him. Such a limitless approach to the human understanding and emotions should not be confused with the restricted influence one human being may have over another. One person may influence the thought of another, but none creates the thought and understanding which He promotes.

A second feature of this teaching ministry of Christ through the Holy Spirit as revealed in this context is the listing of the measureless field of truth which He will disclose. Beyond the general statement that the Spirit will guide into "all truth," the first specified theme in the order as presented by Christ is that the Spirit will show the believer "things to come." Though human teachers, in forming an order in which the truth of God should be comprehended, would hardly place the subject of prophecy first, it remains true that Christ gave it that distinction and with the implication that, apart from this teaching ministry of the Spirit in the heart, there will be little understanding respecting the vast field of prophecy. What relation to the Holy Spirit is sustained by those in the Christian profession who confess no interest in the prophetic Scriptures must be determined by others. Christ asserts that whosoever is taught of the Spirit will be led into the right understanding of prophecy. That which follows in this divine curriculum embraces the whole field of truth respecting the Father, Christ, and all things related to Them. "He shall glorify me." By the reality which these four words represent, the believer may judge himself with respect to attainment in the things of Christ. "He shall receive of mine, and shall shew it unto you." The boundaries of human knowledge appear exceedingly small compared to the things of the Father and Son. What, indeed, could be added to that represented by the words "all truth"? This same fact that the believer is taught by the indwelling Spirit is taken up for a large consideration by the Apostle Paul in 1 Corinthians 2:9—3:3, and there, after having asserted the truth that the Spirit is the Master Teacher, he distinguishes three classes of people who are divided according to their relation to the written Word of God—the unregenerate ($\psi\upsilon\chi\iota\kappa\acute{o}\varsigma$) man, described in 2:14; the spiritual ($\pi\nu\epsilon\upsilon\mu\alpha\tau\iota\kappa\acute{o}\varsigma$) Christian, who discerns all things (2:15); and the carnal ($\sigma\alpha\rho\kappa\iota\kappa\acute{o}\varsigma$) believer, who can receive only the milk of the Word (3:1–3). From this context it is to be seen that the teaching ministry of the Spirit is impossible in those who are unsaved, that it is unhindered in those who are in right relation to Him, and it is greatly hindered in those who are carnal or fleshly in their lives. The student should observe in particular the fact that the great truths related to the presence and work of the Spirit in the world and to the believer were announced by Christ before He went to His cross.

e. A NEW RELATIONSHIP BETWEEN BELIEVERS. The devout mind must stand in awe and wonder when, having contemplated the ineffable mystery of unity in the blessed Trinity, it is told that, in answer to Christ's prayer, believers are related to each other in a unity comparable only to the unity between the Father and the Son. When in the Scriptures a truth is stated twice it assumes important emphasis (cf. John 17:14, 16; Gal. 1:8–9). Should it be declared three times the emphasis is extreme; but, when presented four times in the same context, all human measurements with regard to relative importance are surpassed. It would seem, too, that when speaking to the Father all repetitions on the part of the Son would be superfluous; yet in His High Priestly prayer Christ prays four times for this unity between believers to be wrought by God. In John 17:11 it is recorded that He asked "that they may be one, as we are." In verses 21–23 He repeats this petition three times—"that they all may be one; as thou, Father, art in me, and I in thee . . . ," "that they may be one, even as we are one," and "that they may be made perfect in one." No human mind can comprehend the importance of this fourfold petition voiced by the Son to the Father. The unity desired is that which the Father alone could accomplish; for Christ not only appeals to the Father for its realization, but He indicates its superexalted, divine character—even as the Father is in the Son and the Son is in the Father. That believers should be thus related to each other is a disclosure which staggers the minds of men. In addition to the unity within the Godhead and the unity between believers, the passage—John 17:21–23—presents still a third unity, that which exists between the Persons of the Godhead and the believers. To this truth attention recently has been given; however, the unity of believers has been created by virtue of their position in Christ, and, therefore, both the unity between believers and the unity between the Persons of the Godhead and believers are asked for by the Savior in this prayer. Thoughtless and absurd is the modern notion that Christ was praying that denominations which exist in this remote time and in a country then unknown might become organically united in one, and therefore it is the duty of all sects to unite and thus help to answer this prayer. As indicated before, this unity is sought at the hand of the Father, indicating that it is a divine undertaking. It is that, and it results in a unity as organic and vital as that between the Father and the Son. This prayer began to be answered on the Day of Pentecost when believers were by the Spirit baptized into one Body, and is constantly answered whenever a soul is saved and thus joined as a member to the Body of Christ by the same baptism of the Spirit. The determining truth to be recognized here is that a God-wrought unity exists in answer to Christ's prayer, and one that in magnitude, vital actuality, and heavenly ennoblement is by the Savior Himself classed with that which is highest in heavenly realms. Even though this truth regarding the unity of believers is knowledge-surpassing, a partial response may be given to it, which response is far more commendable than the almost complete neglect of it or the violent opposition to it which arises in the centers which are committed to a program that excludes other believers from its fellowship.

The Apostle Paul arises to the elevated responsibility of amplifying by the Spirit a vital theme advanced in the Upper Room Discourse, when he writes, "I therefore, the prisoner of the Lord, beseech you that ye walk worthy of the vocation wherewith ye are called, with all lowliness and meekness, with longsuffering, forbearing one another in love; endeavouring to keep the unity of the Spirit in the bond of peace" (Eph. 4:1–3). Having declared in chapters 1 to 3 the high positions and possessions of the one who is in Christ, it is needful, lest they be filled with pride, to beseech such to remember to be meek and lowly; also, in view of their true divinely wrought unity, they are besought to exercise longsuffering, forbearance, and love one toward another and by so much "endeavour to keep the unity of the Spirit in the bond of peace." This unity, it will be observed, is that already made by the Spirit and is not a unity which is formed when believers are faithful to each other. Keeping the unity engendered by the Spirit when He united all as members in Christ's Body is far removed from an attempt on the part of believers to make a unity which is no more than the outward exercise of good fellowship one with another. That a unity is divinely accomplished and does exist is demonstrated by the seven cardinal factors which enter into it. These seven the Apostle asserts when he goes on to state, "There is one body, and one Spirit, even as ye are called in one hope of your calling; one Lord, one faith, one baptism, one God and Father of all, who is above all, and through all, and in you all" (4:4–6). The emphasis in this Scripture is on the word *one*. There is one body, one Spirit indwelling, one calling, one Lord, one body of truth, one baptism by which the unity is formed, and one God and Father. In the light of this declaration, the unity is to be kept. Thus, also, in the light of Christ's fourfold prayer that it might exist, to break this unity becomes an immeasurable sin against the work of God and the heart of Christ; yet this unity is broken outwardly when sectarian divisions exist, and inwardly when the divisions are nourished and cherished by Christians. When the same Apostle undertook to correct the wrongs in the Corinthian Church, as set forth in his first Epistle to them, before all else he mentions divisions that existed among them, even before he mentioned immorality and the dishonor to God which was caused by going to law before the unbelieving. The first commandment of Christ given in the upper room is that Christians are under the greatest imperative to love one another (John 13:34–35), and by this love one for the other all men are to know that those who so love are His disciples. Similarly, in His prayer for oneness (John 17:21–23) Christ said that through this unity for which He prayed the world would come to believe concerning Himself. Such an opportunity has hardly been accorded the world in this age, since the early days of the Church. There is little hope that it will be otherwise in a situation characterized by sectarianism and with no apparent disposition to judge and renounce this high crime against God.

It is clear then that a unity does exist which is wrought of God, and that men therefore do not have to make a unity. It is equally clear also that believers are appointed to keep this divinely wrought unity. This they do when they love all other believers perfectly, disregarding class distinctions and rising above prejudice. God alone can evaluate the extent of the sin against Himself which sectarianism has caused—a great sin which is never condoned or commended, but is unreservedly condemned in the New Testament. The correction does not lie in a mere union of organizations or any mass movements, though these might help in the matter of an outward appearance. The injunction to keep the unity of the Spirit, like the one to love one another, is personal in its outworking and is fulfilled when the believer recognizes and loves every other Christian.

f. A NEW GROUND OF PRAYER. The unique character of the Upper Room Discourse is especially seen in its new revelation regarding prayer. A moment's thought respecting the new relations between the Persons of the Godhead and the believers will suggest at once the necessity, arising from those relations, of an entirely new reality in prayer. In other words, the dispensational feature of prayer—so little considered by theologians—is, nevertheless, of paramount import and its recognition is imperative if the scope of the entire field of prayer is to be comprehended. Not only the general significance of prayer but also its new ground is indicated by the fact that Christ returns to this theme five times in this one discourse (cf. 14:12–14; 15:7, 16; 16:23–24, 26).

Since no Christology is complete which does not contemplate Christ's own exercise of the ministry of prayer, attention should be given to that engaging theme. As the humanity of Christ is the divine ideal in the human sphere, it was essential that the Savior fulfill what is man's highest service in the sphere of prayer. Naturally the subjects of Christ's prayer transcend the field of the Christian's praying, but His attention to prayer must ever be an example to His own. Of one occasion it is written, "And it came to pass, that, as he was praying in a certain place, when he ceased, one of his disciples said unto him, Lord, teach us to pray, as John also taught his disciples" (Luke 11:1). Discovering the Lord in prayer, the disciples are impressed with His complete devotion to the exercise of prayer, and they may have reasoned that if He who is so perfect in Himself needed to pray, how much more needful it would be for men like themselves. Hence the request, "Lord, teach us to pray." The force of this petition is sacrificed when it is supposed that they asked Him to teach them *how* to pray. The problem is not one of a better method; it is one of really attending to this limitless ministry. Outside the High Priestly prayer found in John, chapter 17, there is little record, comparatively, covering that which entered into the prayers of the Savior; yet He often prayed all night and at other times arose a great while before day that He might give Himself to prayer. The inner life of any person is revealed in that one's private prayer; and rich indeed would be the revelation could a record be had of Christ's extended prayers.

During His earth ministry Christ taught much concerning prayer, before He came to the upper room. His instructions were largely related to the age of the law, which obtained to the hour of His death. He also anticipated the exercise of prayer in the future kingdom. These instructions, pursuant to both the past and future ages, deserve careful study; but an entirely new ground and manner of prayer was introduced in the upper room. It was thus of necessity. Through Christ's death and resurrection and the new relationship to be wrought by the Holy Spirit following His advent into the world at Pentecost, new privileges and responsibilities were established which determine the whole form and character of prayer. The present measureless advantage is that those who are saved, being joined to the Lord as members in His Body —as all who believe are joined—are in a favored position: they pray in the name of Christ. The disciples are reminded—as are all others who read the record of Christ's words—that "hitherto have ye asked nothing in my name." Since the new ground of prayer provides access to the limitless resources of Him who is infinite, the new appeal which conditions this measureless possibility is important to the last degree, and well it becomes the earnest Christian to enter intelligently and fully into these unbounded provisions. Of Christ's five references to prayer in this discourse, three are of major importance.

John 14:12–14. "Verily, verily, I say unto you, He that believeth on me, the works that I do shall he do also; and greater works than these shall he do; because I go unto my Father. And whatsoever ye shall ask in my name, that will I do, that the Father may be glorified in the Son. If ye shall ask any thing in my name, I will do it."

It is well to observe that this introductory passage establishes, in the first instance, the truth that the believer's relation to Christ is that of a partnership. A great enterprise has been launched into which the child of God of this age is drawn and into which his service has been incorporated. Such declarations as "we as workers together with him" (2 Cor. 6:1) and "God is faithful, by whom ye were called unto the fellowship of his Son Jesus Christ our Lord" (1 Cor. 1:9) serve to amplify this thought of partnership. It is because of the truth that this joint interest exists that the believer is enjoined to be "always abounding in the work of the Lord"; for it is this divine undertaking in which the entire "firm" is engaged. It must therefore be shared alike by all who are within its bounds. It is thus that the significant words of Christ apply, namely, "the works that I do shall he do also; and greater works than these shall he do." The greater deeds, generally speaking, will be accomplished by the partnership formed. At no point does Christ release to another the responsibility for the actual achievement of these greater works. Twice in this context (vss. 13–14) He gives assurance thereof in the words, "I will do." However, as certainly as Christ reserves to Himself the actual doing of the works, as certainly He assigns to the believer-partner the service of prayer. He declares, "If ye shall ask any thing . . . I will do it." Such is the divine arrangement, which carries with it the implication that unless the believer-partner discharges his specific service of asking there may be failure in that which otherwise might be achieved.

The new ground of prayer is seen in the truth that all efficacy depends upon the prayer being presented in Christ's name. Since all depends on the power of that name, it concerns every Christian to understand what is involved in this new basis of prayer. At least two vital relationships are involved: (1) that the believer, being in Christ, must ever pray from that position. He may pray what would of itself prove to be an unworthy prayer; but still he could not pray outside of his position in Christ, and his voice in prayer is heard by the Father even as He hears the voice of His Son, whose every prayer is assuredly answered. As the believer is accounted righteous since he is in Christ (Rom. 3:22; 2 Cor. 5:21), and accepted because he is in the Beloved (Eph. 1:6), and loved as the Son is loved (John 17:23), in like manner he is heard as Christ is heard, being in Christ. (2) It is also to be recognized that the Christian, being in the partnership with Christ, may expect that his prayer, if prompted by the Spirit, will be indited by Christ Himself. It is as though Christ offered the prayer; and that, again, assures the answer. The limitlessness of the promise, "Whatsoever ye shall ask in my name, that will I do," can be guaranteed only as the prayer is such as Christ would present to the Father. Such a prayer is granted directly and specifically for Christ's sake. The believer's acknowledged inability to discern what constitutes an acceptable subject of prayer is overcome, in the divine arrangement, by the ministry of the Holy Spirit. This ministry of the Spirit is vouchsafed to the Christian in other Scriptures of the New Testament which are equally applicable to the child of God in this age. The Apostle declares, "Likewise the Spirit also helpeth our infirmities: for we know not what we should pray for as we ought: but the Spirit itself maketh intercession for us with groanings which cannot be uttered. And he that searcheth the hearts knoweth what is the mind of the Spirit, because he maketh intercession for the saints according to the will of God" (Rom. 8:26–27), and by the same Apostle the Christian is exhorted to be "praying always with all prayer and supplication in the Spirit, and watching thereunto with all perseverance and supplication for all saints" (Eph. 6:18), and Jude speaks of the high privilege of "praying in the Holy Ghost" (Jude 1:20). It is therefore to be concluded that prayer is the exalted service of the believer in his present partnership with Christ, and that to some degree it measures the extent of the achievement to be wrought by the new association formed by Christ and all Christians. It is certain, too, that a new ground of prayer is provided which is not to be compared in its effectiveness with any other ground of prayer that has ever existed before.

John 15:7. "If ye abide in me, and my words abide in you, ye shall ask what ye will, and it shall be done unto you."

This the second major teaching by Christ on prayer in the Upper Room Discourse presents the same unlimited possibility. The phrase, "ye shall ask what ye will," is without bounds; however, in the form that the prayer which is thus unrestricted takes, there are two conditions set forth: "if ye abide in me, and my words abide in you." To have the words of Christ in the heart is to be informed about that which constitutes His will, or that which He elsewhere has termed "my commandments" (vs. 10). That which constitutes His will must be comprehended before it can be undertaken. On the other hand, to abide in Christ is, according to verse 10, not a matter of remaining in *union* with Christ, but rather a matter of remaining in *communion* with Christ through obedience. Having learned His will, it is essential that it be obeyed. It becomes, then, a matter of finding and doing the will of Christ. John in his first Epistle calls attention to the lack of confidence toward God which arises in the believer's heart when he has consciously failed to do Christ's will. He writes, "For if our heart condemn us, God is greater than our heart, and knoweth all things. Beloved, if our heart condemn us not, then have we confidence toward God. And whatsoever we ask, we receive of him, because we keep his commandments, and do those things that are pleasing in his sight" (1 John 3:20-22).

John 16:23-24. "And in that day ye shall ask me nothing. Verily, verily, I say unto you, Whatsoever ye shall ask the Father in my name, he will give it you. Hitherto have ye asked nothing in my name: ask, and ye shall receive, that your joy may be full."

In addition to the limitless scope of prayer which this passage asserts, the order of prayer is here revealed and a final declaration is made of the high privilege of praying in the name of Christ. The momentous phrase, "Hitherto have ye asked nothing in my name," is a plain averment of a fact which may easily go unobserved otherwise. The ground of prayer in Christ's name is strictly a new divine administration and so all former prayer, whatever the basis of its appeal, is lacking in this respect. In this all-inclusive statement Old Testament prayers and even the so-called Lord's Prayer—all of which were familiar to the disciples —are comprehended. This teaching by Christ is also distinctive in that it asserts that prayer is not to be addressed to Him—the Second Person. This is reasonable in view of the truth that Christ is the believer's Partner in the practice of prayer and therefore not the Person to be addressed in prayer. In like manner, the Holy Spirit enables the child of God in prayer and therefore is not the One to whom the believer should pray. The right order or form of prayer is to pray to the Father in the name of the Son and through, or by the power of, the Holy Spirit.

In conclusion it should be emphasized that for all believers the greatest of all service is the exercise of prayer to the Father in the name of the Son and that in the power of the Holy Spirit.

g. THE PROMISED RETURN. "Let not your heart be troubled: ye believe in God, believe also in me. In my Father's house are many mansions: if it were not so, I would have told you. I go to prepare a place for you. And if I go and prepare a place for you, I will come again, and receive you unto myself; that where I am, there ye may be also" (14:1-3).

Earlier in this work (Vol. IV) the student has been reminded of the wide difference between two great events which, though in no way related, are each in their turn rightly styled a coming of Christ. The first in the chronological order is the signless, timeless, and prophetically unrelated coming of Christ into the air to gather the Church, His Body and Bride, to Himself; and that event, which might occur at any moment, marks the termination of the Church's pilgrim sojourn on the earth. By their removal the way becomes clear for the concluding of that portion of the Mosaic age which, as represented by Daniel's seventieth week, yet remains to run its course. The period of Daniel's seventieth week is clearly the time of Jehovah's judgments in the earth and the moment of His fulfillment of all His covenants with His earthly people, Israel. This leads to the second coming of Christ per se, which is His glorious appearing. This event constitutes a major theme of Old Testament prediction, itself continued on into the Synoptics and other portions of the New Testament. It is not until the very end of Christ's ministry, as recorded in the Upper Room Discourse, that the first event—that which concerns the Church alone—is introduced. Since this event is an important feature of the future experience of the Church, it is to be expected that Christ would anticipate it in this discourse. This He did as recorded in John 14:1–3, quoted above. In the main, the passages which relate to the first (in their chronological order) of the two events may be distinguished by the fact that in them the movement is from the earth into heaven (cf. John 14:1–3; 1 Thess. 4:16–17), while the movement in the second event is from heaven to earth (cf. Matt. 24:30; 2 Thess. 1:7–9; Rev. 19:11–16). With this general distinction in mind, the words of Christ recorded in the Upper Room Discourse should not be misconstrued. He said: "I will come again, and receive you unto myself." As revealed in 1 Thessalonians 4:13–18, He comes only to the upper-air spaces and the believers are gathered together unto Him (cf. 2 Thess. 2:1).

It is reasonable that this stupendous event, as it relates itself to each Christian in this age, should be given its introduction as a revelation from Christ Himself; and it is equally reasonable that, as the event concerns only those who make up His Bride, it would not be mentioned by Christ until this company are addressed by Him, as they are for the first time in the upper room. Much, indeed, is introduced in the Scriptures generally concerning Christ's coming again to Israel and to the earth, but His call for His Bride is not foreseen until He speaks to them of it in particular. In this discourse, Christ refers in other portions of it to the relation He will sustain to them after His departure and assures them that He will come to them (cf. John 14:18, 28; 16:16, 19, 22); but the clear, all-important declaration respecting the removal of the Church is found only in the passage under consideration.

Beyond the seven major themes of the Upper Room Discourse, designated above, it will be noted that almost every important doctrine of
theology is directly or indirectly included in these five brief chapters of
John: (1) the truth that the Scriptures are inspired—"I have given them
thy word," "Thy word is truth" (John 17:8, 14, 17); (2) revelation respecting the Godhead, for in this portion the separate, individual activities of the Persons of the Trinity are more evident than in any other
portion of the Bible; (3) of the angels, only a passing reference to Satan
as the evil one is included (John 17:15, R.V.); (4) of man and his sin
it is recorded that the unsaved may be enlightened by the Spirit respecting sin, righteousness, and judgment—and in so far as the message is
addressed to the saved, it concerns their cleansing (13:1–20; 15:1–10);
(5) likewise, being addressed to the saved, there is little about the way
of salvation (cf. John 14:6; 16:8–11); (6) in no other Scripture is the
doctrine of the one Body, the basis of all revelation concerning the
Church, so emphasized (cf. John 13:34–35; 14:20; 17:11, 21–23); (7)
of the future, that which immediately concerns the true Church is announced for the first time, namely, the rapture (cf. John 14:1–3). As the
Sermon on the Mount relates itself to the Old Testament, the Upper
Room Discourse relates itself to the Epistles of the New Testament. An
unrelenting study of this discourse is enjoined upon the student—especially as it relates itself to the Epistles of the New Testament.

II. PARABLES

Contrasts may be drawn between the types of the Old Testament and
the parables of the Synoptic Gospels, and yet both portions are quite
as unsatisfactory with respect to the usual manner of their interpretation and their general neglect. The parables contain within themselves
those aspects of truth which they represent, while the type is dependent
upon its combined relation to the antitype. Essential doctrine is thus
not clearly and finally established by the type, but the truth embodied
in the parables is sufficient unto itself. The parables of the Synoptic
Gospels concern Israel to a large degree, while the types relate to a
wider variety of themes. A standard work on the parables for nearly a
century has been *Notes on the Parables of Our Lord* by Richard C.
Trench; nevertheless, though Trench was a scholar of the highest order
in the field of original languages, he possessed slight understanding of

dispensational distinctions apart from which but little progress can be made in the right interpretation of the parables. In concluding his discussion of the distinguishing marks of a parable, Archbishop Trench summarizes thus: "To sum up all then, the parable differs from the fable, moving as it does in a spiritual world, and never transgressing the actual order of things natural,—from the mythus, there being in the latter an unconscious blending of the deeper meaning with the outward symbol, the two remaining separate and separable in the parable,—from the proverb, inasmuch as it is longer carried out, and not merely accidentally and occasionally, but necessarily figurative,—from the allegory, comparing as it does one thing *with* another, at the same time preserving them apart as an inner and an outer, not transferring, as does the allegory, the properties and qualities and relations of one *to* the other" (9th ed., pp. 15–16).

That Christ employed parables in His teaching is evident. In more modern terminology it might be said that He made large use of illustrations. His use of illustrations not only served to irradiate the truth to those to whom He spoke, but these parables which He employed have become the divinely appointed and provided illustrations of the truth for all succeeding generations; however, in His relation to Israel Christ asserted in answer to the disciples' question, "Why speakest thou to them in parables?" (Matt. 13:10), "Because it is given unto you to know the mysteries of the kingdom of heaven, but to them it is not given. For whosoever hath, to him shall be given, and he shall have more abundance: but whosoever hath not, from him shall be taken away even that he hath. Therefore speak I to them in parables: because they seeing see not; and hearing they hear not, neither do they understand. And in them is fulfilled the prophecy of Esaias, which saith, By hearing ye shall hear, and shall not understand; and seeing ye shall see, and shall not perceive: for this people's heart is waxed gross, and their ears are dull of hearing, and their eyes they have closed; lest at any time they should see with their eyes and hear with their ears, and should understand with their heart, and should be converted, and I should heal them. But blessed are your eyes, for they see: and your ears, for they hear. For verily I say unto you, That many prophets and righteous men have desired to see those things which ye see, and have not seen them; and to hear those things which ye hear, and have not heard them" (13:11–17). In this Scripture it is disclosed that Christ not only anticipated the blindness of Israel, which blindness will extend throughout the present age (cf. Rom. 11:25; 2 Cor. 3:13–16), but He purposely veiled His meaning by the use of parables lest Israel should understand. On the other hand, within the perfect plan of God, Israel is held accountable for the hearing and doing of all that He addressed to them either directly or through parables. Since the precross ministry of Christ is so evidently addressed to Israel and concerning her earthly kingdom, it is to be expected that the parables will, to a large degree, represent truth related to that kingdom. The difficulty is no small one for many expositors when confronted with the teaching relative to Israel's divinely imposed blindness—the judicial withholding of vital truth from their understanding. Such difficulties, though complex as related to the divine way of dealing with His chosen people, are much clarified when the divine purpose in the present age is discerned. The veiling of kingdom truth does not in any way lessen its importance, nor does it supply an excuse for students to be confused—as too often they are—regarding these subjects. The parables of Christ may be divided into two classes: (1) those respecting the Messianic kingdom and (2) those that are general in character.

1. MESSIANIC. As bearing upon the Messianic kingdom parables, no more worthy or discriminating tabulation and classification has been found than that by J. G. Princell, a gifted and Biblically informed theologian of two generations ago. His outline is incorporated at this point.

First, Five Parables concerning the Postponement of the Kingdom—(a) Luke 12:35–40; (b) Luke 12:42–48; cf. Matthew 24:45–51; (c) Luke 19:11–27; cf. Matthew 25:14–30; (d) Luke 21:29–33; cf. Matthew 24:32–35; Mark 13:28–31; (e) Mark 13:34–37.

Second, Five Parables respecting the Preparation for the Coming Kingdom during Previous Times—(a) Mark 4:26–29; (b) Mark 4:30–32; cf. Matthew 13:31, 32; Luke 13:18, 19; (c) Matthew 13:33; cf. Luke 13:20, 21; (d) Matthew 13:44; (e) Matthew 13:45, 46.

Third, Six Parables concerning the Establishing of the Kingdom, Who Will Enter it, and Who Will Be the Ruling Element in It—(a) Luke 14:16–24; (b) Matthew 22:2–14; (c) Matthew 18:23–35; (d) Matthew 20:1–16; (e) Matthew 21:28–32; (f) Matthew 21:33–44; cf. Mark 12:1–12; Luke 20:9–18.

Fourth, Three Parables concerning Cleansing, Separation, and Judgment —(a) Matthew 25:1–13; (b) Matthew 25:14–30; (c) Matthew 25:31–46.

Fifth, Two Parables concerning the Final Separation of Evil from the Good—(a) Matthew 13:24–30, 36–43; (b) Matthew 13:47–50.—Unpublished Ms.

2. GENERAL. These may be listed as follows: of the creditor and two debtors (Luke 7:41–50), of the good Samaritan (Luke 10:30–37), of the rich fool (Luke 12:16–34), of the barren fig tree (Luke 13:6–9),

of the building of a tower (Luke 14:28–30), of a king going to war (Luke 14:31–33), of salt (Luke 14:34–35; Matt. 5:13; Mark 9:50), of the threefold restoration (Luke 15:1–32), of the unjust steward (Luke 16:1–13), of service (Luke 17:7–10), of the unjust judge (Luke 18:1–8), and of the Pharisee and the publican (Luke 18:9–14).

III. SPECIAL TEACHINGS

Very much vital truth is set forth in the special or disconnected teachings of Christ. The more important of these are: the great commandments (Mark 12:28–34), the tribute money (Mark 12:13–17), warning respecting hell (Mark 9:42–50), the law of divorce (Mark 10:1–12), warning respecting riches (Mark 10:23–31), Christ's self-revelation in Nazareth (Luke 4:16–30), prayer (Luke 11:1–13), warning respecting the leaven of the Pharisees (Luke 12:1–15), the rich man and Lazarus (Luke 16:19–34), instruction respecting forgiveness (Luke 17:1–6; cf. Matt. 18:21–35), eternal life (John 3:1–21), the Water of life (John 4:1–45), general teaching to the Jews (John 5:17–47), the Bread of life (John 6:1–71), the Light of the world (John 8:1–59), the Good Shepherd (John 10:1–39), special teaching addressed to Andrew and Philip (John 12:23–50).

IV. CONVERSATIONS

It will be noted that some of Christ's more important declarations were made when engaged in conversation with individuals, and these are: with the lawyer (Luke 10:25–37), with the rich young ruler (Luke 18:18–30; cf. Matt. 19:16–22; Mark 10:17–22), with the Jews respecting tribute money (Luke 20:19–26; cf. Matt. 22:15–22; Mark 12:13–17), regarding His own authority (Luke 20:1–8; cf. Matt. 21:23–27; Mark 11:27–33), on the theme of David's Son (Luke 20:39–47; cf. Matt. 22:41–46; Mark 12:35–37), with Nicodemus (John 3:1–21), with the woman at the well (John 4:1–45), with the Jews (John 7:1—8:59), with the man born blind (John 9:1–39), with Judas (John 12:1–11; 13:27), with Pilate (John 18:28–38; cf. Matt. 27:1–14; Mark 15:1–5; Luke 23:1–7, 13–16).

CHAPTER VIII

THE MIRACLES OF CHRIST INCARNATE

THOSE WHO ARE imbued with supernatural resources should manifest supernatural power. The Christian as being immediately related to God —indwelt, guided, and empowered by God—should not be unaccustomed to supernatural features and experiences in his daily life. Since it follows no well-defined laws of procedure, the supernatural in the Christian is a nearer approach to the miraculous than that in nature which is inexplainable. However, a miracle, in the strict use of the word, is some special achievement which is outside the known laws of either human experience or nature. The Bible draws aside the veil and discloses the truth respecting the living, all-powerful God as well as a whole empire of angelic beings—good and evil—with resources and competences which, in the case of God, reach on into infinity, and which, in the case of the angels, transcend all human limitations. No small deceptions—Satan's "lying wonders"—have been wrought in the past and, according to prophecy, even more will these wonders appear in the future (2 Thess. 2:9; cf. Acts 16:16; Rev. 13:1–18). The cessation of signs and wonders after the first generation of the church has given occasion to counterfeit manifestations. This cessation is not due to lack of faith or faithfulness. The greatest of all saints, though like Abraham and Daniel, have not done mighty works in this age. The usual belief that all supernatural manifestations arise with God gives Satan the opportunity to confirm in the minds of many his misrepresentation of doctrine. Without exception, those manifestations of supernatural power which are acclaimed as divine today appear in support of false or incomplete doctrine. As an example of this, such manifestations as have been published are found among people who receive not enough of the truth respecting saving grace to believe that one once saved is always saved, and such limitation of doctrine so devitalizes the gospel that it becomes "another gospel." Yet these misunderstandings are sealed in the minds of many by what is supposed to be manifestations from God, though serving really as a sanction to the perversion of doctrine.

The Bible is itself a supernatural Book and it records supernatural manifestations without hesitation or apology. The whole field of miracles which the Bible presents may be divided into: (1) miracles which belong to the Old Testament order, (2) miracles wrought by Christ, and by His disciples who wrought miracles by His authority (Matt. 10:1) and in His name as was ordained for kingdom preaching (cf. Matt. 10:7–8; Luke 10:17–19), and (3) miracles wrought by various men of the early church, after the death of Christ and after the Day of Pentecost. The present theme concerns only the miracles wrought by Christ. Of the Old Testament miracles it may be said in passing that, in purpose, they resemble closely the miracles wrought by Christ to this extent, that they served as a sign of the divine presence, an attestation of the truth of God with which they were associated. The Old Testament miracles gather largely around two epochs in both of which a new divine order is being set up. The great majority of Old Testament men, such as Noah, Job, Abraham, David, and Daniel did no mighty works or miracles. But to Moses was given the power of signs and wonders, to the end that he might deliver Israel from Egypt and become their divinely acknowledged leader. The effect of the miracle of the Red Sea is declared in these words, "And Israel saw that great work which the LORD did upon the Egyptians: and the people feared the LORD, and believed the LORD, and his servant Moses" (Ex. 14:31). A later need of the supernatural arose in the time of Israel's apostasy, which apostasy Elijah estimated to have included all but himself (1 Kings 19:10). The miracles wrought by Elijah were continued by Elisha. In fact, as Elisha requested of Elijah that a double portion of his spirit might be upon him, his recorded miracles are double the number of those attributed to Elijah. Thus were the people reminded respecting the God of Israel both in the generation to whom Elijah and Elisha ministered and in all succeeding generations. They, like all of God's wonders, "were done once that they might be believed always." How stupendous is the task of confirming a divine testimony as such, of authenticating a message as word from heaven! The fallen, Satan-energized heart of man would hardly believe though an angel spoke from heaven.

Regarding the miracles wrought by men of the early church, there has been some controversy: Not that the signs then wrought are not believed, but that men disagree over why these miracles ceased, as they did in the first generations of the church. Some are disposed to claim that the discontinuation is due to lack of faith and that if a like faith were exercised now these manifestations would return automatically. Over against this is the fact that the most saintly, spiritually blessed of all these generations have exerted no supernatural power. Such is universally the case and only ignorance would contest such an evident fact. So-called manifestations of speaking with tongues and supposed gifts of healing have constantly reappeared and as an assumed divine sealing of doctrine which is not true to the Bible or complete. Not one of these cults holds enough recognition of the gospel of divine grace to believe that the saved one is by grace so identified with Christ that he is secure forever. Satan is ever active with devices, strategies, and lying wonders; and no greater deception—he deceives the whole world—will be found than that of sealing a false or incomplete doctrine with an apparently divine, miraculous manifestation. Others believe that it has pleased God to withdraw the supernatural once the records of the New Testament were completed, and that it is not the purpose of God that the whole age should be characterized by miracles, but rather that the mighty work of the Holy Spirit is vouchsafed to believers to the end that they may live and serve unceasingly by His indwelling power. The unregenerate are not called to believe some divine works, but they are called to believe the divine Word. This important distinction respecting the object of faith is recognized by Christ when He said, "Believe me that I am in the Father, and the Father in me: or else believe me for the very works' sake" (John 14:11). That the illuminating power of the Holy Spirit in the heart when accompanying the proclamation of the gospel is more advantageous than supernatural manifestations could be is evident. A miracle might incite wonder, argument, or curiosity; but it would not have the power to engender in the heart conviction of sin, of righteousness, and of judgment, nor could it create that inner thirst for the Water of life apart from which there is no personal, intelligent appropriation of Christ as Savior. It might be easy to believe that missionaries to the unevangelized would be benefited in their work by supernatural manifestations; but the work to be done in the heart of the unsaved, be they heathen or civilized, if it is to amount to the complete change which saving grace alone can secure, would not be made possible by signs and wonders, but by the enlightening power of the Spirit. Some believed and some did not when Lazarus was raised from the dead. The miracle of a regenerated life is the missionary's greatest attestation to the message which he proclaims.

Turning more specifically to the miracles wrought by Christ, it may be asserted that they were intended to sustain His claim to be Jehovah, the theanthropic Messiah of Israel, and to give divine attestation to His teachings. The miracles wrought by Christ were largely, if not wholly, a vital feature of His kingdom ministry. Miracles, signs, and wonders are evidently the credentials of those who preach the kingdom gospel. It was commanded as the disciples went forth to preach the kingdom of heaven as "at hand" that they were to "heal the sick, cleanse the lepers, raise the dead, cast out devils" (Matt. 10:7–8), and Joel predicts the supernatural in relation to the oncoming kingdom. He states: "And it shall come to pass afterward, that I will pour out my spirit upon all flesh; and your sons and your daughters shall prophesy, your old men shall dream dreams, your young men shall see visions: and also upon the servants and upon the handmaids in those days will I pour out my spirit. And I will shew wonders in the heavens and in the earth, blood, and fire, and pillars of smoke. The sun shall be turned into darkness, and the moon into blood, before the great and the terrible day of the LORD come. And it shall come to pass, that whosoever shall call on the name of the LORD shall be delivered . . . " (Joel 2:28–32; cf. Acts 2: 16–21). It is true that the miracles of Christ suggest His spiritual power. The healing of the sick suggests His power to cleanse from sin, the feeding of the multitude suggests His ability to care for His own, the raising of the dead suggests His power to raise all when and as He may determine.

The miracles of Christ are themselves worthy of God both in their dignity and scope. In this they are far removed from those human inventions which are found in the Apocryphal writings. Those recorded in the *Evangelium Infantiæ* are not only absurd but are incapable of conveying any corresponding truth whatsoever. Since the miracles wrought by Christ indicate the presence of the omnipotent God, it is to be expected that Satan's opposition will be mustered against these mighty works to discredit them. Such opposition has been voiced by unbelief throughout all generations. Since Christ has come into the world and His Jehovah identity is proved by mighty works which are fully commensurate with His Godhead Person, the consideration of His supernatural power is demanded of all who are of a serious mind. These works should be contemplated in the light of all they demonstrate and the result should be unrestrained worship and adoration. Nicodemus gave feeble though true testimony when he said, "Rabbi, we know that thou art a teacher come from God: for no man can do these miracles that thou doest, except God be with him" (John 3:2). From this recognition which was true as far as it went, Christ led Nicodemus on to a right understanding of His own Saviorhood—"whosoever believeth in him should not perish, but have everlasting life"—and to believe on

Christ to one's eternal salvation is vastly more important than to be impressed with mighty works, even though those works demonstrate His divine origin.

In his work, *Notes on the Miracles of Our Lord,* R. C. Trench has made valuable distinctions respecting the different terms used to indicate the supernatural works. This material is here reproduced.

In the discussion upon which now we are entering, the names are manifold; for it is a consequence of this, that, where we have to do with any thing which in many ways is significant, that will have inevitably many names, since no one will exhaust its meaning. Each of these will embody a portion of its essential qualities, will present it upon a single side; and not from the exclusive contemplation of any one, but only of these altogether, will any adequate apprehension of that which we desire to know be obtained. Thus what we commonly call miracles, are in the Sacred Scriptures termed sometimes "wonders," sometimes "signs," sometimes "powers," sometimes, simply "works." These titles they have in addition to some others of rarer occurrence, and which easily range themselves under one or other of these;—on each of which I would fain say a few words, before attempting to make any further advance in the subject.

To take then first the name *"wonder,"* in which the effect of astonishment which the work produces upon the beholder is transferred to the work itself, an effect often graphically portrayed by the Evangelists, when relating our Lord's miracles (Mark 2:12; 4:41; 6:51; 8:37; Acts 3:10, 11), it will at once be felt that this does but touch the matter on the outside. The ethical meaning of the miracle would be wholly lost, were blank astonishment or gaping wonder *all* which they aroused; since the same effect might be produced by a thousand meaner causes. Indeed, it is not a little remarkable, rather is it singularly characteristic of the miracles of the New Testament, that this name "wonders" is never applied to them but in connection with other names. They are continually "signs *and* wonders," or "signs" or "powers" alone, but never "wonders" alone. Not that the miracle, considered simply as a wonder, as an astonishing event which the beholders can reduce to no law with which they are acquainted, is even as such without its meaning and its purpose; that purpose being that it should forcibly startle from the mere dream of a sense-bound existence, and, however it may not be itself an appeal to the spiritual in man, should yet be a summons to him that he should open his eyes to the spiritual appeal which is about to be addressed to him.

But the miracle, besides being a "wonder," is also a *"sign,"* a token and indication of the near presence and working of God. In this word the ethical end and purpose of the miracle comes out the *most* prominently, as in "wonder" the least. They are signs and pledges of something more than and beyond themselves (Isaiah 7:11; 38:7); they are valuable, not so much for what they are, as for what they indicate of the grace and power of the doer, or of the connection in which he stands with a higher world. Oftentimes they are thus seals of power set to the person who accomplishes them ("the Lord confirming the word by *signs* following," Mark 16:20; Acts 14:3; Heb. 2:4), legitimating acts, by which he claims to be attended to as a messenger from God. We find the word continually used in senses such as these: Thus, "What *sign* showest thou?" (John 2:18) was the question which the Jews asked, when they wanted the Lord to justify the things which he was doing, by showing that he had especial authority to do them. Again they say, "We would see a *sign* from thee" (Matt. 12:38); "Show us a *sign* from heaven" (Matt. 16:1). St. Paul speaks of himself as having "the *signs* of an apostle" (2 Cor. 12:12), in other words, the tokens which should mark him out as such. Thus, too, in the Old Testament, when God sends Moses to deliver Israel he furnishes him with two "signs." He warns him that Pharaoh will require him to legitimate his mission, to produce his credentials that he is indeed God's ambassador, and equips him with the powers which shall justify him as such, which, in other words, shall be his "signs" (Ex. 7:9, 10). He "gave *a sign*" to the prophet whom he sent to protest against the will-worship of Jeroboam (1 Kings 13:3). At the same time it may be as well here to observe that the "sign" is not of necessity a miracle, although only as such it has a place in our discussion. Many a common matter, for instance any foretold coincidence or event, may be to a believing mind a sign, a seal set to the truth of a foregoing word. Thus the angels give to the shepherds for "a sign" their finding the child wrapt in the swaddling clothes (Luke 2:12). Samuel gives to Saul three "signs" that God has indeed appointed him king over Israel, and only the last of these is linked with aught supernatural (1 Sam. 10:1–9). The prophet gave Eli the death of his two sons as "a sign" that his threatening word should come true (1 Sam. 2:34). God gave to Gideon a sign in the camp of the Midianites of the victory which he should win (Judges 7:9–15), though it does not happen that the word occurs in that narration. Or it is possible for a man, under a strong conviction that the hand of God is leading him, to set such and such a contingent event as a sign to himself, the falling out of which in this way or in that he will accept as an intimation from God of what he would have him to do. Examples of this also are not uncommon in Scripture (Gen. 24:16; Judges 6: 36–40; 1 Sam. 14:8–13).

Frequently, also, the miracles are styled *"powers,"* or *"mighty works,"* that is, of God. As in the term "wonder" or "miracle," the effect is transferred and gives a name to the cause, so here the cause gives its name to the effect. The *"power"* dwells originally in the divine Messenger (Acts 6:8; 10:38; Rom. 15:9); is one with which he is himself equipped of God. Christ is thus in the highest sense that which Simon blasphemously suffered himself to be named, "The great *Power* of God" (Acts 8:10). But then by an easy transition the word comes to signify the exertions and separate puttings forth of this power. These are "powers" in the plural, although the same word is now translated in our version, "wonderful works" (Matt. 7:22), and now, "mighty works" (Matt. 11:20; Mark 6:14; Luke 10:13), and still more frequently, "miracles" (Acts 2:22; 19:11; 1 Cor. 12:10, 28; Gal. 3:5), in this last case giving sometimes such tautologies as this, "miracles *and* wonders" (Acts 2:22; Heb. 2:4) and always causing to be lost something of the express force of the word,—how it points to new *powers* which have come into, and are working in, this world of ours.

These three terms, of which we have hitherto sought to unfold the meaning, occur thrice together (Acts 2:22; 2 Cor. 12:12; 2 Thess. 2:9), although each time in a different order. They are all, as has already been noted in the case of two of them, rather descriptive of different sides of the same works, than themselves different classes of works. An example of one of our Lord's miracles may show how it may at once be all these. The healing of the paralytic, for example (Mark 2:1–12), was a *wonder*, for they who beheld it "were all *amazed*"; it was a *power*, for the man at Christ's word "arose, took up his bed, and went out before them all"; it was a *sign*, for it gave token that one greater than men deemed was among them; it stood in connection with a higher fact, of which it was the sign and seal (cf. 1 Kings 13:3; 2 Kings 1:10), being wrought that they might "know that the Son of man hath power on earth to forgive sins."

A further term by which St. John very frequently names the miracles is eminently significant. They are very often with him simply *"works"* (5:36; 7:21; 10:25, 32, 38; 14:11, 12; 15:24; see also Matt. 11:2). The wonderful is in his eyes only the natural form of working for him who is dwelt in by all the fulness of God; he must, out of the necessity of his higher being, bring forth these works greater than man's. They are the periphery of that circle whereof he is the centre. The great miracle is the Incarnation; all else, so to speak, follows naturally and of course. It is no wonder that he whose name is "Wonderful" (Isa. 9:6), does works of wonder; the only wonder would be if he did them not. The sun in the heavens is itself a wonder, but not that, being what it is, it rays forth its effluences of light and heat. These miracles are the fruit after its kind, which the divine tree brings forth; and may, with a deep truth, be styled "works" of Christ, with no further addition or explanation.— 2nd Amer. ed., pp. 9–14

CONCLUSION

In terminating this consideration of the incarnate Son of God in His life and teachings here on earth, restatement is made that, in view of the fact that His earth-ministry occupies almost two-fifths of the entire New Testament, it is fitting that this important body of truth be given a correspondingly extended treatment in any Christology which is true to the Divine Record. Christ came as the manifestation of God to the restricted minds of sinful men. He is God manifest in the flesh— the fullness of the Godhead bodily, but nonetheless God.

Chapter IX

THE SUFFERINGS AND DEATH OF CHRIST INCARNATE

ALL THAT MAY be known respecting the efficacious sufferings and sacrifice of Christ, the Son of God, is contained in the revelation which God has been pleased to release to men; therefore the theology which Christ's death engenders is wholly contained in and wholly dependent upon the Scriptures of truth. In Volume III under Soteriology, the distinctive doctrinal aspects of Christ's death have been presented. The present discussion will be devoted to an analysis of the Sacred Text, from which all right understanding must be derived. Fourteen achievements, stupendous in character, which were wrought by Christ through His death have been indicated already, and the sum of these demonstrates that this great event is the center of all Christian doctrine. Since there can be no saving relation to God apart from the redemption which Christ has accomplished, His death becomes the ground of nearly all aspects of Christian truth. The present approach to this great theme, accordingly, will not be related to aspects of doctrine, as in the previous volume, but instead to the order in which it is found in the progressive revelation of the whole Bible. These proposed divisions are: (1) the death of Christ typified, (2) the death of Christ prophesied, (3) the death of Christ historically declared in the Synoptics, (4) the death of Christ according to John, (5) the death of Christ according to Paul, (6) the death of Christ according to Peter, and (7) the death of Christ according to the letter to the Hebrews.

I. IN TYPES

Reference has been made earlier in this volume (Chap. II) to the types of Christ in general. This consideration is to be restricted to the types of Christ in His death. At least sixteen of these may be identified. These can, at best, be treated with brevity.

Aaron (Ex. 28:1; Lev. 8:12). The priesthood of Christ was foreseen in two types—that of Aaron and that of Melchizedek. The Aaronic type anticipated the offering Christ would make of Himself without spot to God. In this aspect of typology Christ was both the Lamb sacrificed and the officiating Priest who executed the offering (cf. John 10:17). Thus the whole range of truth respecting the death of Christ and His shed blood is foreshadowed in the Aaronic type. However, the Melchizedek type speaks of Christ in resurrection and continuing forever in glory.

The Brazen Altar (Ex. 27:1). Since the Old Testament sacrifice was offered upon the brazen altar, that altar became the type or typical anticipation of the cross upon which Christ died. He, a spotless Sacrifice, was the just One who offered Himself for the unjust.

The Two Birds (Lev. 14:4). As in the instance of the two goats, two creatures are required to complete one type. One bird is slain, which represents Christ as in His sacrificial death; the other bird, dipped in the blood of the slain bird and released, represents Christ in resurrection taking His own blood into heaven on behalf of those for whom He died. His redemptive work which He accomplished by His death having been completed, He arose from the dead. Death had no more claim upon Him (Rom. 4:25).

The Sacrificial Blood (Lev. 17:11). No single type, except it be that of the lamb, is more fraught with meaning than that of the sacrificial blood as it was shed upon the altar. Of this Dr. C. I. Scofield writes on Leviticus 17:11, "(1) The value of the 'life' is the measure of the value of the 'blood.' This gives the blood of Christ its inconceivable value. When it was shed the sinless God-man gave His life. 'It is not possible that the blood of bulls and of goats should take away sins' (Heb. 10:4). (2) It is not the blood in the veins of the sacrifice, but the blood *upon the altar* which is efficacious. The Scripture knows nothing of salvation by the imitation or influence of Christ's life, but only by that life yielded up on the cross. The meaning of all sacrifice is here explained. Every offering was an execution of the sentence of the law upon a substitute for the offender, and every such offering pointed forward to that substitutional death of Christ which alone vindicated the righteousness of God in passing over the sins of those who offered the typical sacrifices (Rom. 3:24, 25; Ex. 29:36)" (*Scofield Reference Bible,* p. 150).

The Sweet Savor Offerings (Lev. 1:1—3:17). In the most exhaustive manner the five offerings of the first five chapters of Leviticus set forth that accomplished by Christ in His death. The first three—the burnt offering, the meal offering, and the peace offering—look forward to that in Christ's death which was well-pleasing—a sweet savor—to the Father. Of these (a) the burnt offering or the whole burnt offering speaks of

Christ offering Himself without spot to God and as a substitute in that the believer has neither obedience nor righteousness of his own to present to God; but both obedience and righteousness, which He is in Himself, were presented by the Savior in behalf of sinners. Quite apart from the remission of sin, the provision of that which is lacking and which the sinner must gain if ever to be accepted of God is released by Christ in His death and made available for all who believe. Salvation thus secures far more than the canceling of evil; it also provides the saved one with that merit or standing which heaven and holiness demand. The details of the whole burnt offering are set forth in Leviticus 1:3–17. (b) The meal offering is described in Leviticus 2:1–16, and represents the perfection of Christ in whom the Father delights and whose fullness is imputed to the child of God (John 1:16; Col. 2:9–10). (c) The peace offering recognizes the truth that Christ has made peace between the believer and God through His sacrificial death. This offering does not magnify the bearing of sin, but rather the result in bringing about a peace relation between God and the believer (cf. Rom. 5:1).

The Non-Sweet Savor Offerings (Lev. 4:1—5:19). Christians generally are more familiar with the truth represented by the non-sweet savor offerings, since these underlie the whole divine freedom to forgive sin, and, as has been before indicated, the gospel as preached by the great majority—if not universally—offers to the unsaved little more than the divine remission of sin. Such, indeed, is not to be esteemed lightly, but far more and of measureless value is the divine provision through Christ's death whereby all the merit of the Son of God is reckoned over to those who believe. It is so reckoned and the sinner is thus blessed when he has Christ as his portion; however, that limitless benefit is as much a message to the unsaved as the remission of sin. It is a vital part of the good news which the gospel represents. It is true that some are saved on a restricted presentation of the divine provisions; but it stands to reason and is experimentally demonstrated that many more may be reached when all the antitype truth of the five offerings—the sweet savor as well as the non-sweet savor aspects of Christ's death—is presented.

The Goat as a Sacrifice (Lev. 1:10). Among the several animals allowed for sacrifice the goat has a peculiar significance. As a symbol of that which God rejects (cf. Matt. 25:33), the goat presents Christ as numbered with the transgressors (cf. Isa. 53:12), made sin and a curse for sinners.

The Two Goats (Lev. 16:5). On the great Day of Atonement a bullock was first offered for the sins of the high priest, which sacrifice finds no antitype in the Savior. That offering was most essential for the preparation of the high priest for the service he was appointed to render that day, as himself a type of Christ. Two goats were selected and one sacrificed. The blood of the slain goat was carried by the high priest into the holiest place, which typified Christ's death and His presentation of His blood in heaven as the divinely provided remedy for the sins of the people. Upon the second goat hands were laid, which ceremony acknowledged the transfer of sin's penalties to the substitute, and then the goat was led away into the wilderness, which serves as a symbol of oblivion, and thus was foreshadowed the perfect disposition of sin by Christ in His death and burial (cf. Rom. 6:2–3; 1 Cor. 15:3–4).

The Kinsman Redeemer (Lev. 25:49; Isa. 59:20). Earlier portions of this work have made much of the Kinsman Redeemer type. It sustains the truth of its antitype, which is that only the great kinsman may redeem. To this end Christ came into the human family. Christ met every requirement of such a redeemer. He was free from any share in the calamity from which He must redeem others, He was of the human family by the incarnation, He was able to pay the price of redemption —which was no less than the shed blood of the Son of God—and He was willing to redeem. In every respect Christ is the one perfect Redeemer.

The Lamb (Isa. 53:7; John 1:29). When tested and proved to be without blemish, the lamb is the type of Christ which is most employed by the Holy Spirit throughout the Word of God. This one type is inexhaustible in all its representation's of the sacrificial, substitutional death of Christ.

The Laver (Ex. 30:18). Every priest was required to be cleansed at the brazen laver before each service. Of how much greater importance it is for the believer-priest of this age to be cleansed constantly if he would be effective in his life and testimony! The blood of Christ constantly applied is the antitype of the Old Testament laver (cf. 1 John 1:7,9).

The Passover (Ex. 12:11). In the Passover type of Christ unlimited riches of truth are involved. The lamb must be without spot, it must be tested with respect to its fitness, its blood must be shed, and the shed blood must be applied. The oft-repeated celebration of the Passover was only a memorial and provided nothing of either salvation or security for those who observed it.

The Red Heifer (Num. 19:2). A peculiar provision in the antitype is foreseen in the type of the red heifer sacrifice. As the ashes were preserved and became the means of a perpetual statute for cleansing, so the blood of Christ is ever the cleansing agent in the believer's daily need (1 John 1:9).

The Rock (Ex. 17:6; Num. 20:8). On this extended type Dr. C. I. Scofield writes, "The rock, type of life through the Spirit by grace: (1) Christ the Rock (1 Cor. 10:4). (2) The people utterly unworthy (Ex. 17:2; Eph. 2:1–6). (3) Characteristics of life through grace: (*a*) free (John 4:10; Rom. 6:23; Eph. 2:8); (*b*) abundant (Rom. 5:20; Psa. 105:41; John 3:16); (*c*) near (Rom. 10:8); (*d*) the people had only to take (Isa. 55:1). The smitten-rock aspect of the death of Christ looks toward the outpouring of the Holy Spirit as a result of accomplished redemption, rather than toward our *guilt*. It is the affirmative side of John 3:16. 'Not perish' speaks of atoning blood; 'but have' speaks of life bestowed" (*Ibid.*, p. 91).

Two Persons (Gen. 22:2). Isaac offered upon the altar represents many specific features of Christ's death. The type is strengthened by the fact that Abraham represents God the Father offering His only Son (Gen. 22:2; Rom. 8:32). Isaac represents Christ obedient unto death, while the ram caught in the thicket (Gen. 22:13) introduces again the ever reappearing theme of substitution.

Joseph (Gen. 37:20–27). A portion only of the extended type of Christ which Joseph provides relates to the feature of death. As Joseph was rejected and all but murdered by his brethren, so Christ not only was rejected but did die at the hand of the rulers of His people.

II. IN PROPHECY

Prediction in the Old Testament concerning the death of Christ is second, in extent, only to that which relates to His first and second advents. Prophecy respecting His death may be divided into four parts for purposes of study: (1) a major historical prediction, (2) a major doctrinal prediction, (3) various lesser predictions, and (4) Christ's own declaration.

1. THE MAJOR HISTORICAL PREDICTION. That the 22nd Psalm is an anticipation of the crucifixion scene can be denied only by blind prejudice—such as is discovered in the unbelieving whether Jew or Gentile. The first portion of this Psalm (vss. 1–21) is evidently a record of what Christ addressed to God the Father during the six hours of His crucifixion suffering. Not one word of this extended context, it will be seen, is uttered by any other than Christ Himself, nor is any

word of His thus spoken directed to any other than the One addressed in the opening words, "My God." Added to the much esteemed seven sayings of the cross, which are recorded in the four Gospels, are these twenty-one verses with their immeasurable wealth of revelation, and all from the lips of the dying Savior. This Psalm was written one thousand years before Christ died and, though it vividly describes a death by crucifixion, it was written many centuries before any human mind had conceived of that manner of torture. The Psalm opens with an address to God inquiring why the Speaker is forsaken of God. This cry with its implied limitations relative to understanding arose from the humanity of the Savior. This truth is evidenced by the fact that His address employs the title *God* rather than *Father*. As has been observed, the First Person is the God of the humanity of Christ, but not the God of His Deity, or of the Second Person. Later in the record He declares, "I was cast upon thee from the womb: thou art my God from my mother's belly" (vs. 10). Having uttered this initial plea, He at once vindicates God by the words, "But thou art holy." This is a word of complete trust and confidence in the midst of such an abandonment. Why, indeed, should He be forsaken at all? Naught had He done amiss in all His years on earth and the Father has declared that in Him He was well pleased. The answer is that the Sufferer was being *made* an offering for sin and from such a thing the Father's face is turned away. The Sacred Text records the experience of two others who in the time of great testing have vindicated God—Job (Job 1:21; 2:10) and the Shunammite woman (2 Kings 4:26).

For a clear comprehension of the redeeming work of Christ on the cross, it is essential that the fact of His humanity with all its actual limitations should be recognized. As God in Christ reconciling the world unto Himself, He knew the full meaning of His suffering and death, but as the suffering Lamb He learned obedience respecting the Father's will in regard to those things which were not known hitherto. That an actually contradictory attitude toward one and the same thing could exist cannot be understood. Nevertheless the unexplainable feature of this fact does not militate against the reality of it; nor should it be allowed to modify to the least degree belief that, on the one hand, Christ's humanity was subject to normal human limitations, or, on the other hand, His Deity was free from limitation with its omniscience and omnipotence. It is a grievous error to suppose that, because of His Deity, His human problems were all but done away; and it is equally erroneous to contend that, because of the presence in Him of His humanity, His Deity was suppressed to any degree.

According to verses 4 and 5 of the Psalm, Christ is reported as saying to His God that He is the first and only individual in all human history to put His trust in Jehovah and find Him to fail. The subsequent addition of nearly two thousand years of history has not changed this fact, that Christ alone has suffered abandonment in the midst of a perfect trust in Jehovah. This stupendous truth only increases the initial problem of *why* this One should be forsaken. It is not difficult to find a reason why a sinner might be forsaken of Jehovah, but in this instance it is the only One in Himself well-pleasing to Jehovah. This is the holy, spotless, undefiled Son of God. The answer respecting why is found only in the fact that He was a substitute for others who were and are meritless before God.

In verses 6 to 8 Christ recounts the utter rejection of Himself by those who are watching His crucifixion. In their eyes He is "a worm, and no man." That which His tormentors actually did say is predicted in verse 8. It reads, "He trusted on the LORD that he would deliver him: let him deliver him, seeing he delighted in him." In no instance of human history is the sovereignty of God and the freedom of the human will so brought into juxtaposition as in the crucifixion of Christ. There could be no doubt that the death of Christ was divinely determined from all eternity, both with regard to the fact of it and the manner of it. He was to be executed by "wicked hands" (Acts 2:23). The very words they would say (vs. 8) and the means they would employ (vss. 16–18) were anticipated in this 22nd Psalm a thousand years beforehand; yet in the most unrestrained manner these men followed what was to them the inclination of their own wills. For this crime, though divinely determined from all eternity, they are declared to be guilty—even the Savior Himself prayed that their sin might be forgiven. Had there been no crime of crucifixion, from all appearances there would have been no redemption from any sin. For the Savior to declare, then, as in verse 15—"and thou [Jehovah] hast brought me into the dust of death" —does not lessen the problem of His suffering and death. The God to whom He speaks is charged with His death. He also at once enters a charge against the wicked who have "enclosed" Him, who have "pierced my hands and my feet." It is thus true that He died at the hands of His Father (cf. Rom. 3:25; 8:32; John 1:29; 3:16), but equally true that He died at the hands of men, who could do no more than commit a tragic crime although no thanks is ever due them for any part they took in this advantageous death. On the other hand, the Father wrought a reconciliation through the sacrifice of His Son, and so to Him be the honor and glory and thanksgiving forever.

2. THE MAJOR DOCTRINAL PREDICTION. The preceding theme is evidence that the doctrinal element could hardly be eliminated from any consideration of the death of Christ. However, the prediction set forth in Isaiah 52:13—53:12, though a statement of facts, is distinctly doctrinal and from that point of approach is all but inexhaustible. Again the humanity of Christ as involved in His sacrificial death is in view. He is, according to the opening declaration (52:13), Jehovah's Servant, One who because committed to do Jehovah's will shall in all things, especially in His death in behalf of others, deal prudently. The reward for so doing is that He shall be exalted very high. Thus, also, it is written in the Philippian Epistle (2:6–11) that He who humbled Himself and became obedient unto death is highly exalted. In His humanity He was made an ignominious sacrifice and His face was marred to the extent that it lost the semblance of a man (52:14); yet this afflicted One shall sprinkle many nations and before Him kings shall be silent (52:15). The 53rd chapter opens with the challenge, "Who hath believed our report?" This will at once be identified as a far look into the future, when the value of that death in the salvation of men shall depend upon a simple response of faith to the gospel report. Not often in the Old Testament are men said to have something to believe (cf. Gen. 15:6); rather they are enjoined to do the whole law of God. Isaiah, chapter 53, is a declaration of that which the Savior wrought in His death and of the benefit secured thereby. It presents no directions for human action or faithfulness. "The arm of Jehovah" is not revealed to every one any more than it is true that all believe the gospel report. To those who do believe, the arm is revealed. The phrase "the arm of Jehovah" is suggestive when compared with Psalm 8:3, which states: "When I consider thy heavens, the work of thy fingers, the moon and the stars, which thou hast ordained." In the one instance the creation of solar systems is likened to God's finger-play; but in the other instance the saving of a lost soul requires the almighty arm of Jehovah to be made bare, to the end that His utmost power may be exercised. No greater exertion could confront the Almighty than that which He has put forth for the salvation of men. That Jehovah might save, He took the sinner's place in the most exact kind of substitution. This is the dominant theme of this entire context. Here it is recorded: "He is despised and rejected of men;

a man of sorrows, and acquainted with grief: and we hid as it were our faces from him; he was despised, and we esteemed him not. Surely he hath borne our griefs, and carried our sorrows: yet we did esteem him stricken, smitten of God, and afflicted. But he was wounded for our transgressions, he was bruised for our iniquities: the chastisement of our peace was upon him; and with his stripes we are healed. All we like sheep have gone astray; we have turned every one to his own way; and the LORD hath laid on him the iniquity of us all. . . . For the transgression of my people was he stricken. . . . When thou shalt make his soul an offering for sin. . . . He shall bear their iniquities. . . . He bare the sin of many." Little wonder that the high priest was moved to say regarding Christ's death: "Ye know nothing at all, nor consider that it is expedient for us, that one man should die for the people, and that the whole nation perish not" (John 11:49–50). The Holy Spirit adds these explanatory words, "And this spake he not of himself: but being high priest that year, he prophesied that Jesus should die for that nation" (vs. 51). Later it is reported of the same Caiaphas, "Now Caiaphas was he, which gave counsel to the Jews, that it was expedient that one man should die for the people" (18:14). The great joy that was set before Him for which He endured the cross and despised the shame (cf. Heb. 12:2) is anticipated in the words with which this doctrinal prediction closes: "He shall see his seed, he shall prolong his days, and the pleasure of the LORD shall prosper in his hand. . . . Therefore will I divide him a portion with the great, and he shall divide the spoil with the strong; because he hath poured out his soul unto death: and he was numbered with the transgressors; and he bare the sin of many, and made intercession for the transgressors" (Isa. 53:10, 12).

3. MINOR PREDICTIONS. Only some of the brief predictions of the Old Testament which anticipate the death of Christ are to be noted.

Genesis 3:15. "And I will put enmity between thee and the woman, and between thy seed and her seed; it shall bruise thy head, and thou shalt bruise his heel."

This proclamation is notable not only for the direct message which it conveys, but for the early time of its utterance. It is a divine pronouncement, quite apart from human agencies, and concerns but one feature of Christ's death, namely, its relation to Satan and through Satan indirectly to all fallen angels. The great crisis of the cross as it bears upon Satan is in view and while Christ was to bruise Satan's head, Satan, in turn, was to bruise Christ's heel. By so much it is manifest that Christ's death was, to an unrevealed extent and in the permissive will of God, an attack by Satan upon the Son of God. The triumph of the latter is sure, as a wound in Satan's head speaks of destruction while a bruising of the heel is at most but an injury.

Isaiah 50:6. "I gave my back to the smiters, and my cheeks to them that plucked off the hair: I hid not my face from shame and spitting."

The details of this prediction are too specific to be misapplied. In the preceding verse the testimony is given by the suffering One that "the Lord GOD hath opened mine ear," which doubtless refers to the sealing of the voluntary slave (cf. Ex. 21:1–6; Ps. 40:6, and all passages bearing on Christ's obedience to the Father's will), and in nothing was He "rebellious, neither turned away back." This obedience led Him into these sufferings and into death.

Zechariah 12:10; 13:6–7. "And I will pour upon the house of David, and upon the inhabitants of Jerusalem, the spirit of grace and of supplications: and they shall look upon me whom they have pierced, and they shall mourn for him, as one mourneth for his only son, and shall be in bitterness for him, as one that is in bitterness for his firstborn. . . . And one shall say unto him, What are these wounds in thine hand? Then he shall answer, Those with which I was wounded in the house of my friends. Awake, O sword, against my shepherd, and against the man that is my fellow, saith the LORD of hosts: smite the shepherd, and the sheep shall be scattered: and I will turn mine hand upon the little ones."

The future mourning of Israel over their part in the crucifixion of Christ occupies an extended place in prophecy (cf. Isa. 61:2–3; Matt. 24:30). This prediction asserts that their mourning will be over the fact that, in His crucifixion, they pierced Him. When He comes again, Israel will recognize Him by the wounds which He bears. Dr. A. C. Gaebelein writes at this juncture in his volume *Studies in Zechariah* (pp. 121, 124) as follows:

The mourning then is described as a universal one. All the families will mourn; family by family apart, and their wives apart. Such a mourning and weeping has never before been seen in the earth nor will there be one like it again. But why mourning and weeping? Should there not rather be joy and feasting, gladness and hallelujahs? The hallelujahs will come during the entire millennium, but the beginning will be mourning, national, by Israel. The mourning is on account of Him, Jehovah, who has appeared in His glory and whom they now behold. The long-expected Messiah has at last appeared, and He is Jehovah. . . . There is still another passage which is in close connection with the appearing of Jehovah, the pierced One, in Zechariah 12, namely, Revelation 1:7, "Behold He comes with the clouds, and every eye shall see Him, and they which have pierced Him and all the tribes of the land shall wail because of Him. Yea. Amen." This passage corresponds with the one before us in Zechariah. The tribes in Revelation are the same as mentioned in Zechariah, and the wailing in Revelation stands for the mourning with which the twelfth chapter in Zechariah closes. . . . They see the sign in the heavens and there will be the glad shout, "Blessed is He that cometh in the name of Jehovah, this is our God, we have waited for Him." And now they behold a person upon that cloud. He is a Son of Man. Again they look and they see that His hands and His feet and His side are pierced. Who can this be with pierced hands, feet and side, who cometh thus in power and glory from the heavens to save His people? The truth so long denied by them flashes upon them, "This is Jesus of Nazareth, the King of the Jews, the rejected One, the One who suffered that shameful death on yonder hill, whose hands and feet were pierced, and from whose loving side and heart the Roman spear drew forth blood and water." Jehovah-Jesus, the pierced One, is seen again.

Dr. H. A. Ironside adds here, as written in his *Notes on the Minor Prophets* (pp. 406–7):

The word "look" might be rendered "contemplate." It implies an earnest attention, beholding with thoughtfulness, that every lineament of His face may be imprinted upon their souls. His once-marred visage, His pierced hands and side—all will be indelibly impressed upon them. When they thus learn that He who was spurned as a malefactor and a blasphemer was really the Lord of glory, their grief and repentance will know no bounds. We have two New Testament pictures of this scene: Thomas the apostle, called Didymus (the twin), believed when he saw. In the remnant of Judah, the other twin— may I say?—will come to the front, equally unbelieving till the marks of spear and nails shall prove convincing. Then in Saul of Tarsus we have a preeminent picture of the same remnant. Hating the name of Jesus, He goes on his way, zealously persecuting all who love that name, till arrested by a light from heaven: his eyes, blinded to earth's glory, peer into the holiest; and there, upon the throne of God, he beholds the Nazarene! Thus he was one born before the time; that is, before the time when, by a similar sight, the remnant will be brought to cry, as he did, "Lord, what wilt Thou have me to do?"

While these references to Christ's death are as a retrospect, when that death is before Israel in the latter times, these Scriptures serve also to indicate that these features—the recognition, the mourning, the smiting of the shepherd, and the scattering of the flock (cf. Matt. 26: 31)—were foreseen many centuries before Christ died.

4. Christ's Predictions. Though Christ repeatedly announced His oncoming death (Matt. 16:21; 17:22–23; 20:17–19; 26:12, 28, 31; Mark 9:32–34; 14:8, 24, 27; Luke 9:22, 44–45; 18:31–34; 22:20; John 2:19–21; 10:17–18; 12:7), it never really reached the consciousness of His disciples. Doubtless it was withheld from them; but a deeper reason for their inability to understand is found in the fact that, up to the

time of His death and even after (cf. Acts 1:6–7), the disciples, like all others who followed Him, were centered in their thought and expectation on the realization of the long-predicted, Messianic, earthly kingdom. Though during the three and one-half years these men preached constantly under the direction and authority of Christ, they could have preached no gospel based upon Christ's death and resurrection. Of those events—so basic in the gospel of divine grace—they knew nothing. This fact is a final answer to those who—too often without due thought—have supposed that the gospel of grace based on Christ's death and resurrection was not only the message of the twelve during Christ's earthly ministry, but was shared by the saints of the Old Testament. The fact that Christ foresaw His death and resurrection while He at the same time announced His kingdom as at hand, does not lend authority to any to assume that these are but one and the same thing. On the contrary, it is thus revealed that Christ with infinite clarity indicated the distinctions between His two advents, though, by the very nature of the case, He could not proclaim these distinctions before the time of His death (cf. Matt. 23:38—25:46; John 14:1–3). He did forecast His coming and kingdom to Peter, James, and John in the mount of transfiguration. It is a study of vital import, yet almost wholly neglected, how the second advent was introduced by Christ both before and after His death and resurrection. The kingdom gospel—unrelated to His death and resurrection—was abruptly terminated before its completion by the death of the King. It is not a function of a king to die. "Long live the king!" However, that very death and resurrection became the ground of a new message of sovereign grace apart from all human works of merit and is the divine appeal for the outcalling of a heavenly people. The hour must come when the Church will be completed and removed from the earth. It is then, without fail, that God returns to the uncompleted purpose respecting a kingdom over Israel in the earth, and that by virtue, not of His death, but by the power and coming again of the King. Christ predicted both His death and the coming again and all that He will accomplish when He returns.

III. IN THE SYNOPTICS

As may be deducted from what has gone before, the Synoptics, since they are largely concerned with His purpose and message, do not feature the death and resurrection of Christ beyond the historical record of that which occurred in connection with His death and resurrection. They do record Christ's prediction respecting His death and also the instituting of the Lord's Supper as a memorial of that death. These Gospels recount the life and action of Christ and His disciples in the days before Christ's death was believed, and therefore before that death could enter into the doctrinal understanding of His followers. In all this the Gospel recorded by John is different, as will be observed in the next division of this chapter. While the testimony of such a portion of Scripture as the 22nd Psalm is concerned with, and restricted to, the thoughts and words of Christ while on the cross, the Gospels, including John, tell the historical facts about that which was said and done by many people. The narrative is a true one indited by the Holy Spirit. The arrest, the trial, the scourging, and the crucifixion are told in terms of perfect accuracy. The death of Christ being central in doctrine, central in history, and central in human life and experience is well sustained by these infallible records. As certainly as a sacrificial body was provided for the greatest sacrifice (Heb. 10:5) and as certainly as all types and prophecies anticipated the blood actually to be shed before it thereby became efficacious, so certainly do the inspired records of the Gospels give final assurance that that which the heart of God required the judgment of angels demanded, and the need of man necessitated, was wrought out perfectly in the sufferings and death of Christ. Thus these historical documents assume an importance far beyond the mere tabulation of immediate facts related to the life and death of a man— though He be the greatest of all. Meditation upon these God-breathed chronicles cannot help but serve a large purpose in the full understanding and heart response to the supreme, divine sacrifice (cf. Gal. 6:14).

IV. IN JOHN'S WRITINGS

This part of the subject in hand may be divided in a threefold manner: (a) as recorded in John's Gospel, (b) as recorded in the Epistles by John, and (c) as recorded in the Revelation.

1. THE GOSPEL. Every attentive student awake to sacred realities recognizes the peculiar spiritual character of the writings by John, as he reports the death and resurrection of Christ. Even his historical narratives of these events, like all of his Gospel, look on into the fathomless depths of divine grace. There are in all, and not including his historical chronicle of the cross, seven momentous and consequential passages to be considered in this Gospel.

John 1:29. "The next day John seeth Jesus coming unto him, and saith, Behold the Lamb of God, which taketh away the sin of the world."

In two recorded utterances, John the Baptist, as declared by the Apostle John, reaches out into the oncoming glories of divine grace made possible through the death and resurrection of Christ. Since the preaching of John the Baptist, as set forth in the Synoptics, is so drastically legal and so clearly a call to a merit system, the recognition of the ground and fact of a grace relationship, presented only in John's Gospel, is significant. The entire context of John 1:15–34 constitutes a rare unfolding of the grace vision accorded in some measure to John the Baptist. But two of these utterances by John may be noted here. In 1:29 one is written as quoted above. The great forerunner—to whom evidently it was not given to understand that the Messianic kingdom which he announced was to be rejected and postponed, with a new heavenly, divine purpose to be ushered in—did, nevertheless, by the Holy Spirit announce the immeasurable declarations of divine grace. John the Baptist could not fail to comprehend to some degree that the title "Lamb of God," which he himself employed, implied a sacrificial death; and the assurance that He would take away the sin of the world measured an achievement far beyond the bounds of his own nation or of the usual Messianic expectation—but then have not prophets often spoken beyond the range of their own understanding? In fact, is not this great proclamation far beyond the understanding of all human minds? It is averred that the sin of the world is taken away by the dying Lamb. The scope of this undertaking—something to affect the whole *cosmos* world (cf. John 3:16)—must not be misinterpreted. There is no reference here to the elect of this age, else language ceases to serve as an expression of truth. The Church is a company saved out of the *cosmos* and therefore not to be confused with the *cosmos*. It is true that the Scriptures specify that Christ died for the Church (Eph. 5:25–27), but it is as clearly said that He died for the *cosmos*. The assumption that Christ could have but one objective in His death has led to much error. His death was as well the judgment of angels, a specific dealing with the sins of Israel past and future, the end of the law, and the ground of heaven's purification. However, the question concerning the sense in which the sin of the world is "taken away" is pertinent at this point. It would be a defenseless contradiction of subsequent New Testament doctrine to contend that the sin of the *cosmos* is so removed by the death of Christ that the individual unregenerate person could not come into judgment. The same, subsequent Scriptures teach that sin has been dealt with in three spheres of relationship—with reference to its power to enslave, Christ has provided a ransom; with respect to its effect upon the sinner, Christ has wrought a reconciliation with God; and with regard to its effect upon God, Christ has achieved a propitiation. These three consummations—redemption, reconciliation, and propitiation—are not things which God *will* do if one believes; they are already finished and constitute the very thing which the sinner must believe. The sin of the world is taken away in the sense that by Christ's threefold accomplishment in His death every hindrance is removed which restrained God from the saving of even the chief of sinners. However, it has pleased Him to require personal acceptance of this Saviorhood of Christ, at which time, and on this sole condition, He will apply all of His saving grace. Even though Christ has completed so perfect a basis for salvation, men are not saved thereby except they believe. Similarly, to claim that men *must* be saved since Christ died for them is equally at fault. The Scriptures teach a finished work for the entire *cosmos* (cf. John 1:29; 3:16; Heb. 2:9; 1 John 2:2), but the same divine revelation asserts that vast multitudes of those who are of the *cosmos* will be lost forever. These are not problems which belong to some one system of theology; they belong to every exegete who receives the words of Scripture in their plain meaning (cf. 2 Cor. 4:2). Through the death of Christ, God has so dealt with the problem of human sin that the *cosmos* stands in an entirely new and different relation to Him. The human family is reconciled, not in the sense that they *are* saved, but in the sense that they may be saved (2 Cor. 5:19). The prison door which Satan would not open (Isa. 14:17) has been unlocked for all (Isa. 61:1; Col. 2:14–15).

John the Baptist announced, likewise, the immeasurable results of divine grace when he said, "And of his fulness have all we received, and grace for grace. For the law was given by Moses, but grace and truth came by Jesus Christ" (John 1:16–17). By the death of Christ—not by His birth—a new reality is secured which he terms "grace and truth." This new thing supersedes the Mosaic system. Grace upon grace, or grace added to grace, accomplishes no less for the believer than experience of the πλήρωμα of Christ for all who come within the range of its provisions. No more all-inclusive statement of the limitless workings of divine grace than this is to be found. The πλήρωμα of the Godhead is that which grace bestows upon those who are saved (cf. Col. 1:19; 2:9–10). Whatever John the Baptist himself may have comprehended is a secondary issue. He did by the Spirit declare the whole basis, scope, and consummation of divine grace.

John 3:14. "And as Moses lifted up the serpent in the wilderness, even so must the Son of man be lifted up."

A most vivid representation of the death of Christ with its essential value was suggested to Nicodemus, whether comprehended or not, by the reference to the lifting up of the brazen serpent in the wilderness (Num. 21:8-9). The serpent serves as a symbol of sin and brass speaks of judgment. The pole on which the serpent was lifted up is a symbol of the cross whereon Christ was made to be sin, or a sin offering, in behalf of those for whom He died. It is also to be noted that as those bitten in the wilderness had but to look at the serpent on the pole to live, so there is life for a look of faith at the crucified One. Hence the essential New Testament doctrine that salvation with all its provisions is secured by faith alone—that faith which Christ went on to emphasize when He said to Nicodemus: "Whosoever believeth in him [the Son of man lifted up] should not perish, but have eternal life" (John 3:15; cf. vss. 16-21). In this declaration to Nicodemus Christ recognizes that, because of His infinite love, God gave His only begotten Son as an offering for man's sin, and that a complete healing from sin's injury is made possible and available for all who believe. So final, indeed, is this one condition—that man's acceptance or condemnation before God depends only upon his believing or not believing—that Christ went on to say, "He that believeth on him is not condemned: but he that believeth not is condemned already, because he hath not believed in the name of the only begotten Son of God" (John 3:18). On this passage Erling C. Olsen in his commentary on John writes:

Jesus Christ did not come into the world to condemn the world; the world was condemned already. The Gospel is preached to men who are condemned because of their sin. Therefore the Gospel is offered to the sinner as the satisfaction for his sins. We can leave the heathen who have never heard about Christ with utmost confidence in the hands of the God of the universe who doeth all things well. But this portion of Scripture teaches that irrespective of the character or lack of character an individual possesses, if he has heard of the name of the only begotten Son of God but refuses to believe on Him, that one is doubly condemned in the sight of God for he has charged God with being a liar. It would be sheer presumption on our part to suggest to any man that he is a sinner and that he is going to hell. Well might such a person say to us, Who made thee a judge? But our Lord said, of the man who *does not believe* in the name of the only begotten Son of God that he "is condemned (or judged) already." If language means anything, that means that any man who does not believe in the only begotten Son of God is already judged, and that judgment is condemnation. Some have an idea that men are on parole and that God is taking a record of men's lives and some day before a great judgment throne

He will examine our lives and there determine whether we are to be condemned or commended. But no such idea entered any man's mind as a result of reading the Bible. There is not even a suggestion of the kind in the Book. Our Lord said that a man is condemned already "because he hath not believed in the name of the only begotten Son of God." But He also said that "He that believeth on him is not condemned . . ." Both statements are remarkable for their absolute assurance. Let me illustrate by a personal reference. I believe on the name of the Son of God. I believe that Jesus Christ was born of a virgin; that he suffered under Pontius Pilate; that he was crucified; that He was buried; and that He arose from the dead on the third day. I believe He died for my sin and put that sin away by His death. I believe God when His Word declares that "He that hath the Son hath life . . ." Thus, I have eternal life. I am not condemned. That fact, however, is not the result of anything I have done except that I have believed God. It has not the slightest bearing upon anything I have ever done or ever shall do. It is a question of faith in the Son of God. It could not be otherwise, for every man in his natural state is condemned already. Man is a sinner; man is lost in his sin; man is absolutely condemned in the sight of God. His lips are sealed, his head is bowed, and his conscience has added its voice to his conviction. How then can a man save himself?—*Walks with Our Lord through John's Gospel*, I, 111–13

John 6:51. "I am the living bread which came down from heaven: if any man eat of this bread, he shall live for ever: and the bread that I will give is my flesh, which I will give for the life of the world."

The mystery of bread becoming physical life when consumed and assimilated by the human body symbolizes the far greater mystery that to those who receive Christ He becomes life everlasting. Manna was divinely sent down from heaven, and of it Christ said, "Your fathers did eat" and though it sustained them for a time, they are all dead (6:49); but the Bread which Christ is, which also came down from heaven, if partaken of, provides eternal life. Of this, Christ stated, "This is that bread which came down from heaven: not as your fathers did eat manna, and are dead: he that eateth of this bread shall live for ever" (vs. 58). The central teaching of this figure is that His flesh must be sacrificed and His blood shed, to the end that He may become that spiritual nourishment which eternal life is. "Then Jesus said unto them, Verily, verily, I say unto you, Except ye eat the flesh of the Son of man, and drink his blood, ye have no life in you. Whoso eateth my flesh, and drinketh my blood, hath eternal life; and I will raise him up at the last day. For my flesh is meat indeed, and my blood is drink indeed. He that eateth my flesh, and drinketh my blood, dwelleth in me, and I in him. As the living Father hath sent me, and I live by the Father: so he that eateth me, even he shall live by me" (vss. 53–57).

John 10:11. "I am the good shepherd: the good shepherd giveth his life for the sheep."

In this, yet another anticipation of His death, Christ indicates that the release of His own life will provide life eternal for those who become His through faith. "I am come," He said, "that they might have life, and that they might have it more abundantly" (10:10); and speaking to the Jews He declared: "But ye believe not, because ye are not of my sheep, as I said unto you. My sheep hear my voice, and I know them, and they follow me: and I give unto them eternal life; and they shall never perish, neither shall any man pluck them out of my hand. My Father, which gave them me, is greater than all; and no man is able to pluck them out of my Father's hand. I and my Father are one" (vss. 26–30).

John 11:49–52. "And one of them, named Caiaphas, being the high priest that same year, said unto them, Ye know nothing at all, nor consider that it is expedient for us, that one man should die for the people, and that the whole nation perish not. And this spake he not of himself: but being high priest that year, he prophesied that Jesus should die for that nation; and not for that nation only, but that also he should gather together in one the children of God that were scattered abroad" (cf. John 18:14).

At this point God by His Spirit introduces a most arresting declaration and uses an unwilling and unsympathetic high priest to announce it. This context discloses the fact that Caiaphas did not originate his utterance, but was rather the mouthpiece of God. The proclamation is far-reaching. First, notice that the Jewish rulers, including Caiaphas, were destitute of understanding concerning what was divinely required and what was about to be accomplished. Second, observe that it was said one man should die for the people. This statement would be justified by reference to Isaiah 53:8, "For the transgression of my people was he stricken," though it is to be doubted whether Caiaphas ever thought of such a truth before. Third, note he predicted that Jesus would die for the nation Israel; and He did die for them in a specific sense. Not only in His death did Christ bear the sins of this people living in past generations which had been covered only by animal sacrifices, but He prepared a basis upon which members of that race along with Gentiles may be saved in this age, and upon which "all Israel" shall yet be saved (Rom. 11:26–27). This prophecy by Caiaphas served in no way to hinder the crucifixion of Christ at the hands of the Jewish rulers and at the hand of Caiaphas himself. It made little impression on the high priest, as is disclosed in Matthew 26:57–68. On this important utterance by Caiaphas, H. A. W. Meyer writes:

Vv. 51, 52. Observation of John, that Caiaphas did not speak this out of his own self-determination, but with these portentous words—in virtue of the high priest's office which he held in that year—involuntarily delivered a *prophecy.*—The high priest passed in the old Israelitish time for the bearer of the divine oracle, for the organ of the revelation of the divine decisions, which were imparted to him through the interrogation of the Urim and Thummim (Ex. 28:30; Num. 27:21). This mode of inquiry disappeared, indeed, at a later time (Josephus, *Antt.* iii. 8. 9), as the high-priestly dignity in general fell gradually from its glory; nevertheless, there is still found in the prophetic age the belief in the high priest's prophetical gift (Hos. 3:4), exactly as, in Josephus, *Antt.* vi. 6. 3, the idea of the old high-priesthood as the bearer of the oracle distinctly appears, and Philo, *de Creat. Princ.* II. p 367, sets forth at least the *true* priest as prophet, and consequently idealizes the relation. Accordingly —as closely connected with that venerable and not yet extinct recollection, and with still surviving esteem for the high-priestly office—it was a natural and obvious course for John, after pious reflection on those remarkable words which were most appropriate to the sacrificial death of Jesus, to find in them a disclosure of the divine decree,—expressed without self-knowledge and will,—and that by no means with a "sacred irony" (Ebrard). Here, too, the extraordinary *year* in which the speaker was invested with the sacred office, carries with it the determination of the judgment; since, if at any time, it was assuredly in this very year, in which God purposed the fulfilment of His holy counsel through the atoning death of His Son, that a revelation through the high-priestly organ appeared conceivable. . . . *For the benefit of* the nation Christ was to die; for through His atoning death the Jews, for whom, in *the first instance,* the Messianic salvation was designed (4:22), were to become partakers by means of faith in the eternal saving deliverance. But the object of His death extended still further than the Jews; not for the benefit of the *nation* alone, but *in order also to bring together into one the scattered children of God.* These are the *Gentiles,* who believe on Him, and thereby are partakers of the atonement, children of God (1:12). The expression is *prophetic* and, just as in 10:16, *proleptic,* according to the New Testament *predestinarian* point of view . . . —*Commentary on the New Testament, in loc.*

John 12:24. "Verily, verily, I say unto you, Except a corn of wheat fall into the ground and die, it abideth alone: but if it die, it bringeth forth much fruit."

A principle is announced in this text which, though working throughout nature generally, is especially evident in Christ's death and resurrection as they reach out in benefit to others. It is through death that life is multiplied (cf. 1 Cor. 15:36). That the principle applies to men is declared by Christ when He went on to say, "He that loveth his life shall lose it; and he that hateth his life in this world shall keep it unto life eternal" (John 12:25). In His death Christ entered the greatest sphere of sacrifice. Of this Dean Alford makes note, "The saying is more than a mere parabolic similitude: the divine Will, which has fixed the law of the springing up of the wheat-corn, has also determined the law of the glorification of the Son of Man, and the one in analogy with the other: i.e., both *through Death*. The symbolism here lies at the root of that in ch. vi., where Christ is *the* BREAD *of life*. it abideth by itself alone, with its life uncommunicated, lived only within its own limits, and not passing on" (*New Testament for English Readers*, I, 572). So, also, R. Govett adds:

> He compares Himself, then, to the grain of wheat which must die before it appears in a new form, and associates others with itself. As the Son of God risen from the dead and ascended to heaven, He can knit to Himself in closest contact both Jew and Gentile, who are made of one spirit with Him. Thus His atonement and His righteousness may be ours. The grain in the granary is possessed of life, but single and limited. If it is to expand, it must die and take a new form. He must, then, die and be buried; like the grain of wheat, which is to spring out of earth in a new shape, having many new grains united with it. Thus He would discover to His persecutors, if they had had eyes to see it, the falsehood of their hopes. They grieved over Jesus' success while *living*, and thought to cut off all by putting Him to death. "Let us *kill* Him, and there will be an end of the matter!" They did so; but it was only to find that the disciples then multiplied by thousands, and filled Jerusalem and the land—nay, and the Gentiles also, with their doctrine. Our Lord, then, knows the counsels of His Father, whose ways are not as ours. Death and resurrection is His plan. And as for Jesus, so for His members. We are familiar with this view of it in the ancient saying, "The blood of the martyrs is the seed of the Church."—*Exposition of the Gospel of St. John*, II, 69–70

John 15:13. "Greater love hath no man than this, that a man lay down his life for his friends."

In this saying Christ not only anticipates His death (cf. John 10: 17–18), but discloses the truth regarding His own devotion to each one who is included in His sacrifice, especially those who would believe on Him. How broad are the objectives in His death! Although that death is effective in immeasurable realms of achievement, it still has its closest personal character. To this the individual should respond and one at least has so responded as recorded in the New Testament. The great Apostle Paul wrote of Christ and himself: "who loved me, and gave himself for me" (Gal. 2:20) and "God forbid that I should glory, save in the cross of our Lord Jesus Christ, by whom the world is crucified unto me, and I unto the world" (Gal. 6:14). Thus the death of Christ at once comprehends the vast issues which reach to creation's outmost bounds and is the joy and hope of the least of individual believers.

2. The Epistles. No direct reference to Christ's death is found in either Second or Third John. The First Epistle presents four important teachings on the subject:

1 John 1:7. "But if we walk in the light, as he is in the light, we have fellowship one with another, and the blood of Jesus Christ his Son cleanseth us from all sin."

In this Scripture the blood of Christ is contemplated as shed and available as a constant benefit to those who "walk in the light." As already seen, this aspect of truth is typified in the red heifer sacrifice (cf. Num. 19). As the ashes were preserved for a perpetual cleansing, so the believer, upon confession to God, is forgiven and cleansed (1 John 1:9). What is involved in "walking in the light" is well stated by Dr. C. I. Scofield in his comment on this passage. To quote: "What it is to 'walk in the light' is explained by vs. 8–10. 'All things . . . are made manifest by the light' (Eph. 5:13). The presence of God brings the consciousness of sin in the nature (v. 8), and sins in the life (vs. 9, 10). The blood of Christ is the divine provision for both. To walk in the light is to live in fellowship with the Father and the Son. Sin interrupts, but confession restores that fellowship. Immediate confession keeps the fellowship unbroken" (*Op. cit.,* p. 1321). The truth remains that sin is ever sinful even when committed by a believer, and the shed blood of Christ is ever available to cleanse perfectly.

1 John 2:2. "And he is the propitiation for our sins: and not for our's only, but also for the sins of the whole world."

With respect to the imperative demands which outraged holiness must otherwise impose upon sinners, God is rendered propitious by Christ's judgment death for them. Propitiation on the part of God is not salvation on the part of sinners. It rather secures the possibility of salvation. God is propitious, therefore the sinner may be saved upon such terms as a propitious God may dictate. The sinner is not called upon by tears and entreaties to persuade God or to influence Him to be well disposed; that much Christ's death as a substitute has wrought to infinite completeness. The sinner has but to believe, by which act he reposes confidence in that which God has provided. In like manner, when the Christian sins, his restoration to divine fellowship is conditioned on the same truth—that, through the death of Christ, God is propitious. The passage under consideration sets forth a primary statement regarding the sins of Christians and only a secondary statement regarding the sins of the unsaved. Preceding this assertion, that God is propitious concerning "our sins," the Apostle John has brought into view two great questions along with their answers: (1) What is the effect of sin upon the Christian himself who commits it? The answer, stated throughout this Epistle and especially in chapter 1, is that fellowship with the Father and Son is lost, as also all spiritual power and blessing. (2) What is the effect of the Christian's sin upon God? This is a most vital problem, for it determines everything with respect to the unchangeable character of the believer's salvation. The answer of a shallow rationalism which argues that, because of God's holiness, He must disown His child is wholly at fault, since it ignores the present ministry of Christ as Advocate in heaven. The believer is told that, when he sins, he has an Advocate in heaven. This is a distinct and sufficient provision. The Advocate is Christ and He stands to plead that He bore the sin on the cross. His advocacy is so absolutely perfect with regard to its equity that He wins in this service a title which is given Him in no other relationship—"Jesus Christ the Righteous" (1 John 2:1). This perfect advocacy in which He pleads His finished work on the cross thus becomes the ground of the propitiation which He is to God, all of which is mentioned in the next verse, the one under consideration. There would be no hope for any sinner—saved or unsaved—apart from the death of Christ; but, sheltered under that provision, divine propitiation is infinitely real and unchangeably effective for man.

1 John 3:16. "Hereby perceive we the love of God, because he laid down his life for us: and we ought to lay down our lives for the brethren."

Again (cf. John 15:13; Rom. 5:8) the immeasurable love of God for those injured by sin is said to be manifested, enacted, and demonstrated by and through the death of Christ. It would be useless indeed for one to seek to discover or comprehend the knowledge-surpassing love of God as expressed in the cross. It is not manifest elsewhere just the same, though the Father's care of His own is prompted by His Love for them. "To know the love of Christ" (Eph. 3:19) is that to which every believer may well seek to attain.

1 John 4:10. "Herein is love, not that we loved God, but that he loved us, and sent his Son to be the propitiation for our sins."

The same theme—God's love expressed in and through the death of Christ—is presented by the Apostle John once more. Nothing could be built on the love of man toward God; but God's love is a perfect basis for all His mighty achievements.

3. THE REVELATION. The Revelation, which looks on to the closing

days of God's dealing with sinful men and which records His final triumph over all evil, also looks backward to the death of Christ in four significant passages.

Revelation 1:5. "Unto him that loved us, and washed us from our sins in his own blood."

The eternal Jehovah character of Christ has been asserted possibly by the words: "from him which is, and which was, and which is to come" (vs. 4). He is "the faithful witness," not only with respect to the character of God, but also with regard to the sinfulness of man and His redemption perfected through the shedding of His own blood. To those who believe in an actual blood-redemption, this passage is a surpassing casket of heavenly jewels. He it is "that loved us," which marvelous truth has been so constantly emphasized in Scripture. He it is that "washed us from our sins," and who shed His blood to that end.

Revelation 5:9. "And they sung a new song, saying, Thou art worthy to take the book, and to open the seals thereof: for thou wast slain, and hast redeemed us to God by thy blood out of every kindred, and tongue, and people, and nation."

The new song is heaven's worship of the Lamb, and is sung only by those who have been redeemed by His blood out from all the peoples of the earth. The song of triumph not only acknowledges that Christ was slain, but its singers are ever reminded of the ground of their acceptance with God and of their right only through the blood of Christ to occupy celestial spheres. Though a modern religious song anticipates a time when the "old, rugged cross" will be exchanged for a crown and though inattentive multitudes lend their voices to such a baseless notion, it remains a fact that the redeemed in heaven recognize their right to be in glory as a privilege extended them only through the blood of the cross, and no intimation is ever given that any other song will be on their lips. Those who sing redemption's song will never reach a place where through some merit of their own they can stand in these celestial spheres. As certain, also, is the truth that only those thus redeemed, who stand in the merit of Christ, will be in glory. All the dreams of Christ-rejecters who hope to be received into glory through the love of God apart from redemption are in vain.

Revelation 7:14. "And I said unto him, Sir, thou knowest. And he said to me, These are they which came out of great tribulation, and have washed their robes, and made them white in the blood of the Lamb."

Those who have attained by His grace to the courts of glory are identified, not by their works, their sufferings, or their personal merit, but they are described as those whose robes have been washed in the blood of the Lamb. This is a figure calculated to represent purification as high as heaven in quality. It is termed a figure of speech, but it is not meaningless on that account; and so there is limitless reality in it. It may be understood only as Christ's blood is seen to be the one divinely provided means whereby the soul and spirit of man may be purified. Cleansing so depends upon the blood of Christ that it may be said to be accomplished directly by that blood (cf. 1 John 1:7).

Revelation 13:8. "And all that dwell upon the earth shall worship him, whose names are not written in the book of life of the Lamb slain from the foundation of the world."

This passage, though so vitally important along with 1 Peter 1:19–20, should create no difficulty. Why should not God anticipate from all eternity the greatest of all His undertakings? Back of the revelation that the Lamb sacrifice has been foreseen is the accompanying disclosure, traced through reason, which is that God also foresaw the evil for which the Lamb must die. The fact thus established, that sin has existed as a divine expectation as long as the purpose of redemption has existed, is not a form of dualism, for sin as a thing merely foreseen is not in active conflict with another reality. The passage does give instruction, however, to the end that it may be recognized that the presence of evil in the world is not an unforeseen fortuity. Because of the immeasurable achievement of Christ in His death, the fact of sin will, when the values of that death shall have accomplished their intended ends, be only a retrospect. God Himself has asserted that, as for His own attitude toward it, sin shall be called no more to remembrance (cf. Isa. 43:25). Because of the indefiniteness of the Greek construction in Revelation 13:8, some have contended that the eternal feature mentioned in this passage refers to the things written in the "book of life." On this combination of words Dean Alford has well said:

They may belong either to **is written**, or to **is slain**. The former connexion is taken by many. But the other is far more obvious and natural: and had it not been for the apparent difficulty of the sense thus conveyed, the going so far back as to **is written** for a connexion would never have been thought of. The difficulty of the saying is but apparent: 1 Pet. 1:19, 20 says more fully the same thing. That death of Christ which was foreordained from the foundation of the world, is said to have *taken place* in the counsels of Him with whom the end and the beginning are one. Ch. 17:8, which is cited by De Wette as decisive for his view, is irrelevant. Of course, where simply the writing in the book of life from the foundation of the world is expressed, no other element is to be introduced: but it does not therefore follow, that where, as here, other elements

are by the construction introduced, that, and that alone is to be understood.—
Op. cit., in loc.

Thus it is seen that from the writings of the Apostle John a wealth of meaning in the death of the Savior is to be gathered. Scarcely any particular meaning assigned to that death is absent from these portions; yet the doctrinal argument of the Apostle Paul extends this testimony still further, to immeasurable length.

V. IN PAUL'S WRITINGS

In the writings of this great Apostle, the death of Christ may be classed as one of four major themes including: Christ's death in all its applications and achievements; Christ's resurrection as the basis of a New Creation with corresponding relations to Israel and the *cosmos* world; Christ in His manifold relation to the Church; and the walk, warfare, and witness of the believer in the present age. Three of these Pauline themes are foreign to this thesis. While the preponderance of evidence points to the Pauline authorship of the Epistle to the Hebrews, it seems best to reserve that book for a special consideration later on. In all the thirteen assured writings of the Apostle, only 2 Thessalonians and Philemon are without reference to that event which in the Pauline system of theology is the basis of all that endures for time and eternity. As there are in the Pauline writings—excluding Hebrews—more than thirty references to the death of Christ, it seems best to consider these as they appear in separate books or related portions of these writings.

1. Romans. The very heart of the gospel of divine grace as grounded in the death and resurrection of Christ is exhibited in the Letter to the Romans.

Romans 3:23–26. "For all have sinned, and come short of the glory of God; being justified freely by his grace through the redemption that is in Christ Jesus: whom God hath set forth to be a propitiation through faith in his blood, to declare his righteousness for the remission of sins that are past, through the forbearance of God; to declare, I say, at this time his righteousness: that he might be just, and the justifier of him which believeth in Jesus."

Having pronounced, by that divine authority which inspiration supplies, that "all have sinned, and come short of the glory of God," the Apostle goes on to describe that divine undertaking which is a complete and final salvation, and in a manner which is without doubt the most perfect and all-inclusive proclamation of it. This affirmation has been preceded in the context by an extended portrayal of the utter ruin of humanity, as seen by the holy eyes of God. Also, in verses 21 and 22 appears that imputed righteousness of God—a theme already introduced in 1:16–17—which is said to be available on no other terms than simple faith in Christ Jesus as a personal Savior. Thus is introduced the greatest of all the divine accomplishments which enter into salvation by grace. Both the forgiveness of sin and the gift of eternal life are important factors in this salvation; but since the Epistle to the Romans is the Magna Carta of the gospel of grace and since that Epistle exhibits the truth of imputed righteousness as its supreme disclosure, it follows that the fact of imputed righteousness ("the gift of righteousness"—Rom. 5:17) is the central revelation in the gospel. The fact that such has not been exalted, and more often not even mentioned, by gospel preachers does not weigh at all against the logic introduced above. This great bestowment of righteousness is properly secured through two divine operations: (a) One in which—as foreshadowed in the sweet savor offerings—Christ through His death offered Himself without spot to God and, by so doing, released and placed legally at the sinner's disposal all that He the Son of God is. (b) One in which, the moment an unsaved person believes, he is invested and furnished with the πλήρωμα ('fullness') of Christ (cf. John 1:16), which is no less than the πλήρωμα of the Godhead (cf. Col. 1:19; 2:9–10). The saved one is instantly "made meet to be a partaker of the inheritance of the saints in light" (Col. 1:12). This measureless enriching is divinely applied through the new union set up between Christ and the believer. Instantly coming to be in Christ by the baptizing work of the Holy Spirit and thus a living member in Christ's Body, the believer automatically becomes what Christ is. God then sees him in His Son and as a part of His Son. Above that exaltation nothing could ever exist. It is the πλήρωμα of the Godhead imputed to the one who believes in Christ as his Savior. Romans 3:24 opens with a new revelation, namely, "being justified"—certainly not merely aspiring to be, or hoping to be, justified. No greater challenge to human conviction could ever be made than that it acknowledge the truth that absolute, immutable justification from God is the present position of everyone who is saved at all. As before demonstrated, justification, as set forth in Romans, is not the fact of righteousness being imputed, but is rather the divine recognition that such righteousness has been imputed. So the believer is righteous because he is in Christ, but is divinely declared to be justified immutably because he is righteous. The added word in this text (3:24) is "freely"—δωρεάν—which, as all have conceded, is better translated "without a cause" (cf. the original of John 15:25; Gal. 2:21). The thought is not that God justifies in a free or generous manner, but rather that He finds no ground or cause for justification in the believer's own self, any more than there was a cause within Christ for the hatred directed against Him. The answer to the question of how a meritless sinner may by simple faith in Christ become immutably justified is at once declared in the very next words, namely, "by his grace." The limits of divine grace, since it is God working with a view to the satisfying of infinite love and now that love set free to act because of Christ's death for the sinner, could never be less than the πλήρωμα of Christ, which fullness is acknowledged by God to be what it is by the decree which proclaims the saved one immutably justified, in response to simple faith in the Savior. Again, if it be inquired how such knowledge-surpassing grace can be exercised toward a meritless sinner without God's holiness being compromised by the making light of sin, the answer is also provided in the same text, with the phrase, "through the redemption that is in Christ Jesus." Thus, if this sequence of doctrine which is compressed into verse 24 be traced backwards, it is seen that, because of Christ's death which satisfies the holy demands of God against the sinner, God's grace—the unrestrained expression of His infinite love—is released toward those who believe and that love will never stop short of a bestowment of the πλήρωμα of Christ, which is itself the πλήρωμα of the Godhead. Since the believer is thus invested with all that infinite holiness can require, God, apart from all merit or demerit in the believer, proclaims the one thus invested to be justified forever. A further word of assurance is added in verse 26, where it is affirmed that God is Himself *just* when He thus justifies the ungodly sinner who does no more than to believe in Jesus. In such a transaction God is not trafficking in mere pretense or fiction. The ungodly are justified (Rom. 4:5) and that without drawing on a supposed divine leniency and without compromising the divine character. So great, indeed, is the redemption which is in Christ Jesus in its outworking toward the meritless and sinful! It should be repeated often that such an exalted position as immutable justification proclaims calls for a heaven-high manner of daily life, not that the sinner can *attain* to or *maintain* by any works of merit a position so exalted, but to the end that he may not *profane* that which God hath wrought in answer to simple faith in Jesus.

Romans 4:25. "Who was delivered for our offences, and was raised again for our justification."

Two important aspects of doctrine are seen in the words "was delivered for our offences"—that by divine authority Christ was a sacrifice and that it was all done for the sins of men. No more fundamental truths are related to Christ's death than these two. The word παραδίδωμι, translated *delivered,* is used to describe a casting into prison or a being brought to justice (cf. Matt. 4:12; 10:17, 19, 21), and is the common term to describe the betrayal of Christ (cf. Matt. 10:4; 17:22; John 6:64, 71). That He was delivered intimates that aspect of His death which reckons it a deed at the hand of God and equally a work of wicked men. There is an aspect in which it is true that no man took His life from Him (John 10:18).

Romans 5:6–10. "For when we were yet without strength, in due time Christ died for the ungodly. For scarcely for a righteous man will one die: yet peradventure for a good man some would even dare to die. But God commendeth his love toward us, in that, while we were yet sinners, Christ died for us. Much more then, being now justified by his blood, we shall be saved from wrath through him. For if, when we were enemies, we were reconciled to God by the death of his Son, much more, being reconciled, we shall be saved by his life."

Here the love of Christ for the lost is in view. He died for those "without strength," the "ungodly," His "enemies." This is indeed a dark picture of the estate of men yet unsaved. These are not prevarications such as men employ; it is the infinite accuracy of an inspired record. Because these words represent the divine estimation of the unsaved, the indictment againt them is by so much augmented; however, even though man represents immeasurable unworthiness before God, for such the Savior died and by so much the love of God in Christ is demonstrated. In this, "God commendeth his love." In the range of human competency it is true that "greater love hath no man than this, that a man lay down his life for his friends," but in the range of divine competency love is expressed thus: "While we were yet sinners" (not, holy), "ungodly" (not, godly), "enemies" (not, friends), "Christ died for us." It is also true, as the latter part of this context reveals, that, being justified and being reconciled—the one said to be by Christ's blood and the other by Christ's death, there is a "much more" attitude of divine devotion than could have existed before; but still that which this passage presents as its primary message is the knowledge-surpassing love of God for those whose demerit, as He sees them, knows no bounds.

Romans 6:3–6, 10. "Know ye not, that so many of us as were baptized into Jesus Christ were baptized into his death? Therefore we are buried with him by baptism into death: that like as Christ was raised up from the dead by the glory of the Father, even so we also should walk in newness of life. For if we have been planted together in the likeness of his death, we shall be also in the likeness of his resurrection: knowing this, that our old man is crucified with him, that the body of sin might be destroyed, that henceforth we should not serve sin. . . . For in that he died, he died unto sin once: but in that he liveth, he liveth unto God."

Various misleading interpretations of this portion of Scripture are given. Some have contended that the purpose of the passage is to establish the supposed importance of a mode of ritual baptism. Others see here a command looking to self-crucifixion, not discerning that the crucifixion referred to is that of Christ already accomplished in which the believer has had his portion. The context sets forth the crucifixion, death, burial, and resurrection of Christ all as deeds wrought in behalf of the believer. This Scripture is not for the unsaved unto justification. (That great aspect of Christ's death, as already indicated above, is presented in Romans 3:21—5:21.) It is, however, for the saved unto sanctification in their daily life. The death, burial, and resurrection of Christ for the unsaved are at the very center of the gospel and so it has been indicated in 1 Corinthians 15:1–4. But the believer, now looking backward upon all that Christ has accomplished, is able to see how it may be all applied to his own heart by faith. It is in this consciousness that he is able to walk upon a new principle of daily living, namely, by the power of the indwelling Spirit. Recognizing his cocrucifixion (which, incidentally, no symbol of ritual baptism ever attempts to represent), his codeath, his coburial, and his coresurrection, the believer finds himself on resurrection ground, indwelt by the Holy Spirit, and, not only logically called upon because of his exalted position to live unto God, but fully equipped to do so. The sin nature, though still alive and active, has been judged by Christ's death unto it (6:10), and, because of that judgment which has no experimental place in the history of the Christian, the Holy Spirit is righteously free to take control of that otherwise-active sin nature. The believer's part is to "reckon" and "let not" (6:11–12). To *reckon* is to count on what is true of one's complete identification with Christ in His crucifixion, death, burial, and resurrection. To *let not* . . . is to depend on the indwelling Spirit for deliverance from the power of the sin nature. Such, indeed, is the walk upon a new principle of daily living. These provisions now obtain under grace, but were never provided under the Mosaic system; therefore the Apostle writes, "For sin shall not have dominion over you: for ye are not under the law, but under grace" (Rom. 6:14).

Romans 7:4–6. "Wherefore, my brethren, ye also are become dead to the law by the body of Christ; that ye should be married to another, even to him who is raised from the dead, that we should bring forth fruit unto God. For when we were in the flesh, the motions of sins, which were by the law, did work in our members to bring forth fruit unto death. But now we are delivered from the law, that being dead wherein we were held; that we should serve in newness of spirit, and not in the oldness of the letter."

Here, as in Galatians 3:13, the one result of Christ's death—its efficacy in terminating for the believer the whole merit system—is in view. It is through the body of Christ as a sacrifice that all law, as a ground of acceptance or as a rule of life, has been abolished. Salvation is now by grace apart from works (cf. Titus 3:5); and the believer's acceptance before God, which acceptance is perfected to infinite proportions, is wholly due to his position in Christ (Eph. 1:6; Heb. 10:14) and not to aught within himself. The sweet savor aspect of Christ's death is again in the foreground, which provides by release to believers the merit of Christ in behalf of those who are without merit. The obligation to merit being ended, the saved one is thus brought into perfect liberty (cf. Gal. 5:1) and sustains no other responsibility than to walk worthy of that estate into which infinite grace has brought him. It is thus that, through the death of Christ, a complete deliverance from the merit system is accomplished.

Romans 8:3–4. "For what the law could not do, in that it was weak through the flesh, God sending his own Son in the likeness of sinful flesh, and for sin, condemned sin in the flesh: that the righteousness of the law might be fulfilled in us, who walk not after the flesh, but after the Spirit."

This is one of three vitally important references to Christ's death within this one chapter. This, the first instance, is a reference to Christ's death unto the sin nature, as considered above under Romans 6. The law made its appeal to the very sin nature which is in the flesh, therefore the law failed because of the "weakness of the flesh" to which it appealed; but Christ by His death unto the sin nature condemned, or completely judged, that nature to the end that the Spirit might be free to control it. When thus sustained and empowered by the Spirit the law —here referring to the whole will of God for the believer—is fulfilled by the Spirit *in* the believer, but is never said to be fulfilled *by* the believer. The one condition imposed is that the believer walk in dependence upon the Spirit (cf. Rom 8:4; Gal. 5:16–17). This, likewise—as in the case of the death of Christ for the believer—is something to believe or reckon to be true. It is not secured by petition or prayer. The sin nature *is* judged, the Spirit now indwells; there remains only the human responsibility of reliance upon the Spirit.

Romans 8:32. "He that spared not his own Son, but delivered him up for us all, how shall he not with him also freely give us all things?"

In the type (Gen. 22:1–14), Abraham the father is called upon to offer his "only son" (22:2) and is in the last moment spared that ordeal; but, in the antitype, God the Father "spared not" His Son, and by this it is again disclosed that the love of God toward sinners is expressed in the gift of His Son (John 3:16; Rom. 5:6–11; 2 Cor. 9:15; 1 John 3:16). With so great a Gift as the Son is and He already given, there is boundless assurance that, in connection with that Gift, the Father will give all else. Expectation respecting lesser things should be free from doubt and hesitation. The Apostle can say that nothing "shall be able to separate us from the love of God, which is in Christ Jesus our Lord" (Rom. 8:39).

Romans 8:34. "Who is he that condemneth? It is Christ that died, yea rather, that is risen again, who is even at the right hand of God, who also maketh intercession for us."

The absolutely substitutionary character of Christ's death is the message of that portion of this verse which bears upon the subject. The dominant theme of the entire eighth chapter to be sure, is announced in the first verse: "There is therefore now no condemnation to them which are in Christ Jesus." Verses 28 to 39 but verify that introductory statement. Justification, it is said (vs. 30), is the portion of all who are called; and, on the ground of the truth that they have been justified, God will bring no charge against His elect whom He has thus declared righteous forever. He may correct or discipline those whom He has thus received, but no condemnation can rest upon them since they are justified on the merit of Another who never fails, He who is the righteousness of God and as such is "made unto them" (1 Cor. 1:30). "Who is he that condemneth?" is the direct question, and the answer is that to those who believe the condemning power of sin is broken, since it has been borne by Christ. Clarity in Soteriology is impossible apart from this basic truth, that sin has already been borne by the Substitute. Too often the impression is created by the preacher that God will do something if He is urged to do so and moved by penitent tears; but, since

Christ has died, there is nothing left for the sinner to do but to believe and there is nothing left for the Christian who has sinned to do but to confess his sin.

2. FIRST AND SECOND CORINTHIANS. *1 Corinthians 1:18, 22–24.* "For the preaching of the cross is to them that perish foolishness; but unto us which are saved it is the power of God. . . . For the Jews require a sign, and the Greeks seek after wisdom: but we preach Christ crucified, unto the Jews a stumblingblock, and unto the Greeks foolishness; but unto them which are called, both Jews and Greeks, Christ the power of God, and the wisdom of God."

The preaching of the cross is God's appointed way of reaching the lost with that very message of His infinite grace. The cross, however, sustains a somewhat different relation to the Jew than it does to the Gentile. Though regarding the cross the Jew has found a stumbling stone (cf. Rom. 9:30–33) and the Gentile, mere foolishness—his most serious effort to explain it, because of spiritual blindness, is so far short of the glory of the cross that it is comparatively foolish, it is nevertheless a perfect display of the wisdom of God and the power of God. In the outworking of the plan of redemption, God has wrought on an infinite plane and has disclosed the unsearchable depths of His wisdom and prudence (Eph. 1:8). In 1 Corinthians 1:23–24, the great transaction of the sacrifice of Christ is declared to be the manifestation of divine power and wisdom. As revealed in the Scriptures, the greatest problem that ever confronted the Almighty is not creation, which in Psalm 8:3 is likened to mere finger-play: it is rather the redemption of a lost soul, which, according to Isaiah 53:1, required the making bare of His great right arm. His *wisdom* is seen in the solving of the problem how God can remain just while being, according to the compassion of His heart, the Justifier of the sinner. His *power* is set free to act in behalf of all who believe on Christ as their Savior; and, when thus set free, He will not stop short of the satisfaction of His measureless love: He will present the saved one in glory, conformed to the image of His Son. God is satisfied with the payment Christ has made; and it is in Him who alone is worthy that we have a perfect redemption, even the forgiveness of sins—not, indeed, a partial forgiveness, which would be no manifestation of infinite grace, but that which, being complete enough to last forever, remains an abiding glory to God. Thus the believer is accepted eternally into the family of the redeemed; yet in that family relationship he will, time and again, need to be forgiven—in the sense of being restored, and that not to the family again, but to the fellowship of the Father and the Son (1 John 1:9).

1 Corinthians 5:7. "Purge out therefore the old leaven, that ye may be a new lump, as ye are unleavened. For even Christ our passover is sacrificed for us."

No forsaking of that which is contrary to the holiness of God or the will of God is too great for the believer, in the light of Christ's sacrifice for him. Evil, which is as leaven, is to be "purged out" even as it was prohibited in the typical offerings of the Old Testament. The one phase of Christ's death—His voluntary yielding of Himself to be the Passover lamb—is presented in this context. Likewise, in 1 Corinthians 6:20 a direct reference is made to Christ's death as a ransom from the divine judgment which must otherwise fall upon those who have sinned.

1 Corinthians 8:11. "And through thy knowledge shall the weak brother perish, for whom Christ died?"

In addition to its renewed reference to Christ's death on behalf of others, this passage imposes the obligation to guard the weak upon those who through knowledge of the truth are strong. In this instance, it is assumed that the weak brother recognizes the superior knowledge of the strong and is misled with good motives. However the facts may be, the true value of a soul is seen here in the immeasurable truth that Christ died for it (cf. 2 Cor. 5:13–16).

1 Corinthians 15:3. "For I delivered unto you first of all that which I also received, how that Christ died for our sins according to the scriptures."

A thoughtful reader of the Scriptures cannot but be impressed with the manifold assurances that Christ died on behalf of or in the stead of others. Repetition of this truth can hardly be avoided in the writing of these lines; in consequence, let it be said that this one text is direct and conclusive and is here related to the gospel as the very heart of it. The wisdom of this world has exhausted its limited field of speculation but still has failed to devise any explanation for the words "Christ died for our sins" which will answer the demands of the text, other than to aver that He died the death which rightfully belongs to the sinner. The great prediction of Isaiah 53:5–6 must be accepted as the understanding of all that Christ's death did accomplish for the lost. No new idea is introduced in the New Testament.

2 Corinthians 5:14–21. "For the love of Christ constraineth us; because we thus judge, that if one died for all, then were all dead: and that he died for all, that they which live should not henceforth live unto themselves, but unto him which died for them, and rose again. Wherefore henceforth know we no man after the flesh: yea, though we have known Christ after the flesh, yet now henceforth know we him no more. Therefore if any man be in Christ, he is a new creature: old things are passed away; behold, all things are become new. And all things are of God, who hath reconciled us to himself by Jesus Christ, and hath given to us the ministry of reconciliation; to wit, that God was in Christ, reconciling the world unto himself, not imputing their trespasses unto them; and hath committed unto us the word of reconciliation. Now then we are ambassadors for Christ, as though God did beseech you by us: we pray you in Christ's stead, be ye reconciled to God. For he hath made him to be sin for us, who knew no sin; that we might be made the righteousness of God in him."

In this great declaration, three features are introduced: (a) Christ's death on behalf of the world, (b) the witness thereunto, and (c) the infinite results of salvation upon those who believe the witness about the all-sufficient death. The outreach of Christ's death is described in the words: "We thus judge, that if one died for all, then were all dead" —that is to say, those for whom He died died in a legal sense in His death. Dean Alford states it thus: "This was true, *objectively*, but *not subjectively* till such death to sin and self is realized in each: see Rom. 6:8 ff. The rendering of the A.V., *'then were all dead,'* is inadmissible both from the construction of the original, and the context: *'One on behalf of all* died, therefore *all* died: if One died the death of [belonging to, due from] *all, then all* died [in and with Him]'" (*Ibid., in loc.*). That which Christ undertook to do respecting the sinner has been accomplished to perfection. As may be seen in verses 18–19, He has wrought for them a complete reconciliation. Their position before God is vitally changed by being those for whom Christ died. God is satisfied with that which Christ has wrought, as a solution of the problem of sin and its required judgments. Whether the sinner will believe and receive this provision to the point of being himself suited with what satisfies God is quite another question. To the end that the unsaved may believe, the reconciling message is committed to ambassadors who are appointed to go forth beseeching the unsaved to be reconciled to God. It is not a mere sentimental appreciation of Christ's death which constrains or impels the gospel messenger. This appreciation, on the contrary, reaches to the point of recognition of the truth that all have received provisionally the benefits of Christ's death for them. This is what "we thus judge" teaches. Verse 15 is of a parenthetical character, and therefore the effect of observing that Christ died for all is not described until verse 16: "Wherefore, henceforth know we no man after the flesh." The soul-winner thus moved by the death of Christ for all men no longer sees them as rich and poor, bond and free, white or black; rather he sees each one as a soul for whom Christ has died. The greatest distinction which could come to any human being has come to every human being, which is that the King of Glory should die for man on the cross. One's appreciation of the value of Christ's death, if experienced at all, is specifically the work of the Holy Spirit in the heart of the witness. By the Spirit, or out from the indwelling Spirit, the love of God for the lost gushes forth (cf. Rom. 5:5), for the fruit of the Spirit is love (Gal. 5:22; cf. John 17:26). Love for lost souls is not a human competency; it is no part of a fallen human being—even for those who are saved it is impossible unaided. It is experienced only as it is inwrought by the Spirit of God. When this dynamic energizing is welcomed by anyone, the witness will be "instant in season [and] out of season" (2 Tim. 4:2). This passage emphasizes again the truth that there was in Christ's death a substitution which secured for the believer the very righteousness of God, and that that righteousness is rightfully gained on the ground of the believer's participation in the new Headship of the resurrected Christ. Thus the Apostle himself asserts it: "Therefore if any man be in Christ, he is a new creature: old things are passed away; behold, all things are become new. And all things are of God" (vss. 17–18); and again, "For he hath made him to be sin for us, who knew no sin; that we might be made the righteousness of God in him" (vs. 21).

2 Corinthians 8:9. "For ye know the grace of our Lord Jesus Christ, that, though he was rich, yet for your sakes he became poor, that ye through his poverty might be rich."

In the preceding context, the Apostle has urged upon the Corinthian believers personal sacrifice for Christ. Now Christ is held before them as the supreme example of sacrifice. What His riches were and to what depth of poverty He descended cannot be comprehended by men; nor can the riches which He thus provides for all who are saved be estimated. As before indicated, John writes of the same truth and in connection with the same theme of generosity: "Hereby perceive we the love of God, because he laid down his life for us: and we ought to lay down our lives for the brethren. But whoso hath this world's good, and seeth his brother have need, and shutteth up his bowels of compassion from him, how dwelleth the love of God in him?" (1 John 3:16–17).

3. GALATIANS. *Galatians 1:4.* "Who gave himself for our sins, that he might deliver us from this present evil world, according to the will of God and our Father."

He who "gave himself for our sins" did so, not only with a view to bearing the guilt of sin, but that "he might deliver us out of this present evil age" (R.V. marg.)—which is none other than the day of the *cosmos* world system. Through the death of Christ, those who believe are delivered from the power of darkness and translated into the kingdom of the Son of God's love (Col. 1:13). The importance of a Scripture which declares that the believer is delivered from the satanic system is evident; however, it is also taught that in addition the believer becomes a rightful sharer in the eternal kingdom of Christ. Elsewhere, the same believer is said to be a citizen of heaven (Phil. 3:20, R.V.).

Galatians 2:20; 6:14. "I am crucified with Christ: nevertheless I live; yet not I, but Christ liveth in me: and the life which I now live in the flesh I live by the faith of the Son of God, who loved me, and gave himself for me. . . . But God forbid that I should glory, save in the cross of our Lord Jesus Christ, by whom the world is crucified unto me, and I unto the world."

It is the personal element in Christ's death linking each sinner with his Savior individually which the Apostle stresses in this testimony. In addition to the constantly reiterated truth that Christ died for others and not for Himself, Paul speaks of this normal, but so unusual, ability to react with great appreciation to the fact of Christ's sacrificial death. Such a heart response may well be sought for by all who would glorify their Lord. On the other hand, this reality in the Apostle's experience must come, by way of contrast, as a rebuke to the vast company of believers. How immeasurable is the obligation to give thanks and glory for and in the cross of Christ!

Galatians 3:13; 4:4–5. "Christ hath redeemed us from the curse of the law, being made a curse for us: for it is written, Cursed is every one that hangeth on a tree. . . . But when the fulness of the time was come, God sent forth his Son, made of a woman, made under the law, to redeem them that were under the law, that we might receive the adoption of sons."

As in Romans 7:4–6, the fact is here presented that Christ's death is a deliverance from the whole merit obligation—whether it be the Mosaic order or the inherent obligation of the creature to the Creator. The Mosaic system was never addressed to Gentiles and therefore it was not addressed to the Galatians; but they, as all Gentile believers, were called upon to recognize the truth that Christ has provided a perfect acceptance for them before God, which satisfies every demand of infinite holiness and thus terminates the entire merit obligation. It is also true that the condemnation which a violated merit system imposes was borne by the Savior. His death was a redemption from the curse of the law. C. F. Hogg and W. E. Vine in their *Epistle to the Galatians* state:

> from the curse of the law, having become a curse—*i.e.*, by becoming; the words describe the means taken for the accomplishment of the redemption. The curse attaches to all under the law, inasmuch as all have failed to meet its requirements, with one exception, Christ, Who was "born under the law," but Who did not Himself incur the curse, because He was "the Righteous One," (Acts 3:14) not in the sight of men, indeed, for they crucified Him as a blasphemer, but in the sight of God Who raised Him from the dead. So being Himself free from the curse, He passed under it voluntarily, that those under it by inheritance and desert might escape. By the death of Christ the unbending rigour of the law is confirmed and illustrated. The law of God makes no exceptions, but demands always the full penalty from all who come within its jurisdiction. In view of that awful exhibition of its terrors, how could the Galatians suppose that their efforts to keep it would result other than disastrously for themselves? The Son of God did not "become a curse for us" in His Incarnation. From before His birth He was called "holy"; He "advanced in . . . favour with God" (Luke 1:35; 2:52); and at the close of thirty years of life in the flesh God spoke of Him from heaven in the words, "This is My beloved Son, in Whom I am well pleased," and later repeated the testimony (Matt. 3:17; 17:5). There is no statement made in Scripture that He became the sin-bearer in His baptism, or in Gethsemane, or at any juncture in His life previous to the Crucifixion. With the Cross alone, then, must these words of the Apostle be associated, and this the quotation of Deuteronomy 21:23 confirms. The language of 2 Corinthians 5:21, "made to be sin," should be compared with this, "became a curse." In each case the reality of the association of the Lord Jesus with the sins of His people, and the completeness of the satisfaction He offered to the law in His death upon the Cross, is vividly set forth.—Pp. 134–35

So also respecting the second passage, Galatians 4:4–5, the same commentators assert:

> v. 5. that He might redeem—as at 3:13, above. Neither the Incarnation of the Son of God, nor His keeping of the law in the days of His flesh availed, in whole or in part, for the redemption of men. Apart from the Incarnation death would have been impossible for Him; hence this was the condition necessary for the accomplishment of the redemption, but was itself no part of that redemption. His redemptive work proper began and ended on the Cross;

accordingly the statement of the Saviour's relation to sin is invariably made in terms that confine that relationship to His death. Hence it is nowhere said in N.T. that Christ kept the law for us. He is not said to have borne sin during any part of His life; it was at the Cross that He became the sin-bearer (1 Pet. 2:24). The first part of Isaiah 53:4 is interpreted in Matthew 8:17, where the context in which these words are quoted makes it plain that they are to be understood not of the death of the Lord Jesus, nor of any vicarious suffering endured by Him, but of His sympathy with suffering humanity and the expression of that sympathy in the alleviation of distress wherever He came in contact with it. Some parts of Isaiah 53 do undoubtedly describe the vicarious sufferings of the Cross, as the closing part of verse 5, *e.g.*, which is quoted in 1 Peter 2:24. These are typical illustrations of the principle that the N.T. is the only guide to the understanding of the O.T. In the first part of Mark 10:45, *e.g.*, the Lord declares the purpose of His life "not to be served but to serve," and of His death, "to give His life a ransom for many." His death was in harmony with His life, and was its fitting climax, but the two are here distinguished by the Lord Himself, and this distinction is observed by each of the N.T. writers.—*Ibid.*, pp. 186–87

Similarly, on redemption from the law Martin Luther in what is termed his greatest work—*Commentary on Galatians*—expresses his understanding of a redemption from the law as this is taught in Galatians. He writes:

Furthermore, this place also witnesseth that Christ, when the time of the law was accomplished, did abolish the same, and so brought liberty to those that were oppressed therewith, but made no new law after or besides that old law of Moses. Wherefore the monks and Popish schoolmen do no less err and blaspheme Christ, in that they imagine that he hath given a new law besides the law of Moses, than do the Turks, which vaunt of their Mahomet as of a new lawgiver after Christ, and better than Christ. Christ then came not to abolish the whole law, that he might make a new, but, as Paul here saith, he was sent of his Father into the world, to redeem those which were kept in thraldom under the law. These words paint out Christ lively and truly: they do not attribute unto him the office to make any new law, but to redeem them which were under the law. And Christ himself, saith, "I judge no man." And in another place: "I come not to judge the world, but that the world should be saved by me" (John 8:15; 12:47); that is to say, I came not to bring any law, nor to judge men according to the same, as Moses and other lawgivers; but I have a higher and better office. The law killed you, and I again do judge, condemn, and kill the law, and so I deliver you from the tyranny thereof. . . . Wherefore, it is very profitable for us to have always before our eyes this sweet and comfortable sentence, and such-like which set out Christ truly and lively, that in our whole life, in all dangers, in the confession of our faith before tyrants, and in the hour of death, we may boldly and with sure confidence say, O law, thou hast no power over me, and therefore thou dost accuse and condemn me in vain. For I believe in Jesus Christ the Son of God, whom the

Father sent into the world to redeem us miserable sinners oppressed with the tyranny of the law. He gave his life and shed his blood for me. Therefore, feeling thy terrors and threatenings, O law, I plunge my conscience in the wounds, blood, death, resurrection, and victory of my Saviour Christ. Besides him I will see nothing, I will hear nothing. This faith is our victory, whereby we overcome the terrors of the law, sin, death, and all evils, and yet not without great conflicts. And here do the children of God, which are daily exercised with grievous temptations, wrestle and sweat indeed. For oftentimes it cometh into their minds that Christ will accuse them, and plead against them; that he will require an account of their former life, and that he will condemn them. They cannot assure themselves that he is sent of his Father to redeem us from the tyranny and oppression of the law. And whereof cometh this? They have not yet fully put off the flesh, which rebelleth against the Spirit. Therefore the terrors of the law, the fear of death, and such-like sorrowful and heavy sights, do oftentimes return, which hinder our faith, that it cannot apprehend the benefit of Christ, who hath redeemed us from the bondage of the law, with such assurance as it should do.—Ed. of 1860, on 4:4–5

4. THE PRISON EPISTLES. This group of Paul's writings—Ephesians, Philippians, and Colossians (with Philemon), known as the Prison Epistles—introduces the truth respecting the believer's exalted position in Christ, which exalted position is grounded upon and made possible through the death of Christ only.

Ephesians 1:7. "In whom we have redemption through his blood, the forgiveness of sins, according to the riches of his grace."

At the very opening of the Ephesian Letter and as a ground of the realization of the eternal purpose of God for each of those chosen in Christ, it is said that redemption is accomplished, which is the basis upon which God can righteously forgive sin. In this text no mention is made of the estate of fallen man, which demands both redemption and forgiveness. That need is assumed and is but a necessary step in the preparation of the more essential manifestation of superabounding grace. In Christ Jesus we *have* redemption. On the divine side, the great redeeming work is accomplished. It is now a completed transaction; therefore, not a thing which God *will* do for man upon some condition of human worthiness, but a thing which He *has* done for man already and when man was without merit, without strength, a sinner and an enemy of God. That there is an elect company in the divine view is no part of the gospel of divine grace which is addressed to a lost world; it is one of God's secrets intended only for those who are saved. On the other hand, the announcement of an accomplished blood-redemption as potentially provided for all is the evangel of infinite grace: "Whosoever will, may come." Redemption has always been by blood alone. Blood is the divinely determined ransom which an outraged holiness must demand. That very blood-ransom was prefigured in all Old Testament sacrifices, as it is now available through the death of Christ; hence, redemption has been offered to man as a benefit throughout the history of the race. Having contemplated the holy nature of God and His uncompromising, unyielding character and righteous government, it is not difficult to accept the solemn decree: "The soul that sinneth, it shall die"; likewise: "The wages of sin is death"; and, again: "Without shedding of blood is no remission." God never deals with sin in leniency or mere generosity. The awful penalty which sin inevitably incurs cannot be lessened in the slightest degree. God's holy demands, which are based on His holy character, are as unchangeable as His nature. Christ paid the required ransom. Divine justice is satisfied, and the way of salvation is now open for all. The responsibility imposed on the sinner is that of believing the record God has given concerning this redemption which is in His Son. This record points to the Redeemer as the only One who is able to save, and calls for nothing less or for nothing more than saving trust in Him. It is in Him that we have redemption. He is our redemption. By the shedding of His blood He made possible a perfect ransom; by His resurrection He proved the completeness of His undertaking, and resumed His life by the same authority by which He laid it down. Thus He ever lives as the all-sufficient Redeemer of those for whom He died. It is God who in infinite grace provided a ransom, and it is man who in infinite sin rejects that ransom. The price is paid and the grace of God is the portion of each one who will receive it, and those who are saved can say with the Apostle: "We have redemption through his blood, the forgiveness of sins, according to the riches of his grace."

Ephesians 2:13. "But now in Christ Jesus ye who sometimes were far off are made nigh by the blood of Christ."

Because of its dispensational import this passage demands special consideration. Having indicated the distinctions which had obtained between Jew and Gentile as set up at the first by God and ever honored by Him—which distinctions were accentuated by human prejudice and hatred—the writer announces a new divine purpose for the present age, a divine purpose specifically revealed to this same Apostle (cf. Eph. 3:1–6). The purpose is realized on the grounds of the death and resurrection of Christ and the advent of the Spirit on the Day of Pentecost. That divine purpose is no less than the forming of a new body of heavenly people drawn from both Jews and Gentiles, each individual in that body perfected in Christ, and the whole company to be to "the praise of the glory of his grace." Therefore, because it is to the glory of His grace, each individual in this company, whether Jew or Gentile, is called and saved upon that same distinct principle of selection—the sovereign grace of God, apart from all human merit. As a basis for this exercise of sovereign grace apart from human merit, the most startling divine decree was announced, startling, indeed, because never before heard of in the world, and because it is so contrary to the hitherto divinely sanctioned exaltation of Israel over the Gentiles. That decree declares that now there is "no difference" between Jew and Gentile: they are all *under sin* (Rom. 3:9). So, again, there is "no difference" between Jew and Gentile, "for the same Lord over all is rich unto all that call upon him" (Rom. 10:12). According to the first declaration, the former distinction between Jews and Gentiles disappears by virtue of the fact that both classes are now, regardless of former relationships to Jehovah, "under sin" (cf. Eph. 2:11–22). According to the second declaration, the way into this highest heavenly glory is open to all who will believe. The estate "under sin" consists in the fact that God now refuses to accept any human merit, national or personal, as a credit or contribution toward that salvation which is offered the individual in and through Christ. God thus strips each human being of all hope in himself and shuts him up to that perfect salvation alone, which is in Christ and which provides the eternal and infinite perfection of Christ. It might seem unkind to take away what little merit one might be supposed to have before God, but in the end it is not unkind. It is rather, "that he might have mercy upon all" (Rom. 11:32). The grace of God is not a thing which adjusts itself to the greater or less degree of human merit, but it is a *standard* whole; that is, since all merit is excluded, it requires the same degree of grace to save one individual as it does to save another. And the result is not to the glory of man in the slightest degree: rather, it is all to the praise of the glory of His grace (Eph. 1:6; 2:7–9). There was little for the Gentile to unlearn in connection with this new age-purpose and plan of salvation. He had no ground for hope before, and the gospel of salvation by grace became to him as life from the dead. But the Jew stumbled over the way of salvation made available through the cross, so only a few, now that their national preference is set aside for this age (Rom. 11:1–36), have been able to abandon their assumed national standing with God and to accept the exceeding grace of God in Christ. This somewhat lengthy restatement of the present ground of salvation by grace for Jew and Gentile alike may clarify the verses which follow in this Ephesians context.

By the words "but now" at the beginning of verse 13, a sharp contrast is drawn between the former estate of these Ephesian Gentiles as that was described in verse 12 and their new position in Christ. Here they are told that they, as Gentiles, who were at a previous time "far off" from God, were right then, because of their new position in Christ, "made nigh," and not by external ordinances or human virtue, but by the blood of Christ. To be *nigh to God* is one of the exalted positions into which each believer is brought at the moment he is saved. The perfection of this position is seen from the fact that one could not be nearer to God in time or eternity than he is already when in Christ. So perfect is the efficacy of the blood of Christ in providing a righteous ground for divine grace, that every desire on the part of God, though prompted by infinite love, can now be satisfied completely in behalf of those who believe on Christ. Verse 13 is closely related to verse 17 (cf. Isa. 59:17). In the former verse of the Apostle's only Gentiles are in view, but in the latter both Jews and Gentiles are seen. The Gentiles are identified as those who, because of no former covenant relation to God, were "far off," while the Jews, because of their covenants, were "nigh," though not nigh to the same degree in which the saved Jew and the saved Gentile are now because of being in Christ and redeemed through His precious blood.

Ephesians 5:1–2. "Be ye therefore followers of God, as dear children; and walk in love, as Christ also hath loved us, and hath given himself for us an offering and a sacrifice to God for a sweetsmelling savour."

In expounding this passage Dr. Charles Hodge states:

As God has placed us under so great obligation, "be ye, therefore, imitators of God." The exhortation is enlarged. We are not only to imitate God in being forgiving, but also as becomes *dear children, by walking in love.* As God is love, and as we by regeneration and adoption are his children, we are bound to exercise love habitually. Our whole walk should be characterized by it. *As Christ also hath loved us.* This is the reason why we should love one another. We should be like Christ, which is being like God, for Christ is God. The apostle makes no distinction between our being the objects of God's love and our being the objects of the love of Christ. We are to be imitators of God in love, for Christ hath loved us. *And given himself for us.* Here as elsewhere the great evidence of divine love is the death of Christ. See verse 25; chapter 3:19; John 15:13. "Greater love hath no man than this, that a man lay down his life for his friends." Gal. 2:20, "Who loved me and gave himself for me." 1 John 3:16, "Hereby perceive we the love *of God,* because he laid down his life for us, and we ought to lay down our lives for the brethren." Christ's death was *for us* as a sacrifice, and therefore, from the nature of the transaction, in our place. Whether the idea of substitution be expressed by ὑπὲρ ἡμῶν depends on the context rather than on the force of the preposition. To die for any one, may mean either for his benefit or in his stead, as the connection demands. Christ gave himself, *as an offering and a sacrifice*, προσφορὰν καὶ θυσίαν; the latter term explains the former. Any thing presented to God was a προσφορά, but θυσία was something slain. The addition of that term, therefore, determines the nature of the offering. This is elsewhere determined by the nature of the thing offered, as in Hebrews 10:10, "the offering of the body of Christ"; or, "himself," Heb. 9:14, 25; by the effects ascribed to it, viz. expiation of guilt and the propitiation of God, which are the appropriate effects of a sin-offering; see Heb. 2:17; 10:10, 14; Rom. 3:25; 5:9, 10; by explanatory expressions, "the one offering of Christ" is declared to be μίαν ὑπὲρ ἁμαρτιῶν θυσίαν, Heb. 10:12; "a sacrifice for sin," and προσφορὰ περὶ ἁμαρτίας, Heb. 10:18; ἀντίλυτρον, and λύτρον ἀντὶ πολλῶν, as in 1 Tim. 2:6, Matt. 20:28; it is called a propitiation, Rom. 3:25, as well as a ransom. Christ himself, therefore, is called the Lamb of God who bore our sins; his blood is the object of faith or ground of confidence, by which, as the blood of a sacrifice, we are redeemed, 1 Pet. 1:18, 19. He saves us as a priest does, i.e. by a sacrifice. Every victim ever slain on Pagan altars was a declaration of the necessity for such a sacrifice; all the blood shed on Jewish altars was a prophecy and promise of propitiation by the blood of Christ; and the whole New Testament is the record of the Son of God offering himself up as a sacrifice for the sins of the world. This, according to the faith of the church universal, is the sum of the Gospel—the incarnation and death of the eternal Son of God as a propitiation for sin. There can, therefore, be no doubt as to the sense in which the apostle here declares Christ to be an offering and a sacrifice.—*A Commentary on the Epistle to the Ephesians*, pp. 277–79

Ephesians 5:25–27. "Husbands, love your wives, even as Christ also loved the church, and gave himself for it; that he might sanctify and cleanse it with the washing of water by the word, that he might present it to himself a glorious church, not having spot, or wrinkle, or any such thing; but that it should be holy and without blemish."

The Letter to the Ephesians unfolds the high place to which the Church, the Body of Christ, has been brought and the corresponding responsibility in daily life which rests upon each member of that Body. At this point in the theme, the Apostle reverts to the order of truth which characterized the opening portion of this Epistle. The Church alone is in view as the one for whom Christ gave Himself to die upon the cross. It is true also that His death is a work provisionally even for those who do not claim its gracious blessing, and that His death is the ground on which God will yet do for Israel what He is now doing for the Church (for God will bring that nation into a place of right relation to Himself and purify her dross—Ezek. 16:2–63; 36:25–29; Isa. 1:25); but the fact of His death for the Church is here, properly enough, given the place of supreme importance. Certainly Jehovah's love for Israel could not be doubted (Jer. 31:3); but the fact that these two great divine purposes—that of Israel's earthly blessing and that of the out-calling of the Church—have so much in common is no argument that these purposes unite in one divine plan in the past, right now, or ever in the future. It is to be expected that Israel's portion would be proclaimed in those Old Testament Scriptures which are addressed to her, and that the portion for the Church would be found in the Epistles of the New Testament. Thus a peculiar application of the death of Christ is introduced by Ephesians 5—it becomes the pattern of devotion which the believing husband should maintain toward his wife. It should be noted that this is a new ideal belonging not to the paganism of Paul's day, but to the Christian home. The high and holy love of Christ for the Church, His Bride, is not degraded by this comparison; rather, the demands upon the husband are exalted to the measure of celestial responsibilities. The message of this passage, which is germane here, is that which is so constantly asserted in the New Testament: it was divine compassion which took Christ to the cross.

Philippians 2:8. "And being found in fashion as a man, he humbled himself, and became obedient unto death, even the death of the cross."

Christ was *obedient* unto death; He was obedient up to the point of death and He was obedient in death. Redemption originated in the Godhead in eternity past, but was consummated by the obedient death of the theanthropic Son. His obedience is always within the sphere of His humanity. His death is the climax of passing from heaven's glory to a felon's execution (cf. Heb. 10:4–7).

Philippians 3:10. "That I may know him, and the power of his resurrection, and the fellowship of his sufferings, being made conformable unto his death."

The personal attitude of the Apostle toward Christ's death is again a theme of his testimony. The whole doctrine of cosuffering with Christ and conformity to His death is doubtless far beyond the power of comprehension, especially in the case of those little disciplined in the ways of God. With Christ's sufferings and death the Apostle sought a likeness in himself. In the substitutionary aspect of His death no mortal may ever share; it is finished forever. But there is a sense in which the sufferings of Christ and His death call for a similar reality in the believer. The same Apostle writes of filling up that which is left behind of the afflictions of Christ (Col. 1:24). This, it would seem, is to signify not mere persecution for Christ's sake (cf. Phil. 1:29), but a like bur-

den for lost men and a willingness, if it were required, to die for them
(cf. Rom. 9:1–3; 1 Cor. 15:31; 2 Cor. 4:10).

Colossians 1:14. "In whom we have redemption through his blood,
even the forgiveness of sins."

This is practically a word-for-word restatement of Ephesians 1:7,
which has already been considered.

Colossians 1:20–23. "And, having made peace through the blood of
his cross, by him to reconcile all things unto himself; by him, I say,
whether they be things in earth, or things in heaven. And you, that
were sometime alienated and enemies in your mind by wicked works,
yet now hath he reconciled in the body of his flesh through death, to
present you holy and unblameable and unreproveable in his sight: if ye
continue in the faith grounded and settled, and be not moved away from
the hope of the gospel, which ye have heard, and which was preached
to every creature which is under heaven; whereof I Paul am made a
minister."

The widest scope for the value of Christ's death to be presented anywhere in the Sacred Text is set forth in this great declaration. It is seen
as a reconciliation of all things in heaven and upon earth. On this vast
theme Dean Alford has written an analysis which is worthy of repro-
duction, though agreement is not accorded it in every particular:

It has been a question, in what sense this reconciliation is predicated of the
whole universe. Short of this meaning we cannot stop: we cannot hold with
Erasmus and others, that it is a reconciliation of the *various portions of creation to one another:* nor, for the same reason, with Schleiermacher, understand
that the elements to be reconciled are the *Jews* and *Gentiles,* who were at vari-
ance about earthly and heavenly things, and were to be set at one in reference
to God. The Apostle's meaning clearly is, that by the blood of Christ's Cross,
reconciliation with God has passed on *all creation as a whole,* including angelic
as well as human beings, unreasoning and lifeless things, as well as organized
and intelligent. Now this may be understood in the following ways: 1) creation may be strictly regarded in its entirety, and man's offence viewed as having,
by inducing impurity upon one portion of it, alienated the whole from God:
and thus *"all things"* may be involved in our fall. Some support may seem to
be derived for this by the undeniable fact, that *the whole of man's world* is
included in these consequences (see Rom. 8:19 f.). But on the other side, we
never find the *angelic beings* thus involved: nay, we are taught to regard them
as our model in hallowing God's name, realizing His kingdom, and doing
His will (Matt. 6:9, 10). And again the terms here used, *"whether . . .
whether . . ."* would not suffer this: reconciliation is thus predicated of each
portion *separately.* We are thus driven, there being no question about *the
things on the earth,* to enquire, how *the things in the heavens* can be said to
be reconciled by the blood of the Cross. And here again, 2) we may say that

angelic, celestial creation was alienated from God because a portion of it fell from its purity: and, though there is no idea of the reconciliation extending *to that portion,* yet the whole, as a whole, may need thus reconciling, by the final driving into punishment of the fallen, and thus setting the faithful in perfect and undoubted unity with God. But to this I answer, *a*) that such reconciliation (?) though it might be a result of the coming of the Lord Jesus, yet could not in any way be effected by the *blood of His cross: b*) that we have no reason to think that the fall of some angels involved the rest in its consequences, or that angelic being is evolved from any root, as ours is from Adam: nay, in both these particulars, the very contrary is revealed. We must then seek our solution in some meaning which will apply to angelic beings in their essential nature, not as regards the sin of some among them. And as thus applied, no reconciliation must be thought of which shall resemble *ours* in its process—for Christ took not upon Him the seed of angels, nor paid any propitiatory penalty in the root of their nature, as including it in Himself. But, forasmuch as He is their Head as well as ours,—forasmuch as in Him they, as well as ourselves, live and move and have their being, it cannot be but that the great event in which He was glorified through suffering, should also bring them nearer to God, who subsist in Him in common with all creation. And at some such increase of blessedness does our Apostle seem to hint in Ephesians 3:10. That such increase might be described as a *reconciliation,* is manifest. In fact, every such nearer approach to Him may without violence to words be so described, in comparison with that previous greater distance which now seems like alienation;—and in this case even more properly, as one of the consequences of that great propitiation whose first and plainest effect was to reconcile to God, in the literal sense, the things upon earth, polluted and hostile in consequence of man's sin. So that our interpretation may be thus summed up: All creation subsists in Christ: all creation therefore is affected by His act of propitiation: sinful creation is, in the strictest sense, *reconciled,* from being at enmity: sinless creation, ever at a distance from his unapproachable purity, is lifted into nearer participation and higher glorification of Him, and is thus *reconciled,* though not in the strictest, yet in a very intelligible and allowable sense.—*Op. cit., in loc.*

The difficulty which this interpretation sets up is to be seen in the fact that there is no revealed reconciliation for fallen angels. These, therefore, cannot be included as having been brought nearer to God. Two distinct points must be kept in mind: (a) The Scriptures declare the ultimate fate of the fallen angels and of unregenerate men. This body of truth respecting the determined destiny of fallen beings must be given its full weight, since it precludes anything which might suggest an ultimate restoration. (b) The word *reconciliation* is too often invested with a meaning which does not belong to it. Its root meaning is that a change has been wrought from the position formerly occupied. A world which is reconciled to God (2 Cor. 5:19) does not mean that all in the world are saved, but rather that their estate before God is changed to the extent that the necessity of condemnation is removed by reason of Christ's death for them. The way is open for their salvation when it was not thus open before (cf. Isa. 14:17; 61:1; Eph. 2:11–12). It is possible that the full effect of Christ's death upon angels has not been revealed and that were it disclosed this matter would be clarified. In this connection it will be admitted by all that little is known of the full meaning of Colossians 2:15, or any other Scripture which deals with the matter of Christ's relationship to the angels (cf. 1 Cor. 15:24–28). It is possible that all angels have been greatly influenced in their relation to God by Christ's death and yet without any feature which involved the restoration of those who have sinned. The death of Christ does not necessitate the salvation of every fallen man. It would seem that Colossians 2:15, rather than suggesting a thorough change in the fallen angelic hosts which would serve to give them hope, intimates a change into a sphere wherein all hope is removed forever.

5. THE THESSALONIAN EPISTLES. Though the Second Thessalonian Epistle does not mention Christ's death, there are two references to it in the First Letter.

1 Thessalonians 1:10; 5:9–10. "And to wait for his Son from heaven, whom he raised from the dead, even Jesus, which delivered us from the wrath to come. . . . For God hath not appointed us to wrath, but to obtain salvation by our Lord Jesus Christ. Who died for us, that, whether we wake or sleep, we should live together with him."

God gave His Son in a sacrificial death (John 3:16) that whosoever believeth on Him should not perish. By reason of Christ's death those who believe are delivered from the wrath to come; the unsaved are not so delivered, but must face that wrath and perish (in the conscious sense that this term as used in the New Testament implies). There is eternal security for those who are delivered. That deliverance is effective in the rapture whether they "wake or sleep."

6. THE PASTORAL EPISTLES. This group of Epistles—1 Timothy, 2 Timothy, and Titus—presents several references to the death of Christ. Two are implications—2 Timothy 1:10; 2:8—and two are direct doctrinal declarations.

1 Timothy 2:5–6. "For there is one God, and one mediator between God and men, the man Christ Jesus; who gave himself a ransom for all, to be testified in due time."

One God and one Mediator between God and men, Christ Jesus, Himself being man, who gave Himself a ransom for all, which ransom is to be testified to in the appointed age: thus the doctrine of a mediator is clearly stated. He being God is, nevertheless, so identified with man through His humanity that He can mediate beween God and man. To that end He gave Himself a ransom. This statement emphasizes the truth, as done already in John 10:18, that Christ laid down His own life voluntarily, and, as done in Hebrews 9:14, that He offered Himself to God; and this witness respecting Christ's death is to be given in an age appointed thereto. It could not be given before. This time, then, is the appointed age of gospel preaching and that for the realization of the heavenly purpose (cf. Heb. 2:10) of God.

Titus 2:14. "Who gave himself for us, that he might redeem us from all iniquity, and purify unto himself a peculiar people, zealous of good works."

Here the same aspect of truth—being redeemed by blood from all iniquity—is set forth. This contemplates the past as something put away and anticipates a people who, because they are redeemed, would be zealous of good works. The passage has a peculiar value in that it relates the good works which become the child of God to the ground of his salvation. As in Ephesians 2:10, so here salvation imposes an obligation to fulfill the will of God on the one He thus saves.

VI. IN PETER'S WRITINGS

The Apostle Peter refers to Christ's death once in each of his recorded sermons—Acts 2:23; 3:14; 10:39—but makes no mention of it in his Second Epistle. In each of these sermons to be recorded, the reference is an accusation of the Jews because of their crucifying Christ. In his First Epistle seven references are made to Christ's death, of which four may be classed as less important—1:2; 2:21; 4:1,13—and three of major import. Attention may well be given to the major passages.

1 Peter 1:18–19. "Forasmuch as ye know that ye were not redeemed with corruptible things, as silver and gold, from your vain conversation received by tradition from your fathers; but with the precious blood of Christ, as of a lamb without blemish and without spot."

As in no other Scripture, the price of redemption is here revealed. The Old Testament type had prepared the way in making it a necessity that the redeeming blood be *shed* and that the lamb be without spot. John the Baptist had identified Christ as the Lamb of God (John 1:29) and now Peter concludes the testimony, which is to the effect that the blood of redemption has been shed and has wrought its immeasurable results in those who have believed. "Without shedding of blood is no remission" (Heb. 9:22). This truth is perhaps more central than any other in the gospel which is to be preached. Men afflicted with unwillingness to be amenable to the Scriptures have spurned the doctrine of redemption by shed blood on the ground that it is offensive to all of our esthetic nature; but what of the offense of their sin as seen by a holy God? The offense to Him is very real and can be cured only by the blood of His own Son. The whole Bible teaches this clearly, and to depart from it is to abandon the Sacred Text in all its parts. The new song in heaven—"Thou art worthy . . . for thou wast slain, and hast redeemed us to God by thy blood" (Rev. 5:9)—would hardly be sung by those whose esthetic natures have blinded them to their need of remission.

1 Peter 2:24. "Who his own self bare our sins in his own body on the tree, that we, being dead to sins, should live unto righteousness: by whose stripes ye were healed."

Here once more the exact meaning of the transaction on the cross is restated. Christ "bare our sins in his own body on the tree." This is God's disposition of human sin. It is wrought through the greatest sacrifice God could ever make, and thrice blessed is he who receives and believes this precious truth, and thrice condemned is he who in unbelief neglects or rejects this good news.

1 Peter 3:18. "For Christ also hath once suffered for sins, the just for the unjust, that he might bring us to God, being put to death in the flesh, but quickened by the Spirit."

Peter's final word of soteriological witness is that Christ "suffered for sins, the just for the unjust" and with a view to bringing the unjust to God. There are many theological problems engendered by this declaration, but not one of these jeopardizes the simple truth that, because of the suffering of the Just, the unjust may be brought to God (cf. Ex. 19:4; Deut. 1:31). There is nothing to be desired beyond that estate wherein man has reached the heart of God; and God's provision through the sacrifice of His Son alone secures this wonderful result. "Believe on the Lord Jesus Christ, and thou shalt be saved."

VII. IN THE LETTER TO THE HEBREWS

The general message and purpose of the Epistle to the Hebrews must be understood if the arguments set forth there are to be given their proper weight. Of the message and purpose, Dr. C. I. Scofield in his introductory words to the book as published in his *Reference Bible* says,

"The doctrinal passages reveal the purpose of the book. It was written with a twofold intent: (1) To confirm Jewish Christians by showing that Judaism had come to an end through the fulfilment by Christ of the whole purpose of the law; and (2) the hortatory passages show that the writer had in view the danger ever present to Jewish professed believers of either lapsing back into Judaism, or of pausing short of true faith in Jesus Christ. It is clear from the Acts that even the strongest of the believers in Palestine were held to a strange mingling of Judaism and Christianity (e.g. Acts 21:18–24), and that snare would be especially apt to entangle professed Christians amongst the Jews of the dispersion" (p. 1291). However, as Dr. Scofield would himself contend, the whole argument of this Epistle hangs on the death and resurrection of Christ as the answer to every claim of Judaism as well as to every need of the human heart. The passages bearing on Christ's death are numerous and some too extended for quotation. They are: 2:9–18; 5:7–8; 7:27; 9:12, 14–15, 26, 28; 10:4–7, 10, 12, 19; 12:2; 13:12. Not all of these may be taken up separately here.

Hebrews 2:9–18. This extended portion introduces several features out of the whole doctrine of Christ's suffering and death. First in order is the truth that Christ came into the world to the end that He might suffer, and that He might bring thereby many sons into glory. He did not stop with descent into angelic spheres through which He passed nor did He take on Him the nature of angels. He was made a little lower than the angels that He might die a ransom death, not for angels but for men. The Spirit of God also asserts that Christ "tasted death for every man." The terminology *every man* is not subject to those distortions which some have imposed upon *world,* when they assert that, as found in John 3:16 and in 1 John 2:2, this expression means the world of the elect or the Body of Christ. The words *every man* will not yield to a cramping torture just to save a theory. To the end that He who created all things and for whom they exist (cf. Col. 1:16–18; Rev. 4:11) might populate heaven with those who are alone capable of singing the redemption song (cf. Rev. 5:9–10), He Himself as the Captain of their salvation needed to be a Savior perfected through the things which He suffered. It is not a matter of any moral change in Him; but as redemption could come only by the sacrifice of Himself it was required of Him that He should suffer and thus become a qualified Redeemer. Redemption's price is the blood of the Lamb of God. The work of Redeemer is not complete until His blood is shed. Thus the incarnation and humiliation brought Him into a Redeemer's relationship to those whom He would save, and of this estate He is not ashamed (cf. Heb. 2:11–12; Ps. 22:22). To redeem He must become "like unto his brethren." Three great doctrines are mentioned in rapid succession here—partaking of flesh and blood to become a saving Mediator, partaking of the seed of Abraham to fulfill His part in the Abrahamic Covenant, and partaking of death (one of many reasons for this step) that He might destroy Satan and His hosts. Of a similar tenor is Hebrews 5:7–9, which reads, "Who in the days of his flesh, when he had offered up prayers and supplications with strong crying and tears unto him that was able to save him from death, and was heard in that he feared; though he were a Son, yet learned he obedience by the things which he suffered; and being made perfect, he became the author of eternal salvation unto all them that obey him." Christ's own sorrow and anguish of soul as seen in the words "My God, my God, why hast thou forsaken me?" arises from His humanity. He appealed unto One who was able to save Him from death, but who did not spare Him—"Remove this cup from me: nevertheless not my will, but thine, be done." Such was His obedience. He learned obedience experimentally by being obedient unto death. As very God Himself He had no obligation to obedience. As very man, that He might be the perfect man, He was of course perfect in obedience. When about to come into the world it is said of Him, "For it is not possible that the blood of bulls and of goats should take away sins. Wherefore when he cometh into the world, he saith, Sacrifice and offering thou wouldest not, but a body hast thou prepared me: in burnt-offerings and sacrifices for sin thou hast had no pleasure. Then said I, Lo, I come (in the volume of the book it is written of me,) to do thy will, O God" (Heb. 10:4–7). Thus He acquired those qualities which belong to a theanthropic Mediator. He has become the source of salvation unto all who obey Him (Heb. 5:9) by responding to His call, "Come unto me" (Matt. 11:28).

Hebrews 7:27; 10:10, 12; 12:2. "Who needeth not daily, as those high priests, to offer up sacrifice, first for his own sins, and then for the people's: for this he did once, when he offered up himself. . . . By the which will we are sanctified through the offering of the body of Jesus Christ once for all. . . . But this man, after he had offered one sacrifice for sins for ever, sat down on the right hand of God. . . . Looking unto Jesus the author and finisher of our faith; who for the joy that was set before him endured the cross, despising the shame, and is set down at the right hand of the throne of God."

In all His sacrifice there is first the voluntary feature—"He . . . offered himself without spot to God"—and, second, the fact that His offering is infinitely effective. The Aaronic type was perfectly fulfilled by His offering of Himself. As the sacrifices of old were efficacious to the degree assigned to them, so the Antitype was efficacious, even perfecting forever those who are set apart unto Him. There was an actuating motive for His sacrifice. The compassion of God moved Him, and, though His suffering was real to the point of anguish and death, there was also a "joy . . . set before him." His was the most desolate and crushed of human lives and at the same time the embodiment of celestial joy. Thus, too, the believer may live, as illustrated in the experience of the great Apostle who could say: "I have great heaviness and continual sorrow" (Rom. 9:1–3) and "Rejoice . . . alway" (Phil. 4:4). Such a paradoxical sort of emotional life is not natural to humanity; it belongs to Deity and can be experienced only through having the characteristics imparted by the Holy Spirit.

Hebrews 10:1–39. The closing portion of this theme—but for Hebrews 13:11–12 wherein Christ is seen to fulfill an important type respecting the location of His cross outside the city walls—carries the attentive student into many features of Christ's death: (a) the contrast between Old Testament sacrifices and that of Christ, (b) Christ a willing sacrifice, (c) the far-reaching benefit of His own death (vss. 10–18), and (d) the practical application, especially to Jewish believers, namely, the obligation in daily life which grows out of that benefit. This fourfold division of this extended portion may be contemplated now, point by point. (a) The contrast between the many offerings and the One divine is greatly heightened by the truth that the many served only as a shadow of the one infinitely efficacious sacrifice, and by the truth that in the many sacrifices God had received no final satisfaction though He did have pleasure in the sacrifice of His Son. It was both in the effectiveness of the offering and in the obedience of the Son that the Father took delight. Why should not the Father take delight in that which opened the way for His immeasurable love to express itself in the saving of lost men? From Adam to Moses there had been no complete realization of the Father's perfect will in any human life. In developing the argument respecting the failure of the many sacrifices—evidently meaning those of the Day of Atonement—the writer asserts that, had any one of those offerings been effectual in the complete sense, there would have been no more need of a repetition, since the worshipers once really purged would have had no more a conscience over sin. Note should be made here of the distinction that exists between the unceasing condemnation for sin which rests upon the unsaved and a grieving of the Spirit by sin which may arise on the part of those saved. In either case there is a consciousness of sin having been committed; but to the unsaved that consciousness is an unceasing sense of condemnation (Isa. 57:21), while of the saved it is said: "There is therefore now no condemnation" (Rom. 8:1). The experience of the saved when they sin is that of being out of fellowship with God (cf. Ps. 32:3–4). Arminianism thrives on the failure to recognize this distinction. These words of Christ spoken when He was about to come into the world are freighted with deepest significance. He looked on to His incarnation, saying, ". . . but a body hast thou prepared me" (vs. 5). This body capable of a blood-shedding sacrifice is held in contrast over against the blood of all the bulls and goats ever slain. "To do thy will" (vs. 7) has reference to the disposition of that body in death. (b) The voluntary character of His death is a crucial feature of this entire doctrine of sacrifice. Those who claim that it would be immoral for the Father to offer His Son have failed to recognize the sublime and determining truth that the Son was infinitely willing. It is even said repeatedly that He gave Himself. All this was predicted in Psalm 40:6–8. (c) The sacrifice of Christ is the basis of a complete perfecting of each believer forever. Much has already been said on this point—even the righteousness of God is imputed to them on the ground of Christ's death and this establishes their justification forever. (d) It could not be otherwise for the believer than to have an obligation to holiness. Any exalted position creates its corresponding responsibility and so here, as elsewhere in the Epistles, the position is first defined and the appeal to live accordingly is based upon it.

In conclusion, seven salient facts respecting Christ's suffering and death may be observed.

(a) While Christ's death is of inestimable value to men, it is of far greater value to God. None but God Himself could realize what it means to Him to have the way clear whereby He may, without tarnishing His own holiness, save and justify those who do no more than to believe in Jesus (Rom. 3:24–26).

(b) The death of Christ represents a sacrifice of infinite proportions. Nothing within the range of finite things can be drawn upon to illustrate such an immolation. No human mind may hope to trace it in its full extent or to grasp its full significance.

(c) The death of Christ was necessary as the only solution of the problem of evil even within the range of divine possibilities; and there is, therefore, no substitute for it, no optional choice, nor any salvation apart from it.

(d) Being God's own devised solution of His greatest problem—the sin question—it is, like all His works, efficacious to the point of infinity. Nothing of man's values need be added to it; nor can it be increased in value by any human effort when once it is applied to an individual.

(e) The death of Christ provides a perfect basis for a perfect salvation apart from all judgments upon the sinner. When the sinner comes to God on the ground of that death, God strikes no blow, offers no censure, and requires no compensation.

(f) By Christ's death there is a perfect redemption sinward, a perfect reconciliation manward, and a perfect propitiation Godward.

(g) Because of the extent of the value of Christ's death and the completeness of that value in all its parts, no other obligation rests upon men who would be saved than that they enter into it by receiving Christ, with all that He is and all that He has done, as their sufficient Savior.

CHAPTER X

THE RESURRECTION OF CHRIST INCARNATE

THE DEATH of Christ and the resurrection of Christ are component parts of one stupendous divine undertaking. Had He not died, there would be no basis upon which those mighty realities which His resurrection provides might rest; and had He not been raised from the dead, there would be no fruition in His death—no Savior, no living embodiment of that which was purposed by His death. Both events are thus seen to be essential in the absolute sense, and that which is essential to such a degree is not with respect to its import properly to be compared with any other thing. It is evident, then, that all attempts to estimate the relative values of these two events only tend to useless speculation. As traced by the so-called Covenant theologians, the death of Christ is given a place of large significance but His resurrection is accounted as little more than something for His own personal convenience, His necessary return from the sphere of death back to the place which He occupied before. In other words, as viewed by Covenant theologians, there is practically no doctrinal significance to Christ's resurrection. That Christ by resurrection became what in Himself He had not been before—the federal Head of a wholly new order of beings and these the primary divine objective as this is set forth in the New Testament—cannot be incorporated into a system of which the cherished and distinctive feature is one unchangeable divine purpose from Adam to the end of time. This simple analysis accounts for the otherwise inexplicable fact that systems of theology which follow the one-covenant idea will be searched almost in vain for any explanation of Christ's resurrection. It is not implied that Covenant theologians do not believe that Christ arose from the dead; it is merely indicated that the resurrection of Christ has for them—and of necessity—no vital doctrinal import. These honored men do recognize that God wrought mightily before Christ's death and of course on the basis of that death as an expectation, and that God works mightily now on the basis of the actuality of Christ's death, but then it is averred by these men that God did the same things for His people on the basis of an expectation as He now does on the basis of reality. Thus the death of Christ, if it were a reasonable expectation, was required at some time. The supposition that God did do in past ages what He is doing now, however, will not stand the test of Scripture. Such views are fanciful and idealistic. This assertion will be demonstrated as this thesis advances. There are certain disuniting events which serve to separate the past Mosaic age from the present age. Conditions and relations between God and man could not be the same after these events have transpired as they were before. The notion of an immutable covenant is rendered void by any one of these determining events, which events may be noted thus. (a) The death of Christ itself. As stated above, Covenant Theology, while magnifying the death of Christ, assumes that His death was just as effective in prospect as it is in retrospect. That He did not do the same work then as now is patent and so indicates a difference, for it is right and reasonable to suppose that God fills to the full the entire field of achievement which at a given time is open to Him. In the old order, sin was covered when animal blood was shed, which sacrifice typified the blood of Christ. The sin was not said to have been "taken away." Accordingly, Hebrews 10:4 asserts, "For it is not possible that the blood of bulls and of goats should take away sins" (cf. John 1:29; Rom. 3:25). However, at the present time upon believing in Christ sin is taken away (cf. Rom. 8:1; Col. 2:13). The Old Testament saint was forgiven, but only as God was able to deal with sin on the ground of the future death of Christ. Sins forgiven, or covered, is not tantamount to sins being taken away. It is really impossible that animal blood should "take away" sin. When about to come into the world the Savior said, therefore, ". . . but a body hast thou prepared me" (Heb. 10:5–7), and to this it is added that "by one offering [of Himself] he hath perfected for ever them that are sanctified"—that is, separated unto God by their salvation received through Christ (Heb. 10:14). "For the law made nothing perfect." Over against this and by the death of Christ, there is the bringing in of a better hope (Heb. 7:19). (b) Christ's resurrection serves also as a demarcation between the old order and the new. If as has been said Covenant Theology ignores the doctrinal aspects of the resurrection of Christ, it is due to the fact that according to that idealism the Church is not a new creation with its headship in the resurrected Christ, but has existed under a supposed uniform covenant from the beginning of human history. Thus for that system the great reality of a heavenly purpose peculiar to this age is ruled out completely. Of this, more anon. (c) The doctrinal aspects of Christ's ascension and present ministry in heaven mean but little to those who are committed to the theory of an unchanging covenant. According to this assumption, the Church obtained without a headship in heaven, even before Christ came; therefore, the inauguration of that headship as something sprung out of His resurrection could not be of any great moment. The Covenant theory cannot be broadened to allow for Christ's new, priesthood ministry in heaven, nor for His immeasurable ministry as Advocate, and for the same reason. Therefore, all this immeasurable truth is not included in their system by Covenant theologians. (d) The advent of the Holy Spirit on the Day of Pentecost constitutes a transformation as vital and far-reaching as any could be. Not only did He take up His residence in the world as definitely as did the Second Person when born of a virgin, but He undertook to form the tabernacle or temple in which He dwells— the whole body of believers, each one of whom is saved to infinite perfection in Christ—and become the indwelling source of life and power in each of those who are saved. By joining each believer to Christ, the Spirit is forming a wholly new thing unforeseen in ages past—a new humanity, a new creation, the realization of a wholly new divine purpose. The advent of the Spirit into the world and His residence in the world cannot be made to conform doctrinally to an unchangeable-covenant theory. Wherever this theory is stressed, there must go along with it a neglect of the most vital truths respecting the present age-characterizing ministries of the Spirit. The same reason may be assigned for this neglect, namely, that if the Church existed and progressed in Old Testament times apart from these ministries of the Spirit they cannot be of vital import in the present dispensation. (e) The disannulling of all Jewish purposes and distinctive features for an age renders a continuous-covenant conception objectionable. The Old Testament history leads on to its consummation in a glorious earthly kingdom in which the elect nation, Israel, will realize her covenants as promises fulfilled. It is, therefore, disruptive to a one-covenant theory to the last degree that a situation should be set up as it has been in this age in which it is said respecting Jew and Gentile that "there is no difference" (Rom. 3:9; 10:12). (f) The opening of the door of privilege to Gentiles as is done in this age introduces a feature wholly foreign to the revealed divine purpose as that was set forth in the Old Testament and renders an immutable, single-covenant idea untenable. (g) The introduction of an age as an intercalation into the midst of the predicted ongoing Jewish and Gentile programs and the new heavenly purpose which characterizes this age cannot be made to conform to a supposed single covenant. Thus it is seen how, to maintain the basic idea of a covenant theology, much that is vital in the whole divine purpose must be renounced and excluded in the interest of that which at best is only a theory; and among the neglected truths is the resurrection of Christ. However, in spite of an almost universal influence of the Covenant theory upon theological thought, the resurrection of Christ is, when seen in its true Biblical setting, properly recognized as the very ground of all the purpose of this age and the basis upon which the new positions and possessions of those in Christ are made to rest. There is a wide doctrinal difference between those who see no special consequence in Christ's resurrection and those who see its momentous significance. Those who observe this significance are not in error, nor do they need to be rebuked as those who have not followed a man-made theological standard. There is little probability that the theologian who by his training has been run into the restricted mold of a Covenant theory would venture far afield in independent Bible research, nor be sympathetic toward those who through years of untrammeled study of the Sacred Text have come to discover more of its meaning.

The Bible doctrine of resurrection is developed in two widely different divisions, namely, the resurrection of Christ and the resurrection of humanity. Being foreign to this discussion the resurrection of humanity, though treated elsewhere in this work, is not included here. In approaching that which is properly germane to this thesis—the resurrection of Christ—the subject will be presented after the following order: (a) the Old Testament doctrine of Christ's resurrection and (b) the New Testament doctrine of Christ's resurrection.

I. THE OLD TESTAMENT DOCTRINE

As recorded in Luke 24:44, following at once upon His appearance in resurrection and as an explanation of it, Christ said: "These are the words which I spake unto you, while I was yet with you, that all things must be fulfilled, which were written in the law of Moses, and in the prophets, and in the psalms, concerning me." Here, then, is intimation not only that Christ is the theme of all parts of the Old Testament, but that these Scriptures anticipate to some extent the resurrection of Christ, whether such references are usually recognized or not. Job makes reference to the resurrection of the body. Such recognition of the resurrection of Christ as is to be discerned in the Pentateuch will be found in the types. If Christ had the matter of type in mind when He spoke of His resurrection as being in the "law of Moses," He has placed notable honor upon this neglected phase of doctrine. Direct reference to Christ's resurrection is not discovered until as late as the Psalms of David, which is a millennium before Christ came into the world. The Old Testament contribution to the doctrine of Christ's resurrection may thus be observed in its two parts—the types and the prophecies.

1. THE TYPES. At least four typical foreshadowings of Christ's resurrection are found in the Old Testament and these occur within the Pentateuch. As indicated above, these appear to be the basis for Christ's own words spoken in relation to His resurrection (Luke 24:44). These foreshadowings are:

The Priesthood of Melchizedek (Gen. 14:18). "And Melchizedek king of Salem brought forth bread and wine: and he was the priest of the most high God."

While the Aaronic priesthood was constantly interrupted by death (Heb. 7:23–24), the priesthood of Christ which is said to be after the order of Melchizedek is wholly upon resurrection ground. Melchizedek himself typified Christ in His eternal character, having, so far as the record goes, no father or mother and no beginning or ending of days. Fulfilling the Aaronic pattern, Christ accomplished a redemption by His death; in the Melchizedek order Christ on resurrection ground looks back upon a finished redemption. This was symbolized in the presentation to Abraham by Melchizedek of bread and wine. The Melchizedek priesthood of Christ begins with Christ's resurrection and continues forever. It is made possible only by Christ's resurrection.

The Two Birds (Lev. 14:4–7). "Then shall the priest command to take for him that is to be cleansed two birds alive and clean, and cedar wood, and scarlet, and hyssop: and the priest shall command that one of the birds be killed in an earthen vessel over running water: as for the living bird, he shall take it, and the cedar wood, and the scarlet, and the hyssop, and shall dip them and the living bird in the blood of the bird that was killed over the running water: and he shall sprinkle upon him that is to be cleansed from the leprosy seven times, and shall pronounce him clean, and shall let the living bird loose into the open field."

Of two birds which together present in one type the whole divine undertaking wrought by Christ through His death and resurrection (cf. Rom. 4:25), the second bird, dipped in the blood of the first bird, signifies Christ in resurrection and ascension taking His blood into heaven. The antitype is clear, since there is no other cleansing which God can recognize except the blood of His Son and that presented in heaven (Heb. 9:11–28).

First-Fruits (*Lev. 23:10–11*). "Speak unto the children of Israel, and say unto them, When ye be come into the land which I give unto you, and shall reap the harvest thereof, then ye shall bring a sheaf of the firstfruits of your harvest unto the priest: and he shall wave the sheaf before the LORD, to be accepted for you: on the morrow after the sabbath the priest shall wave it."

As the sheaf of grain represented all the harvest when waved before Jehovah, so Christ as the First-Fruits in resurrection (1 Cor. 15:23) represents by His resurrected and glorified body all those whom He has saved and who are to follow Him into heaven.

Aaron's Rod that Budded (*Num. 17:8*). "And it came to pass, that on the morrow Moses went into the tabernacle of witness; and, behold, the rod of Aaron for the house of Levi was budded, and brought forth buds, and bloomed blossoms, and yielded almonds."

Writing on this particular type in Numbers 17, Dr. C. I. Scofield declares, "Aaron's rod that budded: Type of Christ in resurrection, owned of God as High Priest. Aaron's priesthood had been questioned in the rebellion of Korah, so God Himself will confirm it (v. 5). Each of the tribe-heads brought a perfectly dead rod; God put life into Aaron's only. So all the authors of religions have died, Christ among them, but only Christ was raised from the dead, and exalted to be a high priest (Heb. 4:14; 5:4–10)" (*Scofield Reference Bible*, p. 190).

2. THE PROPHECIES. While there is much intimation in the Old Testament respecting the resurrection of the human body (cf. Job 14:13–15; 19:25–26; Ps. 16:9–10; 17:15; 49:15; Isa. 26:19; Dan. 12:2; Hos. 5:15—6:2; 13:14; Heb. 11:17–19), there are but three direct predictions in the Old Testament of Christ's resurrection. These are:

Psalm 16:9–10. "Therefore my heart is glad, and my glory rejoiceth: my flesh also shall rest in hope. For thou wilt not leave my soul in hell; neither wilt thou suffer thine Holy One to see corruption."

No more conspicuous example will be found in the Bible of a truth which concerns one person and is at the same time applicable to two persons than is presented in this portion. It is clear that, as the passage reads, David is anticipating his own resurrection; but both the Apostle Peter and the Apostle Paul quote this Scripture as referring to the resurrection of Christ (cf. Acts 2:24–31; 13:34–37). It will be noted that both apostles emphasize the predicted truth that Christ would see no corruption. This He did not see, though in a state of complete death for the period between His death and resurrection. According to the Apostle's distinction recorded in 1 Corinthians 15:42–57, those caught away at the coming of the Lord, though changed from the mortal to the immortal state in the "twinkling of an eye," do not see corruption. Christ is thus classed, in spite of the period in which His body was subject to absolute death, as one who now has immortality (1 Tim. 6:16)—not incorruption, which will be the estate of those who because of death have seen corruption. As it was predicted of Him that not a bone of His should be broken (cf. John 19:36), in like manner it was declared prophetically that He should not see corruption.

Psalm 22:22–31. Writing on the 22nd Psalm, Erling C. Olsen in his commendable *Meditations in the Psalms* states:

The 22nd verse of the 22nd Psalm contains the first words of the risen Christ, "I will declare thy name unto my brethren . . ." From the 17th chapter of John's Gospel, we learn that one of the ministries committed to our Lord was this manifestation of the Father's name. In the sixth verse of that chapter it is written, "I have manifested thy name unto the men which thou gavest me out of the world.". . . But this is not all that is in this 22nd Psalm. Note that our Lord calls us "My brethren." What condescension that He is willing to call us "brethren," and indeed, to say He is not *ashamed* to call us brethren. . . . Now let us look at the last half of verse 22, which reads: ". . . in the midst of the congregation will I praise thee." Have you considered our Lord Jesus Christ as leading a great congregation in songs of praise? That is what this Psalm presents. And it is in harmony with what we learn from the 2nd chapter of Hebrews. You who sing in choruses or lead congregational singing, may it be an added incentive to you, to know that the Lord is the chief Singer, the great choir director. Indeed, no worship, no praise could possibly be acceptable to God unless it went through our Lord Jesus Christ. He is the center of all God's revelation, the center of Christianity. In the 23rd verse we have the various sections of the great choir which our Lord directs. He seems to stand in the midst, instructing each section to render its praise unto God. In the 24th verse we have the substance of the song of praise, as well as the reason for so much singing at Easter time. "For he hath not despised nor abhorred the affliction of the afflicted; neither hath he hid his face from him; but when he cried unto him, he heard." He sings and we sing because of His death and His resurrection. Who wouldn't sing upon experiencing the grace of God in their hearts and the assurance that they have been redeemed from sin?—I, 148, 150

Psalm 118:22–24. "The stone which the builders refused is become the head stone of the corner. This is the LORD's doing; it is marvellous in our eyes. This is the day which the LORD hath made; we will rejoice and be glad in it."

The divine commentary on this portion of the 118th Psalm is found in Acts 4:10–11, which reads: "Be it known unto you all, and to all the people of Israel, that by the name of Jesus Christ of Nazareth, whom ye crucified, whom God raised from the dead, even by him doth this man stand here before you whole. This is the stone which was set at nought of you builders, which is become the head of the corner." The truth that God raised Christ from the dead is illustrated by the rejected stone becoming the headstone of the corner. Such a reversal of the decision of the builders in rejecting the stone is indeed a work of Jehovah. Israel—here said to be the builders who rejected the stone, as the nation did in the crucifixion—found by the resurrection that their deed was reversed. The day of Christ's resurrection—the first day of the week—is peculiarly ordained of God, therefore, as a day in which believers may rejoice and serve. The first word spoken on that morning by the resurrected Christ was χαίρετε (Matt. 28:9), which is translated *All hail,* but, as all will agree, may more literally be translated *Rejoice.* Out of forty-five times as used in the New Testament, in all but six—where it is employed as a salutation—the word is translated in the Authorized Version *rejoice* or *gladness.* The salutation is plainly, therefore, one of rejoicing. Thus the Lord Himself, in compliance with Psalm 118:22–24, is said to have begun the first celebration of His resurrection with rejoicing. Respecting the celebration of the first day of the week, much has been presented already under Ecclesiology and more will be said anon.

It will be observed that, aside from the expectation which the types and predictions present, the Old Testament assigns no specific meaning to the resurrection of Christ as an act related to Israel. David reasoned that, though death was determined for his Greater Son, the Son would be raised to sit on the Davidic throne (Acts 2:23–31). The necessity was not lodged in the resurrection itself, but in the unalterable, oath-bound covenant respecting an unfailing occupant of that throne (cf. 2 Sam. 7:16; Jer. 33:17). The resurrection of Christ in its doctrinal significance, then, belongs alone to the Church, the New Creation.

II. THE NEW TESTAMENT DOCTRINE

The New Testament doctrine of Christ's resurrection may be divided into seven parts: (a) Christ's own predictions respecting His resurrection, (b) His resurrection as subject to valid proof, (c) His an actual resurrection, (d) His resurrection as resulting in a new order of beings, (e) seven reasons for His resurrection, (f) His resurrection as the present standard of divine power, and (g) the Lord's Day as a commemoration of His resurrection.

1. CHRIST'S PREDICTIONS. Unbelieving men have contended it is unreasonable to suppose that with so many direct declarations regarding His own resurrection the disciples could have been so utterly unprepared for it as they were. However, in this connection it should be remembered that up to the time of His death and rising again, a resurrection, being quite supernatural, was not easily expected; but above and beyond this, it is evident that, for important reasons not difficult to recognize, the ability to grasp what Christ said of both His death and resurrection was really withheld from the disciples, though specifically and repeatedly announced. His death and resurrection had no immediate place in the kingdom program to which these disciples were called to give sole attention. Their sincere proclamation of the gospel of the kingdom would have been greatly influenced had they been faced with a certain belief that Christ would be rejected, put to death, and then raised from the dead. Even John the Baptist, as has been noted before, was given no clear comprehension of the oncoming death and resurrection of Christ. On the other hand, as asserted before, it was needful that by the transfiguration exhibition of glory these disciples—especially those appointed to write Scripture, namely, Peter and John—should be encouraged to retain the certainty of His "power and coming" (2 Pet. 1:16) in spite of the disarrangement of the kingdom expectation which the death and resurrection would create. They must know that the kingdom program is not abandoned, but that its realization from that time forth must be associated with His return to the earth in power and great glory. Until their doctrinal significance could be disclosed— and such could not possibly be until these events had actually transpired—the death and resurrection of Christ could have been interpreted by the disciples as only a hopeless cancellation of all they had been taught and all they had proclaimed respecting Messiah's earthly kingdom. The offer of an earthly kingdom, its rejection, the death and resurrection of the King, a new unforeseen age with a new divine purpose, and the return of the King to fulfill all His promises may be comprehended by some as they view it more or less in retrospect, whereas but slight contemplation would convince one of the complexity of all this in the minds of those who passed through its actual outworking. Due thought should be given to the need of divine wisdom in introducing to earnest men the successive steps in the greatest transition the world has ever experienced, namely, one from Judaism to Christianity. The stu-

pendous change which demands the new birth of Nicodemus and the regeneration of Saul of Tarsus is not clarified or even approached by a Covenant theology which, while embracing a unifying idealism respecting a supposed single divine purpose, can ride unconsciously over these mighty changes as though they did not exist. It was required by existing conditions that the disciples should not know of Christ's oncoming death and resurrection until those age-transforming events were experienced and the time had arrived when they should enter into the new values secured for them by these events; yet it was also essential that Christ should predict both His death and His resurrection. Bearing on the inability of the disciples to remember Christ's predictions is John 2:22, which reads: "When therefore he was risen from the dead, his disciples remembered that he had said this unto them; and they believed the scripture, and the word which Jesus had said," but it is also observed how after His resurrection Christ opened their understanding to the Scriptures and that particularly in respect to His death and resurrection. It is written of this: "Then opened he their understanding, that they might understand the scriptures, and said unto them, Thus it is written, and thus it behoved Christ to suffer, and to rise from the dead the third day" (Luke 24:45–46). Of the greatest importance, likewise, is the express declaration of Luke 18:31–34—wherein Christ's declaration regarding His oncoming death and resurrection is recorded—and especially the disclosure in verse 34, which reads, "And they understood none of these things: and this saying was hid from them, neither knew they the things which were spoken." Divine power thus purposely veiled the death and resurrection from their eyes. It is to be noted that, though the disciples were unable to receive Christ's predictions respecting His death and resurrection, the unbelieving Jews did understand and remember. Of them it is recorded that they said to Pilate after Christ's death: "Sir, we remember that that deceiver said, while he was yet alive, After three days I will rise again. Command therefore that the sepulchre be made sure until the third day, lest his disciples come by night, and steal him away, and say unto the people, He is risen from the dead: so the last error shall be worse than the first" (Matt. 27:63–64). Incidentally, it will be seen that this Scripture sheds light on the problem of the time between Christ's death and resurrection. Some have made much of the phrase "after three days," while others have emphasized the phrase "until the third day," but this one passage indicates that these two phrases mean one and the same thing.

Dr. Everett F. Harrison, writing on the resurrection and this point, states:

This much is clear from the whole discussion, that Jesus, both in His predictions and in His teaching following the resurrection, laid great stress upon the time element, and the early church sought to impress the same thing in its witness (Acts 10:40; 1 Cor. 15:4). Yet it must be acknowledged as a singular insistence if the sole basis for it is the necessity of fulfilling the sign of Jonah. That is the only sure link with the Old Testament as far as the three days are concerned. An incident in connection with the raising of Lazarus may shed some light on this problem. When Jesus commanded the removal of the stone, Martha interposed, "Lord, by this time he stinketh; for he hath been dead four days." Why should she be so explicit in stating the period of time? The answer is that among many of the peoples of antiquity, Israel included, it was supposed that corruption began on the fourth day, when all possibility of re-animation by the soul was at an end. This accounts for Jesus' purposeful delay in coming to Bethany (John 11:6, 17) and also for the inability of the Pharisees to deny the reality of the miracle (vs. 47). It accounts also for the emphasis in apostolic preaching upon the fact that Jesus did not see corruption (Acts 2:31; 13:37). Our conclusion, then, is that our Lord deliberately announced a time for His resurrection which would meet every demand of popular understanding—long enough after the death to certify to the reality of the death, yet not so long as to permit corruption to take place.—*The Christian Doctrine of Resurrection,* unpublished ms., p. 55

The passages which record Christ's predictions of His death and resurrection are: Matthew 16:21; 17:23; 20:17–19; 26:12, 28, 31; Mark 9:30–32; 14:8, 24, 27; Luke 9:22, 44–45; 18:31–34; 22:20; John 2:19–21; 10:17–18; 12:7.

2. SUBJECT TO VALID PROOF. Dr. Harrison's introduction to his own treatment of the evidence for Christ's resurrection along with the outline appended is, because of its satisfactory statement, introduced here:

The crucial importance of the resurrection for the demonstration of the divine origin and full authority of the Christian religion has long been recognized, both by friends and foes, perhaps by the latter even more than by the former, since they are on the alert to detect that portion of the foundation which will involve the collapse of the whole edifice in case it can be successfully removed. Though the method of attack has changed through the years and consequently, to a degree, the method of defense, yet the basic facts remain as they have from the very beginning, and to them we make our appeal. The three prominent lines of evidence for Jesus' resurrection are the empty tomb, His appearances to the disciples, and the transformation wrought in them by those appearances. In the background, but no less deserving of consideration as historical evidence, are the very existence of the church and the literature which emanated from it, our New Testament. Finally, though not lying properly within the category of evidence, there is a congruity between His resurrection and all else that we know about Him. The consistent supernaturalism that belongs to Him makes the resurrection a virtual necessity and creates in one who starts from the fact the increasing realization that it was inevitable.—*Ibid.*, p. 56

This sixfold division of the evidences—three major and three minor —though not entering into many details does present the salient features of proof. All evidence functioning through human channels is naturally subject to human limitations. Men are fallible. Their impressions can be erroneous. On the other hand, the honest testimony of a witness must be received and weighed for all it purports to be. "In the mouth of two or three witnesses every word may be established" (Matt. 18:16). No greater line of proof could exist than the fact that Christ did rise. The whole scene was suddenly changed when He appeared and promptly was identified by those who saw Him. The effect produced indicates that there was a sufficient cause and that cause was none other than the truth that He was alive from the dead. His followers were unprepared for His death. That death was not softened by the slightest expectation that He might rise from the dead. They were unprepared for His resurrection and when He arose they responded normally to so great a surprise and joy. They were without a design or plan in acting so. To them the tomb was empty beyond a doubt and the Savior was alive and in their midst again. Angel messengers as well as human witnesses testified to the empty tomb and several hundred testified to His living presence. The apostles began at once to proclaim the resurrection in Jerusalem and to those who had caused His crucifixion. Had there been any proof which men could produce that would demonstrate that Christ was still in the state of death, it would have been forthcoming; but none could be found.

The appearances of Christ were duly recorded by the Apostle in 1 Corinthians 15:5–8, which states: "And that he was seen of Cephas, then of the twelve: after that, he was seen of above five hundred brethren at once: of whom the greater part remain unto this present, but some are fallen asleep. After that, he was seen of James; then of all the apostles. And last of all he was seen of me also, as of one born out of due time." They who knew Him best and could apply uncounted tests to establish His identity were convinced, not so much by the empty tomb as by His actual presence with them. On that confidence which His living presence engendered they preached with all boldness, and Christianity, grounded on the death and resurrection of Christ, was launched with never a recorded doubt on the part of those to whom He appeared. The removal of one man's doubt by a visible appearing of Christ is especially significant. He who had said "Except I shall see in his hands the print of the nails, and put my finger into the print of the nails, and thrust my hand into his side, I will not believe" (John 20:25) saw the actual scars and declared, "My Lord and my God" (John 20:28). Likewise the great Apostle was transformed from the unbeliever he was to the Apostle of divine grace by seeing Christ, and not only risen but enthroned in glory. The men who knew most about Him believed most respecting Christ's resurrection. The entire event bore investigation and it may be assumed that inquest was pursued alike by believers and unbelievers. James Denney in his volume *Jesus and the Gospel* asserts: "The real historical evidence for the resurrection is the fact that it was believed, preached, propagated, and produced its fruit and effect in the new phenomenon of the Christian Church, long before any of our gospels was written" (p. 111, cited by Harrison, *ibid.*, p. 82). Beyond all this—especially for those who have spiritual discernment—is the New Creation reality which is built, not on a mere belief in the resurrection of Christ, but on Him who arose from the grave. A new creation which represents the supreme divine effort and incorporates the interests of heaven and earth is not built on a mere fiction or misguided idealism. The entire Second Testament which proclaims, defends, and stands upon the resurrection of Christ is itself worthy of its claim to be the inspired Word of God. In the course of its message the resurrection of Christ is an essential feature. The greatest divine purpose is being executed upon the reality of Christ's return from the tomb.

3. ACTUAL RESURRECTION. By this caption attention is directed to the truth that Christ really died and that, had He not been raised, He would, so far as His human body is concerned, have remained in the state of death. It is this truth which is misconstrued by unsuitable illustrations. It is probable that nature provides no comparable reality. Sincere men have, without due thought, sought to elucidate the doctrine of Christ's resurrection by comparing it to the hatching of an egg, the manifestation of life in the form of a lily when a dry bulb is planted, or the breaking of the cocoon by the chrysalis and the appearance of a gorgeous butterfly. A moment's consideration suggests the inaptness of all these figures. The egg will not hatch unless it enfolds a germ of life. No dry bulb presents a lily unless it is alive. No chrysalis ever broke its cocoon that was not animated; but there was no life in Christ's tomb. No greater distinction exists than that which obtains between life and

death, and it is tragic indeed when, even by implication—which an ill-considered illustration may very well adumbrate—it is intimated that Christ did not really die, or that even a spark of life was continued in the tomb as the basis of a mere resuscitation. Let it be restated: there is nothing in nature capable of representing a true resurrection from death. Christ went down in despotic death and came up with unimpoverished and inexhaustible life. In the Melchizedek form of His priesthood it is rightly said of Christ: "Who is made, not after the law of a carnal commandment, but after the power of an endless life" (Heb. 7:16). Finite computations can never comprehend that which is in the passage termed "the power of an endless life." Death does not end the consciousness of the human soul and spirit. Death did not end the consciousness of Christ's human soul and spirit, nor did it affect His Deity. Physical death is an experience of the body and only resurrection will restore its life again. Christ entered completely into the state of physical death and from it He came forth by an actual resurrection. Since there is so little upon which to base doctrine at this point, the question of Christ's relation to spiritual death is not discussed at all in this work.

4. A NEW ORDER OF BEING. A sharp contrast exists and should be recognized between the glory of the preincarnate Christ on the one hand and that of Christ in resurrection on the other hand. In other words, His resurrection was vastly more than a reversal of His death. Such reversals, indeed, were the rule for all other so-called resurrections recorded in the Bible. They were, to be strictly accurate, only restorations or resuscitations from the state of complete death. The difference is seen in the fact that other so-called resurrections were a return to the former life and estate wherein those thus revived were subject to a second dying, while of Christ it is said He arose into a sphere of being never occupied or exhibited before. It is not contended that any change was wrought in His Deity other than that which is possible in the realm of association or incarnation. The humanity of Christ—His body, soul, and spirit—instantly became that which had been anticipated throughout all eternity, namely, perfect humanity glorified and exalted to the point that it was not only meet for heaven, but meet as well to be an integral part of the glorified theanthropic Person. It is no small requirement upon that which was itself only perfect humanity that it should become an integral part of the all-glorious, exalted, resurrected Son of God. In other words, Christ is the first and only one of all earth dwellers thus far to put on immortality. The Apostle announces respecting Him: "Who only hath immortality, dwelling in the light which no man can

approach unto; whom no man hath seen, nor can see: to whom be honour and power everlasting. Amen" (1 Tim. 6:16); "Who hath abolished death, and hath brought life and immortality to light through the gospel" (2 Tim. 1:10). Immortality is wholly of the body, never of the soul or spirit, and since no other one from this sphere has yet received the glorified resurrection body, He only hath immortality. That immortal body with a glorified soul and spirit united to Deity becomes the incomparable theanthropic Person, the exalted Savior.

5. SEVEN REASONS. In a section of Soteriology, presented earlier (Vol. III), fourteen reasons for the death of Christ have been listed and examined. In this division of Christology seven reasons for the resurrection of Christ are now to be considered. These, it is believed, will be found to be somewhat comprehensive and are as follows: (1) Christ arose because of who He is, (2) Christ arose that He might fulfill the Davidic covenant, (3) Christ arose that He might become the source of resurrection life, (4) Christ arose that He might become the source of resurrection power, (5) Christ arose to be Head over all things to the Church, (6) Christ arose on account of justification, and (7) Christ arose to be the First-Fruits. These may well be considered separately.

a. BECAUSE OF WHO HE IS. It is recorded of Peter that in his Pentecostal sermon he said, "Whom God hath raised up, having loosed the pains of death: because it was not possible that he should be holden of it" (Acts 2:24). No situation conceivable could be more abnormal than that the theanthropic Person should enter the realms of death. He is the source of all life. "For as the Father hath life in himself; so hath he given to the Son to have life in himself" (John 5:26). This is not a reference to human life, which begins with human generation, but to that life which God is, from everlasting to everlasting. Apart from the experience of animals, this universe knows nothing of death other than as the judgment which it is from God upon a fallen race, and the hour is fast drawing near when that judgment will be lifted and death banished forever. Why, indeed, should the eternal Second Person, even though He took upon Him deathless, unfallen humanity, be found within the shades of death? The question has but one answer and that one answer is the only one given in the Bible, namely, that in infinite love He died for others, the Just for the unjust, that He might bring the unjust to God; but when satisfaction had been rendered on account of those for whom He died, there was no more occasion for the deathless One to continue in the realms of death. It is, therefore, because of who He is that He arose from the tomb.

b. TO FULFILL THE DAVIDIC COVENANT. To the attentive, believing Bible student it is clear that vast issues are contained in the covenant God made with David as recorded in 2 Samuel, chapter 7. To Abraham God covenanted an earthly seed and a land (Gen. 12:1–3; 13:14–17; 15:5–7), and to David God covenanted an everlasting throne, an everlasting King, and an everlasting kingdom. The precise character of that throne and kingdom was revealed to David. His own response to Jehovah's covenant and his impression respecting it (cf. 2 Sam. 7:18–29; Ps. 89:20–37) indicate clearly that it was, as covenanted, none other than the perpetuation of David's earthly throne and earthly kingdom. The student will search in vain for any point in subsequent revelation wherein it is revealed that this throne and kingdom underwent a metamorphosis by which a literal, earthly throne and kingdom, as were promised to David by the oath of Jehovah (cf. Acts 2:30), became the spiritual kingdom which modern theologians fancy exists, and which is so changed that David himself is no longer essential to it. In truth, no subject is more baffling within the range of prophetic themes to those who spiritualize the kingdom than the question why it was prerequisite for Christ to be born of the line of David. If His is a spiritual kingdom, He need be born of no particular human line. The Bible does not follow a program adapted to human ideals. The Davidic covenant promised with an oath of Jehovah's that out of the fruit of David's loins, according to the flesh, God would raise up Christ to sit on David's throne (Acts 2:30). David believed the covenant which Jehovah made respecting his earthly throne and kingdom—what right had he to doubt?—and that is why he spoke of the fact, as recorded in Psalm 16:10, that Christ would not be left in the grave. In the Sacred Text the whole Davidic covenant program moves majestically on with subsequent revelations regarding it quite confirmatory (cf. Isa. 9:6–7; Luke 1:31–33; Acts 2:25–31; 15:16–18), and continues in certain prospect until it is consummated at the return of Christ when He will sit on David's throne in Jerusalem. This is the kingdom proffered by Christ in His earth ministry and preached by His disciples. The same kingdom was rejected by the nation when they rejected their King. In the purpose of God and to the end that redemption might be achieved, the Messiah must die. Of the various reasons here assigned for Christ's resurrection, it is now asserted that He arose because of God's oath to David, lest that be violated—as it would have been had Christ remained in the sphere of death. An oath given to David from Jehovah respecting Messiah as the One to sit on David's throne in Jerusalem bears no relation to a supposed spiritual kingdom. If the kingdom be spiritual rather than literal, what then becomes of Jehovah's oath? And of what import is the Davidic covenant?

c. TO BECOME THE SOURCE OF RESURRECTION LIFE. Of the major factor which constitutes a Christian what he is, much has already been written. It was after His resurrection, however, that Christ breathed on the disciples and said, "Receive ye the Holy Ghost" (John 20:22). In like manner every Christian has been born from above and received the divine nature when he believed. Thereafter Christ is Himself in the heart as the hope of glory (cf. Col. 1:27). "I am come that they might have life, and that they might have it more abundantly. I am the good shepherd: the good shepherd giveth his life for the sheep" (John 10:10–11); "And this is the record, that God hath given to us eternal life, and this life is in his Son. He that hath the Son hath life; and he that hath not the Son of God hath not life" (1 John 5:11–12). It remains only to declare again that the life which is thus imparted is the life of Christ in resurrection and not the preresurrection life of Christ. It is on the ground of this truth that the Christian is contemplated, as he is in the New Testament, as already raised from the dead. Colossians 3:1–4 is direct and conclusive: "If ye then be risen with Christ, seek those things which are above, where Christ sitteth on the right hand of God. Set your affection on things above, not on things on the earth. For ye are dead, and your life is hid with Christ in God. When Christ, who is our life, shall appear, then shall ye also appear with Him in glory." In fact the believer is now blessed with all the values of cocrucifixion, codeath, coburial, and coresurrection with Christ. These great realities are his as completely as they were Christ's, since Christ wrought them as a Substitute for the one who believes. In the most actual sense the child of God has been raised up and seated with Christ in heavenly spheres. Thus it is written: "And hath raised us up together, and made us sit together in heavenly places in Christ Jesus" (Eph. 2:6).

d. TO BE THE SOURCE OF RESURRECTION POWER. After His resurrection Christ said to His disciples, "All power is given unto me in heaven and in earth" (Matt. 28:18). It is His power to "us-ward" who believe, that is measured only by the exceeding greatness of God's power which was wrought in Christ when He raised Him from the dead. Naturally the mind dwells first upon the power that achieved the resurrection of Christ, and that of course is the essential thing to be apprehended; yet the message of Ephesians 1:19–21 presents rather the glorious truth that the power which wrought in Christ is the power that is engaged in behalf of the believer. That power may be directed in various channels, but it is the portion of all who believe. In Romans 6:4 the resurrection of Christ is the measurement of power available for the Christian's walk in "newness of life," or upon a new life principle, namely, the walk in dependence upon the Holy Spirit.

e. TO BE HEAD OVER ALL THINGS TO THE CHURCH. When the resurrected Christ is combined with the Church—they who have been raised with Him and seated with Him (Eph. 2:6)—into one entity, the result is known as the New Creation. It is true that, because of the vital relation to Christ which each believer sustains through the baptizing ministry of the Holy Spirit, each one thus related is himself a new creation. Thus it is said, "Therefore if any man be in Christ, he is a new creature: old things are passed away; behold, all things are become new" (2 Cor. 5:17); but the whole company of the saved ones joined to the resurrected Head and including Him constitute the New Creation of God. This entity is altogether different from any other existing company whether it be composed of angels or men, and its realization constitutes the supreme purpose of God in the present age. As all that enters into the New Creation is established on resurrection ground and is derived directly from the resurrected Christ, it is clear that He Himself was for this cause raised and seated far above angelic spheres and made Head over all things to the Church, which is His Body (Eph. 1:20–23).

f. ON ACCOUNT OF JUSTIFICATION. It will be recognized that this aspect of resurrection truth is drawn from one text of Scripture (Rom. 4:25), which reads: "Who was delivered for our offences, and was raised again for our justification." Above and beyond what has been written previously on this somewhat difficult passage, it may be indicated that, having completed the ground of justification by and through His death and His body having remained the prescribed time in the tomb, Christ arose. Judging from that (the proper) sense of the passage, it is not according to sound doctrine to declare that justification is based upon Christ's resurrection. It, rather, is certain from the testimony of the New Testament that justification is based upon the death of Christ. It is written: "Being justified freely by his grace through the redemption that is in Christ Jesus" (Rom. 3:24); "Much more then, being now justified by his blood, we shall be saved from wrath through him" (5:9). Yet there is a sense in which it may be said too that, since imputed righteousness is the divine reason for that divine pronouncement which justification is and since imputed righteousness accrues to the believer on the sole basis of His union to the resurrected Christ, the believer's justification does rest perfectly on the resurrection of the Lord. It is therefore true that justification is made possible both by the death of Christ and by His resurrection, and so both are essential.

g. TO BE THE FIRST-FRUITS. In this, another instance the theme under consideration has been previously treated in part. However, that the outline of doctrine may be as nearly complete as possible, this wonderful feature of Christ's resurrection should reappear. The term *first-fruits* is used of Israel (Jer. 2:3), of the Spirit's blessing (Rom. 8:23), of the first believers in a given locality (Rom. 16:5; 1 Cor. 16:15), of the saints of this age (James 1:18), of the 144,000 (Rev. 14:4), and of Christ in resurrection. One passage, in which the term is twice applied to Christ, is especially clear as evidence for this last usage: "But now is Christ risen from the dead, and become the firstfruits of them that slept. For since by man came death, by man came also the resurrection of the dead. For as in Adam all die, even so in Christ shall all be made alive. But every man in his own order: Christ the firstfruits; afterward they that are Christ's at his coming" (1 Cor. 15:20–23). That glorified humanity which is to constitute the highest feature of heaven next to the Godhead—they who even in this life being saved have received the $\pi\lambda\eta\rho\omega\mu\alpha$ of the Godhead (Col. 2:9–10) and will yet receive resurrection bodies like unto Christ's glorious body (Phil. 3:21)—are perfectly represented in heaven by the resurrected, glorified man, Christ Jesus. Angels know the estate which will characterize each individual who comprises that unnumbered company which, having received their resurrection bodies, will throng the spacious vaults of heaven. The angels thus know before they appear what each believer will be like, having seen Christ who is to the hosts of heaven a preliminary demonstration of the glorious estate that awaits those who are Christ's. He is thus the "firstfruits." The wave sheaf of the Old Testament anticipated the appearing of Christ in heaven as the Preview or Forerunner of those who were to follow.

6. THE PRESENT STANDARD OF DIVINE POWER. The Bible discloses a standard of divine power for each of the three major ages—past, present, and future. When in the past age God sought to impress His people concerning His mighty power, He reminded them of the demonstration which He made when delivering them from Egypt. The oft-repeated phrase is, "I am the LORD thy God, which brought thee out of the land of Egypt" (Ex. 20:2). In the coming age the standard of divine power is to be that regathering of Israel to be accomplished when Christ returns. Of this Jeremiah writes, "Therefore, behold, the days

come, saith the LORD, that they shall no more say, The LORD liveth, which brought up the children of Israel out of the land of Egypt; but, the LORD liveth, which brought up and which led the seed of the house of Israel out of the north country, and from all countries whither I had driven them; and they shall dwell in their own land" (Jer. 23:7-8). Of this same event Christ said that Israel's regathering would be by angelic ministration. Accordingly it is written: "And he shall send his angels with a great sound of a trumpet, and they shall gather together his elect from the four winds, from one end of heaven to the other" (Matt. 24:31; cf. Isa. 60:8-9). But the measurement of divine power in the present age, between the two advents of Christ, is that of Christ's resurrection from the dead. The Apostle states in Ephesians 1:19-21: "And what is the exceeding greatness of his power to us-ward who believe, according to the working of his mighty power, which he wrought in Christ, when he raised him from the dead, and set him at his own right hand in the heavenly places, far above all principality, and power, and might, and dominion, and every name that is named, not only in this world, but also in that which is to come." There is no means by which a human mind may grasp what is involved in the exercise of the power of God, and this text employs the extreme phrase, "the exceeding greatness of his power." It was power immeasurable which raised Christ from the dead, which took Him into the highest heaven far above angelic hosts, which seated Him on the Father's throne, and gave Him to be Head over all things to the Church. In considering the order of events in the resurrection and exaltation of Christ as here stated, it should be remembered that all that is set forth in this description is stated primarily to the end that the believer may be properly impressed with the *greatness* of the power—the same power which wrought in Christ—which is engaged to accomplish for him everything that God has purposed according to His work of election, predestination, and sovereign adoption. True, the Redeemer and His redemption will be provided, as well as the enabling power to believe; but beyond these issues which are within the boundaries of time the divine, eternal purpose will yet be realized to its full fruition, and is certain because of the "exceeding greatness of his power" which is engaged to that end. Nor should it be forgotten that all this disclosure is but a part of the Apostle's oft-repeated prayer wherein he makes request that, through the teaching work of the Spirit, these marvels which demonstrate the divine sufficiency might be comprehended by those who are the objects of the divine riches of grace and glory. Often in the Scriptures does the Spirit of God bring to one's attention the *certainty* of all things which God hath purposed, and happy indeed is the one who, by divine illumination, enters into the heart-understanding of these things. But what, after all, is the measure of this exceeding great power which is "to us-ward who believe"? The record of it is given for all to understand—if so be that they are taught of the Spirit. Second only in importance is this theme to that of election and predestination with which the Epistle opened. What God hath purposed He will realize, and to an absolute degree. What He hath begun He will complete with that perfection which belongs to infinity. This exceeding great power which is "to us-ward who believe" has already been manifest in four ways in behalf of Christ:

First, *Christ was raised from the dead,* not from a dormant state but from the estate of death. From this estate He was raised to a sphere far above that which He occupied on the earth before His death. As above stated, the resurrection of Christ is more than the reversal of His death, and more, indeed, than a restoration such as characterized all previous so-called resurrections. Christ became a new order of Being. The Second Person of the Trinity was always present in Christ from the moment of His gestation in the virgin's womb to His exaltation in glory; but His humanity presented ever changing aspects. As a child He "grew, and waxed strong in spirit" (Luke 2:40). He who was "from everlasting to everlasting" (Ps. 90:2) came to be "thirty years of age" (Luke 3:23); and that body which was mortal, being subject to death, became immortal and He who was dead is now alive forevermore. He who alone has immortality (1 Tim. 6:16) is now the First-Fruits of resurrection—the only present representation in glory of that host of redeemed ones who will soon be with Him and be like Him. Every power of Satan and man had combined to retain Christ's body in the tomb. The keys of death apparently were in Satan's hands until the resurrection of Christ (cf. Heb. 2:14 with Rev. 1:18). The greatest earthly power had set its seal upon the tomb but none could loose the "pains of death" (Acts 2:24) other than God. Though, in the mystery of the Trinity, it is declared that Christ came forth from the tomb by His own will and power (John 2:19; 10:17–18) and that He was quickened by the Spirit (1 Pet. 3:18), it is stated upwards of twenty-five times that Christ was raised by the power of God the Father. Thus, in this Ephesians passage (vs. 20) it is revealed that the resurrection was due to the exercise of the Father's mighty power which "he wrought in Christ, when he raised him from the dead." This same mighty power, we are assured, is not only engaged to raise the believer from the dead, but is engaged to accomplish *all* that has been divinely predetermined for him unto eternal glory.

Second, *the ascension of Christ* is a measurement of divine power "to us-ward who believe." Though directly presented but three times (Mark 16:19; Luke 24:49–52; Acts 1:9), the ascension of Christ is often referred to in the Acts and Epistles as an important aspect of divine power (Acts 2:33; 3:21; 5:31; 7:55; Rom. 8:34; Phil. 2:9; 3:20; Col. 3:1; 1 Thess. 1:10; 4:16; 2 Thess. 1:7; Heb. 1:3; 1 Pet. 3:22; Rev. 3:21). This body of truth, which is of great importance as evidence of the ascension and present position of Christ, is introduced at this point in the Ephesian Letter as a ground of confidence that what God has purposed for the believer He is abundantly *able* to accomplish. The present exaltation of Christ to a sphere far above all principalities and powers is a theme which transcends the range of unaided human understanding. The Spirit alone can impress the heart with that revelation which is here intended to create assurance in the child of God that he will himself realize all that God has purposed for him. This purpose includes no less than a partaking with Christ of that exalted glory of His. Concerning His own, Christ said, "Where I am, there ye may be also" (John 14:3) and "The glory which thou gavest me I have given them" (John 17:22).

Third, "And hath put all things under his feet" (Eph. 1:22). It was in this same connection that Christ said, "All power is given unto me in heaven and in earth" (Matt. 28:18; contr. Luke 4:5–6); and by Him shall all things be subdued (1 Cor. 15:25–26). Great, indeed, is the power "to us-ward who believe"; for such ones are destined to reign with Christ and share with Him His authority. The Christian experiences little of the exercise of this authority now. At the present time he rather shares the rejection of his Lord; for all who will live godly shall suffer persecution (2 Tim. 3:12).

Fourth, "And gave him to be the head over all things to the church" (Eph. 1:22). Returning thus at the close of the first chapter to the subject which was in view at the beginning—that which has been previously mentioned in this thesis (Vol. IV)—the Apostle makes mention of that group of humanity which, because of being *called out* from both Jews and Gentiles into a heavenly association in Christ, is properly called an ἐκκλησία or Church. The fact which is uppermost here is that Christ, by divine appointment and power, is now Head over all things to the Church. The term *Head* combines two important aspects of truth: (1) Christ now presides over the Church as the One who directs every moment of life and every act of service in those who comprise this heavenly company. He is the bestower of gifts (4:8), and, by the Spirit, directs the exercise of those gifts (1 Cor. 12:4–7). (2) Christ is now Head over the Church in the sense also that from Him she draws all spiritual vitality. Because He lives, the members of His Body live also. He is to the Church as the vine is to the branches, as the shepherd is to the sheep, as the cornerstone is to the building, and as the bridegroom is to the bride.

Special attention should be given to the fact that all the stupendous benefits enumerated in the first chapter of the Ephesian Letter are, on the human side, secured upon the one condition of believing. It is stated that the power of God is "to us-ward who believe." In accordance with the plan of salvation by divine grace, no other condition could be imposed. Not only does God undertake for such all this measureless benefit, but the very faith by which it is received is itself a gift of God.

7. THE LORD'S DAY A COMMEMORATION. It was to be expected, when Covenant Theology has so neglected the fact and meaning of Christ's resurrection, that there would arise much misunderstanding about the reason for the celebration of the first day of the week rather than the seventh. A recent article in a reputable religious journal is entitled, "The Sabbath Permanent but Moveable." By this caption the writer intends to draw attention by stating what after all is a contradiction. The impossible task to which he has appointed himself is to prove that the Jewish Sabbath idea remains intact even though the precise day of the week is changed. His thesis, as for all Covenant theologians, is that the structure of the Jewish Sabbath remains in force—for there is but one covenant—whether it be observed on one day or another. Such blindness respecting the discriminating teaching of the Bible can be accounted for only on the ground that a man-made scheme of supposed continuity is embraced and followed without an unprejudiced examination of the Scriptures. Under the general division of Ecclesiology the entire Sabbath and Lord's day problem has been given extended consideration; but since that issue is of so great import because of its inherent character, because of its doctrinal significance, and because of the existing misunderstanding respecting it, another extended treatment of the whole theme is introduced here, and with a view to establishing the truth respecting the meaning of the Lord's day celebration as that which is in force now and as wholly unrelated to the Jewish Sabbath as grace is unrelated to law or the New Creation is unrelated to the old creation. Beginning with His own work in creation, God has chosen to

sanctify, or set apart, one-seventh of all time. He commanded Israel to observe the seventh day as a day of rest (Ex. 20:8–11), likewise the seventh, or sabbatic year, as a time in which the land was to rest (Ex. 23:10–11; Lev. 25:2–7) and the fiftieth year as a time of jubilee in recognition of seven times seven years (Lev. 25:8–24). In various details both the sabbatic year and the year of jubilee were typically prophetic of the kingdom age, which is the seventh and last of the dispensations and which is characterized by the enjoyment of a sabbatic rest for all creation. Though in the present age the day to be celebrated is divinely changed from the seventh to the first day of the week because of the New Creation's beginning then, the same proportion in the division of time—one day in seven—is perpetuated. The Hebrew word *sabbath* means cessation, or perfect rest, from activity. Apart from the continual burnt offerings and the feasts which might fall on Saturday, the day was in no sense one of worship or service.

A degree of clarity is gained when the Sabbath is considered in its relation to various periods of time:

a. THE SABBATH FROM ADAM TO MOSES. It is recorded that God rested at the close of His six creative days (Gen. 2:2–3; Ex. 20:10–11; Heb. 4:4); but there is no intimation in the Word of God that man was appointed to observe, or ever did observe, a Sabbath until Israel came out of Egypt. The Book of Job discloses the religious life and experience of the patriarchs, and though their various responsibilities to God are therein discussed, there is never a reference to a Sabbath-day obligation. On the other hand, it is distinctly stated that the giving of the Sabbath to Israel by the hand of Moses was the beginning of Sabbath observance among men (Ex. 16:29; Neh. 9:13–14; Ezek. 20:11–13). Likewise, it is evident from the records of the first imposition of the Sabbath (Ex. 16:1–35) that on the particular day which was one week, or seven days, previous to the first recorded Sabbath observed by man the children of Israel finished a Sabbath-breaking journey of many miles from Elim to the wilderness of Sin. There they murmured against Jehovah, and on that day the supply of food from heaven began which was to be gathered for six days, but was not to be gathered on the seventh day. It is evident, therefore, that the day of their journeying which would have been a Sabbath, had a Sabbath obligation been in force, was not observed as a Sabbath.

b. THE SABBATH FROM MOSES TO CHRIST. In this period the Sabbath was rightfully in force. It was embedded in the law (Ex. 20:8–11) and the divine cure for its nonobservance was likewise provided in the law of the offerings. In this connection, it is important to observe that the Sabbath was never imposed on the Gentiles, but was peculiarly a sign between Jehovah and Israel (Ex. 31:12–17). Among Israel's sins, her failure to keep the Sabbath and to give the land its rest are especially emphasized. In the midst of this period of the law, Hosea predicted that, as a part of the judgments which were to come upon Israel, her Sabbaths would cease (Hos. 2:11). This prophecy must at some time be fulfilled, for the mouth of the Lord hath spoken it. As the Mosaic age continued to the death of Christ, His earth-life and ministry were under the law, expounding the law and applying the law. Finding the Sabbath law obscured by the traditions and teachings of men, He pointed out that the Sabbath was given as a benefit to man and man was not to be made a sacrifice for the Sabbath (Mark 2:27). Christ was faithful to the whole Mosaic system, which included the Sabbath, because that system was in force during His earth-life; but that obvious fact is no basis for the claim that a Christian is appointed to follow Christ in His Sabbath observance either in example or precept.

c. THE CHURCH AGE. Following the resurrection of Christ, there is no record in the New Testament that the Sabbath was observed by any believer, even in error. Doubtless the multitude of Judaized Christians did observe the Sabbath; but no record of such observance was permitted to appear in the Word of God. In like manner, following the resurrection of Christ, there is no injunction given to Jew, Gentile, or Christian to observe the Sabbath, nor is Sabbath-breaking once mentioned among the numerous lists of possible sins. On the contrary, there are warnings against Sabbath observance on the part of those who are the children of God under grace. Galatians 4:9–10 condemns the observance of "days, and months, and times, and years." These were usually observed with a view to meriting the favor of God and by those who would likely be thoughtful of God at one time and careless at another. Hebrews 4:1–13 contemplates the Sabbath as a type of the rest (from his own works) into which the believer enters when he is saved. Colossians 2:16–17 plainly instructs the child of God *not* to be judged with respect to a Sabbath day, and implies that such an independent attitude toward the Sabbath is reasonable in view of all that Christ has become to one who is now of the New Creation (Col. 2:9–17). In this passage, most evidently reference is made to the weekly Sabbaths, rather than to those special or extra Sabbaths which were a part of the ceremonial law. Romans 14:5 declares that when the believer is "persuaded in his own mind" he may esteem all days alike. This does not imply a neglect of faithful worship, but rather suggests that, to such a one, *all* days are full of devotion to God. Because of the fact that in the New Testament the Sabbath is never included as any part of the Christian's life and service, the term *Christian Sabbath* is a misnomer. In this connection it may be noted that in place of the Sabbath of the law there is provided the Lord's day of the New Creation, which far exceeds the Sabbath in its glory, its privileges, and its blessings.

d. THE SABBATH IN THE COMING AGE. In full harmony with the New Testament doctrine that the new Lord's day is related only to the Church, it is prophesied that the Sabbath will be reinstated—thus superseding the Lord's day—immediately upon the completion of the outcalling of the Church and her removal from the world. Even in the brief period of the tribulation which must intervene between the end of this age and the age of the kingdom, the Sabbath is again in view (Matt. 24:20); but prophecy especially anticipates the Sabbath as a vital feature of the coming kingdom age (Isa. 66:23; Ezek. 46:1).

The first day of the week has been celebrated by the church from the resurrection of Christ to the present time. This fact is proved by the New Testament records, the writings of the early Fathers, and the history of the church. There have been those in nearly every century who, not comprehending the present purpose of God in the New Creation, have earnestly contended for the observance of the seventh-day Sabbath. At the present time, those who specialize in urging the observance of the seventh day combine these appeals with other unscriptural doctrines. Since the believer is appointed of God to observe the first day of the week under the new relationships of grace, confusion arises when that day is invested with the character of, and is governed by, the seventh-day Sabbath laws. All such teachings ignore the New Testament doctrine of the New Creation.

e. THE NEW CREATION. The New Testament reveals that the purpose of God in the present, unforeseen dispensation is the outcalling of the Church (Acts 15:13–18), and this redeemed company is the New Creation, a heavenly people. While it is indicated that there are marvelous glories and perfections which are to be accomplished for this company as a whole (Eph. 5:25–27), it is also revealed that they *individually* are the objects of the greatest divine undertakings and transformations. Likewise, as the corporate Body is organically related to Christ (1 Cor. 12:12), so the individual believer is vitally joined to the Lord (1 Cor. 6:17; Rom. 6:5; 1 Cor. 12:13). Concerning the individual believer, the Bible teaches that (a) as for sin, each one in this company has been cleansed, forgiven, and justified, (b) as for their possessions, each one has been given the indwelling Spirit and the gift of God which is eternal life, has become a legal heir of God and a joint-heir with Christ, (c) as for their positions, each one has been made the righteousness of God by which he is accepted in the Beloved forever (2 Cor. 5:21; Eph. 1:6), a member of Christ's mystical Body, a part of His glorious Bride, and a living partaker in the New Creation of which Christ is the Federal Head. We read: "If any man be in Christ, he is a new creature [creation]: old things [as respects positions, not experience] are passed away; behold, all things are become new. And all [these positional] things are of God" (2 Cor. 5:17–18; Eph. 2:10; 4:25; Gal. 6:15). Peter, writing of this company of believers, states: "But ye are a chosen generation" (1 Pet. 2:9), which means a distinct heaven-born race or nationality— a stock or kind—which has been directly created by the power of God. As the first Adam begat a race which partook of his own human life and imperfections, so Christ, the Last Adam, is now begetting by the Spirit a new race which partakes of His eternal life and perfection. "The first man Adam was made a living soul; the last Adam was made a quickening [life-giving] spirit" (1 Cor. 15:45). Having partaken of the resurrection life of Christ and being in Christ, the believer is said to be raised already (Rom. 6:4; Col. 2:12–13; 3:1–4). However, as for his body, the believer is yet to receive a glorious body like unto the resurrection body of Christ (Phil. 3:21). In confirmation of this we also read that, when Christ appeared in heaven immediately following His resurrection, it was as the "firstfruits," implying that the whole company that are to follow will be like Him (1 John 3:2), even to their glorified bodies. In the Word of God the New Creation—which began with the resurrection of Christ and consists of a born-again, heavenly company who are in Christ—is everywhere held in contrast to the old creation, and it is from that old and ruined creation that the believer is said to have been saved and delivered. As the Sabbath was instituted to celebrate the old creation (Ex. 20:10–11; 31:12–17; Heb. 4:4), so the Lord's day celebrates the New Creation. Likewise, as the Sabbath was limited in its application to Israel as the earthly people of God, so also the Lord's day is limited in its application to the Church as the heavenly people of God.

f. THE LORD'S DAY. In addition to the fact that the Sabbath is nowhere imposed on the children of God under grace, there are abundant reasons for their observance of the first day of the week.

(1) *A New Day Prophesied and Appointed.* According to Psalm

118:22–24 and Acts 4:10–11, Christ in His crucifixion was the Stone rejected by Israel—the "builders"—but, through His resurrection, He has been made the Headstone of the corner. This marvelous thing is of God, and the day of its accomplishment is divinely appointed as a day of rejoicing and of gladness. In accord with this, Christ's greeting on the resurrection morn was "All hail" (Matt. 28:9, which is more literally, "O have joy!"), and being "the day which the LORD hath made," it is rightfully termed "the Lord's day."

(2) *Observance Indicated by Various Events.* On the first day Christ arose from the dead (Matt. 28:1), on that day He first met His disciples in the new intimacy of fellowship (John 20:19), on that day He gave them instruction (Luke 24:36–49), on that day He ascended into heaven as the "firstfruits" or wave sheaf (John 20:17; 1 Cor. 15:20, 23; Lev. 23:10–12), on that day He breathed the Spirit on them (John 20:22), on that day the Spirit descended from heaven (Acts 2:1–4), on that day the Apostle Paul preached in Troas (Acts 20:6–7), on that day the believers came together to break bread (Acts 20:6–7), on that day they were to "lay by in store" as God had prospered them (1 Cor. 16:2).

(3) *The Day of Circumcision.* The rite of circumcision, which was performed on the eighth day, typified the believer's separation from the flesh and the old order by the death of Christ (Col. 2:11), and the eighth day, being the first day after a completed week, is symbolical of a new beginning.

(4) *The Day of Grace.* At the end of a week of toil, a day of rest was granted to the people who were related to God by law-works, whereas to the people under grace, whose works are finished in Christ, a day of worship is appointed which, being the first day of the week, precedes all days of work. In the blessing of the first day the believer lives and serves the following six days. A day of rest belongs to a people who are related to God by works needing to be accomplished; a day of ceaseless worship and service belongs to a people who are related to God by the finished work of Christ. The seventh day was characterized by unyielding law; the first day is characterized by the latitude and liberty belonging to grace. The seventh day was observed with the hope that by it one might prove acceptable to God. The first day is observed with the assurance that one is already accepted of God. The keeping of the seventh day was fostered by the flesh; the keeping of the first day is fostered by the indwelling Spirit.

(5) *The Day Blessed of God.* Throughout this age Spirit-filled, devout believers, to whom no doubt the will of God has been clearly re-

vealed, have kept the Lord's day apart from any sense of responsibility to observe the seventh day. It is reasonable to suppose that had they been guilty of Sabbath-breaking they would have been convicted of that sin.

(6) *The Day Committed Only to the Individual*. First, notice it is not committed to the unsaved. It is certainly most misleading to the unsaved to give them grounds for supposing that they will be more acceptable to God if they observe a day; for apart from the salvation which is in Christ all men are utterly and equally lost. For social or physical reasons a day of rest may be secured to the benefit of all; but the unregenerate should understand that the observance of such a day adds nothing to their merit before God.

Second, note it is not committed to the Church as a body. The responsibility relative to the observance of the first day is of necessity committed to the individual believer only, and not to the Church as a whole, and the manner of its celebration by the individual is suggested in the two sayings of Christ on the morning of His resurrection: "O rejoice!" and "Go . . . tell." This calls for ceaseless activity in all forms of worship and service; and such activity is in contrast to the seventh-day rest.

(7) *No Command to Keep the Day*. Since it is all of grace, a written requirement for the keeping of the Lord's day is not imposed, nor is the manner of its observance prescribed. By this wise provision, none are encouraged to keep the day as a mere duty; it is to be kept from the heart. Israel stood before God as immature children under tutors and governors and needing the commandments which are given to a child (Gal. 4:1–3), whereas the Church stands before God as adult sons (4: 4–7). Their life under grace is clearly defined, indeed, but it is presented only as the beseechings of God with the expectation that all shall be done *willingly* (Eph. 4:1–3; Rom. 12:1–2). There is little question over how a well-instructed, Spirit-filled believer (and the Scripture presupposes a normal Christian to be such) should be occupied on the day which commemorates Christ's resurrection and the New Creation. If perchance the child of God is not yielded to Him, no unwilling observance of a day will correct his carnal heart nor would such observance be pleasing to God. The issue between God and the carnal Christian is not one of outward actions, but of a yielded life.

In terminating this discussion respecting the truth that a new day has been divinely introduced which is in harmony with the New Creation and that this day celebrates the event which ushered in the new order, namely, the resurrection of Christ, it is further to be asserted that, as the New Creation is the one divine objective in this age and as Israel's covenants are in abeyance until this objective is realized, it is not only reasonable but imperative that the Sabbath with all its own significance as the celebration of the old order should be abrogated and supplanted by the day which belongs to the present divine purpose. This, indeed, is what has been divinely ordered, and the new day obtains whether a Judaized church comprehends it or not. At no point are the distinctions between Judaism and Christianity brought more into juxtaposition than in the different days they celebrate. The Jews never made choice of the seventh day; it was Jehovah's choice for them. Christians never made choice of the first day; it, too, is the appointment of God and is observed by the church in spite of her confused mind regarding it. In fact, the Covenant theologian's problem is not whether the first or the seventh day should be observed; his problem is to account for the fact that the church does observe the first day. Not allowed to recognize the heaven-high New Creation lest it disrupt the theory of one unchangeable covenant, the best that he can do is to invest the new day with the features of the old day and assign to the new day the inappropriate, antithetical, antipodal term, *Christian Sabbath*. Happy are they who understand and do the will of God for the day they observe!

CONCLUSION

Every effort to set forth the doctrinal import of Christ's resurrection must prove inadequate. When the human mind grasps the truth respecting the exalted position to which the believer is brought through his vital union with the resurrected Christ, that mind may then hope to penetrate somewhat into the significance of Christ's glorious *anastasis*.

Chapter XI

THE ASCENSION AND SESSION OF CHRIST INCARNATE

Again the attentive student of the Sacred Text is confronted with major doctrines and age-characterizing ministries of Christ which by theologians generally are neglected to the point of dishonor to Christ; especially is this true of those of a Covenant school who in defense of a man-made theory must avoid all that is distinctive in this age of God's supreme achievements, lest the dead level of a supposed immutable covenant should be brought to disorder and confusion. Why, indeed, should any emphasis be placed on the limitless achievements of Christ's present ministry when, according to this theory, saints of former ages were equally blessed with the saints of this age? Nevertheless, and with no support for a man-made theory, the age-characterizing ministries are recorded on the pages of the Word of God. It is no small issue that the present ministries of Christ which are of the greatest consequence should be disregarded by theological writers. The unfortunate effect of such neglect is that the majority of students accept without question or investigation the doctrinal position and emphasis of their teachers. Even the teachers themselves are run into the mold of their own instructors. For this reason, there is little hope of a new and worthy reconsideration of the interpretation of the Bible. Naturally the student looks upon any truth which was neglected by his teacher as of no great moment or even as dangerous. To many the only body of interpretation which is orthodox is that which was recovered by the Reformers, or that contained in an ancient doctrinal statement. There is, however, a great body of truth which the Reformers were unable to consider and which is lacking in ancient creeds. It is this which worthy expositors have brought to light in subsequent days. Since these expositors are as capable in the field of analysis of revealed truth as were the Reformers, the results of their labors should at least have some consideration. Two schools are developing among orthodox men: one which restricts all doctrine to the findings of men from the very early days of Protestantism, and one which, while accepting the sound teaching of the Reformers, recognizes that much added light has fallen (by reason of the Spirit and His continued ministry) upon the Word of God in later days and that this is as worthy of consideration as the findings of men of former times. Of these two schools, the first-named has too often looked upon the vital truth presented by the other as speculative, precarious, or perilous. The present ministries of Christ, like His resurrection and the Pauline doctrine of the Church, however, must be recognized, weighed, and given a full place regardless of the theories or prejudices of men in any work on theology which purports to be at all complete. As suggested by the caption by which this chapter is designated, there are two aspects of truth relative to Christ to be considered, namely, His ascension and His session. These are sufficiently related to be combined in one general division.

I. THE ASCENSION

The doctrinal importance of Christ's ascension lies not so much in His departure from the world as it does in His arrival in heaven. Yet some attention should be given to His departure from this world, since it occupies a prominent place in the historical narrative. The whole theme of Christ's ascension is divided with reference to two events: the ascension on the resurrection morn and the final ascension after forty days.

1. THE ASCENSION ON THE RESURRECTION MORN. While it is probable that Christ was resident in heaven from the resurrection day onward and only visited the earth as contact with His followers dictated (cf. John 17:16)—in which case there were a number of ascensions—it is generally believed, perhaps without due consideration, that Christ remained in residence on the earth until His final departure on the clouds of heaven (Acts 1:9–11). To many, therefore, the suggestion that Christ ascended on the resurrection morn may cause surprise. That there was an immediate ascension following the resurrection is well indicated in the Scriptures, and that it was at the time of one antitype fulfillment is a certainty. The doctrine of an immediate ascension appears when two passages of Scripture are compared. It is recorded that when Christ came out of the tomb He was met by Mary, who in ecstatic devotion would have embraced His feet and held her Lord. Christ's loving declaration to her was, "Touch me not; for I am not yet ascended to my Father: but go to my brethren, and say unto them, I ascend unto my Father, and your Father; and to my God, and your God" (John 20:17). Yet in

Luke's account of the resurrection it is asserted that the same day in which He arose and at evening He not only appeared in the midst of the frightened disciples, but said unto them, "Why are ye troubled? and why do thoughts arise in your hearts? Behold my hands and my feet, that it is I myself: handle me, and see; for a spirit hath not flesh and bones, as ye see me have. And when he had thus spoken, he shewed them his hands and his feet" (Luke 24:38–40). As no intimation is given why He should not be touched before His ascension, speculation will achieve but little. It is enough to know that He was not to make contact with things of the earth, at least until the exact demands involved in His great redemptive mission were completed and His efficacious sacrifice had been presented in heaven. It is difficult not to believe that there was a sacred continuity to be guarded between His death and the presentation in heaven, which continuity would not permit any contact. Having abandoned the former sphere of relationship with His followers by His death and resurrection, the new and final relationship could not be entered into until He had completed it all by the presentation in heaven. The implication is clear that, since He could not be touched in the morning until He ascended and yet He could be "handled" at evening of the same day, He had ascended during the day. He ascended at once from the tomb and returned for such manifestations as were appointed for that day. "Go to my brethren, and say unto them, I ascend unto my Father" means that He was about to ascend. Had He made reference in this message to His final ascension, there was no need that Mary carry the message of that to His disciples, since He Himself had before Him the entire forty days in which to deliver the news Himself. Of the two recorded ascensions, that of the resurrection morn holds the greater doctrinal significance. He had said to His Father in His final priestly prayer, "And now come I to thee" (John 17:13), and this return is not only momentous in the whole history of the universe, but it is the natural sequence after Calvary. He had come forth from the Father for the purpose of securing man's redemption (Heb. 10:4–7) and now He returned to the Father where He belonged by all right and title. His ascension was no penetration into unexplored regions—it was a going home in triumph, and helpless indeed is the human imagination to picture that welcome, that reunion, and that heavenly ecstasy. The Beloved was returning who was ever the Father's delight; but how much more is He welcome at the end of so great an achievement in which all the Father's desire is realized and the Son's perfect obedience is actualized!

Certain achievements were wrought by the Son of God at the time of His first ascension. These fashion the doctrinal meaning of this event. In so far as human sentiment may be attributed to Deity, it may be recognized as true that there was great celestial joy in heaven when the Son returned from the earth. This would have its fullest manifestation when He first returned directly from the tomb. His appearance—marvelous above anything angels had ever seen—was, as it ever will be, the central glory of heaven itself; but from the doctrinal viewpoint the first ascension accounts for the long-anticipated fulfilling of two foreshadowings of the Old Testament as well as their becoming the eternal reality which the antitypes are.

a. CHRIST ENTERED THE HEAVENLY SANCTUARY. Bearing only on the antitypical meaning of the Day of Atonement when all things were purified by blood and especially on the meaning of the high priest entering into the holy of holies and not without blood, the writer to the Hebrews asserts: "It was therefore necessary that the patterns of things in the heavens should be purified with these; but the heavenly things themselves with better sacrifices than these. For Christ is not entered into the holy places made with hands, which are the figures of the true; but into heaven itself, now to appear in the presence of God for us" (Heb. 9:23–24). No great difficulty arises in connection with the disclosure that mundane things were purified by blood. Of this it is written by the same author: "For when Moses had spoken every precept to all the people according to the law, he took the blood of calves and of goats, with water, and scarlet wool, and hyssop, and sprinkled both the book, and all the people, saying, This is the blood of the testament which God hath enjoined unto you. Moreover he sprinkled with blood both the tabernacle, and all the vessels of the ministry. And almost all things are by the law purged with blood; and without shedding of blood is no remission" (9:19–22). It is evident that, as the typical blood of beasts served to purify all things of the earthly sanctuary, Christ's entrance into heaven itself—typified by the high priest entering the holy of holies and sprinkling the mercy seat—was in some way, not fully revealed, a purifying of "heavenly things" by "better sacrifices." The widest range of interpretations is advanced respecting this heavenly purification. Though extended, the analysis of the passage made by F. W. Grant in *The Numerical Bible* clarifies the issues in several particulars. He writes:

The things to which the Levitical system pointed are now fulfilled, the true Day of Atonement, the Great High Priest of a better tabernacle, who has entered the sanctuary, "not by the blood of bulls and goats, but by His own blood," having found, not an atonement which would last a year, but *"eternal redemption."* Thus the worshiper has at last his conscience purified from dead works, from that which had in it no savor of life; would not satisfy, therefore, the living God. The legalism of the old covenant has been replaced by the grace of the new. The eternal inheritance is secured to those who are called by the grace of the gospel. Christ is thus the High Priest of those good things which were typified in Judaism, things still to come, which its shadows pointed to, but nothing more. The tabernacle is a better and more perfect one, "not made with hands," not belonging to the old creation. The blood of goats and bulls has been replaced by the value of His own blood, in virtue of which He has entered in once for all into the holy places, having found an "eternal redemption." He entered in in the triumph of having done this. There may be need of some additional clearing of the old types which are here interpreted for us, as well as of their application to the things of which they speak. The mercy-seat in the holiest, as being the "propitiatory," or place of propitiation, propitiation or atonement (for the word is the same in the Hebrew of the Old Testament and in its translation in the Septuagint Greek) being made upon it once a year, the question cannot but be raised, How does this affect the question of propitiation for us being really made in heaven, in some sense at least, when our High Priest entered in? It is evident that for Israel the blood upon the mercy-seat was the fundamental condition of all their blessing. Atonement, or propitiation, was then made "for the holy sanctuary, and for the tabernacle of the congregation, and for the altar, and for the priests, and for all the people of the congregation" (Lev. 16:33). Insomuch that this and this alone was the "day of atonement," apart from which no other sacrifice could legally have been offered, or God have remained in their midst at all. Is there nothing, then, in the substance that answers to these shadows, that answers just to this putting of the blood upon the mercy-seat, equally fundamental, that the throne may be for us that "throne of grace" which we know it to be? Or, can this speak simply of the Cross, and what was done there? and was not the blood, in any sense, carried in so as to be presented for acceptance before God in heaven? Now, there is another question that may be asked in return, which, simple as it is, deserves yet serious consideration. Does any one conceive of our blessed Lord carrying in literally His blood into heaven? That will, of course, be denied at once, and wonder expressed even at the suggestion of it. These are figures, it will be rightly said, and must be figuratively conceived; and we may add, as the apostle declares of them, that they are not even "the very image" of what they represent. This must not be taken as license for any avoidance of honest, consistent observance of the very terms in which it has pleased God to reveal things to us, as has many times been said, yet it has to be considered and reckoned with none the less. What could the application of the blood to the various objects to which it was applied in the Levitical ritual mean with reference to us now? When the high priest had completed his work in the tabernacle, he went out to the altar (of burnt-offering) to apply the blood similarly there. Are we to conceive of this as some further presentation of it for acceptance in relation to what the altar typifies? It is plain that this cannot be. The altar was that from which the daily sacrifices went up for

Israel, and the blood put upon it for propitiation simply set forth the righteousness of God in accepting what was done there. Just so by that upon the mercy-seat God's righteousness was set forth in continuing to dwell among a sinful people. In each case it was the blood that made the propitiation (Lev. 17:11); and the application of it gave it no new efficacy, but simply revealed its efficacy in particular relations. It was one of those object-lessons of which the ritualistic service consisted, and which may be easily strained in the endeavor to find in them a kind of exactness which does not belong to them. Thus, because the burning upon the altar followed the slaying of the victim, it was made by many to speak of atoning sufferings on the Lord's part *after* death. It has been forgotten in all such cases that "no parable can teach doctrine." We must find elsewhere the doctrine which the type illustrates, before we can find the ground for a just application. Now it is here that the doctrine thought to be found in Scripture as to this fails so absolutely. Where shall we expect to find it if not in Hebrews, where confessedly the Day of Atonement is the text upon which the apostle is dwelling in all this part? And where is it to be found in Hebrews, or anywhere else in the New Testament, that Christ went into heaven to make propitiation there? to present His work to God for its acceptance, or in any sense to sprinkle the blood upon the Eternal Throne? Quite another thing is, in fact, taught there,—namely, that Christ entered in once into the holy places, *having obtained* eternal redemption. As risen from the dead, raised up by the glory of the Father, He entered once, not the second time, propitiation therefore already accomplished, the resurrection the evidence of the ransom accepted, nothing remaining in this way to be done. The virtue of the blood revealed itself all the way, even as the typical veil of the sanctuary had been rent at the Cross already, before a step had been taken on the triumphant journey. All is as consistent as possible, and as plain as need be. And if it be said, Have we, then, nothing that answers more closely to this priestly action at the Throne? the answer is abundant, that the reality far transcends the type; for not only has the Throne been acting in power thus all along the road, but the Great High Priest, "having made by Himself purification of sins, He seated Himself" *upon* the Throne, "at the right hand of the Majesty on high." No blood is needed further to assure us that the Throne whereon He sits who shed it is a Throne of triumphant, glorious grace. *Christ there* is, as we are told in the epistle to the Romans (chap. 3:25), "set forth a propitiatory" (or mercy-seat) "through faith, by His blood." Christ is HIMSELF, in heaven, the blood-sprinkled mercy-seat. The New Testament, while confirming and interpreting the Old, goes yet far beyond it; and this is an important principle for its interpretation. Where should we find this more than in the light which thus streams out through these opened heavens? —*Heb. to Rev.*, 2nd ed., pp. 50–52

Mr. Grant, it would seem, has hardly considered all that is implied in the problem respecting the taking of Christ's blood into heaven, for the terminology—heavenly things purified by a better sacrifice—indicates a cleansing by blood. Is it only the historical fact that Christ's blood was shed which is accepted as the ground of heaven's cleansing, or is it the actual blood taken into heaven? It is probable that not enough is revealed to help one to a clear understanding and solution of the problem. The two types involved are specific enough: (a) that of the two birds, the second of which is dipped in the blood of the first bird and released, all of this a type of Christ rising and ascending into heaven and taking His blood with Him; (b) the high priest on the Day of Atonement going into the holiest and there applying the blood to the mercy seat. The blood, it is true, becomes the ground of propitiation; but that is hardly the issue here. The fact remains that in both types the blood is carried either into the sky by the bird or into the typical earthly sanctuary by the high priest. In the latter instance, it is plain how an awful throne of judgment becomes a throne of grace.

b. CHRIST THE FIRST-FRUITS. With reference to Leviticus 23:9–14, C. H. Mackintosh writes:

> The beautiful ordinance of the presentation of the sheaf of first-fruits typified the resurrection of Christ, who, "at the end of the Sabbath, as it began to dawn toward the first day of the week," rose triumphant from the tomb, having accomplished the glorious work of redemption. His was a "resurrection *from among* the dead"; and in it we have at once the earnest and the type of the resurrection of His people. "Christ the first-fruits; afterwards they that are Christ's at His coming." When Christ comes, His people will be raised "from among the dead [ἐκ νεκρῶν]," that is, those of them that sleep in Jesus; "but the rest of the dead lived not again until the thousand years were finished" (Rev. 20:5). When, immediately after the transfiguration, our blessed Lord spoke of His rising *"from among the dead,"* the disciples questioned among themselves what that could mean (cf. Mark 9). Every orthodox Jew believed in the doctrine of the "resurrection of the dead [ἀνάστασις νεκρῶν]," but the idea of a "resurrection from among the dead [ἀνάστασις ἐκ νεκρῶν]" was what the disciples were unable to grasp; and no doubt many disciples since then have felt considerable difficulty with respect to a mystery so profound. However, if my reader will prayerfully study and compare 1 Corinthians 15 with 1 Thessalonians 4:13–18, he will get much precious instruction upon this most interesting and practical truth. He can also look at Romans 8:11 in connection.—"But if the Spirit of Him that raised up Jesus from the dead [ἐκ νεκρῶν] dwell in you, He that raised up Christ from the dead shall also quicken your mortal bodies by His Spirit that dwelleth in you." From all these passages it will be seen that the resurrection of the Church will be upon precisely the same principle as the resurrection of Christ. Both the Head and the body are shown to be raised "from among the dead." The first sheaf and all the sheaves that follow after are morally connected. . . . "And ye shall count unto you from the morrow after the Sabbath, from the day that ye brought the sheaf of the wave-offering; seven Sabbaths shall be complete: even unto the morrow after the seventh Sabbath shall ye number fifty days; and ye shall offer a new meat-offering unto the Lord. Ye shall bring out of your habitations two

wave-loaves of two tenth deals: they shall be of fine flour; they shall be baken with leaven; they are the first-fruits unto the Lord" (Lev. 23:15–17). This is the feast of Pentecost—the type of God's people, gathered by the Holy Ghost, and presented before Him, in connection with all the preciousness of Christ. In the passover we have the death of Christ, in the sheaf of first-fruits we have the resurrection of Christ, and in the feast of Pentecost we have the descent of the Holy Ghost to form the Church. All this is divinely perfect. The death and resurrection of Christ had to be accomplished ere the Church could be formed. The sheaf was offered and then the loaves were baked. And, observe, "they shall be baken *with leaven.*" Why was this? Because they were intended to foreshadow those who, though filled with the Holy Ghost, and adorned with His gifts and graces, had, nevertheless, *evil* dwelling in them. The assembly, on the day of Pentecost, stood in the full value of the blood of Christ, was crowned with the gifts of the Holy Ghost; but there was leaven there also. No power of the Spirit could do away with the fact that there was evil dwelling in the people of God. It might be suppressed and kept out of view, but it was there. This fact is foreshadowed in the type by the leaven in the two loaves, and it is set forth in the actual history of the Church; for albeit God the Holy Ghost was present in the assembly, the flesh was there likewise to lie unto Him. Flesh is flesh, nor can it ever be made aught else than flesh. The Holy Ghost did not come down on the day of Pentecost to improve nature or do away with the fact of its incurable evil, but to baptize believers into one body, and connect them with their living Head in heaven.—*Notes on Leviticus,* Amer. ed., pp. 337–39, 341–42

Thus in His first ascension Christ appeared at once in heaven, having finished the work of redemption. The first type fulfilled in that first ascension is that of the high priest entering the holy of holies, while the second type fulfilled is that of the wave sheaf, the first-fruits of harvest.

2. THE FINAL ASCENSION ON THE CLOUDS OF HEAVEN. It is true that the two recognized ascensions of Christ may be, as they often are, contemplated as one event by the Scripture. The first, nevertheless, as indicated above, is the time of the formal presentation and the fulfilling of typical expectation, while the second represents the visible, final departure from earth to heaven and the seating of Christ on His Father's throne. As quoted above, F. W. Grant relates the seating with His presentation in heaven. Doubtless there is a sense in which Christ was hailed as the occupant of the throne when He entered heaven at the time of the first ascension, yet that could hardly have been the moment of His final and permanent occupancy of that throne. His missions to the earth during the succeeding forty days would preclude this.

The pertinent question is raised whether Christ's glory was veiled to any extent during the forty-day appearances, as it had been veiled during His precross ministry. As throwing light upon this, it may be remembered that the Apostle John had seen Christ in His baptism, His earth ministry, His transfiguration, His death, His resurrection, and in His postresurrection appearances; yet when he saw the Christ in heaven, in His present glory and as all will see Him, he fell at His feet as one dead. Of this experience he relates: "And when I saw him, I fell at his feet as dead. And he laid his right hand upon me, saying unto me, Fear not; I am the first and the last: I am he that liveth, and was dead; and, behold, I am alive for evermore, Amen; and have the keys of hell and of death" (Rev. 1:17–18). It would follow that, as all who saw Christ after the resurrection were able to recognize Him, to relate Him to His former appearance, and to endure the sight, His forty-day appearances were also veiled to a large degree.

While, according to the twofold approach to the whole revelation respecting Christ's ascension being followed, each event is characterized by achievements and occurrences peculiar to itself, there are Scriptures which contemplate the ascension as one complete event. In this connection, it is instructive to consider:

Psalm 68:18. "Thou hast ascended on high, thou hast led captivity captive: thou hast received gifts for men; yea, for the rebellious also, that the LORD God might dwell among them."

This passage, quoted by the Apostle in Ephesians 4:8, draws out the following comment from Erling C. Olsen:

Observe that the 8th verse of the 4th chapter of Ephesians is a direct quotation from the 18th verse of the 68th Psalm. David said in that verse: "Thou hast ascended on high, thou hast led captivity captive: thou hast received gifts for men . . ." Of whom was David speaking? The Apostle Paul, through the Holy Spirit, tells us it is the Lord Jesus, for he declares: "(Now he that ascended is he also that first descended into the lower parts of the earth. He that descended is the same also that ascended up far above all heavens, that he might fill all things.)" In other words, the Jehovah of the Old Testament is the Lord Jesus of the New Testament! It is He who first descended into the lower parts of the earth, in order to deliver those who were held captive. Then He *ascended,* taking with Him the spoils of His triumph. Now from that high, exalted place in the heavens He has given gifts to men. To some He has given the gift of apostleship; to some, that of evangelist; to some, pastors; and to others, teachers. For what purpose? For the perfecting of the saints, for the work of the ministry, for the edifying of the body of Christ.—*Meditations in the Psalms,* I, 494

Proverbs 30:4. "Who hath ascended up into heaven, or descended? Who hath gathered the wind in his fists? who hath bound the waters in a garment? who hath established all the ends of the earth? what is his name, and what is his son's name, if thou canst tell?"

Dr. H. A. Ironside writes the following bearing on this passage:

How vast the ignorance of the most learned man, when confronted with questions like these! We are at once reminded of the Lord's challenge to Job, in the 38th and 39th chapters of the wonderful book that bears his name. At the best, human knowledge is most circumscribed and contracted. No man, apart from divine revelation, could reply to the questions here asked. The first never found an answer until the words of our Lord concerning Himself, as recorded in John 3:13: "And no man hath ascended up to heaven, but He that came down from heaven, even the Son of Man which is in heaven." He it was who descended likewise, as it is written. "Now that He ascended, what is it but that He also descended first into the lower parts of the earth? He that descended is the same also that ascended up far above all heavens, that He might fill all things" (Eph. 4:9, 10). How much there is for the believer in the precious truth connected with the Lord's descent and ascension! Because of our sins He died upon the cross, bearing the righteous judgment of God. There He drank the dreadful cup of wrath which we could never have completely drained to all eternity. But because of who He was, He could drink the cup, and exhaust the wrath, leaving naught but blessing for all who trust in Him. He died, and was buried, but God raised Him from the dead, and in triumph He ascended to glory. Enoch was translated that he should not see death. Elijah was caught up in a flaming chariot, and carried by a whirlwind to heaven. But neither of these went up in his own power. Jesus, His work finished, and His ministry on earth accomplished, ascended of His own volition, passing through the upper air as easily as He had walked upon the water. The fact of His having gone up and having been received by the Shekinah—the cloud of divine Majesty—testifies to the perfection of His work in putting away forever the believer's sins. When on the tree, "Jehovah laid on Him the iniquity of us all." He could not be now in the presence of God if one sin remained upon Him. But all have been righteously settled for and put away, never to come up again: therefore He has gone in, in the power of His own blood, having accomplished eternal redemption. "Wherefore He saith, When He ascended up on high, He led captivity captive, and gave gifts unto men" (Eph. 4:8). He had "destroyed him that had the power of death, that is, the devil," that He might "deliver them who, through fear of death, were all their lifetime subject to bondage" (Heb. 2:14, 15). The trembling, anxious sinner is pointed by the Holy Ghost, not to Church or sacraments, not to ordinances or legal enactments, not to frames or feelings, but to a risen and ascended Christ seated in highest glory! "The righteousness which is of faith speaketh on this wise, Say not in thy heart, Who shall ascend into heaven? (that is, to bring Christ down from above:) or, Who shall descend into the deep? (that is, to bring up Christ again from the dead.) But what saith it? The word is nigh thee, even in thy mouth, and in thy heart: that is, the word of faith which we preach; that, if thou shalt confess with thy mouth the Lord Jesus, and shalt believe in thy heart that God hath raised Him from the dead, thou shalt be saved. For with the heart man believeth unto righteousness; and with the mouth confession is made unto salvation" (Rom. 10:6–10). Christ bore our sins on the cross. He died for them. He has been raised from the dead in token of God's infinite satisfaction in His work. He has ascended up to heaven, and His place on the throne of God as a Man in glory, is proof positive, that our sins are gone forever. This it is that, believed, gives deep and lasting peace. When the believer realizes that all has been done in a way that suits God; that He who accomplished it is one with the Father; that man as a fallen creature had no part in that work save to commit the sins for which the Saviour died: then, and not till then, does the majesty of the work of the cross dawn upon the soul. The question, "What is His name, and what is His Son's name?" followed by the challenge, "Declare, if thou canst tell," finds its answer in the New Testament revelation of the Father and the Son.—*Notes on Proverbs,* pp. 435–39

John 3:13. "And no man hath ascended up to heaven, but he that came down from heaven, even the Son of man which is in heaven."

While this passage is not directly on the ascension of Christ, there is much in it about Christ's rightful place in heaven and an anticipation of His return to heaven from whence He came. Dean Alford states here:

The whole verse seems to have intimate connexion with and reference to Proverbs 30:4, "Who hath ascended up to heaven, or descended?" and as spoken to a learned doctor of the law, would recall that verse,—especially as the further question is there asked, "Who hath gathered *the wind* in His fists?" and "What is His name, and what is His Son's name?" See also Deuteronomy 30:12, and the citation, Romans 10:6–8. All attempts to explain away the plain sense of this verse are futile and ridiculous. The Son of Man, the Lord Jesus, the Word made Flesh, *was in, came down from,* heaven,—and was *in heaven* (heaven about Him, heaven dwelling on earth, ch. 1:52), *while here,* and ascended up into heaven when He left this earth;—and by all these proofs, speaking in the prophetic language of accomplished Redemption, does the Lord establish, that *He alone* can speak of *heavenly things* to men, or convey the blessing of the new birth to them. Be it remembered, that He is here speaking *by anticipation,* of *results* of His course and sufferings on earth,—of the way of regeneration and salvation which God has appointed by Him. He regards therefore throughout the passage, the great facts of redemption *as accomplished,* and makes announcements which could not be literally acted upon till they had been so accomplished. See vv. 14 ff., whose sense will be altogether lost, unless this **hath ascended up** be understood of His exaltation to be a Prince and a Saviour, **which is in heaven.** See ch. 1:18 and note. Doubtless the meaning involves *"whose place is in heaven";* but it also asserts the being in heaven of the *time then present:* see ch. 1:52. Thus majestically does the Lord characterize His whole life of humiliation in the flesh, between His descent and His ascent. As uniting in Himself God, whose dwelling is Heaven, with man, whose dwelling is on earth, He ever was in heaven. And nearly connected with this fact is the transition to His being the fountain of eternal life, in vv. 14 ff.: cf. 1 Cor. 15:47–50, where the same connexion is strikingly set forth. To explain such expressions as *"to ascend up into heaven,"* etc., as mere *Hebrew metaphors* (Lücke, De Wette, etc.) is no more than saying that Hebrew metaphors were founded on deep insight into divine truth: —these words in fact express *the truths on which Hebrew metaphors were constructed*. Socinus is quite right, when he says that *those who take* "hath ascended up into heaven" *metaphorically, must in all consistency take* "he that came down from heaven" *metaphorically also;* "the descent and ascent must be both of the same kind."—*New Testament for English Readers*, I, 484

Ephesians 1:20–23. "Which he wrought in Christ, when he raised him from the dead, and set him at his own right hand in the heavenly places, far above all principality, and power, and might, and dominion, and every name that is named, not only in this world, but also in that which is to come: and hath put all things under his feet, and gave him to be the head over all things to the church, which is his body, the fulness of him that filleth all in all."

The span of the ascension of Christ is measured in this Scripture. Not only has He left the tomb and returned to His native place, but He is exalted above all others, with all authority in heaven and on earth committed to Him; yet His humanity is present too. There is a *man* in the glory. His glorified humanity is retained forever.

Ephesians 4:8–10. "Wherefore he saith, When he ascended up on high, he led captivity captive, and gave gifts unto men. (Now that he ascended, what is it but that he also descended first into the lower parts of the earth? He that descended is the same also that ascended up far above all heavens, that he might fill all things.)"

Reference to this portion has been made by the writers quoted above. The text contemplates the whole movement down to the earth and to death and the movement back again with the immeasurable fruits of His conquest. Much emphasis is placed in the New Testament upon the exceeding greatness of the occasion on which the eternal Son of God came into the world. Here, as elsewhere, an equally great achievement is indicated, namely, Christ's return or ascension back to His former place and glory. It is written that He prayed as He was about to leave this world: "And now, O Father, glorify thou me with thine own self with the glory which I had with thee before the world was" (John 17:5).

Acts 1:9–11. "And when he had spoken these things, while they beheld, he was taken up; and a cloud received him out of their sight. And while they looked steadfastly toward heaven as he went up, behold, two men stood by them in white apparel; which also said, Ye men of Galilee, why stand ye gazing up into heaven? this same Jesus, which is taken up from you into heaven, shall so come in like manner as ye have seen him go into heaven."

The historical facts related to Christ's final ascension are here set forth in simple terms. Having indicated the divinely arranged delay in the realization of Israel's earthly kingdom (Acts 1:6–7) and having defined the scope of the responsibility of His own in the world in this age together with the provided power of the enabling Holy Spirit (Acts 1:8), Christ departs into heaven. This Scripture traces His movement no further than that He was removed from human sight. That He ascended above all authorities and powers in angelic realms, that He assumed vast authority, and that He is seated upon His Father's throne must be understood from other portions of the New Testament. Of great significance is the fact that, as His last words in the world, He gives a comprehensive statement respecting Israel's kingdom to the effect that —though it is in no way abandoned—its time of realization is left indefinite relative to human understanding but fully determined in the mind and purpose of God, and a statement that the present age, if wholly indefinite with respect to duration, is to be characterized by a believing witness unto Himself in the power of the Holy Spirit. Such themes are eminently fitting—and they alone would be—for the final word He has left this world. As a theme, Christ's activity and responsibility in heaven belong to the next division of the chapter.

II. THE SESSION

The present ministry of Christ in heaven, known as His session, is far-reaching both in consequence and import. It, too, has not been treated even with a passing consideration by Covenant theologians, doubtless due to their inability—because of being confronted with their one-covenant theory—to introduce features and ministries which indicate a new divine purpose in the Church and by so much tend to disrupt the unity of a supposed immutable purpose and covenant of God's. Since, as will be seen, certain vital ministries of Christ in heaven provide completely for the believer's security, the present session of Christ has been eschewed by Arminians in a manner equally unpardonable. This neglect accounts very well for the emphasis of their pulpit ministrations. The Christian public, because deprived of the knowledge of Christ's present ministry, are unaware of its vast realities, though they are able from childhood itself to relate the mere historical facts and activities of Christ during His three and one-half years of service on earth. That

Christ is doing anything now is not recognized by Christians generally and for this a part-truth kind of preaching is wholly responsible. It yet remains true, whether neglected by one or the other kind of theologian, that Christ is now engaged in a ministry which determines the service and destiny of all those who have put their trust in Him. Various aspects of His present ministry are here indicated.

1. THE EXERCISE OF UNIVERSAL AUTHORITY. An inscrutable mystery is present in the fact that all authority is committed by the Father to the Son. In the light of the complete evidence that the Son is equal in His Person with the Father, it is difficult to understand how authority could be committed to the Son which was not properly His in His own right. Whatever may be the solution of that problem, it is certain that "all power" is given unto Christ (Matt. 28:18). And that power, while it was used in the beginning for the creation of all things in heaven and on earth, visible and invisible, including thrones, dominions, principalities, and powers, is exercised now to the end that all things may hold together (Col. 1:16–17). The very seating of Christ far above all intelligences (Eph. 1:20–21) implies that He is over them in complete authority. Thus, in a similar way, it is written that the Father hath put all things under the feet of the Son, excepting of course Himself (1 Cor. 15:27). This power will be exercised in the coming kingdom age to the end that all rule, authority, power, and every enemy—even death —shall be subdued (1 Cor. 15:24–28); but that same authority is possessed by the Son inherently and then is exercised in those ways in which it is required. It is, therefore, essential that when drawing a picture of the exalted Christ and in contemplating His Person and present activity He should be seen as the One who, under the Father, is above and over all things in the universe in the sense that they owe their very existence to Him, are held together by Him, and are governed by Him.

2. HEAD OVER ALL THINGS TO THE CHURCH. Unavoidably, this theme recurs in this chapter, though considered already under Christ's resurrection. Much, indeed, is made in the prophetic Scriptures of the future relation Christ will sustain as King to Israel and the nations at that time when He shall have returned to the earth; but now in the present age Christ is, through the same exaltation by the Father which placed Him above all intelligences, made to be Head over all things to the Church, which is His Body (cf. Eph. 1:22–23; Col. 1:18). Out of this Headship various responsibilities arise which will, because of their vital import, be traced as major divisions of this theme. The point of present emphasis is the essential fact of Christ's Headship over the one

Church, which is His Body. That it is termed *the Church, which is His Body* differentiates it from every form of the organized or visible church, which organized church at best is no more than an outward representation (with wheat and tares) in one locality and in one generation of that larger company of all believers in every locality and every generation who, being individually joined to Christ and perfected in Him, are one Body. This Headship is organic and real. Into Him are all the saved ones placed by the baptism of the Spirit and He is over them as the Head to that Body which they thus form. It is certain that Christ was not Head over all things to the Church until He ascended into heaven. The Church was not yet formed during His earthly ministry (cf. Matt. 16:18), nor until the descent of the Spirit on Pentecost. This assertion is not only sustained by uncomplicated, direct teaching of the New Testament but by the types as well. It was precisely fifty days after the wave sheaf—the type of Christ in resurrection—when the two loaves were waved which are a type of the Church, yet to be raised also and presented in glory. The loaf represents an uncounted number of particles sealed into one unit. Thus, also, the Church is one though formed out of a multitude of people from every kindred, tongue, and tribe. The Church is the supreme heavenly purpose of God and Christ's Headship over it is as exalted as that which is pre-eminent in the mind of the eternal God could be. The teaching ministry of Christ may well serve as an illustration of His Headship relation to every member of His Body. In John 16:13 it is recorded that complete instruction is ever being given to each yielded believer by the indwelling Spirit. It is clearly pointed out that the Spirit does not originate the message which He imparts, but rather speaks in the believer's heart whatsoever He hears. The One to whom the Spirit listens and whose message the Spirit transmits is none other than Christ, who stated "I have yet many things to say unto you" (vs. 12). It is thus the wonderful privilege of each member of the Body of Christ to receive direct messages of instruction and comfort from his exalted Head up in glory.

3. THE BESTOWER OF GIFTS. According to the New Testament, a gift is a divine enablement wrought in and through the believer by the Spirit who indwells him. It is the Spirit working thereby to accomplish certain divine purposes and using the one whom He indwells to that end. It is in no sense a human undertaking aided by the Spirit. Though certain general gifts are mentioned in the Scriptures (Rom. 12:3–8; 1 Cor. 12:4–11), the possible variety is unlimited since no two lives are lived under exactly the same conditions. However, to each believer some gift is

given, although the blessing and power of the gift will be experienced only when the life is wholly yielded to God. (In Romans 12, then, the truth of verses 1 and 2 precedes that of verses 6–8.) There will be little need of exhortation to God-honoring service for the one who is filled with the Spirit; for the Spirit will be working in that one both to will and to do of His good pleasure (Phil. 2:13). In like manner, certain men who are called His "gifts unto men" are provided and locally placed in their service by the ascended Christ (Eph. 4:7–11). The Lord did not leave this work to the uncertain and insufficient judgment of men (1 Cor. 12:11, 18). The bestowment of gifts is but another instance in which the personal and individual supervision of the exalted Christ over each member of His Body is disclosed. Each one is appointed to the exercise of a spiritual gift and that "as he will" (1 Cor. 12:11).

4. THE INTERCESSOR. This ministry of prayer began before He left the earth (John 17:1–26), is carried on for the saved rather than the unsaved (John 17:9), and will be continued in heaven as long as His own are in the world (John 17:20). As Intercessor, His work has to do with the weakness, the helplessness, and the immaturity of the saints who are on the earth—things over which they have no control. He who knows the limitations of His own and the power and strategy of the foe with whom they have to contend, has become unto them the Shepherd and Bishop of their souls. His care of Peter is somewhat an illustration of this truth (Luke 22:31–32). The priestly intercession of Christ is not only effectual, but is unending. The priests of old failed partly because of death; but Christ, because He ever liveth, hath an unchanging priesthood: "Wherefore he is able also to save them to the uttermost [hence, without end] that come unto God by him, seeing he ever liveth to make intercession for them" (Heb. 7:25). David recognized the same divine shepherding care and its guarantee of eternal safety, when he said "The LORD is my shepherd; I shall not want" (Ps. 23:1). One of the four reasons assigned in Romans 8:34 for the believer's safekeeping is that Christ now "maketh intercession for us." The effectiveness of the intercession of Christ in the preservation of each believer is declared to be absolute. As quoted above, "He is able also to save them to the uttermost," that is, to save and keep saved forever those who come unto God by Him and this on the ground of His ministry of intercession.

5. THE ADVOCATE. The child of God is often guilty of actual sin which would separate him from God were it not for his Advocate and what

He wrought in His death. The effect of the Christian's sin upon himself is that he loses his fellowship with God, his joy, his peace, and his power. On the other hand, these experiences are restored in infinite grace on the sole ground that he *confess* his sin (1 John 1:9); but it is still more important to consider the Christian's sin in relation to the holy character of God. Through the present priestly advocacy of Christ in heaven there is absolute safety and security for the Father's child even while he is sinning. An advocate is one who espouses and pleads the cause of another in the open courts. As Advocate, therefore, Christ is now appearing in heaven for His own (Heb. 9:24) when they sin. It is written: "My little children, these things write I unto you, that ye sin not. And if any man sin, we have an advocate with the Father, Jesus Christ the righteous" (1 John 2:1). His pleading is said to be with the Father, and Satan is there also, ceasing not to accuse the brethren night and day before God (Rev. 12:10). To the Christian, the sin may seem insignificant; but a holy God can never treat it lightly. It may be a secret sin on earth, but it is open scandal in heaven. The Psalmist wrote: "Thou hast set our iniquities before thee, our secret sins in the light of thy countenance" (Ps. 90:8). In marvelous grace and without solicitation from men, the Advocate pleads the cause of the guilty child of God. What the Advocate does in thus securing the safety of the believer is so in accordance with infinite justice that He is mentioned in this connection as "Jesus Christ the righteous." He pleads His own efficacious blood and the Father is free to preserve His child against every accusation from Satan or men and from the very judgments which sin would otherwise impose, since Christ through His death became "the propitiation for our [Christians'] sins" (1 John 2:2). The truth concerning the priestly ministry of Christ in heaven does not make it easy for the Christian to sin. On the contrary, these very things are written that *we be not sinning* (1 John 2:1, Greek); for no one can sin carelessly who considers the necessary pleading which his sin imposes upon the Advocate. The priestly ministries of Christ as Intercessor and as Advocate are directed unto the eternal security of those who are saved (Rom. 8:34).

6. THE BUILDER. One passage of great significance bears upon Christ's present undertaking in heaven as a Builder. He said "I go to prepare a place for you," and this in connection with the statement that in His Father's house, or universe, there are many abodes (John 14:1–3). Evidently not one of those abodes is in His estimation suitable for His Bride. Thus it comes about that He is preparing an abode which

will be even more glorious than all within God's creation at present. He is now thus engaged.

7. CHRIST EXPECTING. Over and above all the stupendous present ministry of the resurrected, exalted Savior already noted is the attitude which He is said to maintain toward the day when, coming back to the earth, He will defeat all enemies and take the throne to reign. Important, indeed, is the revelation which discloses the fact that Christ is now in the attitude of expectation toward the oncoming day when, returning on the clouds of heaven, He will vanquish every foe (cf. Ps. 2:7–9; Isa. 63:1–6; 2 Thess. 1:7–10; Rev. 19:15). Hebrews 10:13 records His expectation, which reads: "From henceforth expecting till his enemies be made his footstool." This will be realized in connection with His return to the earth in power and great glory, which return is the theme of the next chapter in this treatment of Christology.

In concluding this chapter on the ascension and session of the resurrected Christ, attention is again called to the immensity of His undertakings—some accomplished when He ascended from the tomb and others when He ascended visibly on the clouds of heaven. To this may be added the continued saving of souls, even all who come unto Him (Matt. 11:28; John 6:37). As High Priest over the true tabernacle on high, the Lord Jesus Christ has entered into heaven itself there to minister as Priest in behalf of those who are His own in the world (Heb. 8:1–2). The fact that He, when ascending, was received of His Father in heaven is evidence that His earth-ministry was accepted. The fact that He sat down there indicated that His work for the world was completed. The fact that He sat down on His Father's throne and not on His own throne reveals the truth, so constantly and consistently taught in the Scriptures, that He did not set up a kingdom on the earth at His first advent into the world, but that He is now "expecting" until the time when His kingdom shall come in the earth and the divine will shall be done on earth as it is done in heaven. "The kingdoms of this world" are yet to become "the kingdoms of our Lord, and of his Christ; and he shall reign for ever and ever" (Rev. 11:15), and the kingly Son will yet ask of His Father and He will give Him the nations for His inheritance and the uttermost parts of the earth for His possession (Ps. 2:8). However, Scripture clearly indicates too that He is not now establishing that kingdom rule in the earth (Matt. 25:31–46), but that rather He is calling out from both Jews and Gentiles a heavenly people who are related to Him as His Body and Bride. After the present purpose is accomplished He will return and "build again the tabernacle of

David, which is fallen down" (Acts 15:13–18). Though He is a King-Priest according to the Melchizedek type (Heb. 5:10; 7:1–3), He is now serving as Priest and not as King. He who is coming again and will then be King of kings is now ascended on high to be "head over all things to the church, which is his body" (Eph. 1:22–23).

CHAPTER XII

THE SECOND ADVENT OF CHRIST INCARNATE

SINCE CHRIST is the center of all Biblical prediction, there is properly an eschatology to be included in Christology. It contemplates the return of Christ to the earth, the kingdom which He will then set up on the earth, and His eternal reign. The first of these is now to be considered, the second in the chapter following, while the last forms the theme of the closing main division of Christology or chapter XIV.

Though theologians differ about the time and the manner of Christ's second advent, all who receive the Bible seriously do agree that He will return to this earth. The Scriptures clearly teach that Christ will come for judgment and for the setting up of His kingdom on the earth. Over this kingdom He with His Bride shall rule forever. No apology is entered or entertained for taking this vast body of Scripture which presents Christ's coming again and His kingdom in other than its natural, literal, and grammatical sense. All predictions due to be fulfilled before the present time, and they are many indeed, have been fulfilled after this manner and without exception; it is therefore reasonable to believe that unfulfilled predictions will be accomplished as faithfully and as definitely. It is possible that for want of faith some men of the past age of law who were confronted with predictions respecting the first advent when it was yet future were inclined to place some so-called spiritualizing interpretation upon these great prophecies; but it remained true, and would have remained so though no living man had taken God at His Word, that the inspired predictions moved on majestically in their natural, literal, and grammatical fulfillment. For those who have not done so, it may be the introduction into almost limitless fields of divine revelation and into overwhelming demonstrations of divine faithfulness to follow through an investigation which pursues this specific method of interpretation—such, anyway, is this division of Christology designed to be. The theme is as august, majestic, and consequential as the consummation of all divine purposes in mundane spheres must be. If matters of present world crises arrest the attention and spread consternation among all civilized inhabitants of the earth, how much more should believing men be aroused to unprecedented attention by the portrayal of those stupendous realities which constitute the closing scenes—the final disposition of evil and the final enthronement of righteousness and peace unto all eternity to come! However vividly expressed, comparison between any event in the history of the world —unless it be the creation of the universe—and that program which is yet to come is, so far as that which is sublunary is concerned, more an antithesis than a parallel. With reference to the literal fulfillment of prophecy related to the first advent and the probability of literal fulfillment of prophecy related to the second advent, George N. H. Peters writes:

If we were to adopt this principle of spiritualizing the [Second] Coming and the language employed in its usage, *then,* if consistently applied to the whole Bible, it would ignore the *literal, personal First Advent.* This is no caricature, but sober argument. Suppose our opponents are correct in their interpretation; let us then transplant ourselves to a period *before* the First Advent and apply their system to prophecies relating to that Advent and see the result. Let us, taking such an imaginative position, select e.g. Isa. 40:3, "the voice of him that crieth in the wilderness," etc., and according to the system just adopted, this would denote that divine truth would be heard in the earth even in the most abandoned parts of it, etc. Or, select e.g. Isa. 53, and we would have a representation of truth, its treatment, rejection, and final triumph. But what are the facts *as evidenced* by fulfilment? Have we not a literal voice, literal wilderness, literal address to Jews, a literal Coming, humiliation, sufferings, and death of Jesus Christ, etc.? According to the system of our opponents no such literal, personal fulfilment was intended, for if the predictions relating to the Sec. Advent, which are *far clearer, distinctive, and decisive* than those referring to the First, are to be understood as portraying a spiritual or providential Coming, *then surely,* if this measurer of prophecy is applied to the less distinct ones of the First Advent, they too only mean a spiritual or providential Coming. If the rule of interpretation holds good now, it ought to cover all time; for we know of no rules that were applicable to one age and not to another. If it be answered, that fulfilment shows that such and such language must be literally understood, *then* our reply is ready: the fulfilment is evidence that the spiritualistic interpretation on this point is *utterly untrustworthy,* while it gives decisive proof of *the consistency* of that adopted by the early Church.—*The Theocratic Kingdom,* II, 169

There could be no more decisive reason for giving a literal interpretation to the prophecies of the second advent than is set up by the fact that the prophecies of the first advent were thus fulfilled. Those who persist in a change of plan for the interpretation of that which is future have assigned to themselves the unenviable task of explaining why so violent a variation is introduced. At this point candor is challenged. If, perchance, the variation be interposed merely to defend a man-made idealism or to relieve a feeble credence, it deserves only the censure which belongs to unbelief. A phenomenon exists, namely, that men who are conscientious and meticulous to observe the exact teaching of the Scripture in the fields of inspiration and the divine character of the Sacred Text, the ruin of the race through Adam's sin, the Deity and Saviorhood of Christ, are found introducing methods of spiritualizing and vamping the clear declarations of the Bible in the one field of Eschatology. So much has this tendency prevailed in the past two or three centuries that, as respecting theologians, they are almost wholly of this bold class. So great an effect calls for an adequate cause, and the cause is not difficult to identify. As previously indicated, when one is bound to a man-made covenant theory there is no room within that assumption for a restoration of Israel, that nation with all her earthly covenants and glory having been merged into the church. There is but one logical consummation—that advanced by Whitby with all its reckless disregard for the Biblical testimony, namely, that a hypothetical grace covenant will eventuate in a transformed social order, and not by the power of the returning Messiah but by the preaching of the gospel. In the present time there are those who, misapprehending the prediction that the gospel of the kingdom must be preached in all the world (Matt. 24:14), assert that Christ cannot return until the missionary enterprise has reached to all the inhabited earth, not recognizing that the passage in question is found in a context belonging to the future great tribulation and that because of the unending cycle of birth and death there could not be a set time in this age when the missionary enterprise would be completed.

The truth that Christ is coming to the earth again is so emphatically and repeatedly asserted in the Sacred Text that nearly all creeds have included it in their declarations, and only those who are lacking in respect for the verity of the Bible text fail to acknowledge that Christ is to return; however, a wide variation in belief has existed about how and when He will return. A woeful lack of attention to the precise testimony of the Word of God is revealed in these conflicting sentiments more than is found in connection with any other one doctrine. Human notions and fancies have run riot with little apparent attempt to harmonize these ideas with the Scriptures. The assumption must arise that men either do not read the text of the Bible carefully, or, reading it, they are not admonished by it. An example of the human imagination's straying when making no reference to the extended testimony of

Scripture is furnished—and similar quotations might be made from various theologians—by Dr. William Newton Clarke, late Professor of Christian Theology in Colgate University, in his book *An Outline of Christian Theology* (5th ed., pp. 443–46). Having written at some length on certain points and having implied that Christ's second advent is fulfilled in the death of the believer—using John 14:1–3 as the proof-text, by the coming of the Spirit on Pentecost, and by the destruction of Jerusalem, he summarizes as follows:

Christ foretold a coming in his kingdom; the prediction was understood by his disciples to promise a visible coming at an early day, with startling manifestations of visible glory; but the prediction was fulfilled in the spiritual and invisible coming by means of which his spiritual work in the world has been carried forward. Or, to state more fully the view of Christ's coming that the Scriptures seem to warrant:—*a.* When he left the world, the work of Christ for the world, far from being finished, was only begun, and he was expecting still to carry it on toward completion. His prediction of a return, and an early return, was a true prediction, not destined to fail. *b.* Christ came again, in that spiritual presence with his people and the world by which his kingdom was constituted and his work upon mankind was done. This presence is such that his friends are not in orphanage, deprived of him (John 14:18); or, to use a figure frequent in the Scriptures, his Church is not a widow but a bride (Rev. 21:2–4). The New Jerusalem pictured at the end of the Apocalypse as the bride of Christ is not the symbol of the future life, but, as a careful reading is enough to show, represents the ideal Church of Christ in this world. To the production of this ideal state the spiritual coming of Christ tends, and is essential. *c.* Christ's coming was not accomplished in any one event. In reality, the event in which it was announced and introduced was the gift of the Holy Spirit on the day of Pentecost; and its first great providential accompaniment in history was the overthrow at Jerusalem. But his coming is not an event, it is a process that includes innumerable events, a perpetual advance of Christ in the activity of his kingdom. It has continued until now, and is still moving on. Christ came long ago, but he is truly the Coming One, for he is still coming, and is yet to come. *d.* No visible return of Christ to the earth is to be expected, but rather the long and steady advance of his spiritual kingdom. The expectation of a single dramatic advent corresponds to the Jewish doctrine of the nature of the kingdom, but not to the Christian. Jews, supposing the kingdom of the Messiah to be an earthly reign, would naturally look for the bodily presence of the king: but Christians who know the spiritual nature of his reign may well be satisfied with a spiritual presence, mightier than if it were seen. If our Lord will but complete the spiritual coming that he has begun, there will be no need of visible advent to make perfect his glory on the earth. The picturing of Christ's coming as a single event dramatic in its splendors and terrors, attended by resurrection and judgment, has served a useful purpose in keeping the thought of the unseen Christ fresh and vivid to the Church, in times when no other presentation of him, probably, would have been so effective. But at the same time it has been hurtful. It has led multitudes even of Christian people to regard the advent of their Saviour with more of terror than of desire. That great but terrible hymn, the "Dies Irae," has been only too true an expression of the common feeling. The Church has been led to regard herself as the widow and not the bride of Christ, and prevented from perceiving the power and love that were already abiding with her. This misapprehension has made it common for Christians to speak of the absent Lord; whereas he is the present Lord, reigning now in his spiritual kingdom. It has also led to a habitual underestimate of the intrinsic value of the present life and its common interests. Placing the reign of Christ mainly in the future, it has drawn attention away from his desire to fill all life now with the fulness of his holy dominion. Christianity has by no means been the friend to the family, to the nation, to commerce, to education, and to the common social life of man that it might have been if Christ had been recognized as the present reigning Lord, whose kingdom is a present reign of spiritual forces for the promotion of holiness and love. The present need is the need of living faith and love, to perceive the present Lord. It has long been common to call him the absent Lord: but after so long quoting his word of power, "Lo, I am with you alway," it is high time that the Church heard her own voice of testimony, and came to believe in him as the present Lord. The prevailing non-recognition of the present Christ amounts to unbelief. What is needed in order to awaken a worthier activity in the Church is a faith that discerns him as actually here in his kingdom, and appreciates the spiritual glory of his presence in the world. This view of the coming of Christ implies that the apostles grasped the spiritual idea of his kingdom but imperfectly, and that they expected what did not come to pass; and to many this seems inadmissible. Misapprehension on their part was of course a constant thing during his lifetime, but many think it cannot have existed after the Day of Pentecost, when they were taught by the Spirit of God. But it must be remembered that the Master told his disciples that "the times and seasons" were not for them to know (Acts 1:7), and that no man knew the time of his coming save that it would fall within the life of that generation (Mark 13:32). In this matter they were not to be helped by revelation. But apart from all theories of what the apostles were, we have to deal with the plain fact that the writers of the New Testament did expect an advent that did not occur. Wonderful indeed was the clearness of vision, and the trueness of perception, to which Christ's influence raised the disciples who knew him best; but we do not understand them if we overlook the fact that they were men of their own age, who received his truth into minds in which the thoughts of their age had influence. Here indeed was their power: for this enabled them to influence their own age, and send the influence on to ours. The glory of the first disciples lay not in the infallible correctness of their conceptions, but in their spiritual fellowship with Christ their Master.

This work of fiction which does not even draw its material from the Bible—though for remote identification it must introduce Christ and His disciples—is one mass of impossible error in doctrine from its beginning to its end; yet this work on theology has had acceptance with, and commendation from, an unusually large company of ministers and professors of note. Its fallacies should be noted briefly: (a) The entire assumption that Christ's coming is fulfilled by a "spiritual and invisible" program ignores every event connected with His return. These are too numerous to recount; but where, indeed, is the resurrection and translation of saints, the coming as lightning from the east which shines even unto the west, the taking of His earthly throne, the judgment of Israel and the nations, and why should anyone "watch" or "wait" for His coming? (b) The writer confuses Christ's personal coming with His omnipresence. He is in the midst when two or three are gathered unto Him, but that fact does not imply that His promise to come as Bridegroom and Judge has been, or is now, being fulfilled. (c) Dr. Clarke's assertion that Christ's promise to return at an early time was not fulfilled—hence the disciples misunderstood Him on that point—is a restriction on the word γενεά (*generation,* cf. Matt. 24:34, etc.) which a man of Dr. Clarke's scholarship should never have tolerated. When he declares that the disciples expected what did not come to pass, he implies that the writers of the New Testament were misinformed and were permitted to incorporate their misunderstandings into the Sacred Text itself. (d) As for the New Jerusalem of the Apocalypse by "a careful reading" being seen to be "the ideal Church" now in the world, the pertinent questions may be asked, what of its coming down from God out of heaven, its light as a jasper stone, its great wall, its twelve angels, its gates of pearl, its foundation of jasper and other gems, and the city itself being of pure gold like unto clear glass, its freedom from need of the sun as its light, and the lighting of it by the glory of God and the Lamb? (e) As for Christ's coming at the death of the believer, this point, too, lacks any semblance of the eschatological events predicted and confuses "the last enemy" with the "blessed hope." This is almost to transform death, the hideous, divine judgment upon the sin of man, into Christ Himself, and teaches that the blessings that await those who "fall asleep . . . in Jesus" are bestowed by death rather than by Christ. (f) That Christ came at Pentecost is Dr. Clarke's central claim; yet he has overlooked the facts, that his theory confuses two Persons of the Godhead, and that at the time of Pentecost no New Testament book had been written but still all the New Testament writers treat the coming of Christ as a future event. (g) That Christ came back in the destruction of Jerusalem is an unpardonable confounding of Matthew 24:15–22 with Luke 21:20–24. Here Dr. Clarke might with profit have undertaken one of those "careful readings," referred to above. It is true that he sees a "negative" aspect of Christ's coming at this point—a clearing away of the rubbish which Israel represented and a preparation for the setting up of His proposed new order; but the fact remains that a Roman army is not the Person of Christ, nor is the death of a million Jews the "blessed hope." (h) As for the declaration —"If our Lord will but complete the spiritual coming that he has begun, there will be no need of visible advent to make perfect his glory on the earth"—it is to be wondered just what would have become of Dr. Clarke's dream had he lived to see the second World War and a time when careless, inattentive preachers were having more and more trouble to find some reality that would take the place of such phantasms of a perfected social order.

Not a moment's attention would be given to such sentimentalism had it been found in the works of Jules Verne, but when it is advanced by a theologian of repute in all seriousness and acknowledged by contemporary men of influence, there can be no passing over it as mere child's play. The statement previously made is repeated, namely, that good and great men who comprehend much truth are, without a right interpretation of the prophetic Scriptures, given to impossible errors, and are often driven, as Dr. Clarke was driven, to refute the very words of Scripture merely to save a grotesque fancy. How different would have been the history of theology in the past three centuries and its fruits today, had theologians accepted the chiliasm of the apostles and the early church instead of the Federal or Covenant theories introduced by Johannes Cocceius and the postmillennialism of Daniel Whitby— both living a century after the Reformation! The insolvable mystery is that these theological theories, so evidently unsustained by Scripture, were not revalued and judged by sincere men in later generations. The mystery is not relieved at all when it is observed that men of the present day are determined to continue the same errors. Those inclined to "scoff," saying "Where is the promise of his coming?" (2 Pet. 3:3–4), have seized upon two utterly unworthy arguments as a defense for their unbelief—yet arguments accepted by good men who apparently have not weighed the issues involved, namely: (1) that Christ, according to the New Testament writers, promised to return within their own generation, but since He did not so return the writers were mistaken and (2) that the Apostle Paul believed and taught in his early ministry the soon coming of Christ, but that, since the doctrine, they say, does not appear in his later writings, he must have "changed his mind." But then what of the doctrine of inspiration? and what under such treatment of the Scriptures remains of any authority on the part of any New Testament writer? Attention has been called earlier to the generic meaning of γενεά, translated *generation*, showing that it refers to the race or stock and not necessarily just to the people then living; and it is certain from the very last words written by the Apostle that he believed in Christ's imminent return to the very day of his martyr death. He plainly declared: "Henceforth there is laid up for me a crown of righteousness, which the Lord, the righteous judge, shall give me at that day: and not to me only, but unto all them also that love his appearing" (2 Tim. 4:8). To claim that New Testament writers were mistaken and that Paul changed his mind is the traditional and all but universal apology of the school of Whitby—better known as postmillennialism. As incredible as it may seem, such subterfuges were indulged by men who with their next breath sought honestly to defend the inspiration and authority of the Scriptures. Daniel Whitby—never cleared from the charge of holding Socinian views—did not object to such dishonest treatment of the Sacred Text; but such inconsistency is deplorable in worthy men who, having embraced the notion of Whitby that Christ would not return until after a man-made millennium, have no other argument to offer in their efforts to counter the plain assurance of the impending return of Christ. Henry Ward Beecher, who was father of a rationalism which has all but wrecked the denomination to which he belonged, said: "He (Paul) expected to see Christ in this world before he departed; and all the apostles believed that they should; and there are some in our day who believe that they shall. I think that you will see Christ; but you will see Him on the other side. You will go to Him, He will not come to you. And your going to Christ will be spiritual, and not carnal. But the faith of the apostles, and of others, was that they should see Christ in their day. In this matter, however, they were *mistaken*. They believed that which facts and time overthrew. Their conviction was founded on a misinterpretation of the language of our Master" ("The Future Life," a sermon in *Christian Union*, Sept. 5, 1877, cited by Peters, *op. cit.*, I, 475). This challenge of many good men would not need to be made had they evidenced a candid investigation of the Scriptures on these specific themes.

In every Bible doctrine, the truths which make it what it is are contained in the Scriptures which set it forth. No attentive, spiritual mind need be uninformed respecting the teaching of the Bible; however, two other requisites are apparent, namely, an extended, painstaking induction of all the Scripture bearing on a given theme and an unprejudiced mind. Even colossal errors will not be corrected where prejudice exists and imposes human theories upon God's Word. How, indeed, may the Scriptures fulfill their prescribed purpose as a "correction" and a "reproof" in doctrine (2 Tim. 3:16) if, as seen in the experience of Dr. Clarke and with him a multitude of theologians, the apostles are charged with ignorance and error and the Sacred Text itself is arraigned as misleading and untrue, only because their theory will not conform to the truth revealed? The analysis of these conditions is entered at this point as an attempt to discover the true reason why the whole field of prophecy and especially the doctrine of the second advent are so strangely neglected. That doctrine stands whether or not it is ever recognized and accepted by the followers of a Cocceius, Whitby, or Clarke. When the doctrine is rightly attended, a vast array of Scripture arises for consideration and each passage demands that it be viewed in the light of its own precise declaration, in the light of its context, and in the light of all other Scripture bearing upon the same theme (cf. 2 Pet. 1:20–21).

A clear distinction should be observed between the Scriptures which announce the coming of Christ into the air to receive His Bride, the Church, unto Himself thus to end her pilgrim journey in the world and those Scriptures which announce the coming of Christ to the earth in power and great glory, to judge Israel and the nations and to reign on David's throne from Jerusalem. The first event is in no way whatsoever a part of the second event; it is Christ's way of delivering His people from the *cosmos* world before the divine judgments fall upon it. It is true that in this connection He said, "I will come again," but that coming He declared was only to receive His own unto Himself (John 14:1–3). Terms often employed, such as "two phases," "two aspects," or "two parts of His coming," are misleading. Much has appeared earlier in this work on this distinction; and no more need be added here other than to reaffirm that in the first event the movement is upward from earth to heaven, as in 1 Thessalonians 4:16–17: "For the Lord himself shall descend from heaven with a shout, with the voice of the archangel, and with the trump of God: and the dead in Christ shall rise first: then we which are alive and remain shall be caught up together with them in the clouds, to meet the Lord in the air: and so shall we ever be with the Lord," and that in the second advent the movement is downward from heaven to earth, as in Revelation 19:11–16. These events, though not always clearly distinguished in every Scripture, are naturally classified by the character of the conditions and incidents accompanying them.

As previously tabulated, there is a very extended list of passages bearing on the second coming of Christ. The important features of that stupendous, consummating event are directly stated in what may be termed the major passages bearing upon it. These are to be indicated with some comment on each.

Jude 1:14–15. "And Enoch also, the seventh from Adam, prophesied of these, saying, Behold, the Lord cometh with ten thousands of his saints, to execute judgment upon all, and to convince all that are ungodly among them of all their ungodly deeds which they have ungodly committed, and of all their hard speeches which ungodly sinners have spoken against him."

Notable indeed is the fact that the first recorded prophecy by man— though the report of it is reserved until the next to the last book of the Bible—and the last prophecy (cf. Rev. 22:20) proclaim the second advent of Christ. There is much to consider in Enoch's prediction both respecting the features of the event itself and the knowledge that was accorded to the man who was "the seventh from Adam." The statement that he "walked with God" (Gen. 5:24) doubtless indicates that, as was the case with patriarchs who lived before the writing of the Scriptures, he received direct revelation from God including some of that which was yet future in its reference. God would withhold nothing from Abraham (Gen. 18:17). It is certain from Genesis 26:5 that God had revealed much to him. The passage reads: "Because that Abraham obeyed my voice, and kept my charge, my commandments, my statutes, and my laws" (cf. Gen. 18:19; Rom. 5:13). Enoch's prediction anticipates the wickedness of humanity at the time of the second advent and the divine judgment that shall fall upon the world at that time. Little of this could have been comprehended by the people of Enoch's time; but it should not pass unnoticed that this the consummation of the ages—the restoration of God's unchallenged authority in angelic and human spheres—is the first theme of prophecy on the lips of man. Great intervening events were yet to be predicted and fulfilled; but the return of Christ, this prediction indicates, is of supreme import.

Deuteronomy 30:1–8. "And it shall come to pass, when all these things are come upon thee, the blessing and the curse, which I have set before thee, and thou shalt call them to mind among all the nations, whither the LORD thy God hath driven thee, and shalt return unto the LORD thy God, and shalt obey his voice according to all that I command thee this day, thou and thy children, with all thine heart, and with all thy soul; that then the LORD thy God will turn thy captivity, and have compassion upon thee, and will return and gather thee from all the nations, whither the LORD thy God hath scattered thee. If any of thine be driven out unto the outmost parts of heaven, from thence will the LORD thy God gather thee, and from thence will he fetch thee: and the LORD thy God will bring thee into the land which thy fathers possessed, and thou shalt possess it; and he will do thee good, and multiply thee above thy fathers. And the LORD thy God will circumcise thine heart, and the heart of thy seed, to love the LORD thy God with all thine heart, and with all thy soul, that thou mayest live. And the LORD thy God will put all these curses upon thine enemies, and on them that hate thee, which persecuted thee. And thou shalt return and obey the voice of the LORD, and do all his commandments which I command thee this day."

The regathering of Israel, the final possession of the land, and the obedience and blessing they are yet to experience are here said to be accomplished divinely when Christ returns. This is the first reference in the text of the Bible to the second advent, itself uttered, as in the case of Enoch, long before any clear understanding of prophecy was disclosed relative to a second advent. It is also indicated in this passage that Christ's second coming will be preceded by Israel's national repentance, when under the mighty hand of God they call to mind the covenant promises of God while they are yet scattered abroad among the nations. This repentance is deep and real, for they shall return unto Jehovah their God with all their heart and soul (cf. Job. 42:10). Their captivity to which this prophecy refers is that of their present estate, dispossessed of their land and unassimilated by the nations among whom they are scattered. The words "Thy God . . . will return and gather thee from all the nations, whither the LORD thy God hath scattered thee" not only assert the fact of His return—which return implies a previous advent—but dates the time when Israel will return to their land and the Palestinian covenant will be fulfilled in their behalf. As they were dispersed because of disobedience, so, in their return, they will be obedient. This is the order in grace. They are not returned because they are obedient, but they are obedient because of their return. The regathering of Israel into her own land is the theme of at least twelve major Old Testament prophecies, and that event, since it is an important feature connected with the second advent, will reappear in passages to be considered. Next in importance to the promise of Christ's return and the restoration of Israel to her land, according to this prediction, is the assurance of their obedience and the law which they will obey. In Jeremiah 31:31-34 it is asserted that the rule of life contained in the law covenant (cf. Ex. 19:5)—which covenant was given to Israel when they came out of Egypt and which covenant they broke—will be superseded by another covenant which will serve as a rule of life in their kingdom; but according to the Palestinian covenant they will, in addition to what constitutes the features of the new covenant, keep the very laws which Moses gave them before he was taken from them. It is probable that the new will incorporate the righteous requirements set forth in the Mosaic system, much, indeed, as those same righteous principles have been incorporated, though wholly readapted, into the teachings of grace which are now addressed to the perfected (in position) people who comprise the Church.

Psalm 2:6-9. "Yet have I set my king upon my holy hill of Zion. I will declare the decree: the LORD hath said unto me, Thou art my Son; this day have I begotten thee. Ask of me, and I shall give thee the heathen for thine inheritance, and the uttermost parts of the earth for thy possession. Thou shalt break them with a rod of iron; thou shalt dash them in pieces like a potter's vessel."

Here the scene changes from Christ's relation to Israel at His second advent over to His relation to the Gentile nations. The time of these judgments upon the nations is indicated in verse 6, in which it is said that Jehovah places His King upon the holy hill of Zion. The hill or mountain, according to Old Testament imagery, is the throne of government (cf. Isa. 2:1-5), and Zion because a part of the city stands for Jerusalem. Thus the prediction is of Jehovah placing His King (Messiah) on David's throne in Jerusalem. This anticipation is often declared in the prophetic Scriptures. The king is enthroned in spite of the opposition of the nations who are led on by demon-possessed kings and rulers (cf. Rev. 16:13-14). The term *heathen* as employed in the Old Testament is better rendered (as in R.V.) *nations*, since it refers to all peoples who are not Jews. It is equivalent to *Gentiles* as that terminology is used in the New Testament. There is no hint here of Christ returning to a converted world; rather He returns to a world in one supreme rebellion against Jehovah and His Messiah. The judgment of God must fall upon them in tribulation, which is described by the words here (vss. 4-5) "the LORD shall have them in derision. Then shall he speak unto them in his wrath, and vex them in his sore displeasure." When taking the throne by divine determination—which determination is well indicated by the word "yet" of verse 6—the Messiah, now King upon the throne, proclaims that by Jehovah's decree He undertakes that which follows. A similar decree came from heaven when Christ was set apart unto the office of Priest at His baptism and again when He was proclaimed from heaven as Prophet at the transfiguration. Thus, as stated in Psalm 2, again will He be attested and that as King, when He takes the Davidic throne in Jerusalem. Other passages —notably Isaiah 63:1-6; Matthew 25:31-46; 2 Thessalonians 1:7-10; Revelation 19:11-16, yet to be considered—declare the despotic, demolishing judgments which fall upon the nations when the King returns. These opposing, raging nations of Psalm 2:1 are, in the end, made a gift from Jehovah to the Messiah. In an undated past the Father gave each and every believer of this age to the Son (John 17:2, 6, 9, 11-12, 24) and that for the infinite blessing of the Son to rest upon them forever; but in the gift of the raging nations, the objective is that their rebellion against Jehovah and His Messiah may be put down completely. The subduing of angelic antagonists follows the second advent and occupies the entire period of the millennium (cf. 1 Cor. 15:24-26). The strongest expressions are employed in this portion of the Psalm to describe the manner in which the Messiah will act. He breaks them with a rod of iron and dashes them in pieces like a potter's vessel. They are His inheritance and when thus vanquished a portion of them, divinely chosen to that end, will inherit the kingdom prepared for them and be subject to the King (Matt. 25:31-46). Seldom in the Old Testament does God address the kings of the earth, but as this Psalm closes they are admonished to "serve Jehovah with fear, and . . . trembling" and to "kiss the Son, lest he be angry, and ye perish from the way, when his wrath is kindled but a little." His wrath will be released as is described in the following passages.

Isaiah 63:1-6. "Who is this that cometh from Edom, with dyed garments from Bozrah? this that is glorious in his apparel, travelling in the greatness of his strength? I that speak in righteousness, mighty to save. Wherefore art thou red in thine apparel, and thy garments like him that treadeth in the winefat? I have trodden the winepress alone; and of the people there was none with me: for I will tread them in mine anger, and trample them in my fury; and their blood shall be sprinkled upon my garments, and I will stain all my raiment. For the day of vengeance is in mine heart, and the year of my redeemed is come. And I looked, and there was none to help; and I wondered that there was none to uphold: therefore mine own arm brought salvation unto me; and my fury, it upheld me. And I will tread down the people in mine anger, and make them drunk in my fury, and I will bring down their strength to the earth."

This most realistic description of Christ coming in judgment upon the nations is presented in a questionnaire form and, though the identity of the one who propounds the inquiry is not disclosed, the returning Messiah Himself supplies the answers. He styles Himself as the One who speaks in righteousness, mighty to save. His salvation is for true Israel; they, accordingly, are those to whom He refers when He says, "The year of my redeemed is come" (cf. Rom. 11:26–27). "The day of vengeance" is the day of His outpoured judgments upon the nations because of their rejection of Him and their persecutions of His elect people, Israel. The imagery employed in this passage is the strongest of any or all used in the Bible to describe these events. In vengeance He treads the wine press of His anger and fury. He declares that He will make those whom He afflicts to be drunk in His fury; He will bring down their strength to the earth. His garments are stained with the blood of His foes as are the garments stained of the one who treadeth the wine press. Such are the judgments which the King imposes when He returns to the earth. If perchance this scene is a shock to those who have contemplated Christ only as the meek and lowly Savior, the Babe of Bethlehem, it should be remembered that the marvel is not that He thus comes as an outraged, destroying monarch to judge the nations that have rejected Him; rather the wonder is that He ever came in lowly guise enduring the scorn of men and crucifixion.

2 Thessalonians 1:7–10. "And to you who are troubled rest with us, when the Lord Jesus shall be revealed from heaven with his mighty angels, in flaming fire taking vengeance on them that know not God, and that obey not the gospel of our Lord Jesus Christ: who shall be punished with everlasting destruction from the presence of the Lord, and from the glory of his power; when he shall come to be glorified in his saints, and to be admired in all them that believe (because our testimony among you was believed) in that day."

Again language is strained beyond all bounds in the effort to describe that which cannot really be expressed to the full. Accompanied by the angels of His might, the Lord of Glory is revealed from heaven in flaming fire, taking vengeance on them that, without excuse (cf. Rom. 1:19–32), know not God and who have refused to obey the gospel of our Lord Jesus Christ. These shall be punished with everlasting destruction. Little comment is needed respecting this important passage. Its language is certain and the event is rightly identified as the second advent of Christ.

Daniel 2:34–35. "Thou sawest till that a stone was cut out without hands, which smote the image upon his feet that were of iron and clay, and brake them to pieces. Then was the iron, the clay, the brass, the silver, and the gold, broken to pieces together, and became like the chaff of the summer threshingfloors; and the wind carried them away, that no place was found for them: and the stone that smote the image became a great mountain, and filled the whole earth."

These words, taken from Daniel's reconstruction of the king's dream, describe the destruction that shall fall upon the fabric which the great monarchies have woven. The specific contribution which this prediction makes (cf. also vss. 44–45) is the fact that Christ in His second advent as the Smiting Stone will demolish and dismiss every vestige of Gentilism, with all of its principles and factors from the beginning of Gentile times (cf. Luke 21:24) to the hour of His return. These principles and factors which have characterized the whole period of nearly 2,500 years thus far will have their fullest expression in that tribulation period which is terminated by the glorious return of Christ. Dr. H. A. Ironside has the following comment to offer respecting the falling of the Stone:

I desire to trace out a little of what Scripture has to tell us elsewhere about this Stone. It is undoubtedly a figure of the Lord Jesus Christ. Ps. 118:22 tells us, long before He came into this scene, that He would be the Stone set at naught by the builders, and become the head of the corner; and in the New Testament this verse is declared to be prophetic of Christ. When He came to earth He was indeed the Stone set at naught by the builders, the rulers of the Jews; but mark, He did not come as the Stone falling from heaven. That is the way He will come when He returns the second time. He came before to His own; but His own received Him not. He came here as the Foundation Stone, the Head Stone of the corner; but they who should have owned His claims, cried in their unbelief and hatred, "Away with Him; crucify Him; crucify Him!" Now God has taken Him up to heaven. Yonder, in the Father's glory, the eye of faith beholds that exalted Stone. The day is coming when it is going to fall upon His enemies; and when it falls, it will grind to powder all Gentile dominion, and all those who have rejected the precious grace of God. In Isa. 8:14 Christ is prophetically described as a Stone of stumbling and a Rock of offence; and we are told that many will stumble and fall. Thus it was when He came in lowly grace: "They stumbled at the stumbling Stone, as it is written." They were looking for a great world-monarch; and when He came in humiliation, Israel nationally stumbled over Him; and they were broken—and they remain broken to this day. Whenever you see a Jew walking the streets of a Gentile city, you may say in your heart. There is a proof of the truth of what the Lord Jesus has said: "Whosoever shall fall on this Stone shall be broken." Broken, and scattered, and peeled, they have wandered in all the lands of the earth, hardly welcome anywhere, until, in these last days, God has been turning the hearts of the nations toward them, preparatory to their being taken back to their own land. By and by a remnant will return to the Lord; so Isa. 28:16 says, "Behold, I lay in Zion for a foundation a Stone, a tried Stone, a precious corner Stone, a sure foundation: he that believeth shall not make haste." He then goes on depicting Israel's deliverance at the second appearing of this Stone of salvation. He it is who is described by Zechariah—chap. 3:9—as the Stone engraved with the engraving of a signet, upon which shall be seven eyes. But what about the nations in that day? The message of grace has gone out to them; and what has been the result? God has been taking out from among them a people for His name, but the mass have deliberately rejected the Christ of God; and that rejected Lord Jesus is soon going to fall upon them in judgment. Then will the rest of His word be fulfilled, "On whomsoever it shall fall, it shall grind him to powder." Israel stumbled over Him, and they were broken. He is going to fall upon the Gentiles in His wrath and indignation, and they will be ground to powder, and driven away from before His face like the chaff of the summer threshing-floor. Do you ask, "When is the Stone going to fall?" It will be when the countries once occupied by the Roman empire in Europe will make a ten-kingdom coalition, electing one of their number to be their supreme arbiter. We have him set forth in chapter 7 as the little horn rising out of the Roman empire—a passage which has been often applied to the Pope, but which we shall see has no application to him at all. In that day the iron of imperial power will be mixed with the brittle pottery of socialism and democracy; but they will not cleave together. We see this preparing at the present time. When, for instance, I read the account of the Peace Conferences, and similar conventions, I have no thought that lasting universal peace is going to be brought about in that way, while the Prince of Peace is still rejected. But I think I see the shadow on the wall of this revived Roman empire. From my study of the word of God, I quite expect one of two things: either universal war, or universal arbitration; and, as a result of either of these methods, the ten-kingdomed form of the Roman empire brought about.—*Lectures on Daniel*, pp. 39–42

Zechariah 14:1–4. "Behold, the day of the LORD cometh, and thy spoil shall be divided in the midst of thee. For I will gather all nations against Jerusalem to battle; and the city shall be taken, and the houses rifled, and the women ravished; and half of the city shall go forth into captivity, and the residue of the people shall not be cut off from the city. Then shall the LORD go forth, and fight against those nations, as when he fought in the day of battle. And his feet shall stand in that day upon the mount of Olives, which is before Jerusalem on the east, and the mount of Olives shall cleave in the midst thereof toward the east and toward the west, and there shall be a very great valley; and half of the mountain shall remove toward the north, and half of it toward the south."

By this prediction the truth is established that Jerusalem shall again be besieged by the nations and the returning Christ will then go forth to fight against them. It is then that His feet shall stand on the Mount of Olives—perhaps on the same spot from which He ascended into heaven—and the Mount of Olives shall be divided in the midst, forming a great valley. In various respects, nature passes through convulsions and changes when Christ returns. "And there shall be signs in the sun, and in the moon, and in the stars; and upon the earth distress of nations, with perplexity; the sea and the waves roaring; men's hearts failing them for fear, and for looking after those things which are coming on the earth: for the powers of heaven shall be shaken. And then shall they see the Son of man coming in a cloud with power and great glory" (Luke 21:25–27); "Immediately after the tribulation of those days shall the sun be darkened, and the moon shall not give her light, and the stars shall fall from heaven, and the powers of the heavens shall be shaken" (Matt. 24:29); "For the earnest expectation of the creature waiteth for the manifestation of the sons of God. For the creature was made subject to vanity, not willingly, but by reason of him who hath subjected the same in hope. Because the creature itself also shall be delivered from the bondage of corruption into the glorious liberty of the children of God. For we know that the whole creation groaneth and travaileth in pain together until now" (Rom. 8:19–22). It is at the time of the manifestation of the sons of God that creation shall be delivered.

2 Thessalonians 2:8–12. "And then shall that Wicked be revealed, whom the Lord shall consume with the spirit of his mouth, and shall destroy with the brightness of his coming: even him, whose coming is after the working of Satan with all power and signs and lying wonders, and with all deceivableness of unrighteousness in them that perish; because they received not the love of the truth, that they might be saved. And for this cause God shall send them strong delusion, that they should believe a lie: that they all might be damned who believed not the truth, but had pleasure in unrighteousness."

Thus is revealed the important truth that the man of sin, the "lawless one" (R.V.), shall be revealed after (not, before) the removal of the Restrainer, the Holy Spirit, and—it is right to believe—the Church will be removed when the Spirit departs (cf. John 14:16). The "lawless one" is destroyed by the coming of Christ and in the midst of his greatest corruption in the earth. Again, as always, the Word of God testifies that Christ will not come to a converted world. He comes into the midst of the greatest manifestation of evil.

Matthew 23:37—25:46. This particular Scripture—far too prolonged for quotation—has had extended consideration as one of Christ's major discourses. It is His farewell word to Israel in which He informs them of conditions which will obtain before His return. Its several parts include: the time-word to Israel, 23:37–39; the occasion of this address, 24:1–4; the course of this unforeseen age, 24:5–8; the great tribulation, 24:9–22; warnings of impostors, 24:23–28; the description of His return and Israel's supernatural regathering, 24:29–31; assurance of His predicted coming and due warnings to Israel that when they see certain things coming to pass (cf. Luke 21:28) they are to "watch," 24:32—25:30; the judgment of the nations, 25:31–46. The greatest emphasis falls upon Israel's responsibility in that day to *watch.* The people in Noah's day did not watch, the evil servant did not look for his master, the five unwise virgins lacked the preparation they would have made had they really expected the bridegroom's return. This entire section, that is, 24:37—25:30, anticipates Israel's coming judgments. As there are evil servants and good servants in a household, as there are prepared and unprepared virgins awaiting the wedding feast, as there are those who employ talents and those who do not, so Israel will be called into judgment when her Messiah comes (cf. Ezek. 20:33–44). This doctrinally formative discourse closes with one central prediction regarding the judgment of the nations then living on the earth (25:31–46), which judgment, like that of Israel, will occur when the King returns and takes the Davidic throne in Jerusalem.

Out of the above outline, four major features may be selected for special consideration: (a) the great tribulation, (b) the fact of Christ's second coming, (c) the judgment of Israel, and (d) the judgment of the nations then living.

In the present discussion attention is first to be centered upon the fact of Christ's coming again. There can be no confusion here respecting the manner of His coming in each Messianic advent. Coming as lightning from the east that shines unto the west has no resemblance to being born of a virgin in a manger. Again, the manner of His coming in the second advent should create no wonder, but the manner of His coming in the first advent is freighted with mystery, condescension, and simplicity which are not at all the natural rôle of the King of Glory. As He went on the clouds of heaven, so He will return (cf. Acts 1:9–11). Every tribe of Israel will see Him and mourn because of Him. Prophecy anticipates this mourning. He comes with power and great glory and by the ministration of angels Israel is regathered "from the four winds, from one end of heaven [horizon] to the other." As formerly indicated, upon taking the Davidic throne, the King enters upon Israel's judgments. This final judgment for Israel is not only an extended theme of prophecy, but is vitally important in the whole progress of doctrine relative to that elect nation. Though no specific time is set, it seems necessary to believe that there will have been a resurrection of the whole house of Israel and all to appear thus before this judgment. It would be woefully incomplete for this judgment to be restricted to the one generation of Israel then living. Men of Israel in all generations have lived and served with the glorious kingdom in view. Those who have attained to it by their faithfulness will not be deprived of it, and those who by carelessness and sin have failed must be judged and excluded. The entire context of Ezekiel 20:33–44, as before stated, should be considered in this connection (cf. Ezek. 37:1–14; Dan. 12:1–3). That which bears immediately upon the present theme and which completes the history of the times of the Gentiles is the judgment of the nations (Matt. 25:31–46), which judgment, since it precedes the millennial kingdom and involves only the nations then living who will have had their part in the great tribulation, should not be confused with the judgment of the great white throne (Rev. 20:12–15), which assize follows the millennial kingdom and involves the wicked dead of all human history. In the judgment of the living nations, these are first seen in utter subjection standing, after Christ has conquered them, before the throne of His glory. The rod of iron of Psalm 2:9 and the trampling in fury of Isaiah 63:3 will have accomplished its perfect end. The issue in this judgment is not the evil that has characterized all past generations of Gentiles; it is rather the one vital question, namely, the treatment that they will have accorded Israel during the great tribulation, i.e., those whom the King terms "my brethren." No reference is made here to Christians, though they are "joint heirs with Christ" and of the household of God. Christ is not ashamed to call them also His brethren (cf. Heb. 2:11). The Christian is never left in dependence upon the world for his support as in the case of dispersed Israel, nor is there any Scripture which would hold the Gentiles responsible for ministering to the Christians; however, dispossessed Israel is cast upon the world and subject to its bounty for survival. They are Christ's brethren in the most literal physical sense. During the great tribulation some Gentile nations will have proved themselves to have been favorable toward Israel and some will have withheld their aid. Some are thereby qualified to enter with Israel into their millennial kingdom and some are disqualified. Even those who enter with Israel into the kingdom must, as was seen before, take a subordinate position (cf. Isa. 14:1–2; 60:12, 14). It seems incredible to those uninstructed in the Word of God that there is such a thing as an elect nation favored with eternal covenants and a specific glory above all the other nations of the earth, that the treatment accorded this people in the time of their greatest affliction should be the basis upon which the destiny of these living nations will be determined. In the hour of Israel's beginning Jehovah said to Abraham respecting his physical seed that those who blessed that people should be blessed and those who cursed that people should be cursed. It is significant, then, that at the end of Gentile times it should be said to those who have blessed Israel: "Come, ye blessed of my Father, inherit the kingdom prepared for you from the foundation of the world," and to those who curse Israel: "Depart from me, ye cursed, into everlasting fire, prepared for the devil and his angels." It makes little difference whether men accept and profit by the King's predictions in their Bible respecting the future; the determined program of God must be, and will be, executed to all completeness anyway.

Acts 1:9–11. "And when he had spoken these things, while they beheld, he was taken up; and a cloud received him out of their sight. And while they looked stedfastly toward heaven as he went up, behold, two men stood by them in white apparel; which also said, Ye men of Galilee, why stand ye gazing up into heaven? this same Jesus, which is taken up from you into heaven, shall so come in like manner as ye have seen him go into heaven."

This passage, already contemplated when considering the ascension, is also a definite promise of the return of Christ. Not another, but *this same Jesus* which is taken up from you into heaven shall so come in like manner as ye have seen Him go into heaven, that is, visibly, bodily, and on the clouds of heaven. He said of Himself "I will come again," not that death will, the Roman army under Titus, nor even the Holy Spirit (although He came for the *first* time on Pentecost). Thus also the Apostle declares: "The Lord himself shall descend from heaven with a shout." The very fact that He appears the second time (Heb. 9:28) links His identity with the one who came the first time. In the former treatment of this Scripture it has been pointed out that in this context great issues are passing in rapid succession. In verses 6 and 7, Christ answers the covenant expectation respecting Judaism and the hope of Israel. He declared that the realization of Israel's promises awaits the times and seasons which the Father hath kept in His own power. In verse 8 the primary occupation of the believer in this age is announced, namely, witnessing to the ends of the earth. The next and final great event in this program is His own return, which return will end the proclamation of the evangel commanded.

Acts 15:16–18. "After this I will return, and will build again the tabernacle of David, which is fallen down; and I will build again the ruins thereof, and I will set it up: that the residue of men might seek after the Lord, and all the Gentiles, upon whom my name is called, saith the Lord, who doeth all these things."

As recorded in this Scripture, the early church met for its first council with the chief aim in view of determining what the new order of things could mean which, according to Peter, Paul, and Barnabas, had reached as fully and as effectively to the Gentiles as it had to the Jews. What had become of the agelong advantages which Jehovah had bestowed upon Israel, which had continued until the time of Christ's death and resurrection; in other words, what had become of Judaism? The fact that God was doing a wholly new thing, with Gentile now securing equal benefits, was the complete evidence that mighty changes had been accomplished. This council, guided by the Spirit, concluded that the new thing into which Gentiles were freely admitted was a visitation of God's grace in calling out from them, as well as from Jews, a people for His name or Person (vs. 14). The name of Deity is equivalent to the Person, of course, and no more endearing recognition of the Bride of Christ can be set up than to declare that she is for His own Person. A moment's reflection will disclose how utterly foreign to Judaism this new order is. The context, however, goes on with the assurance that Christ will come again and that, at His coming, He will restore the Davidic government which has collapsed or fallen down, which means that the Davidic covenant will then be fulfilled, and Judaism restored thence to continue on to the realization of all that is predicted concerning it. This means that the millennial kingdom will be set up and those Gentiles "upon whom my name is called" will share in that kingdom. That a new order is divinely established is indicated in the context which immediately follows the passage under consideration.

Isaiah 59:20; 60:1–5. "And the Redeemer shall come to Zion, and unto them that turn from transgression in Jacob, saith the LORD. . . .

Arise, shine; for thy light is come, and the glory of the LORD is risen upon thee. For, behold, the darkness shall cover the earth, and gross darkness the people: but the LORD shall arise upon thee, and his glory shall be seen upon thee. And the Gentiles shall come to thy light, and kings to the brightness of thy rising. Lift up thine eyes round about, and see: all they gather themselves together, they come to thee: thy sons shall come from far, and thy daughters shall be nursed at thy side. Then thou shalt see, and flow together, and thine heart shall fear, and be enlarged; because the abundance of the sea shall be converted unto thee, the forces of the Gentiles shall come unto thee."

The Apostle's restatement of Isaiah 59:20 is as follows: "And so all Israel shall be saved: as it is written, There shall come out of Sion the Deliverer, and shall turn away ungodliness from Jacob: for this is my covenant unto them, when I shall take away their sins" (Rom. 11:26–27). In their experience of Christ's return, Israel is to arise and shine, for her light will have come. "The Redeemer shall come to Zion, and unto them that turn from transgression in Jacob." The glory of Jehovah shall rise upon them. Preceding this arising of Jehovah upon Israel, darkness shall cover the earth and gross darkness the people. Thus is described the great tribulation that must cover the whole earth. In the time of kingdom blessing, "Gentiles shall come to thy light, and kings to the brightness of thy rising." The forces of the Gentiles shall come thus unto Israel. All of this, as in unnumbered predictions, will occur when the Messiah returns.

Daniel 7:13–14. "I saw in the night visions, and, behold, one like the Son of man came with the clouds of heaven, and came to the Ancient of days, and they brought him near before him. And there was given him dominion, and glory, and a kingdom, that all people, nations, and languages, should serve him: his dominion is an everlasting dominion, which shall not pass away, and his kingdom that which shall not be destroyed."

The particular emphasis in this description of the second advent is on the truth that by it Gentile world dominion is brought to its end. It will be remembered that, in both chapter 2 and chapter 7 of Daniel, there is prediction respecting the great empires that were to arise in succession beginning with Babylon under Nebuchadnezzar, continuing to Media-Persia and Greece, and ending with Rome, which last-named empire was in power when Christ lived here on earth. The intercalation of the Church age, then, began with Christ's death and continues until the Church is removed from the earth. As this intercalary period began before the Roman empire had quite finished the part predicted of her, she has yet to be revived and to fulfill all that is written regarding her. The feet and toes of the colossal image composed of both iron and clay represent that part of the Roman empire yet to be completed. The same is indicated in Daniel 7 by the ten horns of the fourth beast. All this governmental history must, and will, run its course during the momentous seventieth week, or seven years of tribulation yet to come upon the earth which Daniel foresaw. This brief period not only serves to complete Jewish times reaching up to their kingdom, but serves as well to conclude Gentile times on the earth. All things of responsibility both for Israel and the Gentiles are terminated by the glorious appearing of Christ. Specifically, the passage under consideration, along with Revelation 5:1-7, describes the investiture of the King with His kingdom rule. As King upon His throne—the throne of David in Jerusalem—He will render His judgments upon Israel and upon the nations before the kingdom begins. Daniel 2:34-35, already considered, is a description of the crushing blow that the King will administer to the nations, while Daniel 7:13-14, now being examined, presents the assumption of His authority in connection with which He renders His awful judgments upon the Gentiles.

Malachi 3:1-3. "Behold, I will send my messenger, and he shall prepare the way before me: and the Lord, whom ye seek, shall suddenly come to his temple, even the messenger of the covenant, whom ye delight in: behold, he shall come, saith the LORD of hosts. But who may abide the day of his coming? and who shall stand when he appeareth? for he is like a refiner's fire, and like fullers' soap: and he shall sit as a refiner and purifier of silver: and he shall purify the sons of Levi, and purge them as gold and silver, that they may offer unto the LORD an offering in righteousness."

This passage reveals the inability, true of all Old Testament prophets, to recognize the time period intervening between the two advents of Christ. Thus it is confirmed that, as later revealed in the New Testament, the present age must be reckoned a divine "mystery" or sacred secret before Christ came. The prophets of old foresaw both a suffering Lamb and a world-ruling King. They were perplexed about the time relationships for these. The Apostle Peter writes of it after this manner: "Of which salvation the prophets have inquired and searched diligently, who prophesied of the grace that should come unto you: searching what, or what manner of time the Spirit of Christ which was in them did signify, when it testified beforehand the sufferings of Christ,

and the glory that should follow" (1 Pet. 1:10–11). On this passage—
Malachi 3:1–3—Dr. C. I. Scofield in his *Reference Bible* writes: "The
f.c. of verse 1 is quoted of John the Baptist (Mt. 11:10; Mk. 1:2; Lk.
7:27), but the second clause, 'the Lord whom ye seek,' etc., is *nowhere
quoted* in the N.T. The reason is obvious: in everything save the fact
of Christ's first advent, the latter clause awaits fulfilment (Hab. 2:20).
Verses 2–5 speak of judgment, not of grace. Malachi, in common with
other O.T. prophets, saw both advents of Messiah blended in one hori-
zon, but did not see the separating interval described in Mt. 13 con-
sequent upon the rejection of the King (Mt. 13:16, 17). Still less was
the Church-age in his vision (Eph. 3:3–6; Col. 1:25–27). 'My messenger' (vs. 1) is John the Baptist; the 'messenger of the covenant' is
Christ in both of His advents, but with especial reference to the events
which are to follow His return" (p. 982).

Mark 9:1–9. "And he said unto them, Verily I say unto you, That
there be some of them that stand here, which shall not taste of death,
till they have seen the kingdom of God come with power. And after six
days Jesus taketh with him Peter, and James, and John, and leadeth
them up into an high mountain apart by themselves: and he was transfigured before them. And his raiment became shining, exceeding white
as snow; so as no fuller on earth can white them. And there appeared
unto them Elias with Moses: and they were talking with Jesus. And
Peter answered and said to Jesus, Master, it is good for us to be here:
and let us make three tabernacles; one for thee, and one for Moses, and
one for Elias. For he wist not what to say; for they were sore afraid.
And there was a cloud that overshadowed them: and a voice came out
of the cloud, saying, This is my beloved Son: hear him. And suddenly,
when they had looked round about, they saw no man any more, save
Jesus only with themselves. And as they came down from the mountain,
he charged them that they should tell no man what things they had seen,
till the Son of man were risen from the dead."

Whether all theologians recognize it or not, the transfiguration scene
is as important as the great emphasis given to it in the New Testament
indicates. Each of the three Synoptic writers describes it at length and it
is said by them to be a setting forth of the power and coming of Christ,
that is, His coming in His kingdom (Matt. 16:28; Mark 9:1; Luke
9:27; 2 Pet. 1:16). Peter, one of those chosen to be present at this great
event, writes: "For we have not followed cunningly devised fables,
when we made known unto you the power and coming of our Lord Jesus
Christ, but were eyewitnesses of his majesty. For he received from God

the Father honour and glory, when there came such a voice to him from the excellent glory, This is my beloved Son, in whom I am well pleased. And this voice which came from heaven we heard, when we were with him in the holy mount. We have also a more sure word of prophecy; whereunto ye do well that ye take heed, as unto a light that shineth in a dark place, until the day dawn, and the day star arise in your hearts" (2 Pet. 1:16–19). The transfiguration occurred prior to the death of Christ. The disciples were about to face the utter surprise and shock of that death, which death, though plainly predicted by Christ, was divinely withheld from their understanding. Most emphatic and absolute is the divine veiling of the disciples' minds on this fact of Christ's oncoming death and resurrection. Luke writes in his Gospel: "Then he took unto him the twelve, and said unto them, Behold, we go up to Jerusalem, and all things that are written by the prophets concerning the Son of man shall be accomplished. For he shall be delivered unto the Gentiles, and shall be mocked, and spitefully entreated, and spitted on: and they shall scourge him, and put him to death: and the third day he shall rise again. And they understood none of these things: and this saying was hid from them, neither knew they the things which were spoken" (18: 31–34). No clearer prediction of Christ's death was made than the one with which this passage is associated. All of this is a challenge to the thoughtful student. Why, indeed, should they not comprehend such a clear prediction? During the period of Christ's earthly ministry they had preached by divine authority and with personal sincerity the message regarding the Messianic, earthly kingdom with Christ as King on David's throne—the national hope of Israel. It is most evident that they could not have preached a gospel based on Christ's death and resurrection when they had no understanding of these oncoming events. That which had so engaged them, into which they had invested their lives, was about to be shattered by the violent death of the King at the hands of the very men over whom He was expected to rule. A vision of the coming of Christ in power and in His kingdom was given to Peter, James, and John—two of whom were appointed to write doctrinal portions of the New Testament, the other its first apostolic martyr—that they might the more readily accept the unforeseen delay which the age of grace would require and be assured that the plan and purpose of God respecting the kingdom for Israel was not abrogated. The vision of the transfiguration with all it connoted was not given to John the Baptist. He was allowed to face what seemed to him to be complete defeat. That into which his whole life had been poured, his divine commission as the forerunner of the Messiah, and the early success of his preaching were all swept aside thus, without explanation. Here many have failed to comprehend the situation, however, and have turned on John with the declaration that he was mistaken in all his ministry. Such is not the solution of the problem. At any rate, Peter, James, and John—representatives of the whole apostolic company—were saved from that greater distress which fell upon John the Baptist. It is not probable that the assurance which the transfiguration provided was of much import to the disciples in the hour of Christ's death; but after His death and resurrection it served its purpose in clarifying their minds on the truth that, though a new and wonderful, unforeseen, divine purpose was introduced through the death and resurrection of Christ, the earthly purpose was not abandoned but would, when the new age objective is accomplished, be fulfilled by Christ at His second coming, and not in weakness and humility as in His first advent, but in the power and glory which was previewed at the transfiguration. It is clear then that the transfiguration was not an unveiling of heaven, but of Christ's coming in His kingdom.

Luke 12:35–40. "Let your loins be girded about, and your lights burning; and ye yourselves like unto men that wait for their lord, when he will return from the wedding; that when he cometh and knocketh, they may open unto him immediately. Blessed are those servants, whom the lord when he cometh shall find watching: verily I say unto you, that he shall gird himself, and make them to sit down to meat, and will come forth and serve them. And if he shall come in the second watch, or come in the third watch, and find them so, blessed are those servants. And this know, that if the goodman of the house had known what hour the thief would come, he would have watched, and not have suffered his house to be broken through. Be ye therefore ready also: for the Son of man cometh at an hour when ye think not."

Out of very much which Luke records bearing on the second advent of Christ, this one passage may serve as a good representation. The address is to Israel and, like the larger report of the Olivet Discourse which is given by Matthew, it enjoins the attitude of watching for Christ's return. Watching is the responsibility which will rest on Israel at the time "when ye see these things come to pass" (Luke 21:28, 31; Matt. 24:33). Again an appeal is in order that Israel's obligation to watch for the glorious appearing of Christ when they will be delivered and their covenants fulfilled should not be confused with the agelong obligation resting upon the Church to be waiting for Christ's appearing when He will receive them unto Himself. As in Matthew 25:1–13 where

Israel is likened to ten virgins and their need of burning individual lights is the symbol of preparedness, so in the passage under contemplation they are told to have their loins girded and their lights burning. The specific contribution of this passage to the whole body of doctrine is found in verse 36, wherein it is stated that watching Israel will be awaiting the return of Christ "from the wedding." Too often it has been supposed that Christ's return is to participate in the wedding and that the ten virgins are His Bride. The comment on this same situation which Psalm 45:8–15 supplies is of vital import. Having pictured the millennial palace and those within including the King and His Bride, who is identified throughout as "daughter," it is said that she, the Bride, "shall be brought unto the king in raiment of needlework" and that "the virgins her companions that follow her shall be brought unto thee. With gladness and rejoicing shall they be brought: they shall enter into the king's palace." This description of the millennial scene clearly distinguishes between the Bride and the virgins. The Bride is with the King from the hour of the wedding in heaven. She returns to earth with Him (Rev. 19:11–16), and for His return with His Bride Israel, likened to the virgins, watches upon the earth; later, both the Bride and the five accepted virgins enter the palace with the King and join in the marriage feast (cf. Matt. 25:10, R.V.).

2 Peter 3:3–4, 8, 10–13. "Knowing this first, that there shall come in the last days scoffers, walking after their own lusts, and saying, Where is the promise of his coming? for since the fathers fell asleep, all things continue as they were from the beginning of the creation. . . . But, beloved, be not ignorant of this one thing, that one day is with the Lord as a thousand years, and a thousand years as one day. . . . But the day of the Lord will come as a thief in the night; in the which the heavens shall pass away with a great noise, and the elements shall melt with fervent heat, the earth also and the works that are therein shall be burned up. Seeing then that all these things shall be dissolved, what manner of persons ought ye to be in all holy conversation and godliness, looking for and hasting unto the coming of the day of God, wherein the heavens being on fire shall be dissolved, and the elements shall melt with fervent heat? Nevertheless we, according to his promise, look for new heavens and a new earth, wherein dwelleth righteousness."

This Scripture introduces several distinctive features which contribute to the whole doctrine of Christ's second advent. In the first instance, prediction is made that scoffers will arise who reject the truth respecting Christ's return and on the basis of the claim that all things continue from the beginning without change. Therefore, it is asserted, no change need be expected in the future; but this "they willingly are ignorant of," that there has been a world-renovating judgment from God in the form of the flood, and too it is certain, whether believed by them or not, that the heavens and the earth which now are await destruction by fire and at the precise time when God shall accomplish the judgment and perdition of ungodly men (cf. Rev. 20:11–15). The Day of the Lord, the period of a thousand years which begins with the second advent of Christ and ends with the passing of the old heavens and earth, comes by virtue of Christ's return, which is as unexpected as a thief in the night (cf. Matt. 24:43; 1 Thess. 5:4). When verse 9, which presents the faithfulness of God and is therefore parenthetic to the argument, is omitted to the end that the direct statement of prophecy may be noted here, there is more than accidental relation between the fact that a day with Jehovah is as a thousand years and a thousand years as one day (vs. 8) and the reference to the Day of the Lord which follows (vs. 10). It has been claimed that the only time measurement of the Day of the Lord, which is a reference to the millennial kingdom on the earth, is the one found in Revelation 20:1–6; but while the Revelation passage definitely makes the kingdom reign to be a thousand years, this reference in 2 Peter is evidently a time indication of the same Day of the Lord, for Peter states it will begin "as a thief in the night" and end with the passing of the heavens and the earth. The passage includes also a reference to the manner of life which those who believe such things should maintain. All this program is moving on to that final day, the Day of God, which is eternity to come (cf. 1 Cor. 15:28). The new heavens and the new earth are, alike, to be the abode of divine righteousness—the earth that will be inhabited by the elect people whose covenants respecting their land and the earth are everlasting. The earth will then be as suitable a place for God to dwell upon as heaven has ever been or ever will be.

Revelation 19:11–16. "And I saw heaven opened, and behold a white horse; and he that sat upon him was called Faithful and True, and in righteousness he doth judge and make war. His eyes were as a flame of fire, and on his head were many crowns; and he had a name written, that no man knew, but he himself. And he was clothed with a vesture dipped in blood; and his name is called The Word of God. And the armies which were in heaven followed him upon white horses, clothed in fine linen, white and clean. And out of his mouth goeth a sharp sword, that with it he should smite the nations: and he shall rule them with a rod of iron: and he treadeth the winepress of the fierceness and wrath of Almighty God. And he hath on his vesture and on his thigh a name written, KING OF KINGS, AND LORD OF LORDS."

This is the final description of the second coming of Christ in the Bible and the only description to be found in the Book of Revelation. This account serves to open the stupendous scenes which follow in rapid succession and which constitute God's revealed program reaching on into eternity to come. These events are: the battle of Armageddon (19:17–21), the binding of Satan (20:1–3), the first of humanity's resurrections in relation to the kingdom age (20:4–6), the loosing of Satan and the doom of Gog and Magog (20:7–9), the final disposition of Satan (20:10), the setting of the great white throne (20:11), the resurrection (cf. vs. 5) and disposition of the wicked dead (20:12–15), creation of the new heavens and the new earth (21:1–2), God's abode on the earth as in heaven (21:3), the estate of men in eternity to come (21:4–8), the city from heaven (21:9—22:7), the closing message and appeal (22:8–19), the closing promise and its corresponding prayer (22:20–21). Heaven was opened it was declared in 4:1, and a voice called the Apostle John —who as forerunner of the Church is appointed to see and experience all that awaits the Church upon her entrance into heaven and to write these things for the encouragement and edification of those he represented—to come up hither. Since, from that point on (4:1), the Church is not again seen upon the earth but is seen in heaven and since what follows her removal is all of Daniel's seventieth prophetic week in which the Church could have no part whatsoever, it is made clear that the Church is married to her Bridegroom and enjoys the marriage supper of the Lamb in heaven (Rev. 19:7–10) before heaven is opened again, as the text under consideration describes the time when Christ, accompanied by His saints, returns as Messiah to the earth. The order has been preserved precisely: in the 4th chapter the movement is upwards, while in the 19th chapter the movement is downwards. As it should be, the description of chapter 19 centers on the glorious Person of the returning King. It has been predicted that He would thus return accompanied by the hosts of heaven and with power and great glory (Matt. 24:30). His return, it is declared, will be as lightning that cometh out of the east and shineth unto the west (Matt. 24:27) and with the clouds of heaven (Dan. 7:13). He will be revealed from heaven in flaming fire (2 Thess. 1:7–8). The "great glory" is resident in the four titles under which He comes—"The Word of God," "Faithful and

True," "a name written, that no man knew," and "King of kings and Lord of lords." Notable is the fact that the King returns not only to judge but to make war. He embodies the immeasurable holy indignation of God against evil in the day when His offers of grace have finally been withdrawn. None could comprehend or in any way anticipate the "fierceness and wrath of Almighty God." It is "the wrath of the Lamb." Kings and judges have been admonished to kiss the Son "lest he be angry, and ye perish from the way, when his wrath is kindled but a little." Fully a thousand years before the first advent of Christ, David saw that the King when taking His throne in Zion would receive the nations as a gift from Jehovah and break them with a rod of iron and dash them in pieces as if a potter's vessel. About seven hundred years before Christ's birth, Isaiah prophesied that the returning Messiah would tread down the nations in His anger and trample them in His fury. Both the rod of iron of Psalm 2:9 and the treading of the wine press of Isaiah 63:3 are reasserted in Revelation 19:15, which reads: "And out of his mouth goeth a sharp sword, that with it he should smite the nations: and he shall rule them with a rod of iron: and he treadeth the winepress of the fierceness and wrath of Almighty God" (cf. Rev. 1:16; 2 Thess. 2:8). As the Lord of Glory returns thus to the earth to judge and make war it should be observed also that, in this display of infinite power with its destruction exercised upon every enemy of God, that which is indigenous or inherent in Him—that which pertains properly to Deity as the correlative of infinite holiness—will be released and manifested. Right thinking respecting the Christ of God will lead to the recognition of the fact that the great departure from that which is essentially God was achieved in His first advent, when He came as a helpless child, an unresisting man, an afflicted, dying sacrifice. For this He laid aside His rightful robes of glory and so restrained His powers—such as created all things visible and invisible—that He became the unantagonizing Lamb. All this may well incite awe and wonder in man as it must also have affected the angels. That He should come as the embodiment of the fierceness and wrath of Almighty God should cause no bewilderment when it is remembered that this world has rejected God and His saving grace as exhibited and proffered to it in the first advent of Christ. Infinite love in its adjustments with infinite holiness provided a substitute to bear the immeasurable judgments of divine indignation against those who now elect to stand under the shadow of the cross, but for a rebellious, fallen, Christ-rejecting world which has cast in its lot with Satan and embraced his philosophy of independence of God, there can be nothing else but wrath and indignation as the portion of those who obey not the gospel.

In his excellent exposition of the book of Revelation entitled *The Unfolding of the Ages,* the late Ford C. Ottman presents a graphic picture of this last description in the Bible to portray the second advent. Though unusually extended, it is reproduced here as a fitting close to this chapter on Christ's return:

Christ is coming, and that glorious truth is now to engage our attention. The events connected with it can be discovered only through a thorough and patient examination of Scripture. Our attention is first turned to the opened heavens from which He comes. There can be no possibility of mistake as to the identity of the glorious Rider of the white horse. There is One, and only One, to whom the description could apply. He is "Faithful and True." So was He called at the beginning: so is He called at the last. He is now coming forth to judge the world in righteousness. His eyes are like fire, and nothing shall escape the searching flame. He is crowned with many diadems, and this testifies to other sovereignties than that over the world. He has also an incommunicable name, and He is clothed with a vesture dipped in blood. He is girded with a sword for personal conflict, and He has come to tread the winepress of the fierceness and wrath of Almighty God. "He hath on his vesture and on his thigh a name written, King of kings and Lord of lords." The armies that follow Him are composed of saints both Jewish and Christian. Hitherto they have been seen as the occupants of the four and twenty thrones. The elders, after ratifying the song of the heavenly host, are no longer seen as elders. They now appear as "the armies of heaven" following their Victorious Commander. The mark of their identification is the "white and pure linen" in which they are clothed. To this one point all the beams of prophetic light have steadily and unwaveringly converged. One of these shines forth from the sixty-third chapter of Isaiah. The Hebrew prophet, in the dim ages of the past, stands on one of the hills of Judah. He is, perhaps, on the Mount of Olives where the vision is clear to the Jordan valley. He is looking down towards Edom and he sees coming up through one of the deep ravines a solitary warrior. There is so much of majesty about him that the prophet rings out the challenge: "Who is this that cometh from Edom, with dyed garments from Bozrah? this that is glorious in his apparel, traveling in the greatness of his strength?" There comes sounding back the answer: "I that speak in righteousness, mighty to save." With the *identity* of the warrior dawning upon him the prophet cries: "Wherefore art thou red in thine apparel, and thy garments like him that treadeth in the winefat?" To this cry is given the solemn and glorious response: "I have trodden the winepress alone; and of the people there was none with me: for I will tread them in mine anger, and trample them in my fury; and their blood shall be sprinkled upon my garments, and I will stain all my raiment. For the day of vengeance is in mine heart, and the year of my redeemed is come. And I looked, and there was none to help; and I wondered that there was none to uphold: therefore mine own arm brought salvation unto me; and my fury, it upheld me. And I will tread down the people in mine anger, and make them drunk in my fury, and I will bring down their strength to the earth. I will mention the lovingkindnesses of the Lord, and the praises of the Lord, according to all that the Lord hath bestowed on us, and the great goodness toward the house of Israel, which he hath bestowed on them according to his mercies, and according to the multitude of his lovingkindnesses" (Isa. 63:1-7). This, according to the modern critics, is poetry. Yes, poetry of the loftiest strain, but in that poetry is embedded the Hebrew's conception of the coming Messiah. In this vision of Isaiah there is given only the return of the Warrior from the conflict. Of his journey *to* Bozrah there is nothing revealed. Isaiah has before him the conquering, and not the suffering, Messiah. We look back through the centuries to see the one commanding figure that rises above all others, and, Who can answer to the vision? Edom, lying on the border of Judah, was but a faint reflection of the awful cloud that hung over all men: evil, inveterate, uncompromising, on every hand; against which man could only struggle in utter helplessness. Into this stronghold of the enemy came the Son of God. He had none to help Him. He descended alone into the darkness, suffering what no human mind can ever know; but through it He passed to a glorious victory over sin and death. He is gathering the fruit of that victory now. His acquired glory is increased by every soul that puts its trust in Him, and this also shall add another voice to swell the music of redemption-song. When Jesus ascended to heaven, the conflict was not over. When he entered there, Jehovah said: "Sit thou at my right hand, until I make thine enemies thy footstool" (Ps. 110:1). The Messiah of Isaiah's vision is the Messiah of the Second Advent, and not of the First. Christ has been to the cross, but the prostration by the conquering Messiah of all of Israel's enemies, which is foretold in this prophecy, has never yet come to pass. This shall be accomplished when Christ comes again, and not before. The armies that follow Him are robed in white. He is distinguished from them by His being clothed with a vesture dipped in blood: and we shall know Him, not merely by the marks of His suffering, but by the royal robes, which proclaim His universal sovereignty. He has also, "upon his garment and upon his thigh a name written, King of kings, and Lord of lords." When the Magi came to Jerusalem they said: "Where is he that is born King of the Jews?" Pilate's superscription for the cross was: "Jesus of Nazareth the King of the Jews." Whether born in a manger, or dying on the cross, or riding the white horse of universal conquest, Jesus of Nazareth is a *King*. One very significant variation in the title needs to be noted. The Magi and Pontius Pilate call Him the King of the *Jews*. There is no such limitation in the apocalyptic inscription, for the scepter has been extended over all the surrounding nations, and He is now become, not only the King of the Jews, but *"King of kings, and Lord of lords."* The prostration of the kingdoms of this world shall demonstrate His right to the title. He at once proceeds to judgment,—"Out of his mouth goeth a sharp [two-edged] sword, that with it he may smite the nations; and he shall rule them with a rod of iron; and he treadeth the winepress of the indignation of the wrath of God the Almighty." The two-edged sword is the *word*, now to be used as the instrument of judgment. For the overthrow of the world-kingdoms there is needed but a word. That word is to be now spoken, and these kingdoms are to fall. "He shall smite the earth with the rod of his mouth, and with the breath of his lips shall he slay the wicked" (Isa. 11:4). The Coming of Christ is followed by the utter prostration of the world-powers, and by summary judgment upon the leaders of man's rebellion. In solemn contrast with the invitation given to the marriage supper of the Lamb, an angel is seen standing in the sun, and summoning with a loud voice the birds of heaven to come and feast at the great supper of God. The word translated *fowls* in the common version is the same word used in the second verse of the eighteenth chapter, where Babylon is said to have become the habitation of demons, and the hold of every foul spirit, and the cage of every unclean and hateful *bird*. The same word is used in the twenty-first verse, where the fowls, after the slaughter of the opposing armies, are said to be filled with their flesh. These appear to be the only passages in which this particular word for "bird" is used. It well may represent the literal vultures that shall fatten on the bodies of the slain. In His great prophecy Jesus says: "For as the lightning cometh out of the east, and shineth even unto the west; so shall also the coming of the Son of man be. For wheresoever the carcase is, there will the eagles be gathered together" (Matt. 24:27–28). The eagles referred to are doubtless identical with the carnivorous birds "flying in mid-heaven." Of the awful horrors of this day Isaiah thus speaks: "The indignation of the Lord is upon all nations, and his fury upon all their armies: he hath utterly destroyed them, he hath delivered them to the slaughter. Their slain also shall be cast out, and their stink shall come up out of their carcases, and the mountains shall be melted with their blood. And all the host of heaven shall be dissolved, and the heavens shall be rolled together as a scroll: and all their host shall fall down, as the leaf falleth off from the vine, and as a falling fig from the fig tree. For my sword shall be bathed in heaven; behold, it shall come down upon Idumea, and upon the people of my curse, to judgment. The sword of the Lord is filled with blood, it is made fat with fatness, and with the blood of lambs and goats, with the fat of the kidneys of rams: for the Lord hath a sacrifice in Bozrah, and a great slaughter in the land of Idumea" (Isa. 34:2–6). Solemnly enough this is called the Lord's "sacrifice in Bozrah." In Revelation it is called "the great supper of God." This means the destruction, for the time being, of all of God's enemies; and over their desolation heaven rejoices. As soon as these vultures are gathered together, the beast appears, and he has with him the allied kings of the earth, and their armies. These kings and their armies, as we have already seen, are brought together by spirits of demons. The purpose of their assemblage is made known in the declaration that they are about to make war against Him that sat upon the horse, and against His army. In this daring attempt to rush against the bucklers of the Almighty, they illustrate the last extreme to which Satan shall drive his infatuated victims. How vain and fatuous a thing it is for a man to contend with his Maker! "Who hath hardened himself against him, and hath prospered? Behold, he taketh away, who can hinder him? who will say unto him, What doest thou? If God will not withdraw his anger, the proud helpers do stoop under him" (Job 9:4, 12–13). This confederation against Christ and His armies is the literal fulfillment of the second Psalm. "The kings of the earth set themselves, and the rulers take counsel together, against the Lord, and against his anointed, saying, Let us break their bands asunder, and cast away their cords from us" (Ps. 2:2–3). The gathering point here is undoubtedly the battlefield of Har-Magedon. This battlefield, or its immediate vicinity, was famous in Old Testament history by reason of two great victories: Barak over the Moabites, and Gideon over the Midianites. It was famous also for what was considered two national disasters: the death of Saul, and the death of Josiah. If we are to spiritualize this battlefield into some indefinite region of never-ending conflict between the Church and her enemies, it is useless to speculate about the meaning of John's vision. If Christ when He comes is to find the kings of the earth in banded rebellion against Him, what possible objection can there be to a literal location of this rebel host? That He shall find them in such rebellion is the positive declaration of Scripture; and, without occasioning any confusion of mind, we can conceive of them as brought together literally on this ancient battlefield of Israel. There they are found at the last in royal council. They have passed a resolution to break asunder the bands of God, and to cast away His cords from them; but over against this resolution the voice of God is heard saying: "Yet have I set my king upon my holy hill of Zion." The struggle between good and evil is now to be fought out in the open. There is no longer any disguise of the combatants. At last the kingdoms of this world stand arrayed for direct battle with God and His Christ. The conflict is short and decisive. The beast and the false prophet are taken in red-handed rebellion, and are cast into the lake of fire that burneth with brimstone; and there, after the thousand years of Christ's Millennial reign, they are still. Just and equal are the ways of God. In the beginning He put questions to man who had sinned, but to the serpent that was the instrument of Satan in effecting the ruin He put none. Without any interrogation whatever the serpent was doomed. In like manner, to these willing tools of Satan in the last outburst of their impious wrath God gives no opportunity of self-defense. In their case there are no mitigating circumstances. They have lent themselves to an evil from the consequences of which there is no escape. They are permitted no defense, and in their behalf no word is spoken. Their sin has been deliberate; their alliance with Satan open and undisguised. Now, speechless before Him with whom they have contended in vain, they are taken and judged without mercy, for with such as they no mercy could avail. After this summary judgment of the beast and the false prophet, the rest of the rebels are dealt with in strict accord with the judicial code of the court of God. They are slain with the sword. Judged according to the Word of God, they are found worthy of death. Under the blast of His breath they are swept down, and the vultures strip the battlefield of the slain. Such is the end of earth's rebellion against God. Well may the heavens rejoice when His judgments prevail and everlasting righteousness is ushered in. There is no quiet and gradual merging of things into the peaceful reign of the Messiah. The kingdoms of this world must be cast into the winepress of the fierceness and wrath of Almighty God. Judgment only, and judgment of the most unsparing kind, falling on principalities and powers of evil, can drive from the heavens the stormwind of iniquity. The wrath and judgment of God can alone do this, and establish the kingdom of Christ in everlasting righteousness over the earth,—and failure to see this must come from the refusal to accept the reality of the final rebellion that shall fill up the cup of iniquity, and fit the world for the just judgment of God.—Pp. 417–24

CHAPTER XIII

THE MESSIANIC KINGDOM OF CHRIST INCARNATE

THIS COURSE of investigation turns at this point to one of the greatest of all Bible themes, namely, the Messianic kingdom—known also as the millennial kingdom since it continues a thousand years and as the Davidic kingdom since it is the realization of the kingdom covenanted to David. If it be claimed that Christ holds the central place in such an investigation, this is granted; and a Biblical Christology certainly must include that extended aspect of Christ's Person and work in which He appears as the theocratic King. Though the kingdom occupies so large a place in the Sacred Text, the theme of the kingdom has been more misunderstood and its terminology more misapplied than any other one subject in the Bible. This is directly due to the failure, so inherent and far-reaching in Covenant Theology, to recognize the dispensational aspect of divine revelation. Truth respecting the Messianic expectation as that is set forth in the Old Testament does not imply that the kingdom is the Church, nor does the New Testament, with its objectives centered in heaven, teach that the Church is the kingdom. Similarly, the earthly kingdom that according to the Scriptures had its origin in the covenant made to David, which is mundane and literal in its original form and equally as mundane and literal in uncounted references to it in all subsequent Scriptures which trace it on to its consummation, is by theological legerdemain metamorphosed into a spiritual monstrosity in which an absent King seated on His Father's throne in heaven is accepted in lieu of the theocratic monarch of David's line seated on David's throne in Jerusalem. Again, through careless inattention many modern writers refer to the kingdom of heaven as though it were heaven, and in spite of the absurdities and contradictions which arise when these terms are thus confused.

Under Ecclesiology, already treated (Vol. IV), the distinction in meaning between the terms *kingdom of God* and *kingdom of heaven* has been pointed out. Suffice it to say here that the authority of God over the entire universe is a dominant theme from Genesis to Revelation.

And such, indeed, is the kingdom of God. It extends to all intelligences —angels and men—wherever there is loyal subjection to divine authority. That there are angels as well as men who disown this authority is clearly taught in the Word of God, and as clearly is it asserted that before the millennial, Messianic reign of Christ is ended all opposition to God's rule will have been crushed by the theocratic King (cf. 1 Cor. 15:24–28), and then the kingdom of God will be "delivered up" to God in the sense that His rightful supremacy, government, and empire will resume their former unchallenged sway of ages past. This universal exercise of authority is properly styled the *kingdom of God,* and should not be accounted the same as the Davidic theocratic rule over Israel and the earth, which rule is brought to its consummation and established in the earth before the transformations and restorations which belong to the kingdom of God have begun. Broadly speaking, the Kingdom of God—as defined above—is the universal authority of God from everlasting to everlasting, while the term *Kingdom of Heaven* is fittingly applied to God's rule in the earth—it is heaven's rule on the earth—and is restricted, with respect to time, as has been seen, to limited periods and well-defined situations. The prayer for and in the kingdom of heaven includes the words: "Thy kingdom come. Thy will be done in earth, as it is in heaven." While that kingdom appears in various forms, it had its tangible beginning in the Davidic Covenant and will be fulfilled and consummated with a perfected social order in the earth under the beneficent reign of the King of kings. When the vast distinctions between these two spheres of divine authority are observed there is a solving of many problems in the interpretation of the Bible which would otherwise exist. Faithful recognition of these dissimilarities is beginning to be held by expositors generally as the most effective key to the understanding of the Scriptures. So Dr. Auberlen quotes R. Rothe as saying: "Our key does not open—*the right key is lost;* and till we are put in possession of it again, our exposition will never succeed. The system of biblical ideas is *not* that of our schools; and so long as we attempt exegesis without it, the Bible will remain *a half-closed book.* We must enter upon it with *other conceptions* than those which we have been accustomed to think *the only possible ones;* and whatever these may be, this one thing at least is certain, from the whole tenor of the melody of Scripture in its natural fulness, that they must be *more realistic and massive*" (*Divine Revelation,* p. 387, cited by Peters, *Theocratic Kingdom,* I, 21). This is a confession which is at once both humiliating and significant. That this millennial discussion to follow is related only to the earthly, Davidic, Messianic kingdom of heaven need hardly be pointed out. Consideration of the kingdom of God in its restored, final form will be the theme of the next and closing chapter of this work on Christology. Why, indeed, after centuries of study should so great a proportion of good men be in dire confusion over the divine program for the earth while others are informed and to that extent delivered from such difficulties, unless it be that some hold and use the key to which Rothe refers while others do not? Men of commendable scholarship do hold the key and for them these specific problems are really solved. There are now two schools of orthodox men. For one school, having imbibed the concoction of Whitby which proposes a man-made millennium and, having been run into the idealistic, cramping mold of Cocceius' one covenant of grace, there is little hope that a deliverance will be wrought. Such theological systems, seminaries, and individuals muddle on, transmitting idealism which is unsustained by the Word of God to succeeding generations. On the other hand, those who hold the key are increasing in number; they have their schools and system of theology which generates exposition of the Bible and promotes Bible study over the whole land. Certain obvious facts respecting the kingdom of heaven are now to be listed:

I. ASSURED BY JEHOVAH'S COVENANTS

Jehovah has made oath-bound covenants with Abraham and with David. Not only are these covenants unconditional and binding by the very terms by which they are declared, but extended subsequent Scriptures reaffirm these promises. The Abrahamic covenant records Jehovah's sovereign purpose in, through, and for Abraham. The covenant is unconditional in that no obligation is imposed upon Abraham; he contributes nothing, but rather is the recipient of all that Jehovah proposed to do for him. While this covenant (cf. Gen. 12:1–3; 13:14–17; 15:4–7; 17:1–8) provided personal blessings and great honor to Abraham, its more important features reach out in two other directions, namely, that of Abraham's seed and that of the land of promise. Abraham's seed is threefold: (1) a great nation through Ishmael (cf. Gen. 17:20), (2) a seed like the dust of the earth—realized in his physical seed through Israel and so through Jacob, and (3) a spiritual seed like the stars of heaven for extent and realized on the principle of Abrahamic faith by Jew and Gentile. Of the physical seed it is written: "Who are Israelites; to whom pertaineth the adoption, and the glory, and the covenants, and the giving of the law, and the service of God, and the promises; whose are the fathers, and of whom as concerning the flesh Christ came, who is over all, God blessed for ever. Amen" (Rom. 9:4–5). To this same physical seed pertain also the covenants respecting the land, the earthly Davidic throne, the king, and the kingdom. To this earthly seed the system known as Judaism, with its commandments, ordinances, and statutes, alone was addressed. If all this be acknowledged, as indeed it must be, practically every error relative to covenants, peoples and their destinies will be obviated. Over against all this is the truth that Abraham attained unto the righteousness of God through faith (Gen. 15:6), a stupendous privilege not restricted to Abraham (though not extended to other Old Testament saints) but promised to all in this age who exercise Abrahamic faith to the extent of believing God (Rom. 4:20–24), which righteousness of God Abraham's physical seed utterly failed to secure (cf. Rom. 9:30—10:4). The New Testament declares that all—individual Jews or Gentiles alike—who believe unto righteousness as Abraham did are spiritual children of Abraham. Great is the error when it is supposed that spiritual seed of Abraham ever become physical seed or that physical seed, aside from regeneration, ever become spiritual seed. Of the five eternal features of Jehovah's covenants with Israel—an everlasting nation, an everlasting possession of her land, an everlasting throne, an everlasting king, and an everlasting kingdom—two, the nation and the possession of the land, are covenanted through Abraham, while the remaining three, the throne, the king, and the kingdom, are covenanted through David. That covenanted to Abraham and that covenanted to David may now be considered separately.

1. THE COVENANT WITH ABRAHAM. As noted above, there are in addition to the assurance of personal blessing for Abraham, his posterity, and those who bless his people two far-reaching features covenanted, namely:

a. AN EVERLASTING NATION. Some theologians who seem not to have given close attention to what the Word of God discloses respecting the perpetuity of the earthly seed of Abraham through Isaac and Jacob have asserted that this nation is but a feature of one covenant, by which they are bound into the same divine purpose with the Church of the New Testament and being thus merged into the Church have no distinctive future, while others have declared that, because of their sin, God has cut off His earthly people forever. The Scriptures hardly support these rationalistic notions. Beginning with the covenant made with Abraham as recorded in Genesis, chapter 12 and continuing to the end of the New

Testament, the promise respecting an everlasting earthly seed is ever in view. There is but little said of Abraham's seed through Ishmael and nothing said of his seed which he secured late in life through his marriage to Keturah (cf. Gen. 25:1–4). None would question the endurance of the spiritual seed; but the unending future of the earthly seed through Isaac and Jacob is a matter of divine purpose just as clearly revealed and therefore not subject to human wishes, suppositions, or judgments. Several Scriptures may well be cited at this point. Speaking to Israel through Isaiah, Jehovah said: "For as the new heavens and the new earth, which I will make, shall remain before me, . . . so shall your seed and your name remain" (66:22). Likewise, having declared the terms of His new covenant (Jer. 31:31–34), Jehovah affirms regarding the one nation to whom this covenant will be made: "Thus saith the LORD, which giveth the sun for a light by day, and the stars for a light by night, which divideth the sea when the waves thereof roar; The LORD of hosts is his name: if those ordinances depart from before me, saith the LORD, then the seed of Israel also shall cease from being a nation before me for ever. Thus saith the LORD; If heaven above can be measured, and the foundations of the earth searched out beneath, I will also cast off all the seed of Israel for all that they have done, saith the LORD" (vss. 35–37). Yet again, in Matthew 24:34–35, which reads: "Verily I say unto you, This generation shall not pass, till all these things be fulfilled. Heaven and earth shall pass away, but my words shall not pass away," the line of Israel's descent or posterity will outlive all events which precede the return of the King. Jehovah declared to Abraham, according to Genesis 17:7: "And I will establish my covenant between me and thee and thy seed after thee in their generations for an everlasting covenant, to be a God unto thee, and to thy seed after thee," but there is no basis for an everlasting covenant if there is not an everlasting people to whom it applies. That this same nation, preserved in its identity, continues forever is implied in the several features of their covenants, namely, the everlasting possession of the land, the endless throne, the eternal king, and unending kingdom. The entire 11th chapter of Romans is written to unfold the abiding character of the nation Israel. It is true that, to the end that the Church be called out, Israel has for an age been "broken off" and to them "blindness in part" hath happened (Rom. 11:20, 25), but all this only *until* the present divine purpose connected with the Church is accomplished. After that, "all Israel shall be saved." This last-named Scripture declares in full: "And so all Israel shall be saved: as it is written, There shall come out of Sion the Deliverer, and shall turn away ungodliness from Jacob: for this is my covenant unto them, when I shall take away their sins. As concerning the gospel, they are enemies for your sakes: but as touching the election, they are beloved for the fathers' sakes. For the gifts and calling of God are without repentance" (Rom. 11:26–29).

b. AN EVERLASTING POSSESSION OF THE LAND. The Palestinian covenant, as first announced to Abraham and confirmed to Isaac and Jacob, is set forth in its full character in Deuteronomy 30:3–8. The earlier proclamations are: "And the LORD appeared unto Abram, and said, Unto thy seed will I give this land: and there builded he an altar unto the LORD, who appeared unto him. . . . And the LORD said unto Abram, after that Lot was separated from him, Lift up now thine eyes, and look from the place where thou art northward, and southward, and eastward, and westward: for all the land which thou seest, to thee will I give it, and to thy seed for ever. And I will make thy seed as the dust of the earth: so that if a man can number the dust of the earth, then shall thy seed also be numbered. Arise, walk through the land in the length of it and in the breadth of it; for I will give it unto thee. . . . And he said unto him, I am the LORD that brought thee out of Ur of the Chaldees, to give thee this land to inherit it. . . . In the same day the LORD made a covenant with Abram, saying, Unto thy seed have I given this land, from the river of Egypt unto the great river, the river Euphrates" (Gen. 12:7; 13:14–17; 15:7, 18). In these passages the larger and final boundaries of the land are indicated. Likewise, the confirmations to the seed of Abraham assert: "Sojourn in this land, and I will be with thee, and will bless thee; for unto thee, and unto thy seed, I will give all these countries, and I will perform the oath which I sware unto Abraham thy father; and I will make thy seed to multiply as the stars of heaven, and will give unto thy seed all these countries; and in thy seed shall all the nations of the earth be blessed. . . . And God said unto him, I am God Almighty: be fruitful and multiply; a nation and a company of nations shall be of thee, and kings shall come out of thy loins; and the land which I gave Abraham and Isaac, to thee I will give it, and to thy seed after thee will I give the land" (Gen. 26:3–4; 35:11–12; cf. 28: 13–14). The Palestinian covenant conveys the land to Abraham and his earthly seed through Isaac and Jacob for an everlasting possession. Added predictions modify the covenant only with respect to the time of its final tenure. Three dispossessions were anticipated and three restorations (cf. Gen. 15:13–14, 16; Jer. 25:11–12; Deut. 28:25, 36– 37, 63–68; 30:1–5). All three of the dispossessions are now fulfilled and two restorations. Thus the nation is out of her land for the third and last time. When restored again, as predicted, that people will go out no more forever. It hardly need be stated that no land is promised to the Church, and when Israel's promises of a long life in the land are applied to the Church the incongruity is at once apparent. Those appointed to "wait for his Son [their Lord] from heaven" are not to be looking for a long life in this sphere. Citizens of heaven hold no rights to earth in the sight of God.

2. THE COVENANT WITH DAVID. Since the oncoming theocratic kingdom is the divine objective with respect to the earth and since it forms the national hope of Israel, the covenant with David which introduces the revelation of the kingdom declares the precise nature of all this. From the inception of this dominant theme onward as seen in subsequent Scriptures the subject is held in constant observation and as a feature of unfulfilled prophecy. This earthly kingdom, the throne, and the King are among the dominant themes of the Old Testament. The revelation respecting these great features in the Davidic covenant is both explicit and extended. Difficulty arises only for those who are determined to metamorphose a literal, earthly throne and kingdom into some vague and wholly imaginary spiritual idealism. The acid test to be applied to any such human notion is the pertinent inquiry of why the King must be of David's line. This evident requirement regarding the King is ignored by every theory which rejects the truth concerning the literal throne and kingdom; yet that the King must be born of David's lineage is both asserted and assumed throughout this great highway of prediction— consider, for example, John 7:42, which states: "Hath not the scripture said, That Christ cometh of the seed of David, and out of the town of Bethlehem, where David was?" God said to David, "And thine house and thy kingdom shall be established for ever before thee: thy throne shall be established for ever" (2 Sam. 7:16). There was indeed but one reservation in this covenant, namely, that the sons of David succeeding him would be subject to chastisement, though the covenant itself could not be abrogated. Chastisement did fall in the form of disruption of the kingly line from the time of the Babylonian captivity to the birth of Christ. However, by the explicit terms of the covenant, the kingdom of David cannot be destroyed. It must yet be re-established and abide forever, else Jehovah's oath would fail. Description of David's own reaction, which indicates his understanding of the covenant, follows at once in this context. It is certain that David entertained no other thought than that his own literal throne, kingly line, and kingdom were

to continue forever. He said to God "Who am I, O Lord GOD? and what is my house, that thou hast brought me hitherto? And this was yet a small thing in thy sight, O Lord GOD; but thou hast spoken also of thy servant's house for a great while to come. And is this the manner of man, O Lord GOD? And what can David say more unto thee? for thou, Lord GOD, knowest thy servant. For thy word's sake, and according to thine own heart, hast thou done all these great things, to make thy servant know them. . . . And now, O Lord GOD, thou art that God, and thy words be true, and thou hast promised this goodness unto thy servant: therefore now let it please thee to bless the house of thy servant, that it may continue for ever before thee: for thou, O Lord GOD, hast spoken it: and with thy blessing let the house of thy servant be blessed for ever" (2 Sam. 7:18-21, 28-29). So, also, the Psalmist gives his own apprehension of this covenant when it is quoted at length in Psalm 89: 1-4, 20-37. In this context, which records the words of Jehovah more fully respecting this covenant with David, the literal character of the covenant is assured, the certainty of its fulfillment and the reservation about chastisement are all clearly stated. Though extended, this determining Scripture is quoted in full:

I will sing of the mercies of the LORD for ever: with my mouth will I make known thy faithfulness to all generations. For I have said, Mercy shall be built up for ever: thy faithfulness shalt thou establish in the very heavens. I have made a covenant with my chosen, I have sworn unto David my servant, Thy seed will I establish for ever, and build up thy throne to all generations. . . . I have found David my servant; with my holy oil have I anointed him: with whom my hand shall be established: mine arm also shall strengthen him. The enemy shall not exact upon him; nor the son of wickedness afflict him. And I will beat down his foes before his face, and plague them that hate him. But my faithfulness and my mercy shall be with him: and in my name shall his horn be exalted. I will set his hand also in the sea, and his right hand in the rivers. He shall cry unto me, Thou art my father, my God, and the rock of my salvation. Also I will make him my firstborn, higher than the kings of the earth. My mercy will I keep for him for evermore, and my covenant shall stand fast with him. His seed also will I make to endure for ever, and his throne as the days of heaven. If his children forsake my law, and walk not in my judgments; if they break my statutes, and keep not my commandments; then will I visit their transgression with the rod, and their iniquity with stripes. Nevertheless my lovingkindness will I not utterly take from him, nor suffer my faithfulness to fail. My covenant will I not break, nor alter the thing that is gone out of my lips. Once have I sworn by my holiness that I will not lie unto David. His seed shall endure for ever, and his throne as the sun before me. It shall be established for ever as the moon, and as a faithful witness in heaven.

In his charge to Solomon David said: "That the LORD may continue his word which he spake concerning me, saying, If thy children take heed to their way, to walk before me in truth with all their heart and with all their soul, there shall not fail thee (said he) a man on the throne of Israel" (1 Kings 2:4). In the light of this, Solomon said of himself "Now therefore, as the LORD liveth, which hath established me, and set me on the throne of David my father, and who hath made me an house" (2:24). And Jeremiah writes: "For thus saith the LORD; David shall never want a man to sit upon the throne of the house of Israel; . . . Then may also my covenant be broken with David my servant, that he should not have a son to reign upon his throne; and with the Levites the priests, my ministers. As the host of heaven cannot be numbered, neither the sand of the sea measured: so will I multiply the seed of David my servant" (Jer. 33:17, 21–22).

A notable feature of all this prediction respecting the covenant with David was the divine guarantee that David will never lack one to sit upon his throne. That throne is as literal, historical, and tangible as the throne of the Caesars, the Hohenzollerns, or the Hapsburgs. That throne is more often than not called "the throne of Israel" (1 Kings 2:4) and Christ termed it "the throne of his glory" (Matt. 19:28; 25:31). Jehovah refers to that throne in Psalm 2:6 as "my holy hill of Zion." The Davidic earthly throne has never lacked one to sit upon it and never will. During the five hundred years which followed immediately upon David's own reign, his sons in succession sat upon that throne. Beginning with the Babylonian captivity and continuing until the birth of Christ—a similar period of over five hundred years—there was in every generation a rightful heir to (though no occupant of) that throne. With the birth of Christ there need be no other such, for He was the Heir in His generation and was thus identified (cf. Matt. 9:27; 12:23; 15:22; 20:30–31; 21:9, 15; 22:42; 2 Tim. 2:8; Rev. 22:16). There need be no other, since Christ abideth forever. He is now in heaven, seated upon His Father's throne and "expecting" until the kingdoms of this world shall have become the kingdoms of the Lord and his Christ—not by virtue of evangelizing forces, but by the decree of Jehovah and the gift to Himself of the raging nations. He will then Himself not only conquer those nations, but rule over them. The perpetuity of the literal Davidic throne and kingdom may be traced through various Scriptures. A few are given here.

Isaiah 9:6–7. "For unto us a child is born, unto us a son is given: and the government shall be upon his shoulder: and his name shall be called

Wonderful, Counsellor, The mighty God, The everlasting Father, The Prince of Peace. Of the increase of his government and peace there shall be no end, upon the throne of David, and upon his kingdom, to order it, and to establish it with judgment and with justice from henceforth even for ever. The zeal of the LORD of hosts will perform this."

The government shall be upon Messiah's shoulder, for He shall be upon the throne of David and over his kingdom to order it and to establish it with judgment and with justice forever. No error need be made with respect to this kingdom or this throne. That it will increase without end to both government and peace enters much into the limitless character of its duration. This is clearly a prediction of the reign of Christ in the earth—the kingdom of heaven as it will be when its final form is set up by the returning King. There is no future divine reign over the earth that is not related to and which does not proceed from the Messiah seated on David's throne.

Jeremiah 23:5–6. "Behold, the days come, saith the LORD, that I will raise unto David a righteous Branch, and a King shall reign and prosper, and shall execute judgment and justice in the earth. In his days Judah shall be saved, and Israel shall dwell safely: and this is his name whereby he shall be called, THE LORD OUR RIGHTEOUSNESS."

According to this prophecy, which is of the greatest weight, Christ must be born of David's line and reign and prosper; He must execute judgment and justice in the earth. The same essential features of truth are recorded in Isaiah 11:1–5, where it is said: "And there shall come forth a rod out of the stem of Jesse, and a Branch shall grow out of his roots: and the spirit of the LORD shall rest upon him, the spirit of wisdom and understanding, the spirit of counsel and might, the spirit of knowledge and of the fear of the LORD; and shall make him of quick understanding in the fear of the LORD: and he shall not judge after the sight of his eyes, neither reprove after the hearing of his ears: but with righteousness shall he judge the poor, and reprove with equity for the meek of the earth: and he shall smite the earth with the rod of his mouth, and with the breath of his lips shall he slay the wicked. And righteousness shall be the girdle of his loins, and faithfulness the girdle of his reins." These are not predictions regarding a general rule of God exercised from heaven, as would be true of the kingdom of God, but regarding one Davidic in character as well as earthly in its sphere. Again it may be noted that it is the kingdom of heaven which is anticipated in the Davidic covenant.

Ezekiel 37:21–28. "Thus saith the Lord GOD; Behold, I will take the children of Israel from among the heathen, whither they be gone, and will gather them on every side, and bring them into their own land: and I will make them one nation in the land upon the mountains of Israel; and one king shall be king to them all: and they shall be no more two nations, neither shall they be divided into two kingdoms any more at all: neither shall they defile themselves any more with their idols, nor with their detestable things, nor with any of their transgressions: but I will save them out of all their dwellingplaces, wherein they have sinned, and will cleanse them: so shall they be my people, and I will be their God. And David my servant shall be king over them; and they all shall have one shepherd: they shall also walk in my judgments, and observe my statutes, and do them. And they shall dwell in the land that I have given unto Jacob my servant, wherein your fathers have dwelt; and they shall dwell therein, even they, and their children, and their children's children for ever: and my servant David shall be their prince for ever. Moreover I will make a covenant of peace with them; it shall be an everlasting covenant with them: and I will place them, and multiply them, and will set my sanctuary in the midst of them for evermore. My tabernacle also shall be with them: yea, I will be their God, and they shall be my people. And the heathen shall know that I the LORD do sanctify Israel, when my sanctuary shall be in the midst of them for evermore."

It matters but little at this point whether it is, as some contend, King David who is exalted as a vice regent in the future kingdom or whether the reference is to Christ as David's greater Son, because the prophecy here is exceedingly explicit. The earthly kingdom over Israel in the sight of the nations with kingly authority exercised forever from David's throne is something too specific to allow this passage to be interpreted as a mere fraction of the general reign of God everywhere in His universe. It can be seen that no semblance of a fulfillment of this or any similar prediction was experienced at Christ's first advent, nor has it ever been fulfilled, nor would it be fulfilled even if all Jews and Gentiles were to be saved and brought into the Church.

Daniel 7:13–14. "I saw in the night visions, and, behold, one like the Son of man came with the clouds of heaven, and came to the Ancient of days, and they brought him near before him. And there was given him dominion, and glory, and a kingdom, that all people, nations, and languages, should serve him: his dominion is an everlasting dominion, which shall not pass away, and his kingdom that which shall not be destroyed."

The contribution of this portion of Scripture to this general theme is the fact that in His second advent when coming with the clouds of heaven, rather than in His first advent, He will establish a rule which is universal—so far as the earth is concerned—and everlasting.

Hosea 3:4–5. "For the children of Israel shall abide many days without a king, and without a prince, and without a sacrifice, and without an image, and without an ephod, and without teraphim: afterward shall the children of Israel return, and seek the LORD their God, and David their king; and shall fear the LORD and his goodness in the latter days."

The prophetic Scriptures thus anticipate Israel's present separation from their rightful relations to Jehovah; yet as certainly predict that they will return and seek Jehovah their God and David their king in the latter days—an expectation wholly unfulfilled to the present hour.

Matthew 1:1. "The book of the generation of Jesus Christ, the son of David, the son of Abraham."

The order of the Messianic truth set forth in Matthew's Gospel is here indicated. It presents first a record concerning the King, the Son of David, and then the work of Christ in His death as the surety of the promise which is within the Abrahamic covenant. The title "Son of David" is many times applied to Christ and indicates not merely that He is a son of David, as many were in His generation, but that—as before stated—He is *the* Son, the immediate and rightful Heir to David's throne (cf. Matt. 9:27; 15:22; 20:30–31; 21:9, 15; 22:42). Why, indeed, should the Davidic sonship be emphasized? Is He not as much the son of Solomon or Jacob? There is but one answer to these questions: Christ not only fulfills but fills to the full the expectation contained in the Davidic covenant respecting a throne, a King, and a kingdom, and precisely in that literal sense in which the covenant was committed unto David and in that same literal sense in which it is magnified throughout all subsequent Scripture. Apart from the recognition of this relation between Christ and His human forefather David, there can be no workable interpretation of Matthew's Gospel or other Scripture which bears upon the same theme.

Luke 1:31–32. "And, behold, thou shalt conceive in thy womb, and bring forth a son, and shalt call his name JESUS. He shall be great, and shall be called the Son of the Highest: and the Lord God shall give unto him the throne of his father David."

No more determining Scripture for the point under consideration can be found than this message from the angel Gabriel to Mary. The passage incorporates truth related to each of His two advents. That which did not take place at the first coming will be accomplished at His second advent, namely, the predictions that the Lord God shall give unto Christ the throne of His father David, that He shall reign over the house of Jacob forever (vs. 33), and that of His kingdom there shall be no end (vs. 33). This throne is the Davidic, earthly throne; the house of Jacob is not the Church or any other people than those to whom the term properly applies. An endless reign carries this kingdom beyond the millennial age into eternity to come. It is yet to be observed that the throne which embodies the kingdom is a gift from "the Lord God." This, it is yet to be pointed out in the last chapter of Christology, is mentioned by the Apostle Paul in 1 Corinthians 15:27-28, which declares: "For he hath put all things under his feet. But when he saith all things are put under him, it is manifest that he is excepted, which did put all things under him. And when all things shall be subdued unto him, then shall the Son also himself be subject unto him that put all things under him, that God may be all in all." To the same end the Savior said, "All power is given unto me in heaven and in earth" (Matt. 28:18). The word of the angel to Mary confirms the Davidic covenant and advances the highway of truth respecting that covenant, on its usual literal terms, to the day of Christ's second coming. No shifting into a spiritual idealism can be admitted at any point.

Acts 2:25-31. "For David speaketh concerning him, I foresaw the Lord always before my face, for he is on my right hand, that I should not be moved: therefore did my heart rejoice, and my tongue was glad; moreover also my flesh shall rest in hope: because thou wilt not leave my soul in hell, neither wilt thou suffer thine Holy One to see corruption. Thou hast made known to me the ways of life; thou shalt make me full of joy with thy countenance. Men and brethren, let me freely speak unto you of the patriarch David, that he is both dead and buried, and his sepulchre is with us unto this day. Therefore being a prophet, and knowing that God had sworn with an oath to him, that of the fruit of his loins, according to the flesh, he would raise up Christ to sit on his throne; he seeing this before spake of the resurrection of Christ, that his soul was not left in hell, neither his flesh did see corruption."

The early part of this passage is identified as a quotation from Psalm 16; the latter portion is a direct assertion regarding the Davidic covenant as David himself understood and accepted it. He comprehended that the reference to an unending throne and kingdom contained in the covenant would be linked with the eternal Messiah who was, according to the covenant, to be of his own seed. To David was given some realization of the death of Christ, too. This he expressed in Psalm 22. He evidently reasoned that if his Son, the Messiah, was both to die and to sit upon his throne forever, He, the Messiah, must first die and be raised from death that He might satisfy the interminable feature of the covenant. Certainly Messiah could not occupy the throne forever and then come to die. It is thus that David foresaw Christ's resurrection. The passage also records the fact that God had sworn with an oath to fulfill this literal, earthly, everlasting kingdom which was covenanted to David. Of this the Psalmist writes as a record of Jehovah's declaration: "My covenant will I not break, nor alter the thing that is gone out of my lips. Once have I sworn by my holiness that I will not lie unto David. His seed shall endure for ever, and his throne as the sun before me. It shall be established for ever as the moon, and as a faithful witness in heaven" (Ps. 89:34–37). Objectors, if such there be, would do well to reconsider the insult to divine veracity which a denial of Jehovah's oath constitutes. On this evil Ford C. Ottman has written:

Affirmed it has been—and with great emphasis—that John the Baptist and the disciples of Jesus were "obsessed by popular misconceptions" and saturated with "delusions" concerning the restoration of the Davidic dynasty; and so positively has this been affirmed that many have come to accept the statement as final and no more open to question. But any general acceptance of this affirmation, without examination or understanding of what is involved in it, shows only how easily a people more modern than the Jews may be "obsessed" with a "popular misconception." The Jew knew—and so also do we—that God had sworn with an oath to establish the kingdom of David forever, and to build up his throne to all generations. Deny this we cannot, without denying Scripture that asserts it. If Scripture be of no authority, we may think what we will: if it has authority, our thinking must by it be governed. Despite the covenant and oath of God, the kingdom of David was not—as the prophets had predicted, and as the disciples had expected—restored to Israel under the Messiah. Are we to conclude from this that the national hope was a delusion, and the popular expectancy a misconception of the Messianic mission? Certainly not: and they that labor to maintain such a conclusion prove only that they are under a delusion worse than that charged against prophets, apostles and people.—*Imperialism and Christ*, pp. 81–82

This oath of Jehovah confirms the divine purpose to place the Christ on David's throne (cf. Ps. 2:6), and, according to every Scripture bearing upon it, this was not to occur in connection with His ascension when returning to heaven from the first advent, but in connection with His coming again in power and great glory (cf. Matt. 25:31; Rev. 19:16).

Acts 15:13–18. "And after they had held their peace, James answered, saying, Men and brethren, hearken unto me: Simeon hath declared how God at the first did visit the Gentiles, to take out of them a people for his name. And to this agree the words of the prophets; as it is written, After this I will return, and will build again the tabernacle of David, which is fallen down; and I will build again the ruins thereof, and I will set it up: that the residue of men might seek after the Lord, and all the Gentiles, upon whom my name is called, saith the Lord, who doeth all these things. Known unto God are all his works from the beginning of the world."

In defining Jehovah's new purpose in the present age, which purpose so completely set aside the essentials of Judaism for a time, the first council of the Church at Jerusalem recognized an order of events which were yet future. There was to be an outcalling of the Church from both Jews and Gentiles, which outcalling has already begun and continues to the present hour. This, in turn, was to be followed and terminated by the return of Christ; and Christ in His return would re-establish the Davidic dynasty—a restoration foreseen by Amos, which prediction reads: "In that day will I raise up the tabernacle of David that is fallen, and close up the breaches thereof; and I will raise up his ruins, and I will build it as in the days of old: that they may possess the remnant of Edom, and of all the heathen, which are called by my name, saith the LORD that doeth this" (Amos 9:11–12). There is no support here or elsewhere for the Romish notion that the church is the kingdom. The elders of the early church distinguished here between the Church as the present divine objective and the final return to, and completion of, the Davidic covenant.

Revelation 22:16. "I Jesus have sent mine angel to testify unto you these things in the churches. I am the root and the offspring of David, and the bright and morning star."

This identification of Christ as the Son of David is not a meaningless reference to an indefinite heredity; it proclaims the truth, and that by the glorified Son of God Himself, that the Davidic kingdom will yet be realized through that One who bears the name *Son of David.*

As the opening portion of his masterful volume *Imperialism and Christ,* Ford C. Ottman has written the following:

Imperialism and Christ are separate words of inseverable meaning. They hold each other in encircling grasp that cannot be unbound nor broken. Their disconnection, if this were possible, would throw out of gear, and stop the action of, the machinery of the Universe. Imperialism—a word insistent and resonant in the political vocabulary of today—is, without Christ, beyond the bounds of possibility. Christ—a word central and controlling in the theological vocabulary of the Church—is, without Imperialism, neither regnant nor real. For the Crown Rights of Jesus the martyrs of the Scots Kirk contended, asserting Christ's sole Headship over His Church, till they, bludgeoned and harried by dragoons, lay down on the heather and dyed it with a richer hue than ever had nature given it, the red of the blood of testimony. And yet, the Crown Rights of Jesus do not include nor consist of His Headship over the Church. The Crown Rights of Jesus are substantial and literal, and they appertain to Kingship over Israel rather than to Headship over the Church. Imperialism and Christ, in which are involved the Crown Rights of Jesus, is a phrase of concise and definite meaning: a meaning that is enshrined in the memorable and classic utterance of Andrew Melville, as he shook King James's sleeve, calling him "God's silly vassal"—and adding, "Remember, there are two kingdoms in Scotland. There is King James, whose loyal subjects we are. But there is King Jesus." "The Crown Rights of Jesus" are words that have echoed along the years from the land of the national covenant, through the highlands, and down the glens, and over the moors of Scotland; and they are words whose meaning is now expanding from bud into bloom in the unfolding doctrine of the ever-approaching Eschatology of what we have here laid down as the "logical universe" in which our thoughts are now to move—Imperialism and Christ. Imperialism and Christ are convertible terms, equivalent in meaning, coordinate in rank, cooperative in action. Imperialism and Christ are not twain, but One. Christ without Imperialism is featureless. Imperialism without Christ is formless. It is in this, the correlative Unity of Christ and Imperialism, that all hope for the world is inextricably bound. The negation of this statement dismisses the one and the only clue given to guide us through the perplexing maze and mystery of the Universe. The negation of this statement, that with Christ's Imperialism the world's hope is indissolubly united, criminally drops the thread of the only exodus from the labyrinth of the great cosmic problem that presses upon the human soul for solution. The Crown Rights of the Lord Jesus Christ are positively declared and fully defined in Revelation, and they may not be nullified by speculation nor by pseudo-exegesis, nor, indeed, by these be in the least modified. Were the Bible incoherent or were the Bible vague in its statements of Imperialism and Christ, then we might account for the prevalent misconception of, and the prejudice against, God's Plan and Purpose in the probationary Ages of the world's history. But the Bible is not vague: it is as clear as a sunbeam, as concise as a mathematical proposition: it is positive in statement, plain in meaning, and precise in application: it pledges to the Lord Jesus Christ an Absolutism that has never been consummated in a kingdom spiritual. The real redemption of this pledge, however we may interpret its meaning, lies away in the future, and, whether it means a temporal kingdom on earth, or, whether it means a spiritual kingdom in the hearts of believers, must and can be determined by Revelation alone. Convictions, however profound they may be, have, unless they are sustained by Scripture, neither weight nor value, nor any call at all to be standard and measure of the coming kingdom. Christ in deity was David's Lord: in humanity He was David's Son. His exclusive and indisputable title to the throne of Israel was and is established and sealed by the genealogical tables of the authoritative records in the Gospels of Matthew and Luke, the inspired Chroniclers of His Crown Rights as Son of David and Son of man. . . . "Joseph, thou son of

David, fear not to take unto thee Mary thy wife: for that which is conceived in her is of the Holy Ghost. Then Joseph being raised from sleep did as the angel of the Lord had bidden him, and took unto him his wife." By this marriage Jesus was constituted the adopted Son of Joseph and his legal heir. Thus, in the wisdom of God, Jesus, by natural descent, and by primo-geniture claim, and by legal right, is given title to the throne of His father David. That throne Jesus has never occupied. It was denied Him on earth, and since the ascension He has been seated on the throne of the Father. On that throne He is to remain until His enemies are made His footstool. The Spiritual Absolutism that traditional thought awards Him is neither the precise fulfilment of prophecy, nor the equivalent or substitute of the Temporal Absolutism that has been pledged to Him by the mouth of all the holy prophets since the world began.

The rejection of Christ by the Jews, and His death at the hands of the Romans, were fore-known and fore-told. "He was taken from prison and from judgment"—so centuries before His birth it was written—"and who shall declare his generation? for he was cut off out of the land of the living: for the transgression of my people was he stricken" (Is. 53:8). The same prophet tells us that the government was to be upon His shoulder, and that of the increase of His government and peace there should be no end, upon the throne of David, and upon His kingdom, to order it, and to establish it with judgment and with justice from henceforth even forever. This promise is confirmed by the angel's announcement to the virgin, that the Lord God should give unto Him the throne of His father David, and that He should reign over the house of Jacob forever, and that of His kingdom there should be no end. How are such conflicting statements to be reconciled? Dying without generation, cut off out of the land of the living: yet reigning on the throne of David, and upon his kingdom to order it, and to establish it forever? The theological casuist, who has been trained to work out the subtleties of moral questions, may convince himself that the Church of Christ is that kingdom of David promised to Jesus, but such reasoning, however subtle and specious, is, to the man that believes that the words of the Bible are to be taken at their face value, inconclusive. If Gabriel stood alone in the declaration that Jesus should reign on David's throne there might be some reasonable question—in view of what has come to pass—as to the exact meaning of his words; but Gabriel is not alone in this testimony: the same is believed and is proclaimed by the Hebrew prophets. They predict a kingdom that is to be established in power, in the hands of Messiah, the Son of David; peace is to prevail and the earth is to be filled with the knowledge and glory of the Lord as the waters cover the sea; the house of David is to be reestablished, and Israel, restored to divine favor, is to become the center of refreshment and blessing to all the nations of the earth; the glory of the Lord is to be revealed from Zion, and the throne of Messiah established there—such is the concurrent testimony of all the prophets. In vain would it be to assert that the kingdom has ever assumed such form. We know that it has not. The King was rejected and was crucified. And this also, as well as the overwhelming judgment that should fall upon Israel in consequence of this crowning sin, had been predicted by the Hebrew prophets. The children of Israel, during these long centuries unrolling since the rejection of Christ, have been, as was prophesied of them, "without king, and without prince, and without sacrifice, and without pillar, and without ephod or teraphim" (Hos. 3:4, R.V.). This bereft people, in their wayward and weary wandering from God, have demonstrated and justified the literal application of this prophecy; and yet the prophecy, without a break, continues—"Afterward shall the children of Israel return, and seek the Lord their God, and David their king; and shall come with fear unto the Lord and to his goodness in the latter days" (Hos. 3:5). By what principle of fair interpretation are we allowed to make a literal application of verse 4 and deny the literal force of verse 5? Is it that Israel's long banishment from God has justified the one, and has extinguished all hope of the other? If the "casting away" of Israel is a literal fact, Why should it be thought a thing incredible that God shall restore them again to His favor? And if God restores Israel, Why should it be thought a thing incredible that the kingdom shall be set up and established in the form that the prophets predicted? All believers in the Bible will admit that Jesus came into the world to establish a kingdom. Born King of the Jews was He, and—as the genealogical tables conclusively prove—legal Heir of David's throne He was, and is. Of the character and constitution of His kingdom a true conception cannot be weened from speculation, nor derived from any source beyond or other than from a sound rendering and strict interpretation of Scripture. The primitive form of the kingdom, whatever modifications there may, or may not, have been made subsequently, was a kingdom here upon the earth, during the continuance of which the law should "go forth of Zion, and the word of the Lord from Jerusalem" (Micah 4:2). The kingdom, according to the united testimony of the prophets, is to be set up and established here upon the earth, with Jerusalem as the capital city of the kingdom, the Messiah reigning from the throne of David over restored Israel, and through Israel extending His dominion to the ends of the earth. That is the prophet's field of vision, and there is not the shadow of an intimation that the rejection and death of the King—both fore-known and fore-told —should result in any organic change of the kingdom, or modify in any way the prophet's conception. The form ultimate of the kingdom should be commensurate and concordant with its form primitive. Evidence of this is given by the prophet Micah, who says, "They shall smite the judge of Israel with a rod upon the cheek"—this foretells the King's rejection—"but"—the prophecy continues—"thou, Bethlehem Ephratah, though thou be little among the thousands of Judah, yet out of thee shall he come forth unto me that is to be ruler in Israel" (Micah 5:2).—Pp. 9–21

It is this latter which is the truth, namely, that the norm of the kingdom as covenanted by Jehovah with an oath is its ultimate form on earth. But that hermeneutical legerdemain which can start with a covenant respecting an earthly throne, an everlasting reign and kingdom, or without recognition of such a covenant at all, and emerge at the end with a mere fictitious idealism concerning a spiritual authority over men is borrowed—if concerned with Scripture at all—from the fact of the larger authority of God over His universe, namely, the kingdom of God. All this is but the dregs of Whitby's theory, which persuasion has so woefully ignored the precise teachings of the Bible and by so doing has become the progenitor of modern liberalism with its masquerade as the messenger of God. The indictment is against those who attempt no exposition of the Sacred Text and who present human opinions, more or less ethereal, respecting God's purpose in future ages.

II. ITS VARIOUS FORMS

Since the kingdom of heaven is the rule of God in the earth down through the ages, it may be identified in various forms. These are now to be traced.

1. THE JUDGES. While God has guided the affairs of men from the beginning, there was no established method of His government over a nation until the period of the Judges. Before that time a temporary dictatorship was set up under Moses and continued under Joshua. The divine rule through the Judges is definitely owned of God as that period closes. Jehovah said to Samuel: "Hearken unto the voice of the people in all that they say unto thee: for they have not rejected thee, but they have rejected me, that I should not reign over them" (1 Sam. 8:7; cf. Judges 2:16, 18; Acts 13:20). So, also, according to Isaiah the original method of administering the theocratic government will yet be restored. Isaiah declares "And I will restore thy judges as at the first, and thy counsellors as at the beginning: afterward thou shalt be called, The city of righteousness, the faithful city" (1:26). The rule of the Judges, being Jehovah's government over Israel, is a form of the kingdom of heaven.

2. THE DAVIDIC REIGN AND COVENANT. Though Saul served as king over Israel for a long period, he failed and his reign was evidently an education of the people in preparation for the true exercise of divine authority through David. The reign of David was peculiarly a divine undertaking for it had in view as a pattern the final form of that Davidic reign. It served its greatest purpose, however, as the starting point for all that inheres in Jehovah's covenant with David. Such, indeed, is the start of the great highway of prediction respecting the kingdom of heaven.

3. THE KINGDOM PREDICTED. It is significant that the Old Testament prophets spoke, in the main, during one comparatively brief period.

This was the time in which Israel was approaching and entering her national dispersion under the chastening hand of God. It was in the darkest hour of their nation's history that these seers, as if by contrast, set forth the unprecedented light of the nation's coming glory. This consensus of prophetic vision has never had a semblance of fulfillment; yet the nation is still divinely preserved, and so, evidently, with this consummation in view (Jer. 31:35–37; Matt. 24:32–34).

Some of the prophets spoke before the exile, some during the exile, while others spoke after the exile when a remnant, but not the nation, had returned to their land. While they spoke with individual purpose and style, they were united as one voice on certain great themes. They condemned the nation's sin and predicted the coming chastisement. They saw the judgments about to fall upon the surrounding nations, but these Gentile judgments are in view only as they are related to Israel. Above all they saw their own future blessings, the form and manner of which are too accurately described by them to be misunderstood. Their prophecies expanded into magnificent detail the covenanted reign of David's Son over the house of Jacob forever. In tracing these passages scarcely a comment is necessary if the statements are taken in their plain and obvious meaning. Passages are here selected from the many that were spoken by all the prophets concerning the coming King and His kingdom, and from these Scriptures it will be seen that Emmanuel's government is—

a. TO BE THEOCRATIC. The King will be "Emmanuel . . . God with us," for He is by human birth a rightful heir to David's throne and born of a virgin in Bethlehem.

First, the King will be "Emmanuel . . . God with us": "Therefore the Lord himself shall give you a sign; Behold, a virgin shall conceive, and bear a son, and shall call his name Immanuel" (Isa. 7:14). "Now all this was done, that it might be fulfilled which was spoken of the Lord by the prophet, saying, Behold, a virgin shall be with child, and shall bring forth a son, and they shall call his name Emmanuel, which being interpreted is, God with us" (Matt. 1:22–23).

Second, the King will be heir to David's throne: "And there shall come forth a rod out of the stem of Jesse, and a Branch shall grow out of his roots: and the spirit of the LORD shall rest upon him, the spirit of wisdom and understanding, the spirit of counsel and might, the spirit of knowledge and of the fear of the LORD; and shall make him of quick understanding in the fear of the LORD: and he shall not judge after the sight of his eyes, neither reprove after the hearing of his ears: but with righteousness shall he judge the poor, and reprove with equity for the meek of the earth: and he shall smite the earth with the rod of his mouth, and with the breath of his lips shall he slay the wicked. And righteousness shall be the girdle of his loins, and faithfulness the girdle of his reins" (Isa. 11:1–5). "Behold, the days come, saith the LORD, that I will raise unto David a righteous Branch, and a King shall reign and prosper, and shall execute judgment and justice in the earth" (Jer. 23:5). "And I will set up one shepherd over them, and he shall feed them, even my servant David; he shall feed them, and he shall be their shepherd" (Ezek. 34:23). "And David my servant shall be king over them; and they all shall have one shepherd: they shall also walk in my judgments, and observe my statutes, and do them" (Ezek. 37:24). "For the children of Israel shall abide many days without a king, and without a prince, and without a sacrifice, and without an image, and without an ephod, and without teraphim: afterward shall the children of Israel return, and seek the LORD their God, and David their king; and shall fear the LORD and his goodness in the latter days" (Hos. 3:4–5).

Third, the King was to be born of a virgin in Bethlehem: "Behold, a virgin shall conceive, and bear a son, and shall call his name Immanuel" (Isa. 7:14). "But thou, Beth-lehem Ephratah, though thou be little among the thousands of Judah, yet out of thee shall he come forth unto me that is to be ruler in Israel; whose goings forth have been from of old, from everlasting" (Mic. 5:2).

b. TO BE HEAVENLY IN CHARACTER. "And he shall judge among the nations, and shall rebuke many people: and they shall beat their swords into plowshares, and their spears into pruninghooks: nation shall not lift up sword against nation, neither shall they learn war any more" (Isa. 2:4). "But with righteousness shall he judge the poor, and reprove with equity for the meek of the earth: and he shall smite the earth with the rod of his mouth, and with the breath of his lips shall he slay the wicked. And righteousness shall be the girdle of his loins, and faithfulness the girdle of his reins" (Isa. 11:4–5). "Behold, the days come, saith the LORD, that I will perform that good thing which I have promised unto the house of Israel and to the house of Judah. In those days, and at that time, will I cause the Branch of righteousness to grow up unto David; and he shall execute judgment and righteousness in the land. In those days shall Judah be saved, and Jerusalem shall dwell safely: and this is the name wherewith she shall be called, The LORD our righteousness.

For thus saith the LORD; David shall never want a man to sit upon the throne of the house of Israel" (Jer. 33:14–17). "And in that day will I make a covenant for them with the beasts of the field, and with the fowls of heaven, and with the creeping things of the ground: and I will break the bow and the sword and the battle out of the earth, and will make them to lie down safely" (Hos. 2:18).

c. TO BE IN JERUSALEM AND WORLD-WIDE. First, Emmanuel's kingdom will be in the earth: "Ask of me, and I shall give thee the heathen for thine inheritance, and the uttermost parts of the earth for thy possession" (Ps. 2:8). "For the earth shall be full of the knowledge of the LORD, as the waters cover the sea" (Isa. 11:9). "He shall not fail nor be discouraged, till he have set judgment in the earth: and the isles shall wait for his law" (Isa. 42:4). "Behold, the days come, saith the LORD, that I will raise unto David a righteous Branch, and a King shall reign and prosper, and shall execute judgment and justice in the earth" (Jer. 23:5). "And the LORD shall be king over all the earth: in that day shall there be one LORD, and his name one" (Zech. 14:9).

Second, Emmanuel's kingdom will be centered at Jerusalem:

"The word that Isaiah the son of Amoz saw concerning Judah and Jerusalem. And it shall come to pass in the last days, that the mountain of the LORD's house shall be established in the top of the mountains, and shall be exalted above the hills; and all nations shall flow unto it. And many people shall go and say, Come ye, and let us go up to the mountain of the LORD, to the house of the God of Jacob; and he will teach us of his ways, and we will walk in his paths: for out of Zion shall go forth the law, and the word of the LORD from Jerusalem" (Isa. 2:1–3). "For Zion's sake will I not hold my peace, and for Jerusalem's sake I will not rest, until the righteousness thereof go forth as brightness, and the salvation thereof as a lamp that burneth. And the Gentiles shall see thy righteousness, and all kings thy glory: and thou shalt be called by a new name, which the mouth of the LORD shall name. Thou shalt also be a crown of glory in the hand of the LORD, and a royal diadem in the hand of thy God. Thou shalt no more be termed Forsaken; neither shall thy land any more be termed Desolate: but thou shalt be called Hephzi-bah, and thy land Beulah: for the LORD delighteth in thee, and thy land shall be married. For as a young man marrieth a virgin, so shall thy sons marry thee: and as the bridegroom rejoiceth over the bride, so shall thy God rejoice over thee. I have set watchmen upon thy walls, O Jerusalem, which shall never hold their peace day nor night: ye that make mention of the LORD, keep not silence, and give him no rest, till he establish, and till he make Jerusalem a praise in the earth" (Isa. 62:1–7). "Thus saith the LORD of hosts; It shall yet come to pass, that there shall come people, and the inhabitants of many cities: and the inhabitants of one city shall go to another, saying, Let us go speedily to pray before the LORD, and to seek the LORD of hosts: I will go also. Yea, many people and strong nations shall come to seek the LORD of hosts in Jerusalem, and to pray before the LORD. Thus saith the LORD of hosts; In those days it shall come to pass, that ten men shall take hold out of all languages of the nations, even shall take hold of the skirt of him that is a Jew, saying, We will go with you: for we have heard that God is with you" (Zech. 8:20–23). "And Jerusalem shall be trodden down of the Gentiles, until the times of the Gentiles be fulfilled" (Luke 21:24).

Third, Emmanuel's kingdom will be over regathered and converted Israel:

"That then the LORD thy God will turn thy captivity, and have compassion upon thee, and will return and gather thee from all the nations, whither the LORD thy God hath scattered thee. If any of thine be driven out unto the outmost parts of heaven, from thence will the LORD thy God gather thee, and from thence will he fetch thee: and the LORD thy God will bring thee into the land which thy fathers possessed, and thou shalt possess it; and he will do thee good, and multiply thee above thy fathers. And the LORD thy God will circumcise thine heart, and the heart of thy seed, to love the LORD thy God with all thine heart, and with all thy soul, that thou mayest live" (Deut. 30: 3–6). "And it shall come to pass in that day, that the Lord shall set his hand again the second time to recover the remnant of his people, which shall be left, from Assyria, and from Egypt, and from Pathros, and from Cush, and from Elam, and from Shinar, and from Hamath, and from the islands of the sea. And he shall set up an ensign for the nations, and shall assemble the outcasts of Israel, and gather together the dispersed of Judah from the four corners of the earth" (Isa. 11:11–12). "For the LORD will have mercy on Jacob, and will yet choose Israel, and set them in their own land: and the strangers shall be joined with them, and they shall cleave to the house of Jacob. And the people shall take them, and bring them to their place: and the house of Israel shall possess them in the land of the LORD for servants and handmaids: and they shall take them captives, whose captives they were; and they shall rule over their oppressors" (Isa. 14:1–2; cf. 60:1–22). "In his days Judah shall be saved, and Israel shall dwell safely: and this is his name whereby he shall be called, THE LORD OUR RIGHTEOUSNESS. Therefore, behold, the days come, saith the LORD, that they shall no more say, The LORD liveth, which brought up the children of Israel out of the land of Egypt; but, The LORD liveth, which brought up and which led the seed of the house of Israel out of the north country, and from all countries whither I had driven them; and they shall dwell in their own land" (Jer. 23:6–8). "Behold, I will gather them out of all countries, whither I have driven them in mine anger, and in my fury, and in great wrath; and I will bring them again unto this place, and I will cause them to dwell safely: and they shall be my people, and I will be their God" (Jer. 32:37–38). "And I will cause the captivity of Judah and the captivity of Israel to return, and will build them, as at the first. And I will cleanse them from all their iniquity, whereby they have sinned against me; and I will pardon all their iniquities, whereby they have sinned, and whereby they have transgressed against me. And it shall be to me a name of joy, a praise and an honour before all the nations of the earth, which shall hear all the good that I do unto them: and they shall fear and tremble for all the goodness and for all the prosperity that I procure unto it" (Jer. 33:7–9; cf. Ezek. 36:16–38). "And say unto them, Thus saith the Lord GOD; Behold, I will take the children of Israel from among the heathen, whither they be gone, and will gather them on every side, and bring them into their own land: and I will make them one nation in the land upon the mountains of Israel; and one king shall be king to them all: and they shall be no more two nations, neither shall they be divided into two kingdoms any more at all: neither shall they defile themselves any more with their idols, nor with their detestable things, nor with any of their transgressions: but I will save them out of all their dwelling places, wherein they have sinned, and will cleanse them: so shall they be my people, and I will be their God. And David my servant shall be king over them; and they all shall have one shepherd: they shall also walk in my judgments, and observe my statutes, and do them. And they shall dwell in the land that I have given unto Jacob my servant, wherein your fathers have dwelt; and they shall dwell therein, even they, and their children, and their children's children for ever: and my servant David shall be their prince for ever" (Ezek. 37:21–25). "In that day, saith the LORD, will I assemble her that halteth, and I will gather her that is driven out, and her that I have afflicted; and I will make her that halted a remnant, and her that was cast far off a strong nation: and the LORD shall reign over them in mount Zion from henceforth, even for ever. And thou, O tower of the flock, the strong hold of the daughter of Zion, unto thee shall it come, even the first dominion; the kingdom shall come to the daughter of Jerusalem" (Mic. 4:6–8).

Fourth, Emmanuel's kingdom shall extend to the nations in the earth:

"Yea, all kings shall fall down before him: all nations shall serve him. . . . His name shall endure for ever: his name shall be continued as long as the sun: and men shall be blessed in him: all nations shall call him blessed" (Ps. 72:11, 17). "All nations whom thou hast made shall come and worship before thee, O Lord; and shall glorify thy name" (Ps. 86:9). "Behold, thou shalt call a nation that thou knowest not, and nations that knew not thee shall run unto thee because of the LORD thy God, and for the Holy One of Israel; for he hath glorified thee" (Isa. 55:5). "I saw in the night visions, and, behold, one like the Son of man came with the clouds of heaven, and came to the Ancient of days, and they brought him near before him. And there was given him dominion, and glory, and a kingdom, that all people, nations, and languages, should serve him: his dominion is an everlasting dominion, which shall not pass away, and his kingdom that which shall not be destroyed" (Dan. 7:13–14). "And many nations shall come, and say, Come, and let us go up to the mountain of the LORD, and to the house of the God of Jacob; and he will teach us of his ways, and we will walk in his paths: for the law shall go forth of Zion, and the word of the LORD from Jerusalem" (Mic. 4:2). "Yea, many people and strong nations shall come to seek the LORD of hosts in Jerusalem, and to pray before the LORD" (Zech. 8:22). "And I will plant them upon their land, and they shall no more be pulled up out of their land which I have given them, saith the LORD thy God" (Amos 9:15).

d. TO BE ESTABLISHED BY THE RETURNING KING. "That then the LORD thy God will turn thy captivity, and have compassion upon thee, and will return and gather thee from all the nations, whither the LORD thy God hath scattered thee" (Deut. 30:3). "Our God shall come, and shall not keep silence: a fire shall devour before him, and it shall be very tempestuous round about him. He shall call to the heavens from above, and to the earth, that he may judge his people. Gather my saints together unto me; those that have made a covenant with me by sacrifice" (Ps. 50:3–5). "For he cometh, for he cometh to judge the earth: he shall judge the world with righteousness, and the people with his truth" (Ps. 96:13). "Sing and rejoice, O daughter of Zion: for, lo, I come, and I will dwell in the midst of thee, saith the LORD. And many nations shall be joined to the LORD in that day, and shall be my people: and I will dwell in the midst of thee, and thou shalt know that the LORD of hosts hath sent me unto thee. And the LORD shall inherit Judah his portion in the holy land, and shall choose Jerusalem again. Be silent, O all flesh, before the LORD: for he is raised up out of his holy habitation" (Zech. 2:10–13). "Behold, I will send my messenger, and he shall prepare the way before me: and the Lord, whom ye seek, shall suddenly come to his temple, even the messenger of the covenant, whom ye delight in: behold, he shall come, saith the LORD of hosts. But who may abide the day of his coming? and who shall stand when he appeareth? for he is like a refiner's fire, and like fullers' soap: and he shall sit as a refiner and purifier of silver: and he shall purify the sons of Levi, and purge them as gold and silver, that they may offer unto the LORD an offering in righteousness. Then shall the offering of Judah and Jerusalem be pleasant unto the LORD, as in the days of old, and as in former years" (Mal. 3:1–4).

e. TO BE SPIRITUAL. The kingdom is not incorporeal or separate from that which is material, but still it is spiritual in that the will of God will be directly effective in all matters of government and conduct. The joy and blessedness of fellowship with God will be experienced by all. The universal, temporal kingdom will be conducted in perfect righteousness and true holiness. The kingdom of God will again be "in the midst" (Luke 17:21, R.V. marg.) in the Person of the Messiah King and He will rule in the grace and power of the sevenfold Spirit (Isa. 11:2–5). Judah shall be saved, and Israel shall dwell safely, and the nations shall walk in the light of the city of God. "Yea, many people and strong nations shall come to seek the LORD of hosts in Jerusalem, and to pray before the LORD." The trees of the field shall clap their hands in accord with man's joy.

These passages, which might be multiplied many times, may serve to outline the prophet's vision of the features of Messiah's earthly kingdom which was covenanted to David. This kingdom has ever been Israel's only hope and was the consolation for which she waited when Christ was born (Luke 2:25).

4. THE KINGDOM OFFERED. In subject matter the division between the Old Testament and the New occurs at the cross of Christ, rather than between Malachi and Matthew. The Gospels, in the main, carry forward the same dispensational conditions that were in effect at the hour when Christ was born. Especially is this true of the Gospel of Matthew, Christ being set forth in that Gospel, first of all, as a King with His kingdom in full view. The Spirit has faithfully selected those deeds and teachings of Christ from the complete manifestation He made in the flesh which portray Him in the dominant character to be reflected in each individual Gospel. In Matthew He is presented as the King, in Mark as Jehovah's Servant, in Luke as the perfect Human, and in John as the very Son of God. In all these narratives, this one Person is seen acting and teaching under the same conditions which existed for centuries before the cross. There is some anticipation of what would follow the cross, as there is reference after the cross to what had gone before. Whatever preceded the cross, in the main, fell under those conditions linked with and colored by "the law [which] was given by Moses," for Jesus not only held up Moses as the authority for the time but also expanded his teachings. The great division between the Old Testament and the New, therefore, lies in the fact that "grace and truth came by Jesus Christ," and this became effective with the cross of Christ rather than with His birth. Matthew opens with an emphasis upon Christ as the Son of David: "The book of the generation [γένεσις—ancestry or line of descent; cf. the kindred term γενεά, Matt. 24:34] of Jesus Christ, the son of David, the son of Abraham." Although in this Gospel Jesus is also presented as "the son of Abraham" in His sacrificial death, the primary purpose of the writer is to set forth the nation's King, this being the only office that is ever assigned to a firstborn "son of David." The tracing of the divinely appointed kingdom thus proceeds from the Old Testament into the New without a change other than the appearance of the long-expected King, accompanied by His forerunner whose

predicted ministry had occupied the closing words of the Old Testament revelation. There is no break in the narrative, then.

The fact that Jesus was David's Greater Son, the fulfiller of all the nation's kingdom blessings, is not based on human opinion. It was announced by the angel Gabriel before the birth of Christ as recorded in Luke 1:31–33: "And, behold, thou shalt conceive in thy womb, and bring forth a son, and shalt call his name JESUS. He shall be great, and shall be called the Son of the Highest: and the Lord God shall give unto him the throne of his father David: and he shall reign over the house of Jacob for ever; and of His kingdom there shall be no end." This treats distinctly of the "throne of . . . David" ruling over the "house of Jacob," and proclaims of this kingdom that "there shall be no end." No Gentile blessings are in view here; nor need the Gentiles seek to intrude. Gentile blessings will eventually flow out of this very throne, but these are not in view; nor are any Gentile blessings endangered by a faithful recognition of this distinctly Jewish purpose. The same is clearly stated in Romans 15:8: "Now I say that Jesus Christ was a minister of the circumcision [i.e., Israel] for the truth of God, to confirm the promises made unto the fathers." He did not come to *disannul* those promises, but He did come to *confirm* them. The promises made unto the fathers are well defined; no promises were made to Gentiles. The terminology "the fathers" can mean none other than God's chosen men, or Israel. By these promises Israel was to be redeemed and placed in her own land and that by Emmanuel, who should be the final Prophet, Priest, and King. He should be King over her covenanted kingdom. These promises made unto the fathers were the nation's only hope, as is clearly indicated: "We trusted that it had been he which should have redeemed Israel"; "Lord, wilt thou at this time restore again the kingdom to Israel?" In Christ, then, the kingdom covenant made to David had its confirmation as well it might, being one of the promises made unto the fathers. How certainly that covenant must stand today! It is recorded of Jesus that He was "born King of the Jews" (Matt. 2:2). To this throne He made final claim at His trial (Matt. 27:11). And under this accusation He suffered (Matt. 27:29) and died (Matt. 27:37). One needs only to search the Scriptures to discover the fact that He is never mentioned as King of the church, nor even King of the nations until He comes again as "KING OF KINGS, AND LORD OF LORDS" (Rev. 19:16). He fulfilled every prediction that described Israel's Messiah King and the manner of His coming—that at a time when all the records and genealogies were intact. He came from the tribe of Judah, ranked as a first-born Son of David, born of a virgin in Bethlehem of Judea. Such claims could not have been made then by an impostor without arousing the violent opposition of the rulers of the nation. His claim to be King was never challenged, so far as title was concerned. He met every prediction concerning Israel's Emmanuel-King. He was that King.

Four centuries before the birth of Jesus, Malachi had prophesied the coming of a forerunner to prepare the people for their King: "Behold, I will send you Elijah the prophet before the coming of the great and dreadful day of the LORD: and he shall turn the heart of the fathers to the children, and the heart of the children to their fathers, lest I come and smite the earth with a curse" (4:5–6). This had a certain fulfillment in John the Baptist according, again, to angelic testimony: "But the angel said unto him, Fear not, Zacharias: for thy prayer is heard; and thy wife Elisabeth shall bear thee a son, and thou shalt call his name John. And thou shalt have joy and gladness; and many shall rejoice at his birth. For he shall be great in the sight of the Lord, and shall drink neither wine nor strong drink; and he shall be filled with the Holy Ghost, even from his mother's womb. And many of the children of Israel shall he turn to the Lord their God. And he shall go before him in the spirit and power of Elias, to turn the hearts of the fathers to the children, and the disobedient to the wisdom of the just; to make ready a people prepared for the Lord" (Luke 1:13–17). Furthermore, another Messianic claim was met in the faithful ministry of John, for the first message of this divinely foreseen witness is recorded thus: "In those days came John the Baptist, preaching in the wilderness of Juda, and saying, Repent ye: for the kingdom of heaven is at hand" (Matt. 3:1–2). This, too, was the first message recorded of Christ: "From that time Jesus began to preach, and to say, Repent: for the kingdom of heaven is at hand" (Matt. 4:17). So, again, it was the only message committed to His disciples when He first sent them forth to preach: "These twelve Jesus sent forth, and commanded them, saying, Go not into the way of the Gentiles, and into any city of the Samaritans enter ye not: but go rather to the lost sheep of the house of Israel. And as ye go, preach, saying, The kingdom of heaven is at hand" (Matt. 10:5–7). This message, it is clear, had no application to Gentiles; the messengers were to go only "to the lost sheep of the house of Israel." It can scarcely go unnoticed that, while every detail of the manner of their journey was subject to the most careful instruction by the King, there is no record of their being given instruction on the meaning of this first, or kingdom, message committed to them. Evidently they did not need such instruction concerning the kingdom. Had not the kingdom hope been passed from father to son for generations? Had it not been sung to them at their mother's knee? Had it not been the one great theme of synagogue instruction? Was it not their national hope? How much in contrast to this was the prolonged inability on the part of these same disciples to grasp, later on, the new message and world-wide commission of the cross! This focusing of the testimony of Jesus, of John, and of the disciples upon one solitary message "The kingdom of heaven is at hand" places that message under an unusual emphasis, and its actual meaning should be carefully considered.

The phrase "the kingdom of heaven" is found only in Matthew, the Gospel of the King, and there it appears with different shades of meaning. Only one of these shades of meaning is used in chapters 1 to 12 of this first Gospel. Here it seems to refer to the same earthly Davidic kingdom with which the Old Testament had closed its Messianic prophesying in Malachi. As has been stated, whatever was meant by this New Testament announcement of "the kingdom of heaven," it was clearly understood by the preachers who first proclaimed it and by their hearers. No other kingdom message could have thus been received by Jewish people in that day. So, also, it was addressed to one nation, Israel, and to them as a whole rather than to individuals. Thus "the kingdom of heaven" as a message must ever be distinguished from the message of the gospel of grace which came by reason of the cross. The gospel of grace Israel as a nation has never understood, and furthermore it is addressed to all peoples and to them as individuals only. The message of "the kingdom of heaven" as first set forth by Matthew had, therefore, a limited and national meaning, limited in the time of its application because a new message has since come in from God, and national because for the time being it was addressed to Israel alone. The message of "the kingdom of heaven" did not concern itself so much with the Person of the King as it did with His kingdom. But then Israel had never dreamed of a kingdom apart from the presence and power of the expected King. Thus Jesus could say of Himself, in the light of the accepted close relation between the Person of the King and His kingdom: "the kingdom of God is within you" ("in the midst of" Israel in the Person of the King, Luke 17:21). To assert the imminency of the kingdom was, to them, to assert the imminency of the King.

This kingdom message conforms in another respect, also, to the conditions of the Old Testament prophecy of a government. There must be a great national heart-turning, or repentance, to God as an immediate preparation for the kingdom, as seen in the Old Testament (Deut. 30: 1–3; Isa. 42:7; Hos. 3:4–5; 14:8; Zech. 12:10—13:1; Mal. 3:7). Repentance, therefore, became an imperative part of the message concerning the imminency of the kingdom. So each of these kingdom messengers called upon that nation to repent. A "generation of vipers" must "bring forth . . . fruits meet for repentance." They must turn about in heart as a prerequisite for this covenanted kingdom blessing. This they, by His grace, are yet to do, "in his time." It is to be regretted that this required national repentance of Israel has been so often misapplied as a necessary preliminary step in an individual's salvation by grace.

As certainly as the message of "the kingdom of heaven" was consistent with the nation's hope, so, also, the rule of life presented in connection with this message by both John the Baptist and Christ was in harmony with the Old Testament predicted kingdom's rule of life. The kingdom as foreseen in the Old Testament had ever in view the righteousness in life and conduct of its subjects (Isa. 11:3–5; 32:1; Jer. 23:6; Dan. 9:24). "The kingdom of heaven" as announced and offered in the early part of Matthew's Gospel is also accompanied with positive demands for personal righteousness in life and conduct. This is not the principle of grace; it is rather the principle of law. Kingdom teaching extends into finer detail the law of Moses and never ceases to be the very opposite of the principle of grace. Law conditions its blessings on human works, grace conditions its works on divine blessings. Law says "If ye forgive . . . your heavenly Father will also forgive you," and in that measure only (Matt. 6:14–15), while grace says "Forgiving one another, even as God for Christ's sake hath forgiven you" (Eph. 4:32). So, again, law says "Except your righteousness shall exceed the righteousness of the scribes and Pharisees, ye shall in no case enter into the kingdom of heaven" (Matt. 5:20). This is not a present condition for entrance into heaven. Present conditions are wholly based on mercy: "Not by works of righteousness which we have done, but according to his mercy he saved us" (Titus 3:5). So the preaching of John the Baptist, like the Sermon on the Mount, was on a law basis as indicated by its appeal, which was only for a correct and righteous life: "Then said he to the multitude that came forth to be baptized of him, O generation of vipers, who hath warned you to flee from the wrath to come? Bring forth therefore fruits worthy of repentance, and begin not to say within yourselves, We have Abraham to our father: for I say unto you, That God is able of these stones to raise up children unto Abraham. And now also the axe is laid unto the root of the trees: every tree therefore which bringeth not forth good fruit is hewn down, and cast into the fire. And the people asked him, saying, What shall we do then? He answered and saith unto them, He that hath two coats, let him impart to him that hath none; and he that hath meat, let him do likewise. Then came also publicans to be baptized, and said unto him, Master, what shall we do? And he said unto them, Exact no more than that which is appointed you. And the soldiers likewise demanded of him, saying, And what shall we do? And he said unto them, Do violence to no man, neither accuse any falsely; and be content with your wages" (Luke 3:7-14). This, like the Sermon on the Mount, is an appeal for a righteous life and cannot be confused with the present terms of salvation without nullifying the grounds of every hope and promise under grace. The present appeal to the unsaved is not for better conduct; it is for personal belief in, and acceptance of, the Savior. There are directions concerning the conduct of those who are saved by trust in the Savior; but these cannot be mixed with the law conditions of the Old Testament, or the New, without peril to souls. Later on, the same people said to Christ "What shall we do, that we might work the works of God?" and to this He replied "This is the work of God, that ye believe on him whom he hath sent" (John 6:28-29). John the Baptist looked forward to the blessings of grace when he said "Behold the Lamb of God, which taketh away the sin of the world," but his immediate demands were in conformity with pure law, as were the early, kingdom teachings of Jesus. Thus the legal principles of conduct of the Old Testament predicted kingdom are carried forward into the revelations of the same kingdom as it appears in the New Testament. The right division of Scripture does not destroy the usefulness of these legal passages for today, but it does fully classify them with the other Scriptures relating to the kingdom, both in the Old Testament and the New. There are many elements in this body of truth that indicates the required manner of life in the kingdom which will be found likewise under the consistent walk in grace; but whatever is carried forward to be a life-governing principle under grace is there restated in its own place and with its own new emphasis. Thus the two widely differing systems are meant to be kept distinct in the mind of the faithful student of God's Word. It should be borne in mind that the legal kingdom requirements as stated in the Sermon on the Mount are meant to prepare the way for, and condition life in, the earthly Davidic kingdom when it shall be set up upon the earth, and at that very time when the kingdom prayer "Thy kingdom come. Thy will be done in earth, as it is in heaven" has been answered. These kingdom emphases appear in the early ministry of Jesus, since He was at that time faithfully offering the Messianic kingdom to Israel.

It has been objected that such stipulations as "Resist not evil," "Whosoever shall smite thee on thy right cheek . . . ," "Whosoever shall compel thee to go a mile . . . ," and ". . . persecuted for righteousness' sake" could not be possible in the kingdom. This challenge may be based upon a supposition that the earthly Messianic kingdom is to be as morally perfect as heaven. On the contrary, the Scriptures abundantly testify that, while there will be far less occasion to sin, for the sufficient reason that Satan is then bound and in a pit and the glorious King is on His throne, there will be need of immediate execution of judgment and justice in the earth, and even the King shall rule, of necessity, with a "rod of iron." It is said that "All Israel shall be saved" and "They shall all know me [the Lord], from the least of them unto the greatest," but it is also revealed that at the end of that millennium, when Satan is loosed for a little season, he is still able to solicit the allegiance of human hearts and to draw out of the multitudes within the kingdom an army for rebellion against the government of the King (Rev. 20:7-9). In that kingdom age "the sinner being an hundred years old shall be accursed" (Isa. 65:20). The saints of that age will doubtless have heaven before their eyes and be looking there for their reward. And they will be the "salt of the earth." These kingdom commands and principles were given to Israel only and it is the same distinct nation that shall stand first in her predicted kingdom when it is set up in the earth. Jesus was first "a minister of the circumcision," consequently is it an unnatural interpretation of Scripture to understand that He was performing this divinely appointed ministry at that very time when He was offering the kingdom to that nation and when He, with His forerunner, was depicting the principles of conduct that should condition life in that kingdom? Nothing is lost by such an interpretation; on the contrary, everything is gained, for the riches of grace—which alas so few apprehend—are thus kept pure and free from an unscriptural admixture with the kingdom law.

It may be concluded that the term "the kingdom of heaven" as used in the early ministry of Jesus referred to the Messianic, Davidic, earthly kingdom foreseen in the Old Testament. As has been noted, the Jewish preachers used by Christ needed no instruction in the details of that message. It was the hope of their nation, and it was addressed to that nation alone. So, also, an appeal was made with this message for the anticipated national repentance which must precede the setting up of their kingdom in the earth, and the requirements set forth were legal rather than gracious. Israel's kingdom was faithfully offered to them by their King at His first appearing.

5. THE KINGDOM REJECTED AND POSTPONED. The suggestion that God has deferred any feature of His program of the ages engenders objection in some minds, assuming that such action on His part is unworthy of Him. The difficulty is removed at once when it is remembered that the postponement was not an afterthought or unexpected necessity, but was itself a part of the original plan of God—that is, to the end that an age might be introduced which had been kept secret in the counsels of God, that Messiah might be crucified and raised from the dead to be the Redeemer of both Israel and the Church, likewise the Judge of all created beings, and that Israel's rejection of Jehovah might assume its final, concrete form as it did in the death of Christ. The setting up of Messiah's kingdom, though first faithfully offered to Israel, was deferred and now awaits the return of Messiah for its realization. The question which presents difficulty to some is how the kingdom could be offered to Israel in sincerity and yet Jehovah Himself know, as He did, that it would not be accepted and that it would be deferred. Was the whole divine purpose in redemption by so much rendered uncertain? Much has been written on this problem in an earlier portion of this theological work. It is evident that, as the present age was a divine secret, it could not have been revealed until the rejection of Christ was consummated in His death and resurrection. Similarly, there is a natural disposition to judge the entire question, which the postponement of the kingdom creates, from the finite viewpoint alone. Whatever occurs is usually directly or indirectly due to man's action in free will; it is therefore natural to suppose that God is in some way subject to human determination, not realizing that God not only knows beforehand the choice His creatures will make, but is Himself able to work in them both to will and to do of His own good pleasure. The Scriptures present many incidents which disclose the fact that the will of God is executed by men even when they have no conscious intention to do the will of God. Within their own sphere of recognition they act in perfect freedom. With reference to other situations in which God's sovereign purpose seems for a time to depend on the free-will action of men, it will be remembered that God ordained a Lamb before the foundation of the world and that Lamb to be slain at God's appointed time and way. By so much it is made clear that God anticipated the sin of man and his great need of

redemption. God, however, told Adam *not* to sin; yet if Adam had not sinned there would have been no need of that redemption which God had before determined as something to be wrought out. Was God uncertain whether He would save life on the earth until Noah consented to build an ark? Was the nation Israel a matter of divine doubt until Abraham manifested his willingness to walk with God? Was the birth of Christ dubiety until Mary assented to the divine plan respecting the virgin birth? Is God censurable for determining that Christ should be born of the virgin Mary before she was even born? Is the virgin Mary deprived of her own volition through God's sovereign choice of her as the mother of Jesus? Was the death of Christ in danger of being abortive and all the types and prophecies respecting His death of being proved untrue until Pilate made his decision regarding that death? From these propositions, which might be multiplied indefinitely, it can be seen that in the greatest issues of time and eternity—all predetermined before the foundation of the world—God has realized His purposes in and through man—often unsympathetic to God's will—who, so far as human determination is concerned, could have frustrated the whole divine program by the action of his free will. Could God promise a kingdom on the earth knowing and so planning that it would be rejected in the first advent but realized in the second advent? Could God offer a kingdom in the first advent in sincerity, knowing and determining that it would not be established until the second advent? After all, what constitutes divine sincerity under such circumstances? Who is in a position to measure what, from the divine side, enters into the seeming conflict between divine sovereignty and human free will? To inquire what would have become of the divine plan respecting the death of Christ and of this entire age had the Jews accepted the offer of the kingdom, is equivalent to asking what would have become of God's purpose in redemption through a divine Lamb slain had Adam not sinned? Beyond all these confusing crosscurrents of determinations is the simple fact of revelation which asserts that the kingdom was offered as it was predicted it would be offered by Messiah's forerunner, it was rejected, it was delayed until the immediate value of Christ's death and resurrection as seen in the outcalling of the Church could be made effective. In this connection it will not be overstressed that, so far as the vision accorded the prophets of the Old Testament is concerned, there was in the program for Israel, as predicted, no separation between the two advents. But for the Church intercalation—which was wholly unforeseen and is wholly unrelated to any divine purpose which precedes it or which follows it—Israel would be expected to pass directly from the crucifixion to her kingdom; for it was not the death of Christ and His resurrection which demanded the postponement, but rather an unforeseen age. It should require no great effort to note that the recognition of this age—wholly unforeseen, wholly unrelated, and itself a strict intercalation—is the key to the understanding of the entire program of God in the ages, and without that key only confusion can result. It is not claimed that many spiritual truths may not be drawn from the life and death of Christ by those who do not concern themselves with the deeper problems of interpretation; it is claimed, however, that the vital issues of the divine purpose as far as it has been revealed and the clear apprehension of the doctrines involved depends upon the recognition of the truth which constitutes the above-mentioned key. It requires no profound study to observe that the earthly, Messianic, Davidic kingdom was offered by John the Baptist, by Christ, and by His disciples, that it was rejected even to the murder of John and the crucifixion of the King, and that it was not set up in connection with the first advent, nor is it being set up in the present age. Nevertheless, every oath-bound covenant of Jehovah will yet be consummated, His kingdom will come, and His bidding be done on earth as it is done in heaven.

6. THE PRESENT FORM. Since, as earlier defined, the kingdom of heaven is the rule of God in the earth, it follows that it is now present to the extent to which He is exercising authority over the affairs of the *cosmos*. Assuredly God is not at this time executing a preannounced Jewish program, nor is He extending Jewish blessings to Gentiles; rather He is calling out a heavenly people from both Jews and Gentiles on equal terms of privilege and to the heights of glory never extended to any people in past ages. In such unprecedented and momentous undertakings God, of necessity, must govern the affairs of men to an extended degree. This present exercise of divine authority is styled "the mysteries of the kingdom of heaven" (cf. Matt. 13:11). A New Testament *mystery* is a hitherto unrevealed purpose of God. It therefore follows that God's direct authority is now exercised in the realization of the features of this age which are thus termed *mysteries*. On the Church in her relation to the New Testament mysteries, Dr. Rollin Thomas Chafer has written: "The Church does not appear in the Old Testament. As something new in God's provision for Jew and Gentile, the true Church and some of its unique characteristics are spoken of by Paul as *mysteries*. These mysteries were withheld from Old Testament saints, but are freely revealed to New Testament believers, hence the church is

not found in the Old Testament. These mysteries include the Church itself, its Head, its message of grace, the Body of Christ as an organism made up of saved Jews and Gentiles, indwelt by Christ as the hope of glory, its ministry controlled by the Lord Himself, its ultimate removal from the earthly scene by resurrection and translation, and its approaching marriage as the Bride of the Lamb. Not a hint of these things appears in the Old Testament. On the contrary, this is the ethnic group which the Lord spoke of when he said, 'I will build my church,' an accomplishment which was still future at the time of its announcement. Never does the Scripture confuse it with Israel—past, present or future" (*The Science of Biblical Hermeneutics*, p. 43). In each of these mysteries which Dr. R. T. Chafer enumerates—the Church itself, its Head, its message of grace, the Body of Christ an organism indwelt by Christ as the believer's hope of glory, its ministry, its ultimate removal, and its approaching marriage as the Bride of the Lamb—it is to be noted that the originating of it, its progress, and its consummation are wholly wrought of God. In this He exerts His sovereign control. Thus the "mysteries of the kingdom of heaven" represent the present sphere of divine authority. It is true that, to the end that they may cooperate in His primary purpose, God is in authority over governments and all the affairs of men, both collectively and individually; but the divine objective is the kingdom in its mystery form. When the Church is completed and removed from the earth, every secondary feature of divine authority will automatically reach its termination too. In other words, the Church is not waiting for some crisis to be reached in the sphere of human governments, but instead the governments are muddling on until the divine purpose in the Church is consummated.

The moral character of this mystery age at its beginning, like its moral development and end, is clearly presented in the New Testament. At the very beginning the inspired writers spoke of it as an evil age: "Who gave himself for our sins, that he might deliver us from this present evil world" (or *age*, Gal. 1:4), "And be not conformed to this world" (or *age*, Rom. 12:2), "For Demas hath forsaken me, having loved this present world" (or *age*, 2 Tim. 4:10), "In whom the god of this world [or *age*] hath blinded the minds of them which believe not" (2 Cor. 4:4). So the church was fully warned from the beginning about the nature of this age, and taught concerning her pilgrim character while here and her holy calling and separateness from the "evil age."

A portion of the time during which Israel was to be dispersed and deprived of national blessing had been divinely accounted for by the "seventy weeks" revelation given to Daniel. The fact and purpose of the present mystery age was not mentioned in this revelation; hence there was need that this sacred secret should be revealed when its time had fully come. This Jesus does in the seven parables of Matthew 13, it being ever God's method to give a foreview of all His great purposes and undertakings. The course and moral development of this age are divinely presented in these parables. Three distinct features or elements of this age are to be seen in these seven parables, while each of the three are elsewhere said to be terminated by one and the same event. These are to be noted and the single conclusion they have, namely, Christ's return. (1) The blindness of Israel, mentioned in Romans 11: 25, is followed by the promise: "And so all Israel shall be saved: as it is written, There shall come out of Sion the Deliverer, and shall turn away ungodliness from Jacob: for this is my covenant unto them, when I shall take away their sins" (Rom. 11:26–27). (2) The career of the "man of sin," who is said to be the consummation of the "mystery of iniquity," is ended thus: "whom the Lord shall consume with the spirit of his mouth, and shall destroy with the brightness of his coming" (2 Thess. 2:8). (3) So, also, it is written concerning the completion of the calling out of the Church: "After this I will return" (cf. Acts 15:13–18). These great sacred secrets, it will be noticed, constitute the very elements in the parables which define the character and object of the age.

In the first of the parables a sower goes forth to sow, but only a fourth part (no reference, of course, to a percentage basis) of the seed thus sown comes to full development. The parable is interpreted by Christ and so permits of no speculation: "Hear ye therefore the parable of the sower. When any one heareth the word of the kingdom, and understandeth it not, then cometh the wicked one, and catcheth away that which was sown in his heart. This is he which received seed by the way side. But he that received the seed into stony places, the same is he that heareth the word, and anon with joy receiveth it; yet hath he not root in himself, but dureth for a while: for when tribulation or persecution ariseth because of the word, by and by he is offended. He also that received seed among the thorns is he that heareth the word; and the care of this world, and the deceitfulness of riches, choke the word, and he becometh unfruitful. But he that received seed into the good ground is he that heareth the word, and understandeth it; which also beareth fruit, and bringeth forth, some an hundredfold, some sixty, some thirty" (Matt. 13:18–23). In full agreement with experience during the past nineteen hundred years of Christian history the parable teaches that a great portion of those to whom the Word is preached are not saved by it; and lest it might be concluded by His hearers that, while this was the condition at the beginning of the age, it would not be so at the end, the second parable, that of the wheat and the tares, immediately follows. This, like the first, is interpreted by Christ Himself and its meaning is made plain: "He answered and said unto them, He that soweth the good seed is the Son of man; the field is the world; the good seed are the children of the kingdom; but the tares are the children of the wicked one; the enemy that sowed them is the devil; the harvest is the end of the world [or *age*]; and the reapers are the angels. As therefore the tares are gathered and burned in the fire; so shall it be in the end of this world [or *age*]. The Son of man shall send forth his angels, and they shall gather out of his kingdom all things that offend, and them which do iniquity; and shall cast them into a furnace of fire: there shall be wailing and gnashing of teeth. Then shall the righteous shine forth as the sun in the kingdom of their Father. Who hath ears to hear, let him hear" (Matt. 13:37–43). In this parable the born-again ones, the members of His Body, are seen as the "wheat" or the "children of God" amidst the whole sphere of religious profession and assumption. It is important to note how the age closes according to this divine inter-pretation: "So shall it be in the end of this world" (or *age*). Certainly this does not depict a regenerated world. It clearly pictures an outcalled people together with the full ripening of iniquity in the unregenerate portion of humanity. The third parable is not interpreted, nor is any parable following it explained; but enough has been revealed by the two interpretations to furnish a key to all that follows. The parables all present aspects of the kingdom of heaven in the one mystery form it now possesses, and so must be in fullest agreement. In the third parable Christ presents truth through the figure of the mustard seed and tree. Again the testimony of history and the teaching of the parable agree. The very small beginning in the early days of the church has developed out of all due proportion in mere members and includes all professing Christendom. The great tree now shelters even the birds of the air. It is significant that the birds of the first parable are represented as catch-ing away the good seed. The truly saved ones are still a "little flock" compared with the multitude of nominal church supporters. The fourth parable is of the three measures of meal which all became leavened. Throughout the Bible, leaven symbolizes evil and Jesus fully defined His use of the word on other occasions. He used the word to represent evil doctrine to the extent of formality (Matt. 23:14, 16, 23–28), unbelief (Matt. 22:23, 29; Mark 8:15), and worldliness (Matt. 22:16–21; Mark 3:6). Paul uses the same word with reference to "malice and wickedness" (1 Cor. 5:6–8). Its process of working is by a subtle permeating of the mass into which it is introduced. This much-misunderstood parable teaches, in accord with the other parables and all related Scripture, that which has proved to be consonant with experience in the history of the age, namely, that even the true believers—and certainly the mass of professors—will be sadly influenced by these various forms of subtle evil. There can be no question that this has been true to the present hour. The fifth parable is evidently a teaching concerning Israel because she is His "treasure" (Ex. 19:5; Deut. 14:2), including all the twelve tribes, though now they are hid in the field, which is the world—all places where the nation is scattered. When He shall call forth His "treasure" it will be by virtue of the fact that He hath, as the Lamb of God, taken away the sins of the world, theirs included. One, we are told, sold all and purchased that field containing the treasure. What Jehovah may do now, or of course at any time in behalf of any people, will be because of the atoning value of the priceless blood of His Son as the purchase price for sinners in their need of redemption. The Only Begotten Son was given for the world. The mystery of the Church, the pearl of great cost as set forth in the sixth parable, has already been considered. She is not now hid in the field, i.e., the world; but is being formed there and is awaiting her bridal glory when, in the ages to come, she shall display His glory and grace. She, too, is redeemed at the same priceless cost as Israel (1 Pet. 1:18–19). The last parable restates the fact of the outworking of the two great mysteries—the outcalled Church and the mystery of iniquity—as two coexisting on to the time of the end. The good fish shall be gathered into vessels and the bad shall be cast away. "So shall it be at the end of the world" (or *age*). Thus the three great mystery purposes of this mystery age (Israel's blindness, the Church's formation, the man of sin's appearance) were related in the teachings of Jesus to the beginning, course, and end of the present age respectively.

The following Scriptures give added light on the thought and expectation of Christ and the apostles concerning the course and end of this age:

"And Jesus answered and said unto them, Take heed that no man deceive you. For many shall come in my name, saying, I am Christ; and shall deceive many. And ye shall hear of wars and rumours of wars: see that ye be not troubled: for all these things must come to pass, but the end is not yet. For nation shall rise against nation, and kingdom against kingdom: and there shall be famines, and pestilences, and earthquakes, in divers places. All these are the beginning of sorrows" (Matt. 24:4-8). "But as the days of Noe were, so shall also the coming of the Son of man be" (24:37). "I am made all things to all men, that I might by all means save some" (1 Cor. 9:22). "Now the Spirit speaketh expressly, that in the latter times some shall depart from the faith, giving heed to seducing spirits, and doctrines of devils" (1 Tim. 4:1). "This know also, that in the last days perilous times shall come" (2 Tim. 3:1). "But evil men and seducers shall wax worse and worse, deceiving, and being deceived" (3:13). "For the time will come when they will not endure sound doctrine; but after their own lusts shall they heap to themselves teachers, having itching ears; and they shall turn away their ears from the truth, and shall be turned unto fables" (4:3-4). "Knowing this first, that there shall come in the last days scoffers, walking after their own lusts, and saying, Where is the promise of his coming? for since the fathers fell asleep, all things continue as they were from the beginning of the creation" (2 Pet. 3:3-4).

To this may be added the other parables of Jesus regarding the kingdom in its mystery form and the whole divinely given history of the church as previewed in Revelation 2:1—3:22. So, also, the more detailed description of the age-ending scenes as given by Daniel and Revelation 4:1—20:3. There is an age of universal blessing coming upon the earth; but it is in no way represented in Scripture as any part, or product, of this mystery age. On the other hand, it is revealed that it will be ushered in by the same divine movements that form the closing scenes of this age. The impelling motive for the service of saints at the present time must be nothing less than the world-wide testimony to the gospel of God's grace through which Christ may finish the gathering out of a people for His Person and soon complete His Bride. The great soul-winners of past generations have been actuated by this vision and purpose, and there could hardly be a ministry in the mind and power of the Spirit that did not wholly agree with the revealed purpose of God in the present mystery age.

7. THE KINGDOM OF HEAVEN REALIZED AND MANIFESTED. Since it is a major theme of both the Old and New Testaments, the kingdom of heaven provides an almost inexhaustible study. In the introduction to his massive work *The Theocratic Kingdom*—about 2,100 pages of at least 750 words to the page—George N. H. Peters writes regarding the text he has produced: "This work is far from being exhaustive. Here are only presented the outlines of that which some other mind may mould into a more attractive and comprehensive form" (I, 15). Yet, but recently—and to demonstrate by way of contrast how restricted the modern theological understanding may be—a professor of New Testament

in a reputable seminary said, "I can tell all I know about the kingdom in fifteen minutes." This drastic restriction in the knowledge of vital truth does not, however, hinder this professor from sitting in condemnatory judgment against the vast array of truth with all its adaptations and evident soundness of exposition to be set forth by Peters. Because of its comprehensiveness, a very real problem arises when a summarization of this subject is called for, as it is when closing this entire prophetic discussion. The essential character of the earthly, Davidic, millennial, Messianic kingdom yet to be set up on the earth by the power of Christ in His second advent has had some consideration in this chapter and still more in Ecclesiology (Vol. IV). It now remains only to present the following recapitulation.

According to prophecy, there will be two realities in the world especially to be reckoned with as the present age draws to its close, namely, the completion and removal of the Church and the increase of lawlessness in the world. Immediately after the removal of the Church and immediately before the establishment of the millennial kingdom is the brief period of incomparable trial in the earth. In relation to Israel, it is known as "the time of Jacob's trouble" (Jer. 30:7), and in relation to the Gentiles it is the hour when their governments and institutions as represented in Nebuchadnezzar's colossal image shall be ground to powder and blown away as the chaff of the summer threshing floor (Dan. 2:34-35, 44-45). It is the hour of God's judgments upon a Christ-rejecting *cosmos* world—a world which will have produced the final manifestation of abomination in the person of the man of sin. Upon such a world as upon its god—Satan—the judgments of God must fall. As His consummation of those judgments and into the scenes of earth's most wicked repudiation of God, the King returns in the clouds of heaven accompanied by His Bride and the holy angels. He utterly destroys all opposition to God and conquers the nations of the earth (cf. Ps. 2:1-9; Isa. 63:1-6; 2 Thess. 1:7-9; Rev. 19:11-21). Satan is bound and placed in the abyss (Rev. 20:1-3), and the King takes His throne—the throne of His glory, the throne of David in Jerusalem. He gathers and judges Israel (cf. Ezek. 20:33-44; Matt. 24:37—25:30) and those accepted by the King are saved and enter their kingdom (cf. Rom. 11:26-27). He also judges the nations from that same throne—the nations whom He will have conquered (Matt. 25:31-46). A portion of these nations then upon earth shall be ushered into His kingdom, which is prepared for them by the Father from the foundation of the world. The remainder of these nations are dismissed to the lake of fire. Those Gen-

tile nations that are allowed to enter Israel's kingdom are given a place
as servants of Israel (cf. Isa. 14:1–2; 60:10, 12, 14, 16). Thus by the
glorious return of Christ as Judge and King is ushered in the Day of
Jehovah so long and explicitly foretold by prophets of old. That Day
begins with the coming of Christ to Israel "as a thief in the night" (cf.
Matt. 24:43; 1 Thess. 5:4; 2 Pet. 3:10), that is, to Israel His coming is
at a time when they look not for Him (Matt. 24:50). With this in view,
they are told to *watch,* which injunction does not apply to Israel in the
present or in any past age but only at the time when they "shall see
all these things" which have been named by Christ as characterizing
the tribulation period (cf. Matt. 24:9–28, 37–51; 25:1–13). The Day
of Jehovah is that long period of Christ's rule and judgments over the
earth which begins with His return as a thief in the night and ends, in
certain particulars, with the passing away of the heavens and the earth.
Of this period and its boundaries and in connection with the comment
that Jehovah's Day may in His eyes be as a thousand years, Peter declares: "But the day of the Lord will come as a thief in the night; in the
which the heavens shall pass away with a great noise, and the elements
shall melt with fervent heat, the earth also and the works that are
therein shall be burned up" (2 Pet. 3:10). This passage because connected directly with verse 8 intimates that the Old Testament Day of
Jehovah, that is, Israel's age of kingdom glory, is to continue a thousand years, which is but a confirmation of the time measurement for
the kingdom later given in Revelation 20:4, where it is seen that the
saints who are resurrected "live and reign with Christ a thousand years."
Truth to be especially noted at this point is that after a certain manner
Christ reigns a thousand years. That His reign is Israel's day of glory
is abundantly declared throughout the prophetic Scriptures. The conclusion is that the thousand-year period of Revelation 20:1–6 and the
intimation of 2 Peter 3:3–8, 10 are references to the time when Israel's
covenants will be fulfilled under the long-expected reign of Messiah, and
that His reign will continue in this precise form a millennium.

To outline fully the character and blessedness of that coming age
would require the quotation of great portions from the messages of the
prophets in which language seems not to suffice to paint adequately the
glory of the transformed earth. A selection of passages, indicating
the character of the Messianic kingdom, has been given already in this
chapter of Christology, and another selection follows here. By these
Scriptures this kingdom is seen to be theocratic. The King will be Emmanuel and by human birth a rightful heir to David's throne, Himself

born of a virgin in Bethlehem of Judea. Emmanuel's kingdom will be heavenly in character in that the God of heaven will rule in the earth, His will to be done on earth as it is done in heaven. Emmanuel's kingdom will be in the earth, rather than in heaven, and centered at Jerusalem. His blessed reign will be over regathered and converted Israel and extend through them to the nations. Emmanuel's kingdom will be realized only by virtue of the power and presence of the returning King. Emmanuel's kingdom, though material and political, will be spiritual as well in that its subjects will walk on the earth in the undimmed light of God. The animal kingdom will be subdued: "The wolf also shall dwell with the lamb, and the leopard shall lie down with the kid; and the calf and the young lion and the fatling together; and a little child shall lead them. And the cow and the bear shall feed; their young ones shall lie down together: and the lion shall eat straw like the ox. And the sucking child shall play on the hole of the asp, and the weaned child shall put his hand on the cockatrice' den. They shall not hurt nor destroy in all my holy mountain: for the earth shall be full of the knowledge of the LORD, as the waters cover the sea" (Isa. 11:6–9). So, among other things, the physical creation shall be changed:

"For ye shall go out with joy, and be led forth with peace: the mountains and the hills shall break forth before you into singing, and all the trees of the field shall clap their hands. Instead of the thorn shall come up the fir tree, and instead of the brier shall come up the myrtle tree: and it shall be to the LORD for a name, for an everlasting sign that shall not be cut off" (55:12–13). "When the poor and needy seek water, and there is none, and their tongue faileth for thirst, I the LORD will hear them, I the God of Israel will not forsake them. I will open rivers in high places, and fountains in the midst of the valleys: I will make the wilderness a pool of water, and the dry land springs of water. I will plant in the wilderness the cedar, the shittah tree, and the myrtle, and the oil tree; I will set in the desert the fir tree, and the pine, and the box tree together: that they may see, and know, and consider, and understand together, that the hand of the LORD hath done this, and the Holy One of Israel hath created it" (41:17–20). "For the earth shall be filled with the knowledge of the glory of the LORD, as the waters cover the sea" (Hab. 2:14). "The meek . . . shall inherit the earth" (Matt. 5:5). "And he shall judge among many people, and rebuke strong nations afar off; and they shall beat their swords into plowshares, and their spears into pruninghooks: nation shall not lift up a sword against nation, neither shall they learn war any more" (Mic. 4:3). "Then the eyes of the blind shall be opened, and the ears of the deaf shall be unstopped. Then shall the lame man leap as an hart, and the tongue of the dumb sing: for in the wilderness shall waters break out, and streams in the desert" (Isa. 35:5–6). "But this shall be the covenant that I will make with the house of Israel; After those days, saith the LORD, I will put my law in their inward parts, and write it in their hearts; and will be their God, and they shall be my people. And they shall teach no more every man his neighbour, and every man his brother, saying, Know the LORD: for they shall all know me, from the least of them unto the greatest of them, saith the LORD: for I will forgive their iniquity, and I will remember their sin no more" (Jer. 31:33–34). "For unto us a child is born, unto us a son is given: and the government shall be upon his shoulder: and his name shall be called Wonderful, Counsellor, The mighty God, The everlasting Father, The Prince of Peace. Of the increase of his government and peace there shall be no end, upon the throne of David, and upon his kingdom, to order it, and to establish it with judgment and with justice from henceforth even for ever. The zeal of the LORD of hosts will perform this" (Isa. 9:6–7). "He shall have dominion also from sea to sea, and from the river unto the ends of the earth. They that dwell in the wilderness shall bow before him; and his enemies shall lick the dust. The kings of Tarshish and of the isles shall bring presents: the kings of Sheba and Seba shall offer gifts. Yea, all kings shall fall down before him: all nations shall serve him. . . . His name shall endure for ever: his name shall be continued as long as the sun: and men shall be blessed in him: all nations shall call him blessed. Blessed be the LORD God, the God of Israel, who only doeth wondrous things. And blessed be his glorious name for ever: and let the whole earth be filled with his glory; Amen, and Amen" (Ps. 72:8–11, 17–19).

Chapter XIV

THE ETERNAL KINGDOM OF
CHRIST INCARNATE

THE PASSING from the kingdom age to the eternity which follows is
marked by mighty transforming events. Such, indeed, has been the
divine method of action when other major dispensational changes have
been wrought—such changes as inaugurate and necessitate a whole new
order and relationship between God and man. It will be remembered
that there were seven days involved in creation, seven features to the
covenant made with Noah, seven features to the covenant made with
Abraham, seven features to the Palestinian covenant, and seven features
to the covenant made with David. The last three of these covenants
secure everything of blessing for Israel through all time and eternity.
Seven stupendous age-transforming events serve as a cleavage between
the Mosaic age of law and the present age of grace. Conditions could
not be the same after these occurrences as they had been before. These
events are: (1) the death of Christ, (2) the resurrection of Christ, (3)
the ascension of Christ, (4) the advent of the Spirit on Pentecost, (5)
revelation of a new divine age and purpose, (6) the placing of Jews and
Gentiles on the same level as objects of divine grace, and (7) the scattering of Israel far and wide in her last dispersion. Similarly, there are
seven stupendous age-transforming events which serve as a demarcation and cleavage between the present age of grace and the kingdom age
that is to follow. These are: (1) removal of the Church from the
earth, (2) the great tribulation, (3) the glorious return of Christ, (4)
the judgment of Israel, (5) establishment of Israel's kingdom under
the new covenant, (6) the judgment of living nations, and (7) binding
of Satan. Again, and with the same transforming effect, there are seven
stupendous events which mark the transition to be wrought between
the kingdom age and eternity to come: (1) the release of Satan from the
abyss, (2) the revolt on earth with judgments upon Satan and his armies,
(3) the passing of the old heaven and the old earth, (4) the great white
throne judgment, (5) creation of a new heaven and a new earth, (6)
the descent of the bridal city from God out of heaven, and (7) the sur-

render of the mediatorial aspect of Christ's reign and adjustment to the eternal state following immediately. These last-named events, which divide the kingdom age from the eternity to come, may be contemplated in the above order and with a special objective respecting the truth set forth in the final division—the surrender of the mediatorial reign—as properly the consummation of Christology.

I. THE RELEASE OF SATAN

No small mystery gathers around the fact that Satan is released from the abyss even for "a little season." Whatever solution may be found for this will lie within the sphere of the divine permission of sin in the world. Evidently, to the end that a final demonstration may be made of evil as represented by Satan, that sinister being is not only released but unhindered in His renewed program of war and attack upon God and His people. This strange release and the outbreak of evil doubtless serve in some measure to consummate the whole program of iniquity both as it exists in Satan and in the human heart. Armies are to be formed again and the curse of war revived. During the prophesied thousand years the earth will experience a perfect outward peace. Both righteousness and peace will have covered the whole earth. Weapons of warfare will have been forged into weapons of husbandry. It should be noted that the fact of Satan's release and the program he will then introduce have been predicted for thousands of years before their fulfillment. That all this will be enacted cannot be questioned when it resembles, and consummates, the program of evil in the universe. Its importance when seen in that light cannot be measured by the human mind.

II. THE REVOLT ON EARTH

While the astounding revolt on earth is closely related to the release of Satan, as intimated above, it stands much alone as a demonstration that the millennial age will not have changed the temptable character of the human heart. The revelation concerning this revolt is limited to the following words: "And when the thousand years are expired, Satan shall be loosed out of his prison, and shall go out to deceive the nations which are in the four quarters of the earth, Gog and Magog, to gather them together to battle: the number of whom is as the sand of the sea.

And they went up on the breadth of the earth, and compassed the camp of the saints about, and the beloved city: and fire came down from God out of heaven, and devoured them. And the devil that deceived them was cast into the lake of fire and brimstone, where the beast and the false prophet are, and shall be tormented day and night for ever and ever" (Rev. 20:7–10). Much stress is thus placed on the fact that the nations are deceived by Satan and this is the cause of their defection. Such deception is not new. When Satan is bound for a thousand years it is said that as a result of that binding "he should deceive the nations no more, till the thousand years should be fulfilled: and after that he must be loosed a little season" (Rev. 20:3). Thus it is intimated that Satan is ever deceiving the nations, excepting for the period of his binding and until his final dismissal to the lake of fire. Much like the unceasing pressure of the sin nature on the individual's life is the influence of Satan upon the mass of humanity, inciting to war, greed, self-manifestations, and impious conduct. What even a day's release of the individual from the pressure of the sin nature would mean in actual experience or a day's release for humanity from the deceptions of Satan cannot be imagined; but humanity, whether released from the sin nature or not, will be released from satanic deceptions during the kingdom reign of Christ on the earth. It will be noted that the last army ever to be assembled will be drawn from the four quarters of the earth and "Gog and Magog," which designation is perhaps more a reference to the event in question than to any locality or specific peoples. This vast assembled army will be "as the sand of the sea" for number. It is difficult to understand how such an enterprise will be possible with Christ upon the throne and in immediate authority, as described in Isaiah 11:3–5, which text declares: "And shall make him of quick understanding in the fear of the Lord: and he shall not judge after the sight of his eyes, neither reprove after the hearing of his ears: but with righteousness shall he judge the poor, and reprove with equity for the meek of the earth: and he shall smite the earth with the rod of his mouth, and with the breath of his lips shall he slay the wicked. And righteousness shall be the girdle of his loins, and faithfulness the girdle of his reins." There is no solution to this problem other than that of a divine permission in the consummation of evil in the universe. To the same end it may be inquired why with Him upon the throne of the universe He ever permitted the evil which He hates. When, in the light of heaven's understanding, the one problem is solved, the other will be solved also.

III. THE PASSING OF HEAVEN AND EARTH

If but a moment's consideration be given to the prediction that the present heaven and the present earth are to pass away and disappear forever, few would fail to be impressed with the immensity of the proposed undertaking or to be conscious of the fact that men and their institutions are not all that must exist in this universe. There are other objectives to be gained no doubt which have served no part in the human program. This is God's universe. It is planned and executed, and will be consummated to answer reasons which are within His infinite Being. Before such a disclosure, man may well bow in that humility which becomes the creature and find his only existing consolation in the fact that he is cast upon and sustained by the grace of God. Just what may become of dwellers in heaven and upon the earth when these vast spheres of abode fold up and are dismissed forever? God alone is equal to this problem. The command will go forth, possibly, for all such dwellers to stand apart and there witness both the passing of the old and the creation of the new. There is no intimation that agencies will be employed either angelic or human; yet all such beings pass through these mighty transformations and appear on the other side in the new glory that is to be. The Scriptures are explicit respecting the great event to come when the heavens and the earth shall pass away: It is written:

"Heaven and earth shall pass away, but my words shall not pass away" (Matt. 24:35); "And, Thou, Lord, in the beginning hast laid the foundation of the earth; and the heavens are the works of thine hands: they shall perish; but thou remainest; and they all shall wax old as doth a garment; and as a vesture shalt thou fold them up, and they shall be changed: but thou art the same, and thy years shall not fail" (Heb. 1:10–12); "But the heavens and the earth, which are now, by the same word are kept in store, reserved unto fire against the day of judgment and perdition of ungodly men. . . . But the day of the Lord will come as a thief in the night; in the which the heavens shall pass away with a great noise, and the elements shall melt with fervent heat, the earth also and the works that are therein shall be burned up. Seeing then that all these things shall be dissolved, what manner of persons ought ye to be in all holy conversation and godliness, looking for and hasting unto the coming of the day of God, wherein the heavens being on fire shall be dissolved, and the elements shall melt with fervent heat?" (2 Pet. 3:7, 10–12); "And I saw a great white throne, and him that sat on it, from whose face the earth and the heaven fled away; and there was found no place for them" (Rev. 20:11).

IV. THE GREAT WHITE THRONE JUDGMENT

Placed in the Sacred Text between the account of the passing of the heaven and the earth and the creation of the new heavens and the new earth is the description of the awful final judgment. The account reads: "And I saw the dead, small and great, stand before God; and the books were opened: and another book was opened, which is the book of life: and the dead were judged out of those things which were written in the books, according to their works. And the sea gave up the dead which were in it; and death and hell delivered up the dead which were in them: and they were judged every man according to their works. And death and hell were cast into the lake of fire. This is the second death. And whosoever was not found written in the book of life was cast into the lake of fire" (Rev. 20:12–15). In Revelation 21:4, as in 1 Corinthians 15:26, it is declared that there shall be no more death. This arresting statement evidently reaches beyond the mere idea that from that time forth there shall be no more death; it rather reaches backward and asserts that all death ever to have taken place in human spheres—excepting of course the case of those raised at the second coming of Christ —shall be reversed, repealed, and annulled. There is but one way in which so great an end may be attained, and that is by the resurrection of all the remaining dead no more to die. This universal and final resurrection is a theme of prophecy. Of it Christ said, "Marvel not at this: for the hour is coming, in the which all that are in the graves shall hear his [the Son's] voice, and shall come forth; they that have done good, unto the resurrection of life; and they that have done evil, unto the resurrection of damnation" (John 5:28–29). The Apostle writes concerning the prophesied schedule of resurrections, "Then cometh the end"—that is, the last resurrection (1 Cor. 15:24). So, also, John writes, "But the rest of the dead lived not again until the thousand years were finished" (Rev. 20:5). In the text under consideration—Revelation 20:12–15—it is declared that "the dead, small and great, stand before God." The position of standing which is assumed here by the dead after death has done its work is certainly an evidence of resurrection. Unlike the judgment of the living nations, as that is described in Matthew 25:31–46, these people are of all the generations who have seen death. "The first resurrection," so far as humanity is concerned, will have been past a full thousand years (Rev. 20:4–5); but at the end of the thousand years this the last and all-inclusive resurrection will take place. The number of those to be resurrected is incomprehensible. It is estimated that for every living person now on the earth at least one hundred have died and been buried. So far from being "the land of the living," strictly speaking, earth is now the greatest cemetery that could ever be conceived. It is out of this state of bodily death that the dead will rise to judgment. Their resurrection serves to bring all of remaining humanity before God in judgment and to prepare them for their conscious destiny in the lake of fire. The books are opened and men are judged according to their works. It will be remembered that in all ages—unless saved from it as Christians are in this age—men have been under the inherent law or obligation to satisfy the design and purpose of their Creator. The believer has been perfected before God forever and therefore answers in his Christ-wrought perfection every demand of God upon him. In the present age, however, men are condemned not only for their unholy estate, but on the ground of their failure to respond to divine grace as it is offered them in Christ. At the present time evil works are wholly climaxed through an attitude of unbelief toward the Redeemer. The Lamb's book of life is opened—evidently to demonstrate that no mistake has been made; for there will be none present whose names are written in that book. God's irrevocable answer to human sin is the lake of fire, which is the second death. He may save men from it only as a Substitute answers the holy demands made of them and they receive that Provision for them. Too often men are blinded by the awfulness of this divine judgment against sin and contend that, since God is love, He will not finally execute all that is here predicted; but be it said again that, if God could save even one lost soul on the ground of His compassion apart from the righteous judgments wrought out by Christ in His death, He could save all lost souls by mere compassion, in which case the death of Christ becomes not only needless, but the greatest blunder of this universe. The glorious truth which needs ever to be proclaimed is that lost souls may be saved, which truth is good news indeed, but they may be saved only in and through Christ. Apart from Christ as Savior, there is no salvation. Even infinite wisdom, power, and love can provide no other escape from the holy judgments of God against sin. What God may do with those who die having never heard the gospel is not revealed, nor could it be revealed. The Scriptures present the unevangelized as wholly lost. Their estate is the impelling call to missionary endeavor. If men might be saved by their ignorance of the gospel, it were well never to take the gospel to them lest, being enlightened, they reject the message and come to be lost forever. Christians being instant in season and out of season are to present this gospel to all who are yet living on the earth. This judgment scene lends no support to the fancy that men who reject Christ in this life will have another chance in realms beyond death. The unsaved remain what they were when death intervened and until they stand thus before God's great white throne to be judged according to their works.

V. THE CREATION OF A NEW HEAVEN AND A NEW EARTH

Again, as always, the clear declaration of the Bible is the only dependable source of information. The greatness of the event in which God repeats His mighty creative act—including both heaven and earth and upon a more marvelous scale—will grow more impressive to a devout mind as it is contemplated. Great, indeed, is the anticipation of the coming day when this great act of God will be executed before the hosts of the redeemed and the holy angels. So far from there always being a fading memory of what now exists, what lies beyond will be attuned to the greater glory of the New Creation. Isaiah declares regarding the new heaven and the new earth that they will be of such exalted character that the former creation will not be brought to mind. This statement, speaking as it does for Jehovah, is: "For, behold, I create new heavens and a new earth: and the former shall not be remembered, nor come into mind" (65:17). Isaiah speaks for Jehovah again when he asserts that the nation Israel will continue as long as the new heavens and the new earth abide (cf. 66:22). It is clear that Israel will dwell in their own land forever. If it is to be an unending residence, that dwelling in the land must transcend the millennial kingdom and thus continue into the new earth that shall be. Following directly upon the description in Revelation of the passing of the old order and the setting up of the Judge upon the great white throne, John the seer writes, "And I saw a new heaven and a new earth: for the first heaven and the first earth were passed away; and there was no more sea" (21:1), and this in turn is followed by a delineation of the new earth. That it is the new earth which is presented is made evident in that it is said tears and crying, sorrow and death are removed; and, to be sure, these have belonged to earth and not to heaven. Thus it appears that the writer is referring to the earth and not to heaven, where tears, pain, and death have never entered. He says: "And I heard a great voice out of heaven saying, Behold, the tabernacle of God is with men, and he will dwell with them, and they shall be his people, and God himself shall be with them, and be their God. And God shall wipe away all tears from their eyes; and there shall be no more death, neither sorrow, nor crying, neither shall there be any more pain: for the former things are passed away" (21:3–4). It may yet be observed that, in this picture of the new earth, the all-important feature is that "the tabernacle of God" will be with men. Such a situation has not obtained before. Earth has been the sphere of sin and corruption unsuited to the presence of God; but it will then be as holy as heaven, and in the new earth He will delight to dwell among men and to be their God. The term *men* is evidently in contradistinction to the Biblical term *saints*. Heaven will be, as now, the abode of the saints, while earth will be the abode of men. God is said now to dwell among men too. Peter asserts that righteousness will dwell in both the new heaven and the new earth alike (2 Pet. 3:13). In the present age, righteousness *suffers;* in the kingdom age, though some may suffer for righteousness' sake (cf. Matt. 5:10), righteousness shall *reign* (cf. Isa. 11:4–5); but in the eternal new heaven and new earth righteousness shall *dwell*.

VI. THE DESCENT OF THE BRIDAL CITY

Measured by the space given to it in the Sacred Text, the city from God is of surpassing import. Doubtless this very city "which hath foundations" is the one that so engaged Abraham the tent dweller (cf. Heb. 11:8–10). It is described in Hebrews 12:22–24, and Christ refers to it in His message from heaven to the church in Philadelphia, saying: "Him that overcometh will I make a pillar in the temple of my God, and he shall go no more out: and I will write upon him the name of my God, and the name of the city of my God, which is new Jerusalem, which cometh down out of heaven from my God: and I will write upon him my new name" (Rev. 3:12). So, again, in Revelation 21:2 John testifies: "And I John saw the holy city, new Jerusalem, coming down from God out of heaven, prepared as a bride adorned for her husband." And for a third time in the last great prophetic book it is referred to: "And he carried me away in the spirit to a great and high mountain, and shewed me that great city, the holy Jerusalem, descending out of heaven from God" (21:10). The description of the city, which now follows, has been interpreted in many ways. Some contend that the descriptive matter of the book returns for the time being to the millennial age because of the statement that "the nations of them which are saved shall walk in the light of it: and the kings of the earth do bring their glory and honour into it" (cf. vs. 24); but to revert at this point to the age that will have been completed already is far from a reasonable contemplation of the text. The chronological order of events in the closing pages of the Revelation is of great significance in the right understanding of it all. It is to be recognized that there is much here which the human mind cannot fully grasp; but still the description of the city falls in the context which has to do with the new heavens and the new earth that appear in eternity to come—unless the order of the truth as presented is abandoned altogether. An extended exposition of this descriptive passage is not permissible here. Suffice it to say that in full correspondence with the description as given in Hebrews 12:22-24, the Church is present, the angels are present, a company of "just men made perfect"—to which class Israel would belong—is present, Christ the Mediator and Lamb is present, and God the Father—the "Judge of all" and the Light of the temple thereof—is present. If the measurements of the city are taken literally, the length and breadth and the height are equal and so each dimension is 12,000 furlongs, which would be over 1,500 miles. That it is of pure gold is wholly within the creative power of God and an intimation may be found here respecting the glory of the new heaven and the new earth. The city descends from heaven and is therefore to be considered, to some degree, as something apart from heaven. It is named for the Bride of Christ and probably because she has some superior right to it; yet other peoples and beings enter her gates. It becomes a cosmopolitan center. The text, though extended, is here given in full:

And there came unto me one of the seven angels which had the seven vials full of the seven last plagues, and talked with me, saying, Come hither, I will shew thee the bride, the Lamb's wife. And he carried me away in the spirit to a great and high mountain, and shewed me that great city, the holy Jerusalem, descending out of heaven from God, having the glory of God: and her light was like unto a stone most precious, even like a jasper stone, clear as crystal; and had a wall great and high, and had twelve gates, and at the gates twelve angels, and names written thereon, which are the names of the twelve tribes of the children of Israel: on the east three gates; on the north three gates; on the south three gates; and on the west three gates. And the wall of the city had twelve foundations, and in them the names of the twelve apostles of the Lamb. And he that talked with me had a golden reed to measure the city, and the gates thereof, and the wall thereof. And the city lieth foursquare, and the length is as large as the breadth: and he measured the city with the reed, twelve thousand furlongs. The length and the breadth and the height of it are equal. And he measured the wall thereof, an hundred and forty and four cubits, according to the measure of a man, that is, of the angel. And the building of the wall of it was of jasper: and the city was pure gold, like unto clear glass. And the foundations of the wall of the city were garnished with all manner of precious stones. The first foundation was jasper; the second, sapphire; the third, a chalcedony; the fourth, an emerald; the fifth, sardonyx; the sixth, sardius; the seventh, chrysolyte; the eighth, beryl; the ninth, a topaz; the tenth, a chrysoprasus; the eleventh, a jacinth; the twelfth, an amethyst. And the twelve gates were twelve pearls; every several gate was of one pearl: and the street of the city was pure gold, as it were transparent glass. And I saw no temple therein: for the Lord God Almighty and the Lamb are the temple of it. And the city had no need of the sun, neither of the moon, to shine in it: for the glory of God did lighten it, and the Lamb is the light thereof. And the nations of them which are saved shall walk in the light of it: and the kings of the earth do bring their glory and honour into it. And the gates of it shall not be shut at all by day: for there shall be no night there. And they shall bring the glory and honour of the nations into it. And there shall in no wise enter into it any thing that defileth, neither whatsoever worketh abomination, or maketh a lie: but they which are written in the Lamb's book of life. And he shewed me a pure river of water of life, clear as crystal, proceeding out of the throne of God and of the Lamb. In the midst of the street of it, and on either side of the river, was there the tree of life, which bare twelve manner of fruits, and yielded her fruit every month: and the leaves of the tree were for the healing of the nations. And there shall be no more curse: but the throne of God and of the Lamb shall be in it; and his servants shall serve him: and they shall see his face; and his name shall be in their foreheads. And there shall be no night there; and they need no candle, neither light of the sun; for the Lord God giveth them light: and they shall reign for ever and ever.— Rev. 21:9—22:5

The last two chapters of the Bible not only describe the future eternal state of all things—Peter designates it as the coming "day of God"— but they indicate that there are then at least four different abodes: (a) the new heaven, (b) the new earth, (c) the bridal city, which may be anticipated in John 14:1–3, and (d) "without" (cf. Rev. 22:15), which may be identical with the lake of fire that is the second death (cf. 20: 14–15; 21:8; 22:15). It should be considered carefully that in this changed situation with its varied abodes the place of residence is no more subject to change. This is the end of revealed things; it is God's last word, reaching on with its prophecy into an unchanging eternity to come.

VII. THE SURRENDER OF THE MEDIATORIAL ASPECT

In the light of much prediction on the one hand and of one passage standing alone on the other hand, there has arisen a problem in many minds over the duration of Christ's reign upon the throne of David. All predictions of the Messianic rule give assurance that He will be King forever; yet one passage—1 Corinthians 15:24–28—has been interpreted by many worthy expositors as teaching that Christ will resign or withdraw as King at the end of the millennial period. Great inconsistency, accordingly, has been indulged at this point. Not a few writers, when considering the prophecies regarding David's throne, assert that His reign is eternal, and yet, when confronting this one Scripture, as definitely assert that the reign is terminated with the completion of the thousand years. The Scriptures are definite and conclusive with regard to the eternal character of Christ's reign. To David it was said, "And thine house and thy kingdom shall be established for ever before thee: thy throne shall be established for ever" (2 Sam. 7:16). To this David replied: "And now, O Lord GOD, thou art that God, and thy words be true, and thou hast promised this goodness unto thy servant: therefore now let it please thee to bless the house of thy servant, that it may continue for ever before thee: for thou, O Lord GOD, hast spoken it: and with thy blessing let the house of thy servant be blessed for ever" (vss. 28–29). So, also, the Psalmist makes fuller record of Jehovah's covenant: "I have made a covenant with my chosen. I have sworn unto David my servant, Thy seed will I establish for ever, and build up thy throne to all generations. . . . My covenant will I not break, nor alter the thing that is gone out of my lips. Once have I sworn by my holiness that I will not lie unto David. His seed shall endure for ever, and his throne as the sun before me. It shall be established for ever as the moon, and as a faithful witness in heaven" (Ps. 89:3–4, 34–37). Psalm 45:6 states, and it is applied to Christ in Hebrews 1:8, "Thy throne, O God, is for ever and ever: the sceptre of thy kingdom is a right sceptre"; and in Psalm 72, a Psalm of the kingdom reign of Christ, it is written, "They shall fear thee as long as the sun and moon endure, throughout all generations. . . . His name shall endure for ever: his name shall be continued as long as the sun: and men shall be blessed in him: all nations shall call him blessed" (vss. 5, 17). Isaiah is exceedingly explicit when he says, "For unto us a child is born, unto us a son is given: and the government shall be upon his shoulder: and his name shall be called Wonderful, Counsellor, The mighty God, The everlasting Father, The Prince of Peace. Of the increase of his government and peace there shall be no end, upon the throne of David, and upon his kingom, to order it, and to establish it with judgment and with justice from henceforth even for ever. The zeal of the LORD of hosts will perform this" (9:6–7). So Jeremiah testifies for Jehovah, saying: "Behold, the days come, saith the LORD, that I will perform that good thing which I have promised unto the house of Israel and to the house of Judah. In those days, and at that time, will I cause the Branch of righteousness to grow up unto David; and he shall execute judgment and righteousness in the land. In those days shall Judah be saved, and Jerusalem shall dwell safely: and this is the name wherewith she shall be called, The LORD our righteousness. For thus saith the LORD; David shall never want a man to sit upon the throne of the house of Israel; . . . Thus saith the LORD; If ye can break my covenant of the day, and my covenant of the night, and that there should not be day and night in their season; then may also my covenant be broken with David my servant, that he should not have a son to reign upon his throne" (33:14–17, 20–21). In describing the final regathering of Israel and the perpetuity of the Davidic kingdom, Ezekiel gives the following as Jehovah's message to Israel, His people: "And David my servant shall be king over them; and they all shall have one shepherd: they shall also walk in my judgments, and observe my statutes, and do them. And they shall dwell in the land that I have given unto Jacob my servant, wherein your fathers have dwelt; and they shall dwell therein, even they, and their children, and their children's children for ever: and my servant David shall be their prince for ever. Moreover I will make a covenant of peace with them; it shall be an everlasting covenant with them: and I will place them, and multiply them, and will set my sanctuary in the midst of them for evermore. My tabernacle also shall be with them: yea, I will be their God, and they shall be my people. And the heathen shall know that I the LORD do sanctify Israel, when my sanctuary shall be in the midst of them for evermore" (37:24–28). Daniel declares: "I saw in the night visions, and, behold, one like the Son of man came with the clouds of heaven, and came to the Ancient of days, and they brought him near before him. And there was given him dominion, and glory, and a kingdom, that all people, nations, and languages, should serve him: his dominion is an everlasting dominion, which shall not pass away, and his kingdom that which shall not be destroyed. . . . And the kingdom and dominion, and the greatness of the kingdom under the whole heaven, shall be given to the people of the saints of the most High, whose kingdom is an everlasting kingdom, and all dominions shall serve and obey him" (7:13–14, 27; cf. 2:44). Thus the word of Gabriel to Mary is of special note: "And the angel said unto her, Fear not, Mary: for thou hast found favour with God. And, behold, thou shalt conceive in thy womb, and bring forth a son, and shalt call his name JESUS. He shall be great, and shall be called the Son of the Highest: and the Lord God shall give unto him the throne of his father David: and he shall reign over the house of Jacob for ever; and of his kingdom there shall be no end" (Luke 1:30–33). Paul's ascription to Christ begins "Now unto the King eternal" (1 Tim. 1:17), and finally the voices in heaven declare at the sounding of the seventh trumpet: "The kingdoms of this world are become the kingdoms of our Lord, and of his Christ; and he shall reign for ever and ever" (Rev. 11:15).

Over against this array of positive Scriptures which so clearly assert the everlasting duration of Christ's reign on David's throne is the one passage thought by many to teach the limitation of Christ's reign to the thousand-year kingdom age. The passage reads: "Then cometh the end, when he shall have delivered up the kingdom to God, even the Father; when he shall have put down all rule and all authority and power. For he must reign, till he hath put all enemies under his feet. The last enemy that shall be destroyed is death. For he hath put all things under his feet. But when he saith all things are put under him, it is manifest that he is excepted, which did put all things under him. And when all things shall be subdued unto him, then shall the Son also himself be subject unto him that put all things under him, that God may be all in all" (1 Cor. 15:24–28).

Obviously this question regarding the perpetuity of Christ's kingly reign is, from the Christological viewpoint, of great importance. The subject has not been without consideration in past years and many might be quoted regarding it. There are those, such as the Anabaptists, who have held that Christ's reign terminates completely with the thousand years. However, the majority of worthy expositors, because of the extent of Scripture cited above, are compelled to recognize the continued rule of Christ beyond the millennial age. Some have sought the solution in a strained construction of the phrase, *a thousand years,* asserting that prophetic periods are implied by the word *years,* thus to make the millennium continue into hundreds of thousands of years. Others suggest that the term is symbolical, representing eternity itself; but then the related revelations such as a binding of Satan, the accomplishment of angelic judgments, and the complete subjection of all enemies would indicate a restricted period of time—one which the inspired text of Revelation 20 declares to be a thousand years—and since there is no absurdity involved when the literal time period is accepted, the literal interpretation should be received until it is proved untenable. To those who argue that the words *eternal, everlasting,* and *forever* are sometimes limited in respect to the time element depending on the obvious duration of the situation with which these words are associated, it may be said that these words, as used in this connection, create the very situation itself; that is, the effort of this language in every instance is to declare the timeless character of Christ's reign. There can be no uncertainty attached to the words of the angel to Mary, "Of his kingdom there shall be no end" (Luke 1:33), or "They shall fear thee as long as the sun and moon endure, throughout all generations" (Ps. 72:5), and, again, "Of the increase of his government and peace there shall be no end" (Isa. 9:7). Granted that God desires to announce a reign of Christ throughout eternity to come, there are no words available other than these or their like to express such a revelation. It is a notable fact that the Jews gave to Messiah's kingdom the character of endless duration (cf. Ps. 89:34–37).

In 1 Corinthians 15:24–28, the passage under consideration, the Apostle is presenting truth in general respecting both the resurrection of Christ and the resurrection of humanity. Having indicated that there is an order or procession in resurrection with several distinct groups and that Christ's resurrection is the first in the series and that "afterward" there shall be a resurrection of "they that are Christ's at his coming"—a period between His and theirs already measuring nearly two thousand years and to be terminated only by Christ's coming—the Apostle declares, "Then cometh the end." Recognizing that various interpretations of the terminology, *the end,* have been advanced, it is nevertheless held that—as the whole purport of the Apostle's message at this point is to set forth the program of resurrection which follows a certain "order" and as the naming of but two of the events without a third would hardly call for any recognition of a procession or any distinction with respect to groups and as the words "every man in his own order" imply that there are more in resurrection than the group designated as "they that are Christ's"—the only tenable interpretation of the phrase, *the end,* is that it indicates the end of resurrection's order and refers to the resurrection of all those who are not included in the first company, styled here "they that are Christ's." How else can "every man" be accounted for, if only a limited company is included in the first of humanity's resurrections? The whole program of resurrection is thus divided into three events. In this enumeration Christ's resurrection stands first; however, when only humanity's resurrections are in view, as in Revelation 20:4–6, the resurrection of those who are Christ's is termed "the first resurrection," and of "the rest of the dead" it is said that they "lived not again until the thousand years were finished." Christ declared that there will be two distinct classes in resurrection, though their time relationship is not indicated by Him (cf. John 5:25, 28–29). After a like manner Daniel anticipated a similar division of his own people when they are raised (cf. Dan. 12:1–3). Besides, the Apostle asserts that, before the end resurrection can come to pass and after the resurrection of those who are the saved in Christ, great angelic judgments are to take place and all to the end that every opposition, whether it be from men or angels, be put down, thus to restore the rightful rule of God over His universe. The Scriptures are faithful in disclosing the truth that there are those among both angels and men who have repudiated the authority of God. It is difficult to understand that sin could thus be suffered to enter into God's creation; but it would be even more difficult to comprehend were it implied that this rebellion must never be judged or corrected. In His judgments of humanity, Christ first deals with the living nations in what seems the briefest time, when seated on the throne of His glory (Matt. 25:31–46). Similarly, the wicked dead shall come up for judgment at the great white throne (Rev. 20:12–15); but the judgment of angelic opposition to God—including Satan, who will accordingly have been confined to the abyss for the duration of the kingdom—will be achieved during the thousand-year period. The text of the prophecy declares: "He shall have put down all rule and all authority and power. For he must reign, till he hath put all enemies under his feet. The last enemy that shall be destroyed is death." This leads on to the marvelous declaration set forth in verse 28: "And when all things shall be subdued unto him," then He will continue to reign by the authority of the Father. It is evident from 1 Corinthians 6:2–3 that the judgment of men and the judgment of angels come after the marriage of the Lamb, for His Bride is associated with Him in those judgments. The passage reads: "Do ye not know that the saints shall judge the world? and if the world shall be judged by you, are ye unworthy to judge the smallest matters? Know ye not that we shall judge angels? how much more things that pertain to this life?" Returning to the passage in question, it will be noted from verse 27 that the Son is to rule during the thousand years by the authority of the Father and that, therefore, the Father is excepted from the authoritative rule of the Son. This verse reads: "For he [the Father] hath put all things under his [the Son's] feet. But when he saith all things are put under him [the Son], it is manifest that he [the Father] is excepted, which did put all things under him" (i.e., the Son). The declarations of verses 24 and 28 become the point of misunderstanding. The delivery to God of a now unmarred kingdom does not imply the release of authority on the part of the Son. The truth asserted is that at last the kingdom is fully restored—the kingdom of God to God. The distinction to be noted lies between the presentation to the Father of a restored authority and the supposed abrogation of a throne on the part of the Son. The latter is neither required in the text nor even intimated. The picture presented in Revelation 22:3 is of the new Jerusalem in the eternal state, and it is declared that "the throne of God and of the Lamb shall be in it." The translation in the Authorized Version of 1 Corinthians 15:28 is not clear. It reads: "And when all things shall be subdued unto him, then shall the Son also himself be subject unto him that put all things under him, that God may be all in all." The statement is meant to signify that, when all is subdued and divine authority is restored in full, the Son, who has ruled by the authority of the Father throughout the thousand years and has put down all enemies, will go on ruling under that same authority of the Father's as subject as ever to the First Person. This more clarified meaning of the text removes the suggestion of conflict between an everlasting reign and a supposed limited reign of Christ. He will, as so fully assured elsewhere, reign on the throne of David forever.

George N. H. Peters' extended treatment of this theme is also added:

There is only *one passage* in Scripture which is supposed to teach the yielding up or ending of the distinctive Messianic Kingdom, viz., 1 Cor. 15:27, 28. Whatever view is engrafted upon or derived from these verses, nearly all (excepting those which utterly degrade Christ, and hence are unworthy of notice) admit, whatever delivering up is intended, that Jesus Christ *still reigns*, either as God, the humanity being subordinate, or as God-man deprived of His dominion and occupying a lower station, etc. Neander (*His. Plant. Ch. Church*, vol. 1, p. 529) more cautiously than many, says: "The Kingdom of Christ in its peculiar" (i.e. mediatorial) "form will come to an end, when it has attained this object, when, through the efficiency of the glorified Christ, the Kingdom of God has no more opposition to encounter, and will no longer need a Redeemer and Mediator." "The Mediatorial Kingdom of God will *then* merge into the immediatorial, such is the declaration of Paul in 1 Cor. 15:24–28." Lange (*Com.* Matt. 3:1–12, doctrinal), more unguardedly, remarks: "At last when the Kingdom of God shall have been perfected, it will also have reached its full and final development, and be ripe for *self-annihilation* which awaits it," thus, as he explains, giving place to a Kingdom of glory. Barnes (*Com. loci*) incautiously says: "It means the Incarnate Son, the Mediator, the man that was born and that was raised from the dead and to whom this wide dominion had been given, *should resign* that dominion, and that the government should be re-assumed *by the Divinity* as God." Stephenson (*The Atonement*) makes Christ reigning first as "*an independent King*" and afterward as "*a subordinate King.*" Thus David's Son, who is *One* with the Father, actually as Theocratic King seated on the Davidic throne adopted and incorporated by the Father as His throne, is made to yield up a throne and dominion which in many other places is pronounced—*in view of this very relationship to the Father—never ending*. Can there be a contradiction between Scripture such as these interpretations present? After careful consideration of the various passages directly bearing upon the subject, we unhesitatingly—in the name and for the sake of David's Son—answer, that it does not exist saving in the interpretations thus attached to it. In giving our reasons for no such antagonism, let the reader notice, that we do not present for our criticisms those of persons favorable to Millenarianism, lest we might be chargeable with seeking out an accommodation for our doctrinal position. Instead of urging our own views of the passage in question, it is sufficient to let *others* specify them and thus indicate *the wonderful harmony* preserved in Holy Writ. . . . The phrase, *"for He must reign till He hath put all enemies under His feet,"* does not limit—as is shown by examples (Bush, etc.) of Scripture phraseology and the admissions of all that some kind of a reign continues—the reign of Christ. The 28th verse, *"And when all things shall be subdued unto Him, then shall the Son also Himself be subject unto Him that put all things under Him, that God may be all in all."* In the reasoning of the apostle he had just replied to an objection that might be alleged, that if Christ has *"all things"* put under Him, His supremacy might exceed that of the Father, by saying that *"He is excepted which did put all things under Him,"* and, in consequence, it follows, as an inevitable result, that if the Father is excepted and has put all things under the God-man Jesus Christ, He will retain His pre-eminence and that Christ is *still subordinate,* even after He has acquired His greatest power and glory in His Kingdom. Bush well observes: "A delegated authority necessarily implies a supremacy to him who conferred it. This is undoubtedly the force of the original (τότε καὶ) 'then also' i.e. then, just as now—which the rendering of the common translation entirely fails to represent." "As Christ, in the great mediatorial scheme, now holds a place inferior to the Father, so, notwithstanding all the grandeur and glory that is predicted to accrue to Him from the final subjection of His enemies, He is still ordained to occupy that subordinate station." Storr and others explain the 28th verse as follows: The adverbs ὅταν and τότε being regarded as influenced by the word translated "shall be subject" not as a future of time, but merely as a logical future denoting an inference, the verse is correspondingly rendered: "Since (ὅταν), therefore, all things have been (by a Divine decree) put under Him, it will follow (τότε) that the Son Himself is or is to be, subject to Him that put all things under Him, that God may be all in all." Having thus hastily passed over the passage, giving the impartial, unbiassed views of Post and Anti-Millenarians, instead of finding it, as alleged, teaching the ending of the Kingdom, it stands *in harmony* with the prophetic announcements proclaiming *the perpetuity* of the Kingdom. In the language of Van Valkenburg (*Bib. Repos.*, vol. 2, *"Essay on Duration of Christ's Kingdom"*), "As the Father was excepted when all things were put under the Son, so also shall He be excepted when all things are subdued unto Him. It appears, then, that this passage does not even intimate that there *will ever be a termination of Christ's Kingdom, or that He will ever deliver up His Kingdom to the Father.* The dominion shall indeed be rescued from His enemies, and restored to the Godhead, but not in any such sense, but that His dominion is *an everlasting dominion,* and that of His Kingdom *there shall be no end."* Storr (*Diss. on Kingdom*) takes the ground that "the government which it is said, verse 24, He shall restore to God, even the Father, *must not be supposed to mean Christ's government,* but that of every opposing power, which is evidently declared to be destroyed, that the power may be restored to God"—adding truly and most forcibly (as our Propositions abundantly prove) *"the government is restored to God when it is restored to Christ."* Thus the passage is made by them to be in accord with Rev. 11:15, *"The Kingdoms [or Sovereignty] of this world are become the Kingdoms [or Sovereignty] of our Lord and His Christ,"* and when this is done, Father and Son *united* in this Theocratic ordering and Personage, *"He shall reign forever and ever."* It is the fulfilment of Dan. 7 and other predictions, from which we learn that the Father gives Him dominion, that He exerts it until all His enemies are subdued, and reigns with acknowledged supremacy (subordinate as this passage teaches in His God-man rulership to One only) over all the earth. One thing must be self-evident to the believer, that this passage, so difficult of interpretation (universally so acknowledged), ought not to be pressed against the testimony *of a multitude* of other passages, either to the separation of the Christ, or to the removal of His distinctive kingship as the Christ, or to the diminishing of any honor, etc., conferred upon Him. The *honor* of both the Father and the Son are identified with the perpetuity of this Theocratic Kingdom, for it is just as much the Father's Kingdom as it is the Son's—the most perfect union existing between them constituting *a Oneness in rule and dominion.—The Theocratic Kingdom,* II, 634–36

Thus endeth the eschatological portion of Christology. Messiah was born into David's line, the fulfiller of the Davidic covenant respecting one to sit on David's throne, was born King of the Jews, was rejected, and is coming again, will at His second advent judge Israel and the nations, establish His promised kingdom over all the earth, judge angelic beings, and reign by the authority of the Father on David's throne forever and ever. Let all who adore the eternal Son ascribe to Him, joining in with the great Apostle, the doxology of adoration and worship: "Now unto the King Eternal, Immortal, Invisible, the Only Wise God, Be Honour and Glory for Ever and Ever. Amen."